Sir John Drummond has been involved in the Arts for forty years, making radio and television programmes, writing for publications and sitting on councils and committees. He was Director of the Edinburgh International Festival for five years, and Director of the Promenade Concerts for ten seasons. In charge of arts programmes on BBC 2 in the seventies, he was later Controller of Radio 3. He is widely known for his commitment to the arts of the 20th century.

D1361999

Speaking of Diaghilev

JOHN DRUMMOND

faber and faber
LONDON · BOSTON

First published in 1997
by Faber and Faber Limited
3 Queen Square London WC1N 3AU
This paperback edition first published in 1998

Photoset by Parker Typesetting Service, Leicester
Printed in England by Clays Ltd, St Ives plc

All rights reserved

© John Drummond, 1997

John Drummond is hereby identified as author of this
work in accordance with Section 77 of the Copyright,
Designs and Patents Act 1988

*This book is sold subject to the condition that it shall not,
by way of trade or otherwise, be lent, resold, hired out or
otherwise circulated without the publisher's prior consent in
any form of binding or cover other than that in which it is
published and without a similar condition including this
condition being imposed on the subsequent purchaser.*

A CIP record for this book
is available from the British Library

ISBN 0-571-19549-0

2 4 6 8 10 9 7 5 3 1

Contents

Illustrations

Acknowledgements

The original Diaghilev project could not have been realised without the support of three remarkable figures in the world of dance: Tamara Karsavina, Lydia Sokolova and Marie Rambert. I owe them a great deal and remember them with profound respect and affection.

I am also greatly indebted to David Wilson Johnson, Stephen and Marion Cox and Asa and Susan Briggs, who lent me their temporarily unoccupied houses in France and Scotland to provide the necessary tranquillity to write.

Above all, this book would not have been written without the persistent promptings of my friend Bob Lockyer, who worked with me on the project and who has gone on to make such a valuable contribution to the development of dance in the intervening years.

The *Omnibus* programmes *Diaghilev: The Years Abroad* and *Diaghilev: The Years in Exile* were first broadcast on BBC1 in 1968. Transcripts are reproduced by kind permission of the BBC.

Introduction

In 1967 I made two documentary films for BBC Television about Diaghilev and the Ballets Russes. In preparing them I came to know many of the survivors of that extraordinary period, and eventually interviewed more than twenty of them – some at very great length. These interviews, of which only brief excerpts were used in the films, have never been published, and cannot now be shown, since the film negative is lost. They form the main part of this book. However, I should explain why I was so interested in the Diaghilev story and why, in the face of considerable difficulties, I persisted in trying to gather the material.

Diaghilev is for me almost a synonym for artistic authority. Artistic authority is of real importance, yet in recent years has been undermined in many different ways. It has little to do with democracy and even less with accountability. It depends on the judicious exercise of limited tyranny. Limitations may be necessary, but so is the power to decide and enforce. How, in our day, is that power achieved: does any individual have the right?

Purely creative artists have it, for it is all they have – the obligation to do what they must, as well as possible, with the minimum of compromise. The interpretative artist works in a different way, but also has an internal imperative. The facilitator, the producer, the impresario, the artistic director, call it what you will, has a more complicated role. He or she should, ideally, know as much if not more than both the creator and the interpreter so as to understand, protect and to some extent control. But what level of understanding, what kind of protection and what degree of control? These are the underlying themes of this book.

The early years of the twentieth century were remarkable not only for the surge of creative energy which informed all the arts, but for the emergence of a new kind of artistic leader. Not always a performer, but always someone of knowledge, wide experience, taste and vision. Meyerhold in Moscow, Florenz Ziegfeld in New York, Max Reinhardt in Vienna, Oswald Stoll in London were all in their different ways representative of this new tendency. But the most extraordinary example was Sergei Pavlovich Diaghilev, whose Ballets Russes in the twenty years from 1909 to 1929 not only revolutionized the world of dance, but radically altered ideas of theatre design and produced some of the greatest music of the time. Diaghilev's influence was felt all over Western Europe, and even in North and South America. Only in pre- and post-revolutionary Russia was it ignored. The more surprising, since Diaghilev and his original collaborators were all Russian. Diaghilev came to typify a new figure in the arts, the artistic director, and his influence both then and now is considerable. His career suggests that, without being primarily creative, it is all the same possible to influence even great artists and the path that they take in their creative life.

Artistic authority of this kind is mysterious in its origins, and very hard to explain in its execution. But, understandably, it continues to fascinate. I am no besotted hero worshipper, since there are many aspects of Diaghilev's personality that I find uncongenial. I am nevertheless convinced that in little more than twenty years at the start of this century a degree of artistic *progress*, in all senses, was achieved by one man on behalf of many others. How or why he did it had never been properly discussed thirty years ago.

What happened is now well enough known, though it was not so familiar when I started to become involved. Despite Richard Buckle's celebrated exhibition at the Edinburgh Festival in 1954 and subsequently in London, when I set out to explore this field in the mid-1960s, intelligent colleagues still looked fairly blank when the name Diaghilev came up. Since then enough material has been generated to fill a bookcase – indeed, I have one filled with memoirs, autobiographies, biographies, critical studies, exhibition catalogues, sale catalogues, video and gramophone projects. The Diaghilev industry grinds on relentlessly – so why add to it?

It seems to me that key questions not only have never been answered, but were never asked. Buckle's two huge volumes on Nijinsky and Diaghilev total more than a thousand pages, yet the view is almost entirely that of the critic in the stalls, looking at the finished product. Buckle has little interest in the technical side of theatre. There is virtually nothing in his two volumes on organization, on rehearsals, on lighting, on contracts or most of the practical details that underpinned the achievement. There is also very little evaluation as to why one view prevailed. This is not to say that Buckle is not fascinating and particularly well researched – in fact, it has for me too much research material and too little judgement. But it is typical of the external view, with much less interest in how things are made than how they appear when finished.

The autobiographies of the members of the Diaghilev circle range from self-justifying nonsense to the very remarkable, but only one – the memoirs of Lydia Sokolova, also edited by Buckle – gets close to the daily life of the company, where there was a constant process of activity, creativity, renewal and experiment. Where can such a policy be found today? I cannot think of a single company in the world which focuses on all four elements. The absence of strong artistic directorship in most classical companies, combined with the worldwide dearth of choreographic talent, has meant that most of them manage 'activity' but little else. Even renewal is at risk, since everything, especially in Britain, seems to be forgotten so quickly, despite advances in choreographic notation and sophisticated visual records. Creativity depends on a context which facilitates it, and on the right choices as to who is to be encouraged. The desperate search for new material allows too much to be entrusted today to entirely unready hands.

But why are companies no longer producing choreographic talent in the classical field? Has the language refused to develop, or is it merely a temporary problem? Millions in every currency across the world are riding on these huge companies that have been created, and everywhere I see rubbish passed off as innovation, fading artistic standards and a feeling of moribund imagination. In many ways it feels just like 1900 – plenty of good dancers, with nothing new for them to dance. Can we learn a sense of direction from the example of the past, or do we have to reject everything, the way the young seem to demand – experimenting all the time without anything on which to base the experiment? The best is always learned from the past, even in knowing what to reject, and continuity shows.

Dance has, perhaps unexpectedly, proved in this century one of the most effective areas in the arts for broadening understanding, by giving pleasure as well as psychological insight. It has the huge cultural advantage of involving several art forms – music, design, choreography and sometimes storytelling. It has often rejected some of those elements, but it has still shown a capacity far beyond that of opera to move and involve large numbers of people. We are always being told how few great ballets there are, but the operas written since the First World War that have made any impact at all on a wide audience can be counted on the fingers of one hand. Despite the patronizing attitude of musicians, dance is worth under-standing. It is therefore relevant to ask why it seems to have lost its sense of direction, and to examine a period when it seemed to have clarity. I say 'seemed', since historical hindsight always suggests patterns that may not have existed in the past and which do not exist in the present. Yet, if one takes any other twenty-year period in this century, it is impossible to find achievements which match those of the twenty years of the Ballets Russes of Sergei Diaghilev from 1909 to 1929. I therefore suggest that the questions raised by the Diaghilev years are still valid for our generation and ones to come, for they involve key issues. What is the nature of artistic direction? How can artistic collaboration be constructively achieved? Wherein lies artistic authority?

I must in some sense – a sense that I can no longer recall with precision – have felt the need to examine not just the facts but these ideas when, with much reluctance on the part of my employers, I became preoccupied with the Diaghilev story in the mid-1960s. And that, I suppose, is the point of departure.

PART I

The Project

1 The Background to the Project

But who was I to care or know enough to get involved? In 1965 I was one of a small group of producers who were making programmes for BBC Television in the field of music and the arts. The department, a new one, was headed by Humphrey Burton, who had left the BBC1 arts magazine *Monitor* to create a new unit when BBC2 began in 1964. *Monitor* had been part of the old Talks Department, which had been run for years by Grace Wyndham Goldie, a fearsome dragon whose influence was then considerable, but who ultimately can be seen to have backed a group of people who proved less able than herself. By the time I was in a position to suggest programme ideas an alternative group had emerged in which the key figure was Huw Wheldon, with whom I enjoyed (if that is the word) a tiresomely abrasive relationship. Having turned me down for a job on *Monitor*, he always behaved as if he resented my knowledge, which frankly, in a number of areas, outran his own. No opportunity was ever lost to put me down, and I found it very difficult to discuss anything with him. But Humphrey Burton was nearer my own age, and a helpful and gifted editor. I learned a great deal from him. He liked the idea that new areas could be opened up. We did not so much make music programmes, as programmes about music. I made my mark very happily with the first series of television master-classes in the United Kingdom. Humphrey's choice had fallen on the French cellist Paul Tortelier. I had been living and working in France in the early 1960s, and it seemed a pleasant continuation of my involvement with the arts in Paris.

During my time there I had become very close to a number of dancers, through my friendship with the Danish *premier danseur* of the Paris Opéra, Flemming Flindt, whom I had first met when he had been with Festival Ballet in London. Always interested in dance, I found the Paris scene more lively than London, and was fascinated by Flemming and his partner and girlfriend, Josette Amiel, a quintessential Parisian, of great wit and allure. Their daily accounts of the battles which went on in the artistic direction of the Paris Opéra were almost unbelievable. Through them I had met Harald Lander, who was living in Paris, having been removed from his post as director of the Royal Danish Ballet, and by then divorced

3

from his brilliant ballerina wife, Toni. I also got to know Erik Bruhn, for me, quite simply, the best male dancer of my time. I sensed something extraordinary about the tradition of these Danish dancers and choreographers. It was not just Bournonville in the nineteenth century, though that was excitingly different, but also something about the whole role of the male dancer in their tradition. So much male dancing in Britain was limp-wristed, and, as Flemming used to say, 'I don't care what they are off-stage – on-stage they are men.' As a historian by training and attitude, I wondered if there were not lessons to be learned in Copenhagen, which I had then never visited.

In Paris, on one memorably drunken evening, we spent four hours with Balanchine – he was there to supervise the final rehearsals of one of his ballets, which was going into the repertory of the Opéra Ballet. Flemming, Josette and I collected him from his hotel, took him to a small but very good restaurant, where he somewhat shocked me by drinking large whiskies throughout the meal, and then he insisted on a nightcap. 'We must go to that place that Tchaikovsky liked so much,' he said. We looked blank. It turned out to be Fouquet, on the Champs-Élysées. There he ordered two bottles of Roederer Cristal, and unbuttoned. The chilly, remote Balanchine, who usually refused interviews (and later did to me), who seemed at ease only with his own dancers, was nowhere to be seen. We asked him all the questions, why this, why not that, why this music, why never narrative? 'I will not do narrative ballets until it is possible in purely choreographic terms to say "this is my brother-in-law".' I know he said it often, but he said it that evening to us, and Flemming and I spent the next two weeks devising endless sibling scenarios. Flemming had introduced me to Eugène Ionesco, whose play *The Lesson* he had got permission to adapt as a ballet. In the summer of 1963 I went to Copenhagen to see it being produced in the studios of Danish Television. Watching class at the Royal Danish Ballet and exploring the magical Theatre Museum in the disused Court Theatre confirmed my belief that this is where what I cared about started. Paris may have had spectacle, Milan bravura, but Copenhagen had a tradition, which was the key to the origins of the school that fascinated us all, and had produced Balanchine: the school of St Petersburg. I had at that time not been to Leningrad, but I had spent several weeks in Moscow in 1961, and had seen not only the Bolshoi as often as I could, but other dance companies as well. Of course, to see *Swan Lake* on the stage of the Bolshoi where it started, albeit unsuccessfully, was unforgettable. But I saw the whole range of the Bolshoi output, old and new, from *Giselle* to *Flames of Paris* and from older dancers such as Semyonova to the very young Kondratieva, and I started to reflect on another problem, that of a great tradition that continued but seemed to be creatively blocked. Was it only politics – was there a deeper malaise? Much as I admired *Romeo and Juliet*, Lavrovsky was no Petipa when it came to steps.

By the time I returned to England in late 1963 I knew that I wanted to look at ballet in England again. The first company I had seen was the Anglo-Polish Ballet in, I suppose, 1940. I was five. I can only recall *Les Sylphides*, because the male dancer, the memorably named Rovi Pavinoff, wore a carrot-coloured wig which I thought hilarious. But there was Chopin, and moonlight, and amazing women suspended in mid-air. I can still remember a sense of wonder. Lydia Sokolova told me years later that she had produced that version for the company, and that the revival was very sound. Long before I was born, my mother had become friendly in Australia with an English dancer in Pavlova's company, Harcourt Essex, known to dance as Algeranoff. After he joined Mona Inglesby's International Ballet, towards the end of the war, Algie and his young French wife, Claudie, stayed with us whenever the company came to Bournemouth. I went to as many performances as possible, often standing. I came to know *Coppélia, Swan Lake* and *Giselle*, in versions reproduced by Sergeyev, who had been regisseur at the Mariinsky Theatre in Petersburg. I bought Arnold Haskell's King Penguin *Ballet* for two shillings, and rather shocked my prep school teachers by delivering a short talk on the history of ballet. Camargo, Taglioni, Pavlova – I knew it all.

After the war I went to Paris and saw Roland Petit's company with Zizi Jeanmaire as *Carmen*, the very young John Gilpin with Colette Marchand doing classical *pas de deux*. I was profoundly affected by dramatic new works, among them *Le Jeune Homme et la Mort*, with Jean Babilée and Nathalie Philippart. Of course, I saw the Sadler's Wells Ballet as well, but without a great deal of enthusiasm. I found Helpmann grotesque, and Fonteyn, with her limited dramatic range and fixed smile at that time, efficient but unremarkable, especially after seeing Danilova, and then the Ballets Russes de Monte Carlo, and later the Ballet of the Marquis de Cuevas, with Vyroubova, Hightower, Skibine and Skouratoff, not to mention Yvette Chauviré and Alicia Alonso. I had become a balletomane. Then in 1953, when I was in the navy, and studying Russian at London University, the Martha Graham company came to the Saville. I no longer know how often I went, but in retrospect it feels like every night for weeks.

The theatre was almost empty – there were so few of us that one got to know the rest of the audience by sight. The regulars included such critics as Richard Buckle and Peter Williams and such enthusiasts as Lord Harewood and Robin Howard. For several years I found the idea of *Coppélia* almost intolerable compared with *Klytemnestra* or *Cave of the Heart* or *Errand into the Maze*. Here was dance for our time, out of the museum. I ceased to be a balletomane, and became a lover of dance.

All that baggage was in my head in 1965 when I approached Humphrey Burton with a few ideas about dance for television. It was quite clear that documentary was to be my field, rather than directing dancing itself. This was for two reasons, one good and one ultimately unacceptable. The good reason was that, though I knew a great deal about dance and its history, and had by then got to know and occasionally work with a number of dancers, I had no training, and no status in a field that was jealously guarded. The second and unacceptable reason was BBC Television's only full-time dance producer, Margaret Dale. I cannot really remember her as a dancer with Sadler's Wells, though programmes tell me I saw her quite often, but she had achieved a very powerful position in the BBC, in charge of all dance except the occasional *pas de deux* that appeared in Patricia Foy's *Music for You*, or a few programmes made by Charles Rogers, usually with Festival Ballet. Anything strictly classical, and anything to do with what had become the Royal Ballet, was hers, and hers alone. Maggie was extremely good at one thing, and that not negligible. She took into the studio existing stage productions and reproduced them for television. Ludicrous union rules meant that the sets had to be redesigned by BBC designers, but to all intents and purposes they were the productions that could be seen at Covent Garden or on tour. In my first months in the BBC her big production was *Giselle* with Nadia Nerina. Fadeyechev was imported from Moscow, and I was allowed to sit at the back of the gallery and watch camera rehearsals. I realized for the first time how very difficult it is to achieve a sense of space, movement and pattern on the small screen, still then in black and white.

Margaret Dale had a powerful protector in Huw Wheldon. He flirted outrageously with her, constantly embracing her publicly, and set her up as a cynosure of production expertise for us 'new boys'. Well, up to a point, Lord Copper. I soon realized that Margaret Dale had absolutely no creative imagination, however good she was at literal transposition. She was totally opposed to any of us getting involved in dance, and, of course, Wheldon backed her. Later Peter Wright came to work in the department, and quite rightly was given the chances that I, and one or two others, had hoped for. Peter brought John Cranko and Kurt Jooss to the studios, and with characteristic generosity encouraged us to sit in and learn. I was, however, largely confined to music documentaries, not without enjoyment, but still very determined to broaden the base. I was not a trained musician in the accepted sense either, though I had always played the piano and had taken composition lessons for several years. But I found and still find music insufficient if it is the only thing I am involved in. I want a wider context. Dance documentaries seemed, despite Miss Dale, a possible way forward.

Eventually I made two proposals to Humphrey Burton. One was that I should make a film about Flemming Flindt, who by now had been appointed director of the Royal Danish Ballet, and whose version of *The Lesson* had won the Italia Prize and been shown successfully all over the world. The second was that I might research the possibility of doing something about Diaghilev, given that so many leading members of his company were not only alive, but living in London.

Humphrey agreed that I should have a small amount of money to explore the willingness of these people to become involved. If I could get agreement from half a dozen key figures, then it might be considered. But two things were essential: I needed the support of a recognized expert, and clear decisions had to be taken as to whether the resulting programme would contain dance sequences. I was fairly hostile both to an outside expert and the idea of a historical documentary containing sequences of dance by living dancers. I was not interested in trying to explain Nijinsky by having the newly arrived Rudolf Nureyev, however exciting, dance his roles. It seemed to me a nonsense. This was to have a long-lasting effect on the outcome of the project. As to the expert, despite my reservations, I was practical enough to recognize that if I could find a shortcut to the survivors, all of whom were old, some reclusive and many suspicious of people they did not know, then I might make quicker headway. So, at Humphrey's suggestion, I contacted Richard Buckle.

We had a brief meeting at his flat in Henrietta Street, high above Covent Garden Market, then a not very good lunch at a restaurant in South-ampton Street, the nearest to his flat. Later meetings took place in ritzier surroundings. He asked for a fee of £200 to act as artistic consultant to the project. In terms of 1965 it was a large sum, but it was the price of Humphrey Burton's support. My subsequent relations with Dicky were for a time so frosty that I have to force myself to recall that at the beginning he was quite helpful and trusting. He quizzed me pretty thoroughly on my knowledge of the period, and was surprised to find that I had done my homework and also spoke both French and Russian. He undertook on my behalf to write a number of letters of introduction, and got out his address book. He warned me that some people were unlikely to help, others to overstate their role. He left me largely alone. Increasingly, after I had made the initial contact, I found less need for him. I think it was an unsatisfactory situation for both of us. Although he had not yet written his two massive volumes on Nijinksy and Diaghilev, he was an acknowledged expert in the field, but no one had asked him to write the programme, just to advise someone whose credentials he probably questioned. My reservations were twofold. In the first place there were a number of aspects of his famous Diaghilev exhibition, which I had seen in London at Forbes House, that I had not liked. Despite the marvellous and revelatory things it contained, I found the decorative context and the juxtaposition of historical material with newly created settings bizarre. I recall with particular distaste a *Sleeping Beauty* tableau of the Awakening designed by Leonard Rosoman, rather a good painter and designer; but what on earth was it doing alongside genuine Bakst costumes, which evoked one of the most extraordinary episodes in the entire Diaghilev story, that moment when the great innovator turned back to the past? For all its success, I found parts of the Diaghilev exhibition in questionable taste.

I also have to say that I was not much taken with Dicky as a person, and to tell the truth, I do not think he cared much for me either. Somehow the chemistry was not right and it never became a comfortable relationship. I found that in spite of his observant eye, and his flair for the telling phrase, he lacked warmth. During the two years, on and off, that I worked on the Diaghilev project, we drifted apart. At one cool session in a very costly restaurant at my expense he referred to someone and, perhaps too quickly, I said, 'Yes, I know about her.' He said glacially, 'You know it all, don't you?' I could not see any point in future reference to him. By this time Humphrey had moved on to London Weekend Television and no one checked up on whether I was using my consultant. Eventually I made two films, and in the week in 1968 when the first was to be transmitted in the *Omnibus* series on BBC1 I met Dicky on the stairs at Covent Garden, and said, 'Hope you'll watch.' 'Watch?' he said. 'What do you mean? I thought it was on the radio.' Now older and perhaps wiser, I am grateful to Dicky, for one thing in particular – he let me get on with it, and did not block my way, which he could easily have done. His £200 was easily earned, and was four times as much as almost everyone who featured in the programmes got.

2 Looking for the Survivors

So what did I have in mind? I was quite certainly not interested at that stage in just telling the Diaghilev story. That, I felt, was well known, and much of it could be taken as read. This, of course, was extremely naïve – not only was the story not well known, but no interpretation of any story can have interest for a wider public without the basic facts being established. Wheldon's dictum about television, 'Tell them you're going to tell them and tell them and then tell them you've told them', had much to be said for it, given the potential breadth of the new audience. These were the years of rapid and exciting growth in the audience for arts programmes. Viewing figures for major performances and, indeed, for documentaries on BBC1 were very much higher than they are today. Fonteyn and Nureyev on *Music for You* delivered 12 million. Even a documentary that I made on Chopin which, unusually, was shown on BBC1 at 9.25 p.m. in the regular Tuesday documentary slot collected over 7 million viewers. *Omnibus*, which succeeded *Monitor* in the slot which I was hoping for, on Sunday nights (right round the year rather than for the few weeks only that it is today), was, despite its late placing, capable of reaching 4 to 5 million viewers. Today one and a half is normal. But then, there were remarkable programmes and programme makers – Ken Russell, Jonathan Miller, David Jones, Patrick Garland, Tony Palmer. Russell's *Elgar* film, for *Monitor* in 1963, was a major breakthrough. His film on *Delius* still seems to me one of the best programmes ever made. I was nowhere in this league, but I was learning, in spite of Wheldon's truculence, and because of Humphrey Burton's help, and the very lively, creative atmosphere of a new department, where practically every programme broke new ground, since so little had been done before other than short magazine items.

Yet there was obviously a problem with the scale of the Diaghilev project. If the man's life story and the twenty years of the Ballets Russes were to be covered adequately, fifty minutes was not much time, especially since my mind was firmly set on interpreting the story rather than just telling it, as did so much of the published available material. The two full-length biographies of Diaghilev, by Arnold Haskell and by Serge Lifar, had both been written in the 1930s and were by this time out of print, though most public libraries had them. The easiest reference book was by Serge Grigoriev, who had been the regisseur of Diaghilev's company. His book, *The Diaghilev Ballet 1909–1929*, was published first in 1953, and then issued in paperback by Penguin in 1960. Despite his closeness to the subject, his was a very plain and uncolourful account. There were other books in print, but not widely accessible. Even given my interest in the subject, I had read only the most obvious – Karsavina's marvellous *Theatre Street*, first published in 1930 and then in a revised edition in 1950; or C. W. Beaumont's *Diaghilev Ballet in London*; or *The Memoirs of Alexandre Benois*. Understandably, all these books told the story from the viewpoint of their author. There was little dispute about the facts, but not always much analysis. The facts were, nevertheless, extraordinary.

Sergei Pavlovich Diaghilev, from a middle-class background in provincial Russia, had become, first through editing a magazine, *The World of Art*, then through putting on exhibitions, sufficiently influential to raise enough money to present Russian painting, music, opera and dance outside Russia, most notably in Paris, in the first decade of this century. Almost everything he put on was being seen for the first time outside Russia, including Mussorgsky's *Boris Godunov* with Chaliapin. In 1909 the Ballets Russes de Serge Diaghilev opened in Paris to extraordinary success, and with only a short break during the First World War continued for twenty years, until Diaghilev's death in 1929. It involved some of the best creative artists of the day: composers such as Rimsky-Korsakov, Stravinsky, Debussy, Ravel, Prokofiev; designers such as Bakst, Picasso, Matisse and Braque; writers such as Cocteau and Hofmannsthal; and the greatest dancers Europe had seen since the mid-nineteenth century, Nijinsky, Karsavina, Pavlova, Massine, Spessivtseva. Even the conductors were of the calibre of Monteux and Ansermet. Of the sixty-eight ballets premièred or first given in the West by the company, over half are still danced. Many, for example *Les Sylphides, Petrushka, The Firebird*, have become the backbone of a worldwide expansion of ballet. Even those that have been forgotten, by their innovation and ambition added several new chapters to the history of the theatre. Then, as suddenly as it had appeared, the Diaghilev company died. After Diaghilev's death no one succeeded in holding it together, or ever again bringing together such a constellation of creative heavyweights. How was it that a man who was neither a composer nor a choreographer, neither designer nor dancer, could become the indisputable archetype of the artistic director? It must have depended on Diaghilev's personality, on his knowledge and the authority he gained over so many outstanding creative artists of different disciplines. But who was he? What was his motivation? And how had he achieved it? That was what intrigued me.

I already knew enough about the complexity of running companies, of creating new work and seeking artistic collaboration, to be daunted by this side of the operation. Diaghilev did it all without a fixed base, without secure funding, without a wide or knowledgeable audience. I had provisionally entitled my project 'The Diaghilev Mystery', since my version could not be just what had happened, but why things had happened, and by extension why it mattered then, and why the example mattered still. It was ambitious, but so much more rewarding than the basic 'he was born, lived, died' kind of tele-biog that involves a mere recitation of facts. I was also aware that the Diaghilev Ballet, though never filmed, had been much photographed, even in the early years. I had seen Baron de Meyer's exquisite photographic record of Nijinsky's *L'Après-midi d'un Faune*. There seemed to be many photographs of *Le Spectre de la Rose*, and Buckle's exhibition had been full of costumes and set designs by Picasso, for instance, for *The Three-cornered Hat, Parade* or *Pulcinella.* I was convinced that there must be a way to animate these photographs and designs, and that there was no need at all for living dancers to ape their predecessors. The essence of the story lay in the music, in these images and in the memory of the survivors. And what an extraordinary number of them were still living in the 1960s, even though I kicked myself that I had never discussed the Diaghilev Ballet with Jean Cocteau, who had died in 1963, but whom I saw quite often when I lived in Paris. Alexandre Benois had died in 1960, but the fact that his studio remained largely unchanged was something I had learned through working with his great-nephew Peter Ustinov.

Buckle had been in touch with all the principal figures ten years earlier when preparing his exhibition. His account of it, *The Search for Diaghilev*, gave strong clues as to who might be helpful and who not. I knew already, from a previous attempt for other purposes, that trying to get to Picasso would probably be a time-wastingly fruitless exercise, and so it proved. But in London alone, Tamara Karsavina had been busily coaching Fonteyn in *The Firebird*; Marie Rambert was still running her school and company; Ninette de Valois was very much in evidence at the Royal Ballet, though no longer director. In Europe and America the great choreographers Massine and Balanchine were still very active, and many of the leading dancers of the later Diaghilev years were teaching in Paris, London, New York or Los Angeles. Without a substantial number of these surviving witnesses the programme I wanted to make would lack authority. Some of them were easily accessible – Madame Rambert I saw frequently for she was a near neighbour, already someone with whom I was on chatting terms. She talked readily, even endlessly. Others were more reticent. Would Karsavina remember me from a meeting the previous year about a programme to celebrate her eightieth birthday, and if so would she allow herself to be photographed? What about Maynard Keynes's widow, the witty and elusive Lydia Lopokova, star of *Boutique Fantasque*, who was now an almost total recluse? What about Sacheverell Sitwell, who had written the scenario for *The Triumph of Neptune*, and whose brother, Osbert, had been one of Diaghilev's few English friends? The more I read, the longer the list became.

My secretary started a card index, a small green box which is in front of me now as I write. First of all there is a blue card for every ballet, with the dates and circumstances of its creation. Then a pink card, which was gradually filled with the references to each ballet, both visual and written, which emerged during the research. Then there are white cards for people – names, addresses, often thanks to Dicky Buckle, and potted biographies. There were soon more than a hundred names on the cards, most of them members of the company or those who worked closely with it. There were others who had been in the Diaghilev circle, who had written about the ballet either as critics or as observers of the social scene. Where did one start? The research had been agreed only on a provisional basis, and I was fully employed at the time on other programmes. But the water had to be tested. It seemed essential to produce a shortlist of the indispensables, and here I was helpfully guided by Dicky as to who had a good memory and who was able to remember only their own part of the story. Dancers are not always the most reliable of witnesses, and many of them never saw the work in which they danced, except from the middle of the mêlée. But some, such as Sokolova, seemed to have retained everything. Some memories were very selective. Grigoriev's book made much more frequent reference to the dancer Lyubov Tchernicheva than could be justified, if it were not for the fact that she was his wife.

My first list contained the following names:

in London: Tamara Karsavina, Marie Rambert, Lydia Keynes, Lydia Sokolova, C. W. Beaumont, Serge Grigoriev;
in Paris: Boris Kochno, Serge Lifar, the Benois family;
in the USA: Igor Stravinsky and George Balanchine.

I set about getting Dicky to make a first approach, which, if not instantly rejected, I would follow up with a letter. My files contain a number of letters dated 21 June 1966, all roughly similar, saying that I was involved with Dicky Buckle in a project concerning the Diaghilev Ballet and would like to meet and talk with them. The responses were prompt, but varied. Madame Rambert said neither yes nor no, but she was too busy at the moment; Madame Sokolova would be delighted to see me; yes, Madame Karsavina did remember me 'with pleasure'. Hooray! She suggested a meeting – would I call her next week? C. W. Beaumont would be happy to help – please ring him. Grigoriev's friend and translator, Vera Bowen, replied rather guardedly, but offered a meeting with herself, 'a close friend of Diaghilev'. My former secretary in Paris found numbers for Kochno and Lifar, and the daughter of Alexandre Benois, Anne. Yes, they would see me when I was in Paris. Lady Keynes was, however, adamant. I had written her a very tentative letter, and this was her reply:

June 26, 1966

Dear Mr Drummond,

Your own sensitivity and Richard Buckle's promptings have obviously given you a very true picture of my attitude to this kind of request. I feel that all has been said about Diaghilev that can be said. No doubt through the new medium of television it can be said in rather a different manner, but fundamentally it will remain the same.

So to preserve my privacy, I must refuse you, hoping you will not think me a rude and stubborn old lady. Give my regards to Dicky (sic).

Yours sincerely,

Lydia Keynes

Was she right – not to refuse to see me, but to think it had all been said? I was unconvinced, and in the following weeks I visited the other former dancers in London, including Madame Rambert. In principle, they were in favour of something being done. It was quite clear that they thought a new generation ought to be told about Diaghilev, but there was a major problem when it came to the question of their participation. Elderly as they were, they were extremely nervous of being photographed. Karsavina ruled it out within minutes of our first meeting; it was no good my reassuring her that she still looked wonderful, which she did. She had, after all, been one of the great beauties of the century, but was now eighty-one and, despite a rather pretty mauve wig, did not, I suppose, look as she had. As another great beauty, Diana Cooper, said to me after a similar request, 'I will not allow the public to see the ruins.'

Noticeable everywhere I went was the extent to which Karsavina was held in real reverence. Of course, it was extraordinary that this great dancer, who had created some of the most famous ballets of the twentieth century, was not only still alive, but living quietly in Hampstead. Quietly was the key word – she did not go out much, was very selective as to whom she saw and rather gave the impression that 'all that ballet business' was far in the past, like an exiled aristocrat who no longer wanted to talk about life before the Revolution. She lived in Frognal, in a very beautiful and quite large early eighteenth-century house, set back from the road by a big lawn. I mention the lawn only because it became quite a feature of our relations. On the appointed day I parked the car with difficulty, and rang the bell. I was very nervous, partly through sheer amazement that here was the original ballerina of *Petrushka*, the girl in *Le Spectre de la Rose*, the Miller's Wife in *Tricorne*, and of *Thamar* and so many other roles that I knew, or half knew. Part also was that I had read with enthusiasm her splendid account of her childhood and early years, *Theatre Street*, and knew that however much she would talk about dance, she was essentially a private person, and would certainly say little in the way of revelations or indiscretions to a perfect stranger. After all, there is no mention anywhere in *Theatre Street* of the name of her first husband. At one stage she is suddenly married, later she has gone off with someone else, no names given. The 'someone else' was a British diplomat called Bruce, who had been in our embassy in St Petersburg on the eve of the Revolution. She always signed her letters 'Tamara Bruce'. He was apparently a charmer, but not a high-flyer. By the early 1920s he had become first secretary in the embassy in Tangiers, and she lived there with him, occasionally interrupting a diplomatic life to return to Diaghilev who, like everyone else, seems to have adored her. 'Tata' she was called by her very few intimates. To me she was quite simply that very rare thing – a true living legend.

She opened the door after a longish wait. Accustomed as I am to dancers in real life being very much smaller than they appear on the stage, I was never quite prepared for how very small Karsavina was. She could hardly have been much above five feet. She was by then rather stout, and rather breathless. She apologized for being slow, saying she found the stairs a trial. We went down a panelled corridor, then upstairs to the first-floor drawing room, a long, lovely room with yellow walls, quiet and, with windows on both sides, sunny. On the landing I noticed a small painting of a theatre. I paused, and she said, 'Serf Theatre – very pretty. Prince Argutinsky Dolgorukov gave it to me.' Somehow I felt we were back in Russia, fifty, sixty, seventy years earlier. I asked about the Prince, known to me as an early supporter of Diaghilev. She looked pleasantly surprised that I had heard of him. I mentioned that I had visited the Serf Theatre at Ostankino, on the outskirts of Moscow, the home of the Sheremetiev family, where even the scenery painted by serfs, and the little dressing rooms of the serf dancers, had been wonderfully preserved. She seemed delighted to hear that it still existed. We sat down, she in a high-backed chair with her legs crossed at the ankles and hands folded in her lap. All the famous photographs swam in front of me. Her huge eyes were still bright, though heavily lidded, and the hands so small and rather square-tipped, but the hands, nevertheless, of the girl holding the rose in the opening tableau of *Spectre*. I was in turn daunted, thrilled and very moved. There was something about Karsavina that was redolent of intelligence as well as charm, of humour as well as dignity. Despite the brief programme Margaret Dale had made for her eightieth birthday, in which she appeared only for a tiny sequence, rehearsing the Harlequin Ballet, I wondered why she was so little known, and why no one had made a real film about her. I sensed an unusual mixture of humility and greatness, without any artifice at all, except for the mauve wig.

'Now,' she said, 'how can I help? Dicky says you are to be helped.' The most noticeable thing about Karsavina was her voice – an unmistakable, individual voice, rather deep and from the back of the throat. Occasionally, as she laughed, there was a gargle, like water running away. Beyond that was the accent. She had, of course, like all the Russians I knew, a very pronounced accent. They seemed never to lose it, no matter how long they lived elsewhere, or in any language, German, French or English. One heard the same sounds, the liquid 'l', the rolling 'r', the throaty 'ch' as in 'loch', so hard to transliterate into other languages. On top of this with Karsavina there was a rather grand, precise upper-class English accent, so a simple phrase such as 'I said to him' came out as 'Yah syed ta chyem'. The English 'e' was always pronounced as a Russian 'e', with a 'y' before it. 'He' became 'chyea'. It was captivating.

I told her of my hopes, and all the reasons why I thought re-examining the Diaghilev legacy was important. 'Yes,' she said ruminatively, 'very important, but surely understood, don't you think?' 'I'm not sure,' I ventured, and suddenly, quite without self-consciousness, we were chatting. Names cropped up from seventy years earlier as if they had been in the room yesterday, Mikhail Fokine in particular. It was obvious from the start that she gave him the credit for almost everything she had become.

Diaghilev's genius was to have understood how remarkable and original Fokine was as a choreographer, even though he had never much liked him as a man. Why was Fokine so different? She talked for almost an hour about the nineteenth-century tradition, about the ballets she had known as a child and danced as a young soloist at the Imperial theatres. Her background was entirely that of the dance. Her father, Platon Karsavin, had been a dancer, 'quite a good one'; her godfather was Pavel Gerdt, born in 1844, the original Siegfried in the first Petersburg *Swan Lake* in the Petipa–Ivanov version that we all knew then so well, before two generations of less talented producers mucked it about. Gerdt was also the first Prince in the *Sleeping Beauty*, though already over fifty years of age by that time. He had partnered Karsavina in her graduation début, a great honour for a young beginner. 'A mark of belief in you?' I suggested. She shrugged. 'It was kind.' In no time at all she was dancing small roles, yet it was not until Fokine came along that she felt liberated. I asked her about forgotten ballets, of which then we knew only excerpts, *Raymonda*, *La Bayadère*, *Le Corsaire*. '*Corsaire*,' she cried very excitedly, and proceeded to run through the entire work, with appropriate gestures and arm movements from her sitting position. Then suddenly she leapt up and dashed across the room to visualize 'le rapt'. She paused. '*Rapt* is always a difficult word for me . . . It is, you know, abduction, not rape. My English!' She flapped her hands. Her English was marvellous; precise, economical and always absolutely understandable. She wrote beautifully as well, with no sense of grammatical strain. I learned more in that hour about the tradition against which Diaghilev rebelled than from any history book.

'Tea,' she said, suddenly looking tired. We went downstairs to a small but charming morning room, where silver kettles, pretty cups, the thinnest cucumber sandwiches were waiting, and in the middle of the table a caddy. I hardly knew anyone in those days who still used a caddy. This was a beauty; mid-eighteenth century, walnut, the several compartments containing different types of tea. She asked me to choose. I picked a highly perfumed China tea, and we sipped it from the little cups. I can scarcely recall ever being so happy. It was only when the question of photography came up that she seemed ruffled. She was very sorry, but no, it was not possible.

On subsequent visits I found out much more about her life and its problems, of which the principal at that time was the house. She clung to it with a fierce affection, but it was far too big for her modest needs, and crumbling away. The roof leaked, the garden had become a jungle, she really could not cope. It was at this stage that I offered to mow the lawn for her. 'Not this time, perhaps another day,' she smiled. It was to become a running theme; in fact, I never mowed the lawn, and thirty years later still feel guilty. Behind all her anxiety was lack of money. One never knows what elderly people who have been in the theatre live on. At least Karsavina had a son and daughter-in-law, and a much-loved grandson, who had previously shared the house with her and would visit her from time to time. Karsavina had certainly had offers in her day – she told me of a dinner given by the Aga Khan, who doted on her. When she unfolded her napkin, there was a huge emerald concealed in it. She gently but firmly pushed it away. No scandal ever attached itself to her name. She remained faithful to her husband, and in due course other friends told me that they thought Karsavina's family could have done more for her. Eventually an American balletomane, Howard Rothschild, who knew all the old dancers, paid for the roof, insisting on anonymity, and the Royal Ballet Benevolent Fund helped with other expenses; but she seemed at this time to depend on an American librarian, a girl who lived on the top floor, and who was quite possibly leaving soon to go home, and she was worried.

I went away full of concern for this very extraordinary creature who, it seemed to me, could and should have been used more in middle age and better looked after in old age. In Russia or in Denmark they value their senior artists more, and find proper roles for them. I longed to help her, but the small fee I could offer for her participation was not going to solve any of her problems, and she had not yet, by any means, agreed to more than meeting me occasionally and giving me advice and help. But it was something, and I felt perhaps that time was on my side. There were anyhow no plans to film anyone or anything before the autumn at the earliest and it was now only July. Vera Bowen had indicated that, despite language problems, Grigoriev might take part, if I submitted the questions in advance. I did, impeccably translated into Russian by the GB USSR Association. I did not trust my handwriting and had no Cyrillic alphabet typewriter.

Karsavina, Sokolova, Rambert, it was a start. I knew that Ninette de Valois, Dolin and Alicia Markova would be less of a problem and could wait until I was more certain of what I was doing. But what about Stravinsky? That, above all, was the name I needed, not just for historical reasons. Stravinsky was the key to the money I would require to film in America as well as Europe.

Looking back nearly thirty years it is extraordinary how cheap everything seems. The budget for the Diaghilev project was, if it went ahead, to be £5,000 to cover everything: contributors' fees, my travel, photographic copyright, film titles, commentary, the lot. With probably twenty or more contributors at fifty guineas each, the suggested fee, and expensive photographic and musical copyrights, there was barely enough to film in England, let alone add on the days I knew I would need in Paris, Monte Carlo and Venice. America was out of the question unless someone else came in on the deal. These were the early years of co-production. The BBC's main partner was Bayerischer Rundfunk in Munich. The friendly, helpful head of documentaries, Kurt Hoffmann, was a passionate Anglophile, and eventually bought into too many BBC programmes for his own good in Bavaria. They were very willing to come in on the project, but required commentary in both German and English and, hopefully, one or two interviews in German. I was not worried about the commentary, as I had decided to ask Peter Ustinov to do it and German posed no problem for him. But I could not see any chance of interviews in German. We would already have to cope with some interviews in French, and possibly Russian, which would need subtitling. If we were not careful, the German version would cost as much as they gave us, and hardly help the total budget.

The other possible source of money was public broadcasting in America, particularly WNET's Channel 13 in New York, where a number of music and dance programmes had been generated by a committed staff. But they were much more interested in performance than documentary, and pretty sceptical about my ideas. However, preliminary contact by Humphrey Burton suggested that the presence of Stravinsky in the film might make a difference, so I had two very strong reasons for going in pursuit of the great man.

His connections with Britain at that time were, to say the least, tenuous. On the publishing side, Faber and Faber had produced Eric Walter White's huge index of all his works, and were publishing the conversation books with Robert Craft as they appeared. But in terms of performing, the situation was much less orthodox. Stravinsky had become, for reasons I have never understood, patron of the English Bach Festival, an annual event held initially in Oxford, but later in London as well, run by Lina Lalandi, a Greek harpsichordist and one-time singer. She endeavoured to get Stravinsky to come each year and conduct something. In 1965 he had conducted *The Firebird* with the London Symphony Orchestra and the BBC had televised it; I had hung about with the crowd, and at least been in the same room, but it was not a real contact. Moreover, Madame Lalandi was hardly a help. When I had met her some months earlier at a party at the German Embassy, she asked what I did. I said I worked for the Music and Arts Department of BBC Television. 'You mean you're one of Humphrey's boys? You can't be, I don't know you,' she said, and stalked off. Lina is one of those people who has achieved a certain amount, despite rather than because of her personality.

Even odder, Stravinsky was represented in Britain by a young South African impresario called Robert Patterson, whose track record was pretty thin. I had first met Patterson through my friend the American pianist Julius Katchen, in Paris. Katchen knew Robert's parents in South Africa. Out of the blue, at just this time, Robert wrote to Humphrey Burton to say that Stravinsky was keen to make a television programme about Dylan Thomas, whom he admired, and even to go to Laugharne to conduct a performance of his *In Memoriam Dylan Thomas* in the village hall. Unfortunately nothing came of this bizarre idea, but I pursued Robert fairly relentlessly to get to see Stravinsky on his European trip that summer. Dates were suggested in various places, then cancelled or postponed – a real dance. Then one evening Robert rang me at home towards 9.00 p.m. and said, 'If you come to Paris tomorrow, I think I can get you in to see him.' I cannot remember now whether I got permission to go, or who paid for or provided the ticket, but I do recall wondering if indeed I should go. Happily, sense prevailed and I went. Stravinsky was staying with his wife and Robert Craft in a hotel in the Rue Royale. He had not been well, and up to the last minute it was touch and go. I hung around for several hours, and eventually in the mid-afternoon I was ushered in and introduced to Vera Stravinsky and Robert Craft, who then said they were going out. Stravinsky was not very well; he would see me, but I was not to tire him. Craft seemed suspicious of me, and his not staying I interpreted as a bad sign, since I knew that the Stravinskys were already very much controlled by Craft as to what they did and whom they saw. However, for some reason Stravinsky had agreed, and joined us in pyjamas and dressing gown, with a rather yellowish Chilprufe vest under the pyjamas. The others left, and I sat down in a chair next to Stravinsky. Patterson remained in the room but at a distance, and took no part in the conversation that followed.

I suppose it is not distance or romanticism which retains that afternoon in my memory as one of the most extraordinary of my life. There was, first of all, a sense of real awe at being in the presence of one of the greatest composers of Western history. He was fascinating to look at and to watch as he talked, with his tiny body, huge domed head, immense glasses and prominent teeth. His hands were also disproportionately large, and within minutes he was clawing my arms to emphasize points. I can no longer recall how it was established that I spoke the four languages in which he habitually conversed, choosing words or phrases where most appropriate in French, German, Russian and English, and occasionally asking for translations into English of Russian or French words. I remember clearly that what most impressed him was that I seemed to have the support of Karsavina – 'Une très grande dame,' he muttered several times. I set out my story, and told him how crucial he was to my enterprise, in more ways than one. He said nothing to encourage or discourage, but started talking very frankly about Diaghilev and their association. He spoke of the famous first night of *The Rite of Spring*, of *Les Noces*, of his respect for Nijinska and, of course, of Balanchine, for whom he had a passionate admiration. Was Balanchine going to help? 'Well,' I said cagily, 'he probably would if Stravinsky did!' He snorted, baring the huge yellow teeth. 'Why does it all matter?' he asked. I made a short but emotional speech, at the end of which he took my hand and said, 'Ask me questions, my dear.' I plunged in.

How did they meet, he and Diaghilev? – something I genuinely did not know. His answer is still fresh in my memory after thirty years. 'It was in Petersburg. They had been playing my *Fireworks* in the orchestral version at a concert in the conservatory. Afterwards he sent round his card with a note, asking me to call the following day at 3.00 p.m. Of course, I knew who he was, everyone did, so I went. The door was opened by a servant, whose attitude was very . . . *nadmyenny* . . . What is that in English?' 'Haughty,' I replied, thanking London University for my education. 'Haughty' . . . he repeated the word several times. 'He said, "Sit down and wait." There was a small entrance hall, I sat and waited. Laughter could be heard from an inner room. Time passed. You know, I was young, but already impatient. I grew restless. After twenty minutes I got up and moved to the street door. As I grasped the handle, a voice behind me said, "Stravinsky, *pridite, pridite*", come in. I went in. You know, my dear, I've often wondered, if I'd opened that door, whether I would have written *Le Sacre du Printemps*.'

The hair on the back of my head stood up. No one I knew had ever heard that story before. And so it continued; Diaghilev's insistence that *Petrushka* was not a piano concerto, it would become a ballet; his miserliness; the problems Stravinsky always had in being paid; and so on. I do not know precisely how long we talked, but it was getting dark when Vera Stravinsky and Robert Craft returned. He said to her in Russian, '*Ochen interyesno –* very interesting, he knows a lot.' There was a pause. 'So will you help me?'

I asked in Russian. 'How much do you pay?' he replied in English. 'Fifty guineas – the same fee for everyone.' He snorted with laughter. 'Guineas,' he said, relishing the word, 'guineas, not pounds. Fifty guineas.' A long silence . . . and then, very quietly, with great emotion, and entirely in English, relishing the words, 'Diaghilev and I were on good terms and bad terms, in good times and bad times, but, after all, he was my brother. Yes, I'll help you, for fifty guineas.' We went on quickly to discuss where. In California in the late autumn was best for him, not while travelling, when he was tired. So it was settled that I would go to Los Angeles in the autumn. Vera, large and still beautiful, looking very like the photographs of herself as the Queen in *The Sleeping Princess* production of 1921 said, 'When you come to California, bring your trunk.' I looked puzzled. 'Yes,' she said, 'bring your trunk, we have very big pool!' He said goodbye, and in a skittish way retreated to the bedroom. Robert Patterson and I bade farewell and left. On the landing outside I burst into tears.

3 Delays and Dramas

In July 1966 I went with the Katchens and David Oistrakh and his wife to Prades, to the Casals Festival. Julius had voiced his suspicion that this might be the last festival there, and he was correct. For a week I sat at the feet of these great musicians, turning the pages for Katchen in rehearsal, spending the evenings talking to Rudolf Serkin and listening to David Oistrakh's unbeatable repertory of Jewish jokes. Tamara Oistrakh, who taught English and spoke it well, was intrigued by my Diaghilev project. 'You see, he's quite unknown to us,' she said. The simple fact that the Diaghilev company had never appeared in Russia, and the Revolution had banned all his collaborators, such as Stravinsky, from Russian experience, was, of course, well known. But for the first time I realized its implications. Here were some of the greatest artists of the twentieth century, all Russians, and none of their works had been shown in their own country. Even Prokofiev's ballets for Diaghilev, *Pas d'Acier*, *Chout*, *The Prodigal Son*, were completely unknown. No wonder the Bolshoi seemed so dated and so unconnected with the twentieth century. Diaghilev, and all the ramifications, had completely bypassed them.

My summer was planned. After Prades I was to have a short holiday on the Côte d'Azur, which would allow me to look at possible locations in Monte Carlo, where the Diaghilev ballet had been based for some months of the year in the 1920s. And then I was going to Leeds, to make a film about the second Leeds International Piano Competition. After that I would return to Diaghilev and, hopefully, film some interviews in the late autumn, including the one in America with Stravinsky. But it did not work out like that. In early August my mother had a stroke, and I had to return in mid-holiday. Then, shortly after I covered the Leeds Competition, she died. My time was divided between complex editing sessions on film and video of the Leeds material, visits to the hospital and coping with my father, who showed little sign of being able to cope on his own. Any further work on Diaghilev was postponed. Then in addition, in October, unexpectedly my other dance project suddenly became a possibility. Flemming Flindt, in Copenhagen, was to choreograph a new version of *The Miraculous Mandarin*, and this provided the obvious opportunity for me to film him and the Royal Danish Ballet. The Leeds Competition film was shown in early October. It was by far the most successful thing I had done, and for the first time I felt that I had made my mark as a director. It was repeated soon after, and went on to win the 'Best Director' award at the Prague Festival the following year, at that time the main European prize for music programmes. The Flindt film, on the other hand, was a disaster. I learned once and for all never to make films with, or about, my close friends. The choreographic sessions were hard to cover, especially with a rather unsupportive Danish crew, and in interview Flemming refused to answer any of the important questions. It was a depressing experience. In the end the intended film bcame little more than an introduction to a performance of *The Miraculous Mandarin*, and I felt all the ground I had gained with Leeds had been lost again.

With one thing and another, and several short-term studio projects, it was not until the spring of 1967 that I was able to take up the threads of the Diaghilev story again. A flurry of apologetic letters had been sent to reassure the old ladies that I would be back in a few months. Stravinsky, on the other hand, had gone cold on the idea – or had Craft intervened? I would never know. In a desperate attempt to get the American end going Humphrey Burton arranged for me to see WNET in New York in April 1967. By now the list of acceptances in Europe was quite long, bringing in *corps de ballet* dancers, as well as musicians such as Ansermet and Diaghilev's last protégé, Igor Markevich. Even the remote Sacheverell Sitwell had shown willing. I was confident that a trip to Paris in May would deliver the French contingent, including possibly the 96-year-old Mathilde Kchessinska, who had been too tired to see me the previous year – exhausted by the celebration of her sister's one hundredth birthday.

America beckoned, not only for Stravinsky, whom I was sure I could get on my side again, but for Balanchine, Danilova, Doubrovska, Nemchinova and other dancers still teaching or working there. It was quite clear that it was up to me to persuade WNET, as there was no more money coming from the BBC or Bayerischer Rundfunk.

Curtis Davis of WNET was a nice man, and well disposed, but knew nothing of the subject matter. He deferred entirely to the executive producer responsible for dance programmes, Jac Venza. I think Venza must be the only person in this long saga who is today in the same post as he was nearly thirty years ago. We had a brief meeting. He warned me there was a late-morning screening of a new video of a dance work by John Butler. He invited me, and I assumed we would continue our meeting afterwards, over lunch. The screening took place, and then Venza disappeared. I was left entirely alone in the viewing theatre, not knowing what to do or to expect. He did not return that day. The following day what little interest he had shown in my project was entirely dissipated. 'Who the hell cares about these old ladies?' he asked. He was sure Balanchine would not talk, and as for Stravinsky, they had had him in a widely shown documentary the previous year. What is more, the idea of using still photographs was a non-starter. The programme would work only if we had Fonteyn and Nureyev, Villella and Farrell dancing the key excerpts from the Diaghilev ballets. Nothing I said would shift him. He would be happy to look at the finished film, but would not invest. In the end, eighteen months later, they bought the finished programmes and showed them, and had the nerve to tell me they were 'quite interesting'. I returned to London, not having met any of the New York survivors, and not at all sure whether I could hold on to Stravinsky. Humphrey Burton eventually decided that if Stravinsky agreed, I could go to Los Angeles and film him, but nothing else. Could the story be told entirely by the European survivors, in European locations? It might have to be.

I turned my attention to Paris. There were three composers of Diaghilev ballets living there at that time: Georges Auric, director of the Paris Opéra; Darius Milhaud, who divided the year between Paris and Mills College in California; and Henri Sauguet, less well known, but whose music for the ballet *Les Forains* had enchanted me when I first saw Roland Petit's company after the war. I had no luck with Auric. He was 'too busy', or possibly at that stage too drunk. His formidable wife, Nora, barred the door. I had already met her in Paris earlier and knew the score. Milhaud was entirely happy to help, but was leaving in three days for California – could I not see him there? When I saw Stravinsky? Perhaps. Sauguet was a charmer, and our subsequent conversations among the happiest.

As to dancers – Kchessinska, I was advised, was 'past it'. She had appeared with Diaghilev in only one season, in 1910, and, having read her autobiography, I was now doubtful about how much she could, or would, say. Her book is typified by one sentence which I always remember: 'It is a source of profound moral satisfaction to me that Nijinsky was so grateful to me for all I did for him.' No doubt there about who mattered most. The former mistress of Nicholas II when tsarevich, she had later married his cousin, the Grand Duke Andrei, and was known as the Princess Romanovsky Krasinsky. She had certainly been a great dancer, and had appeared in London as late as 1937 in the Coronation Gala. Sokolova remembered her Russian Dance. But she had been, in the main, pretty hostile to Diaghilev, since she felt he betrayed, through innovation, the great tradition of the Imperial theatres. Karsavina, nevertheless, recalled her with affection. I once questioned her about the famous Mathilde – 'Very kind,' said Karsavina. 'Taught us about forks.' 'Forks?' Karsavina explained patiently that the graduate girls, who led a convent-like life at the Imperial Ballet School, were, on joining the company, thrown into a world of glamour and high society with very little preparation. 'At big dinners,' Karsavina said, 'there would be as many as ten forks. Matilda told us which we should use.' Who were we? 'Oh, Pavlova, Egorova, myself.' Pavlova, of course, was long dead, but Egorova was still living in Paris in 1967. She had become the Princess Troubetskoi, a little hunched figure in a peasant-style shawl, who proudly produced a brooch of tiny diamonds in the shape of a double-headed eagle. 'Notre Czar m'a presenté ça sur scène du théâtre Mariinsky,' she confided. But she had little to say about Diaghilev that hadn't been said by others, though she had been one of the stars of *The Sleeping Princess*, alternating the role of Aurora with Spessivtseva and Trefilova. I had a taste of imperial Russia as we talked in her studio on the edge of Montmartre, but there were no revelations here.

Revelation was exactly what I hoped for from Boris Kochno, who had been Diaghilev's secretary in his later years, as well as the librettist of several ballets. After Diaghilev's death Kochno became the companion of the great designer Christian Bérard. In many ways Kochno was the godfather of new dance in France after the war, at the opposite pole from Lifar, whom he hated, who ran the Paris Opéra Ballet.

I knew from Dicky that Kochno was quite a handful. He had come to Edinburgh for the exhibition, but had disappeared on a drunken binge in the docks of Leith in highly dubious company. We had corresponded the previous year; I was fascinated by his highly wrought and exquisite handwriting, so remarkable as to be almost entirely illegible. It was known that he had been on the bottle for years, and it was suggested probably also on drugs. What was not known was what he still owned. He had at one time had a vast collection of Diaghilev memorabilia, salvaged after Diaghilev's death in a manner I was later to learn from Serge Lifar. I telephoned him on arrival in Paris, as arranged. The first sentence was daunting. 'Monsieur, dîtes-moi, par quel droit osez-vous faire ce film?' Well, I was not sure, in fact, that I had any rights as such; I just had ambition, enthusiasm and a great deal of support. I mentioned some of those who were helping me. 'But you don't even speak Russian!' I answered in Russian that I did. There was a long silence. 'Bien. Demain à cinq heures chez moi.' And the phone was rapidly replaced. I and my assistant Bob Lockyer, who had joined me the previous month and who was in charge of all the picture research, duly turned up at the appointed hour. We were shown in by Kochno's North African companion and servant, Jean. The house was in a small street, near Les Halles. It had a little tower, and a big wooden door; we stepped straight into the main room, which was hung closely with drawings, designs and masks. We were told to wait. In my mind's eye was a photograph of Kochno as a young man, dark, saturnine, extraordinarily good-looking, very slim.

Vera Stravinsky had told me how he came to be Diaghilev's secretary. In her version, he had come to her as a starving young Ukrainian poet, with a passionate desire to meet Diaghilev. She took one look at him, and thought he might well get noticed, so she placed him strategically in the foyer of the theatre. Diaghilev indeed noticed him, and he was swept up into the entourage. Vera indicated that the relationship had not been platonic; a few weeks later Kochno came to her and said, 'Verushka, I can't stand it, but I don't want to go away entirely!' 'Well,' she said, 'you could always be secretary.' This is very far from the familiar version of their meeting, which has Kochno sent to Diaghilev's hotel in Paris to deliver a parcel. I have not the slightest idea whether Vera's version is the true one, and there is no one left to ask. But Vera had no reason to lie.

Eventually Kochno appeared. He was seventy, totally bald, very fat, and with a drooping tartar moustache. He looked just like the Polovtsian Khan in *Prince Igor*. He was, however, wearing a smart dark-grey three-piece suit, which obviously came from a good tailor. He sent Jean out to get a bottle of whisky. I told him about the project; he looked unimpressed. He then started to talk about an aspect of Diaghilev that I knew about, but which was not exactly central, Diaghilev's obsession in his later years with collecting first editions. He produced a first edition of Pushkin's *Mavra*, inscribed to him by Diaghilev, with the date of the first performance of Stravinsky's and Kochno's version in 1922. It was fascinating, but not enough. Did I know, he asked tantalizingly, that Diaghilev had written his autobiography? This, though known to Dicky, was news to me. Would I like to see a chapter? He produced a typescript of about ten pages, in French. It described in great detail Diaghilev's reaction to the death of Tchaikovsky in 1893, and how Diaghilev, who idolized Tchaikovsky, had gone to his house to pay his last respects, not knowing his death was supposedly caused by cholera. On his arrival the house was deserted, the street door open. Diaghilev entered, and found himself alone in the dining room, with Tchaikovsky's body laid out on the dining table. I was suitably impressed; he snatched it back. How much more was there? He shrugged. A leather bucket was produced, full of eighteenth-century maps of Russia. Very interesting, but we were getting nowhere. I asked him if he still had many drawings or designs. He looked suspicious. 'Why?' Well, we might want to photograph some rare ones. Silence. It was getting frustrating. Bob, who spoke little French, looked baffled; we had met such charm and enthusiasm elsewhere. 'Will you pay?' Kochno asked. Well, yes, according to normal copyright rates, and so on – the usual BBC plea of poverty. He got up suddenly. 'Come back in two days, and we shall see.'

Two days later we returned. This time the wait was interminable. At last, after over thirty minutes, which we had used to take a good look at what was on the walls – fascinating, but little to do with the Diaghilev Ballet – he came slowly down the stairs, dressed in an exquisite eighteenth-century Chinese mandarin coat. The effect was extraordinary. He was, in fact, still wearing the waistcoat and trousers of the three-piece suit, and the shirt, without a collar or tie. I doubt whether he had changed his clothes since our last meeting. He was very unsure of his foothold on the stairs, and it rapidly became apparent that he was extremely drunk. I found it almost impossible to understand anything he said. He seemed in any case quite uninterested in me, and started talking to Bob, in heavily accented but quite reasonable English. This had not been vouchsafed at the previous meeting. I thought quickly, and asked if I could use the bathroom. He waved in the direction of the stairs. I went up, without any need of the bathroom, but simply to see if I could see anything on the walls upstairs that might give a clue as to whether he still had anything of value, or, as I was beginning to suspect, had sold it all to pay for the drinks bills. I nosed around discreetly for as long as was possible, but saw nothing. When I came downstairs, Bob was standing in the middle of the room, scarlet in the face. Oh dear, I thought, I can just imagine what's happened here. By now Kochno looked as though he was about to pass out. Bob said to me through clenched teeth, 'Just how much do I have to do to make this film happen?' We were leaving for London the following day, and I saw no point in trying to talk any more. We left, depressed and fairly sure that we would get nowhere with Kochno. As we walked rather disconsolately down the street, Bob said, 'Poor Diaghilev.' It was a new view. I had tended to believe that Diaghilev had been surrounded by genius, but it was slowly becoming clear that some of his associates, although they had talent, were not always very nice, to put it mildly. It was over a year later, and through Marie Rambert, that I learned from Parmenia Migel Eckstrom that Kochno still had a vast collection. It was subsequently exhibited in France and New York, and later bought by the French government, and can now be seen in the Paris Opéra library.

My failure with Kochno was serious, for he was one of the very few people who had been part of Diaghilev's inner group, the so-called committee, who discussed and decided everything, and whom Diaghilev trusted. Even if Kochno had not had the weight of some of his predecessors, for example Benois or Bakst, he had been close to Diaghilev in all the later years. It was dispiriting, and it seemed increasingly that we would get charming reminiscences from people such as Sauguet, but probably nothing on film from the important collaborators.

It was, anyhow, in such contrast to our visit a few days earlier to the studio of Alexandre Benois, Diaghilev's first great supporter and champion. Benois had now been dead for seven years, but his daughter, Anne, still lived in the studio in the fifteenth arrondissement. This had been Benois's home for the last twenty years of his life. It was a treasure house, and she let us look at everything. There were a small number of sets of costume designs; they had mostly been sold. Hardly surprising, for goodness knows what the old man had lived on in his later years. We had already discovered the huge confusion that exists around the various versions of *Petrushka*, which Benois had designed first for Diaghilev in 1911, then in Stockholm for Fokine in the 1920s and in later versions in France, Germany and England. Naturally the 1911 ones were the most valuable, and we discovered instances of tampering with dates on some of the designs. Anne Benois was a widow – it was said that her husband had shot himself after finding her *in flagrante* with a family friend. She certainly had been beautiful, as we saw from the marvellous family scrapbooks which she produced. One in particular concentrated on summer holidays in the Crimea before the Revolution. There were drawings by Benois, photographs of family and guests, drawings by other guests, including Bakst, of the Benois family, snapshots of well-known faces: Karsavina after her elopement with the young British diplomat who would become her second husband. There was also a complete set of *Mir Isskustvo* (*The World of Art*), the magazine that Diaghilev had edited from 1898 to 1904, and which had first brought him to the attention of Russia, and then gave him his entrée into the West as well. Most remarkable of all was the catalogue of Diaghilev's first great exhibition of historical portraits, in 1905 in St

Petersburg in the Tauride Palace. I had learned how Diaghilev had travelled the length and breadth of Russia, visiting houses in remote provinces, to bring together this first-ever evaluation of the portrait in Russian art history. Not only had Benois kept the catalogue, but he had meticulously noted in his copy exactly what happened to the portraits at the Revolution – which had passed into public collections, which were lost, which destroyed. Benois had, after all, been director of the Hermitage for the first years after the Revolution, and was largely responsible, with Lunacharsky, for saving many of the works of art in private hands, including the great impressionist collections of Mamontov and Schukin.

All this Anne Tcherkessova laid out for us, and in due course let us borrow to have photographed. What would happen to it all? Anne had a son, a feckless man, who looked very like his cousin, Peter Ustinov, and who earned his living as a film extra in the studios of Boulogne Billancourt. Was he interested? Not in the least. She decided it should all go back to Russia, to the Theatre Museum in Leningrad. We felt close to Benois in that crowded studio, but, of course, he was no longer around to be questioned. His memoirs, civilized and modest, show quite clearly, though in an understated way, how far Diaghilev eventually moved from Benois's world. To the younger generation, such as Kochno, Benois was a figure from the nineteenth century or even, through his taste, from the eighteenth.

Perhaps the most exotic of my Paris meetings was with the Princesse Marthe Bibescu. I knew from friends that she had seen the Diaghilev Ballet, and had known all of that group of rich French society women who had helped fund Diaghilev, the Princesse de Polignac, the Comtesse Greffuhle, Misia Sert. Unexpectedly, Princesse Bibescu spent part of each year in Cornwall, where her daughter had married another Romanian prince. Her Paris apartment was on a high floor at the very prow of the Île St Louis. I was shown into a room of no great size, but extreme elegance, by a maid. There was no sign of the Princess. The flat seemed small; where was she? Suddenly a door burst open, and there she was. It must have been a little antechamber, but at the time I was convinced it was a wardrobe out of which she stepped, wearing a hat and gloves, to take up a position on a *chaise longue*, inclining herself at exactly the same angle as the one white lily in an art nouveau vase.

She was riveting about the social world of Paris on the eve of the First World War. She had known everybody, especially the Proust circle, but of Diaghilev her recollections were so sketchy that they could have come from accounts by others. She did, on the other hand, remember vividly the first night of the Diaghilev Ballet, 19 May 1909, at the Châtelet Theatre, because she had been there. She could not recall what had been danced, but she knew the company she was in, and with good reason, for she shared a box with two former imperial mistresses – the mistresses of Alexander II and Alexander III. One of them was called Lobanov Rostovsky, the name of the other I have forgotten; they had both been pensioned off and were living in Paris in some state. It was a wonderful story, marvellously told, though little help except for one telling detail. The Châtelet was not a smart theatre, more a home for operetta. Diaghilev had gone there only because he had failed to get the Paris Opéra, where his previous season of Russian opera had been presented in 1908. Something had to be done to smarten it up. So large sums were spent on flowers. There were tubs of them in the corridors, filling the foyers, all to make the place look worthy of the setting Diaghilev wanted. Needless extravagance? Snobbery? It seemed to Princesse Bibescu very clever, and she recollected clearly the impression it made, nearly sixty years later, even if she had forgotten the ballets.

Of course, I had already visited the Châtelet, and decided that the film should begin on-stage there, where the story started. I had also spent time in the archives of the Paris Opéra, and found at least one photograph of Nijinsky I had never seen before. Bob went off to photographic studios to look at sheets of contacts from the later years. One company, Lipnitzki, produced dozens of photographs of *The Prodigal Son* of 1928. I was becoming convinced that, quite apart from the words, there would be pictures too. But the story was still obstinately the facts, and little more.

It was time to dig deeper, into the memories of the London survivors. They at least would tell their stories in English. I also knew that the New York City Ballet was coming to the Edinburgh Festival, and that perhaps we could catch Balanchine there. My letter to Massine elicited a response which was not a refusal; I had spoken to Serge Lifar; Markova, based in New York, was coming to London; Dolin, temporarily in Australia, was on his way back soon. If I could only get Mesdames Karsavina, Sokolova and Rambert to face the camera, I thought I was on to something, as by now I had realized how exceptionally intelligent they were, and how much more they had to say than I had initially suspected.

4 Memory and Illusion

Intelligence was not, however, the hallmark of another elderly lady who turned up that summer. This was Nijinsky's widow, Romola. She was going the rounds, trying to raise money to film her version of the Nijinsky story. Her biography of her husband, and her selections from Nijinsky's diaries, had been very influential in the 1930s and the 1940s. The glamour of Nijinsky's short career and the tragedy of his madness was still something people remembered. I had learned from Marie Rambert that Romola came to London quite often, and always wanted to see Karsavina, who sought to avoid this, but was too well mannered to refuse to Romola's face. One morning Humphrey Burton asked me to come to his office. And there she was, in a mangy fur coat, her hair suspiciously Venetian red, and with the hawk nose that I knew so well from photographs. Later I took her down to the foyer to wait for a taxi and she asked me about my project – Humphrey had mentioned it. 'Yes,' she said, with a faraway look, 'Diaghilev was wonderful. And, you know, they all got it wrong; I was the only woman Diaghilev liked.' There seemed no point in pursuing her.

She eventually made her film in Norway. Humphrey bought it for the BBC, but I refused to show it unless it was given some sort of introduction or follow-up to point out the dozens of factual errors it contained. Romola's version was entirely unreliable, yet inevitably people would believe her. How could she be wrong, when she had been there? How could I be right, when I had not? Romola had, as Benjamin Britten once said of Ronald Duncan, 'a very creative memory'. I never dared tell Karsavina of Romola's ludicrous claim that Diaghilev liked her, but Sokolova hooted with derision. She, unlike Karsavina, had been on the boat to South America when the extraordinary courtship took place, in Diaghilev's absence. In fact, Sokolova later produced her invitation to the wedding, and some previously unseen photographs. Sokolova had become by now a real friend. It was impossible not to love her, with her hilarious frankness about everything. She was the perfect counter-balance to Karsavina. Karsavina always seemed to me loftily above the sweat and effort. Sokolova, from her ordinary background in Essex, had never quite got over the extraordinary thing that had happened to her.

Little Hilda Munnings from Wanstead, at first Munningsova, later Sokolova – a name chosen for her by Diaghilev as a huge compliment, since it was the name of a great nineteenth-century Russian ballerina – was a witness to the best and worst moments of the Diaghilev Ballet's history. She had even danced *Spectre* with Nijinsky on his last tour of America with the company in 1916. Massine had choreographed his version of *Le Sacre* on her, and also *The Three-cornered Hat*, though the première went to Karsavina. Sokolova had lived in England ever since illness and endless operations had ended her career in the 1930s, in a tiny cottage in a narrow street in the village of Riverhead, which ribbon development had virtually joined on to Sevenoaks. She had been married since the late 1930s to a delightful man, Ronnie Mahon, some years her junior, who worked for the Royal Bank of Scotland, and travelled daily to London.

Sokolova was practically never really well. She had almost died giving birth to a daughter in the difficult years of the First World War, when she had stayed with Diaghilev at first in Switzerland and then in Spain and Latin America. She was married to a Russian character dancer in the company called Kremnyov, who had a nasty reputation and who, she implied, not only drank heavily, but knocked her about. She saved the child, but after an abortion in 1920 complications recurred, and throughout the 1920s, while still dancing major roles, she was in and out of clinics and hospitals in both France and England. By the late 1920s she was living with one of the stars of the last years of the Diaghilev Ballet, the Polish dancer Leon Woizikowski, a compulsive gambler, who also gave her a hard time. (They had remained in contact after the war, which he had spent in Poland, and occasionally corresponded or talked on the phone; Woizikowski was ballet master in Cologne.)

Everything about Lydia was both natural yet incredible. She would sit in her overcrowded little sitting room, and with almost instant recall describe people, ballets, situations from the early days. She was one of the longest-serving members of Diaghilev's company, the first English dancer to be recruited in 1913 and, except for very small breaks, with him until the end. Her view was many-faceted. She had been at times very close to him in adversity, and then suddenly as remote as most of the dancers. Like everyone, she was sometimes rather frightened of him. He always won her round. I remember a story of an evening when she was scheduled to appear as one of the twelve Princesses in *The Firebird*, a very small role for a principal dancer. She complained that *Le Sacre* took it all out of her, and she begged to be let off *The Firebird* to keep up her strength for her main roles. Diaghilev was adamant, so on she went. At the end a huge basket of flowers was presented to this minor-seeming person, one of a group of girls at the back; the public must have been mystified. To her it typified Diaghilev's authority and, of course, his charm, when he wanted to exercise it.

No one talked more than Sokolova, or more freely. No aspect of the company was beyond her recollection, but even she did not know how it had all happened. She had never been part of the small inner group who had decided on repertory and new creations, or who should be commissioned. She would never have discussed these things with Sergei Pavlovich, though he used her quite often as an interpreter. Diaghilev never mastered the English language, and especially in Spain, when Diaghilev was negotiating the company's return to England in 1918, Sokolova worked hard, translating letters from Oswald Stoll. Both her Russian and her French had been rather good; they still were when she wished, even though she had never studied either language. She had a natural intelligence and quickness that had seen her through a tough professional life, and a tricky private one. She, of all the people I saw, was the one most determined that my project should prosper.

The more I got to know Sokolova, the more outrageous it seemed that she had been allowed to contribute so little to the development of ballet in Britain. With the exception of a brief appearance in a revival of *The Good-humoured Ladies* in 1962, the Royal Ballet had made no use of her whatsoever. She, and many other Diaghilev survivors, held the view that Ninette de Valois did not want anyone around who might have known more than she did. They all respected Ninette's achievement, but it stopped short of affection. Grigoriev and his wife, and Karsavina, had eventually been brought in to help with the restaging of *The Firebird* and *Petrushka*, but Sokolova's much more remarkable memory was untapped. However, Buckle had encouraged her to write, and her book *Dancing for Diaghilev* is far and away the most engaging and informative about the life of the company. Sokolova gave me endless assistance, and took to writing or telephoning nearly every week for the rest of her life. She became a close and dear friend. My powerful dislike of Rudolf Nureyev was in part caused by his once sneering at Sokolova in my presence, claiming that she tried to pass herself off as Russian. Nothing was further from the truth, and I told him that no one spoke of her like that in front of me. My host was furious that I had ruined his dinner party, but I am quite unashamed.

Sokolova always knew where everyone was, who was or was not

speaking, which saved me time and potential embarrassment. I can hear her now saying, 'Oh, I wouldn't bother, dear, he never had anything to say.' This of the virtuoso dancer of the Massine years, Idzikowski, a tiny and brilliant technician, but no great mind. He lived in Penge with the rather larger Madame Evina. Lydia speculated wildly on their relationship. She and Tchernicheva had once found some condoms in Idzi's coat pocket – 'The very smallest size, dear, and you know Evina was huge – I don't know how they managed!' On my only meeting with Idzikowski, unprofitable as Lydia had foreseen, the mention of Sokolova's name caused him to seize a chair and smash it into pieces. Lydia later speculated in a letter that perhaps he kept the chair especially for that purpose. None of Lydia's racy stories got into the film, and fewer into her book than I dare say she wished. They are lodged in my memory. Every time I saw her she had had other ideas, thought of another angle, found something else in the trunk in the garage called Pandora's box; but still she would not face the camera. Her appearance was, indeed, rather odd. She had never been a beauty, but the total removal of her eyebrows and their replacement with two blue lines on her forehead did not help. However, she wore a pretty blond wig, and always looked as if she had made an effort. I watched her creatively using her memory when she assisted Sotheby's in promoting the sales of recently discovered Diaghilev costumes by posing young dancers in the right positions both to show off the costumes and to evoke the choreography. 'Now, dear,' she would say, of some obscure work which had been danced only a few times some forty years earlier, 'what did we do? . . . Oh, yes!' and within moments it all came into sudden fitful life.

Of course, the fact that Sotheby's had become heavily involved in sales of Diaghilev-related material was evidence of the way that the story was becoming better known, yet the prices were extremely low compared with today: a Bakst Odalisque, a genuine one, for one hundred pounds; costumes for less than fifty pounds. But there were buyers: George Howard of Castle Howard, Bengt Hager of the Swedish Theatre Museum, the Australian National Gallery in Canberra. I have never forgotten Lydia's face when the Chanel bathing costume she wore in *Le Train Bleu* was unwrapped from the tissue paper. It was full of holes, and looked more like a dishcloth than anything by Chanel. Lydia shrieked, then said, 'Well, you know, dear, it was very chic at the time!' Eventually I became intense and emotional with her after two or three gins in the local pub. 'I cannot do this film unless you agree to be filmed!' She said she would think hard, and a few days later she wrote to me: 'I will do your programme on condition you do me a Dietrich, and put me behind a gauze. I shall have to get the dentist to pad out my gums somehow, then maybe I shall not appear to be an old witch!' I told Karsavina this, and she sighed. 'Very well, but you must tell me what questions you want to ask.' How could one not love them, these extraordinary women?

Someone else who had become a friend was Sacheverell Sitwell. I wrote him a tentative letter, knowing how much he valued his privacy and how rarely he came to London. I received a postcard in response, saying he was intrigued, and would I ring? So I rang Weston Hall, near Towcester, and spoke to the butler. Mr and Mrs Sitwell were in London, perhaps I could call them there? They were at the International Sporting Club. I rang; a deep voice answered; I went into my carefully prepared speech; there was a pause . . . 'This is Mrs Sitwell. I'll get my husband.' Another pause, then a high-pitched, fluting voice said, 'Hello.' It was Sachie. I was asked down to lunch the following week. I had always been interested in the Sitwell story; all three had been around in my youth. I had heard Edith recite several times. On one memorable night she read 'Still Falls the Rain', and then Benjamin Britten and Peter Pears performed Britten's setting of it. Unlike some, I found much of her writing far from silly. I had seen Osbert often, since he lived close to me, and seemed the last person in London always to wear a hat. But Sachie I had never met or even seen.

I was let in by the butler. Sachie greeted me, very courteously, then offered a drink. He went to a trolley in the dining room, above which on the wall was a portrait of a ringleted girl of the early Victorian period. 'Oh yes,' I said, 'Louisa Hely-Hutchinson.' Sachie spun round. 'How do you know that?' 'Well,' I said, 'it's illustrated in *Left Hand! Right Hand!*, or is it *The Scarlet Tree*?' – two of the five volumes of Osbert's autobiography. At that moment Mrs Sitwell appeared. 'Do you know, darling, Mr Drummond recognized Louisa. Isn't that splendid?' Mrs Sitwell looked a little less impressed. I had been warned to be careful of her as most people thought her very difficult. She looked the archetypal English aristocrat *d'un certain age*, well-cut grey hair, tweed skirt, twin set, pearls, excellent shoes and handbag. Nothing could seem more English, except she was not; she was Canadian, the sister of the actress Frances Doble, friend of Noël Coward. Yet forty years of English country-house life had left its mark on her appearance and her voice.

They started to quiz me. Who did I know? Karsavina – 'Divine!' Marie Rambert – 'Very extraordinary – did you know her name was originally Rambam?' No, I did not, I thought it was Ramberg. 'No, not at all, Cyvia

Rambam.' This led to a lengthy discussion of Jewish names, and how they evolved. 'Do you know you can spell Ashkenazy five or six different ways?' and Sachie the polymath was off. I loved it. I had always admired his eclecticism, in a sense much more than his actual writing. I had read him on every subject from Mozart to Liszt, from southern baroque art to Dutch tulips. It seemed he had the life I would have liked. He asked me if I knew Spain. 'A little,' I said, having been once in a wet autumn to the nastier end of the Costa Brava. 'I prefer Italy.' 'Yes,' he said, 'so do my family, which is probably why I love Spain. I had to do something different.' After a simple but excellent lunch, when Georgia had left the room, he told me a bizarre story about Paganini. The deformed, twisted hip in the well-known statuette, of which Sachie had an example in the library, was a delicate reference not to any known deformity, but to a tradition that Paganini always became so excited by his performances that he got an erection. Oh yes, and by the way he would like to take part in the film, he had much admired Diaghilev. He then retired for a post-prandial rest.

Georgia walked me out to the car, took my arm and said, 'Come again; Sachie likes you. I like you. Just ring.' It was the first of many happy visits to Weston, always with some memorable story or observation. Once Sachie said unexpectedly, 'Do you watch wrestling on television?' I replied guardedly with something about ritual theatre. He brushed it aside: 'No, no, I love it for itself. We have it here in the Midlands on Wednesdays and Saturdays. You know Edith was buried on a Wednesday, and it was rather a lowering occasion. I thought as we drove back, well at least there's wrestling tonight, and do you know, it was quite a solace.'

The last time I saw Sachie, nearly twenty years later, he was driven over for lunch to a friend with whom I was staying near by. I had not seen him since Georgia's death. 'How are you coping?' I asked. 'Not well,' he said. 'I am becoming very eccentric.' This from a Sitwell. 'In what way?' I asked. 'I talk to myself all the time, out loud.' 'We all do,' I answered, 'who live alone.' 'No, but John, you don't understand. I say the most bizarre things. The other day I heard myself say to myself, "I shouldn't do that if I were you, darling!"' 'Well, at least you didn't say, "Have another drink, dear",' I suggested. He smiled wanly. In the intervening years I had interviewed him about Diaghilev, about William Walton, who wrote *Belshazzar's Feast* at Weston, and about other friends. I proposed on his seventy-fifth birthday that we might record an interview about his life. 'Not ready for the obituaries,' he said tartly. The sad thing was how riven his family was by the terrible dislike between Sachie and Georgia and their daughter-in-law,

Penelope, wife of the eldest son, Reresby. It seemed to me quite inexplicable. I had wanted to take Sachie to Renishaw to talk about his parents and his brother and sister. With some embarrassment he walked me round the garden and said he was *persona non grata* at Renishaw. He could not go there at all.

Meanwhile, I had been there, and for an odd reason. I had been looking for a great classical ruin to film for the Diaghilev project which would stand symbolically for the Russian Revolution and the destruction of the old order, to which Diaghilev referred in a rare recorded speech. It was to represent Petersburg and the changed world of post-revolutionary Russia. Leafing through my many volumes of Pevsner's *Buildings of England*, I stumbled on a house in Derbyshire called Sutton Scarsdale. It was grand, and wonderfully roofless, or so the photograph suggested. I telephoned the county archivist in Derby to find out to whom it belonged. Sir Osbert Sitwell was the unexpected reply. I rang Sachie. Indeed, Osbert had bought it for £1,500 to save it from the demolition men. It had belonged to the Arkwrights of spinning-jenny fame. The last Arkwright had been kicked in the head by a horse, and had become very bizarre, ending up living in the butler's pantry and selling off the house piecemeal. Years later I was to find one of the marvellous plasterwork interiors in Philadelphia. Eventually nothing was left but the walls; deserted, the roof fell in and, as in *Sleeping Beauty*, vegetation took over. Osbert now lived in recluse at Montegufoni, near Florence. Like all his English property, the house had passed to Sacheverell's son, Reresby, to avoid death duties. I called Reresby. Might I visit the ruins? 'Civil of you to ask,' he said, 'but you can walk in off the road. Be careful, it's pretty dangerous.' He suggested that I visit the following week, when he would be at Renishaw, a few miles away. 'You might care to dine and stay over?' I leapt at the chance to see a house I felt I knew well from Osbert's autobiography and John Piper's illustrations.

I arrived in the late afternoon, having seen Sutton Scarsdale, which was everything I had been looking for. I rattled on about Sachie and Georgia and how good they had been to me. We dined *à trois* in the vaulted dining room, waited on by a self-selected servant, I think the manager of the local colliery, whose parents had been in service at the house, and who took pride in helping out. After dinner Reresby went to try to get him to accept some form of payment. He never would, and tonight Reresby had on offer a copy of the book he had recently written with his friend John Julius Norwich on Mount Athos. I was left alone in the drawing room with Penelope, seated under the huge John Singer Sargent portrait of Sir George and Lady Ida Sitwell and their three children. What, asked Mrs Sitwell, did I think of the older generation of Sitwells? 'Well,' I stammered, 'I didn't really know your Uncle Osbert; I found Edith rather daunting, but your father-in-law has been marvellously kind to me.' A silence hung in the air. She said, firmly, 'Osbert's a bore, Edith's a terrible old phoney and my father-in-law, quite simply, the most unpleasant man in Europe.' At that moment Reresby returned and, sensing a hiatus, said, 'What's going on?' Penelope said chattily, 'I was just telling Mr Drummond how much we loathe your family.' Time for bed, I thought. I do not believe either Penelope or Reresby has any recollection of this visit, and on subsequent meetings over the years they have never shown any sign of knowing who I was, or that we had ever met before.

With hindsight I can imagine that a typical upper-class boy such as Reresby must have found it appalling at Eton to be linked with his loony aunt and her mad costumes and even madder poetry. Too embarrassing for words. He and his brother had probably heard Sachie's stories over and over again. Nevertheless, I found it hard to believe that when, after Georgia's death, the younger son, Francis, and his wife took over Weston, Sachie should insist on the house being divided down the middle and a new kitchen inserted, so that they would not have to share anything. Luckily, he shared with me his memories and his anecdotes, and unencumbered by familial associations we became friends. There was always so much to ask about and learn.

5 Three Dames and an Eventual Knight

The two principal figures in dance in London in the 1960s were the two dames, Marie Rambert and Ninette de Valois. Both of them, I knew, could make a considerable contribution, for they both thought as well as reacted in relation to their memories. Rambert, for survivors of the Diaghilev world, was a controversial figure. Many of them felt that she had based a long career on limited exposure to rigorous training or technique. It was all very well, Sokolova said, Rambert rolling down hills, her favourite pursuit until her eighties, if she couldn't teach First Position. Rambert had come into the Diaghilev Ballet by a curious sidestep from the Dalcroze Institute in Dresden, brought in to help Nijinsky work out the rhythmic complexity of *The Rite of Spring*. Dalcroze's theories of eurhythmics were fashionably avant-garde in pre-First World War Germany. Diaghilev visited his school at Hellerau and met this young Polish former medical student. Rambert knew little of classical dance, but in the way of things, after her exposure to and experience of *The Rite of Spring*, she joined the company and went on the South American tour of 1913 on which Nijinsky got married. When the First World War broke out, she moved to London and married the writer Ashley Dukes. She eventually studied with Astafieva, who was later to teach both Markova and Dolin, and after the war with Diaghilev's ballet master, Cecchetti. But it was surprising to someone such as Sokolova that Rambert should have founded a school which, however forward-looking, based its work on classical technique.

Rambert, known to everyone as Mim, had not always been beautiful or much admired. She became both with the passing years. Earlier her constantly restless manner irritated as many as it charmed. She had a habit of talking all the time at the theatre. Lydia Sokolova, seated some rows behind her at a gala at the Royal Opera House in the 1930s, could not stand it any longer. She went up to Mim in the interval, seized her by the chignon she always wore in those days on her head and shook her like a terrier with a rat. 'Silly little bun,' she shouted, 'silly little bun! Wouldn't stop talking, would it?' They did not speak for years.

By the time I got to know her, in 1960, when I was for a brief period a lodger in the flat of her secretary, Erica Bowen, she had mellowed. What was now clear was the extraordinary instinct she had for recognizing talent. Frederick Ashton had been a member of her company, and arranged his first dance piece for her as long ago as 1928. Then Anthony Tudor had been her principal choreographer in the 1930s, before going off to America. Rambert found them, encouraged them, pushed them, forced them and then they left. It was true of dancers also. Although this must have caused her bitterness, she never let it show. I enjoyed seeing her, and she took to telephoning me at odd hours, to chat about people, places and most especially Pushkin, her idol. For a Pole educated in Paris and resident in London for over forty years, she had become surprisingly Russian. I once said to her, 'I know who you are, you're the Grand Duchess Anastasia!' She took to signing her postcards to me Anastasia, and on one occasion 'V. I. Lenin, secretary to the Grand Duchess'. One evening, in the last year of her life, I drove home with her from Covent Garden, and quite by chance asked her if she knew the words of the French cabaret song that pops up in the First Act of *Petrushka*. I thought it was called 'Elle Avait une Jambe de Bois'. Rambert threw her head back and sang about five verses, each ruder than the last, as to what the lady had done with her wooden leg. One always came away from seeing Mim somehow enlivened. Her life cannot have been easy, keeping the company and the school going for all those years, yet she loved the young men to whom she had handed over, Norman Morrice, John Chesworth and Christopher Bruce, and though I am sure she often drove them mad, she fought for them. It was only late in life that she admitted she had been in love with Nijinsky, and then it became a kind of party piece, trotted out whenever wanted. Was there a touch of hindsight and rewriting history, or had she wanted to protect her husband and children in a world less given to emotional confessions? Watching her turn the pages of her copy of Baron de Meyer's photographs of the *Faune*, there was an extraordinary feeling of closeness and tenderness. She had a copy of the four-handed piano arrangement of *The Rite of Spring* and in it she had marked all the choreographic movements she could remember. By the time the Joffrey Ballet sought to revive it in 1980 I had lost trace of what happened to that score, but I suspect it is in some American collection.

Most of the people who left Rambert in their earlier years had joined de Valois at Sadler's Wells, Ashton most significantly. I, of course, had seen de Valois in the theatre and on television, heard her speaking at meetings and on the radio, but I had never met her. As I have already stated, I was not the greatest admirer of the Sadler's Wells company, despite the presence of some good dancers. There were few men, it must be said, but some very striking women, such as Beryl Grey or Moira Shearer. But when Beriosova joined the company in the 1950s, and then Nureyev in the 1960s, I realized that at last I could see what had been missing – the grand style of the Russian tradition. Beriosova had acquired it from her father, Nicholas Beriosoff, a wonderful teacher. Nureyev had grown up inside that tradition in Leningrad.

It was always said that Ninette was a good general, rather than a great artist. Her choreography was well made and serviceable, sometimes, as in *Checkmate*, much better than that. But I felt something lacking in the whole set-up. I hated then, and still do, the way they called her Madam. Madams run brothels. Diaghilev, who admired her dancing very much (according to Karsavina, it had been brilliant and effective), hated the name she had chosen. 'Half tart, half royal family of France', he said. Yet the former Edris Stannus from Ireland had fought a long and tenacious battle to establish classical ballet on a national scale in England, and had achieved it, with a royal charter and Covent Garden, long before the opera caught up. Even though she had officially ceased to be director of the Royal Ballet in 1963, she still went in every day, advising, helping, suggesting and arguing. No one could stop her. I have never been able to decide whether her successors, Frederick Ashton, Kenneth MacMillan, Norman Morrice or Anthony Dowell, despite their considerable and varied talents, were the right people for the job, or whether somehow she prevented them from doing it, or using their full authority. She was constantly there with access to the board, with very firm views and very public status as founder-director.

My approach to de Valois in 1967 was through Ursula Moreton, a former Diaghilev *corps* dancer, who had been a mainstay of the Royal Ballet and its school. I was not allowed to meet Dame Ninette until the day of the interview. We spoke briefly on the phone. She insisted on being interviewed in her old office at the Royal Ballet School in Talgarth Road on the Cromwell Road extension, with the traffic thundering by outside. When we arrived, she erupted like a Roman candle when she saw the film crew. 'But it is a radio interview,' she stormed. 'How can I be filmed? I haven't been near a hairdresser for days!' I did not believe a word of it; she was applying her usual technique of wrong-footing everyone else to show who was in charge. We were sent to the canteen to wait. Then we were summoned, and with great seriousness and intelligence she gave one of the most thoughtful appraisals of the Diaghilev years and their legacy of all the interviews I was to record.

It is impossible not to have the most profound respect for Dame Ninette and her achievements, yet it is also possible to find her less than approachable. Over the many years that I have been meeting her, even been to her home to interview her, she has never recalled my name. After I joined the board of Governors of the Royal Ballet, she would always turn to Pamela May if I spoke and ask very audibly 'Who's that?' I think her whole life has been centred on the company and if you are not part of that, then you are not really of any significance. But this matters less than the fact that, even in her late years, she often spoke more sense than anyone else.

I will never forget the governors' meeting at which a decision had to be taken as to whether the Sadler's Wells Ballet would move to Birmingham. I was entirely for it, but almost everyone else was, for one reason or another, opposed. Even Peter Wright, who could see some advantages, feared that he would lose his best dancers. There was a great deal of sentimental tosh talked about Sadler's Wells, that most uncomfortable of theatres on both sides of the curtain. Then Ninette started banging the table, as was her wont; she told everyone that Sadler's Wells may have been the past, but Birmingham was the future. To Birmingham they would go. She was ninety-one years of age. There was a pause, then a collective chorus of agreement. 'Of course, Madam. If you say so, Madam.' And off to Birmingham they went. She was certainly a director still, but how much had she been truly an artistic director? It is the continuing relevance of that question which has ultimately made me cool about the significance of the English ballet school. The problem showed less when great creative artists such as Constant Lambert or Frederick Ashton were around, but once they had gone, what was left? It seemed much less than Balanchine had achieved in New York, despite the international acclaim the Royal Ballet had won, especially in America.

There were two internationally renowned English dancers still working in the 1960s who had been with Diaghilev and later with de Valois in the years at Sadler's Wells. They were Alicia Markova and Anton Dolin. Both had moved on, but since they came near the end of the Diaghilev story they were almost the only Diaghilev dancers I had seen often. It is fair to say that by the time I saw them, after the war and in the 1950s, neither was exactly young, yet they surely provided a crucial link between the world of Diaghilev and the British dance experience that I knew.

Markova joined Diaghilev while still almost a child. He had been notably fond of her, and she saw a tender, human side of him denied to many others. My memories of Markova as a dancer have not faded.

43

Though not classically beautiful of face or figure, she had a rare sense of poetry in movement. Few dancers in my experience were so good in both acts of *Giselle*. Most are strikingly better in one or the other. She could be a simple peasant girl in the First Act, and then a vision of romanticism to put beside the engravings of Taglioni in the second. Only Chauviré and Ulanova, in my view, came as close to the heart of this essential classic of the repertory. *Giselle* had been virtually forgotten in France where it was created, but had been preserved in Russia, and then it was returned to the West by Karsavina and Nijinsky in Diaghilev's second season in 1910.

I knew Markova's younger sister, Doris, quite well. She was a jolly, engaging woman who worked for years assisting Hughie Green in his terrible television show, *Opportunity Knocks*. Their older sister had married Arnold Haskell, doyen of dance writers, whom I had heard lecturing and, of course, read. Haskell was extremely odd-looking, with a goatee beard, bow-ties, a high-pitched voice and (can I really remember it correctly?) spats. He was still alive in 1967, but I never approached him. I cannot now remember why. Was I warned off by Dicky Buckle, or did I just decide not to? I simply do not know.

But Markova I had to see. She was at that time in charge of the ballet company of the Metropolitan Opera in New York. Elegant, petite and ageless with her geisha-like hairdo, she came to London and we had a meeting. It was very cordial, but it was hard to get her to speak above a whisper or, indeed, to tell any story that lasted less than fifteen minutes. I was looking for shorter statements, and in the end I used only a brief extract from the interview we filmed – a rather trivial story about a constructivist ballet called *La Chatte*, in which she had taken over from two dancers who were injured. The photos of the set, by Gabo and Pevsner, were beautiful; Sauguet had written the music and talked about it well, so I included Alicia's story about why the others had accidents, slipping on a floor covered in shiny American cloth, an unsuitable surface for dancing. Alicia solved the problem by sticking rubber soles on her pointe shoes. After the film was shown, Lydia Sokolova commented on the phone, 'Good old Alice! Exposed to the full splendour of the Russian Ballet and all she can talk about is her rubbers!' It was unfair, but made us all laugh.

The thing with Dame Alicia was that you needed time, and then in her little-girl voice she would come out with amazing things. Once, when we were both on the Dance Panel of the Arts Council, I drove her back from a performance in Oxford, and she started talking about make-up, especially for white roles, and how the make-up she wore for *Giselle*, *Swan Lake* or

Les Sylphides was all different. It was a real page of nineteneth-century theatre history. I begged her to record it for the Institute of Recorded Sound, or the archives of the Royal Ballet. She could not be bothered, and I wish today that I could still remember the exact details of how she dressed her hair slightly differently for each role, and why she believed it mattered. Had she learned it all from Olga Spessivtseva, the greatest classical ballerina of the 1920s and 1930s, whose tragic mental breakdown and subsequent history had been charted in a book called *The Sleeping Ballerina* (1966) by Markova's long-time partner and friend, Anton Dolin?

I wish I had seen Dolin in his youth. Everybody, including Karsavina and the very critical Sokolova, had admired him. In *Le Train Bleu* in 1924 his cartwheels and acrobatics as Le Beau Gosse had typified the new iconoclastic world of the 1920s. I had seen him partnering Markova in *Giselle* with Festival Ballet, and in other roles in the 1950s; I had admired his evocation of romantic ballet in *Pas de Quatre*. He was a wonderfully considerate partner, and a generally helpful teacher; Flemming Flindt had picked up several tips from him about the role of Albrecht in *Giselle*, including the highly dramatic fall at the end of Albrecht's solo in the Second Act, to suggest exhaustion. And yet, I have to say, I never found his presence on-stage in later years comfortable. I think I first saw him being noble in that curious farrago *Where the Rainbow Ends*, but I cannot forget him dancing a solo to the *Boléro* music of Ravel, which was painfully embarrassing. He had been the first British leading male dancer of this century, but his appearance had not worn well. His 1930s film-star looks – big nose, scraped-back brilliantined hair – were out of fashion in the age of the mop-headed Nureyev. Dolin had been not only for two periods a principal dancer with Diaghilev's company, but for a time his companion and lover. Could he bring me any closer to understanding how Diaghilev worked?

We had a great deal of toing and froing about getting together. He was constantly travelling, teaching, reviving ballets, visiting companies. Eventually we settled on a meeting in the south of France, where he was spending some weeks teaching at Rosella Hightower's school in Cannes. This had the advantage that we could film him in Monte Carlo, the scene of many of his successes, and of his closest period with Diaghilev. I went to Monte Carlo to sort out filming locations with the Opera House. Dolin had been responsible, through his friendship with Princesse Antoinette of Monaco, the sister of Prince Rainier, for the bust of Diaghilev which stands on the terrace above the sea, behind the Opéra. I do not know who chose the portentous inscription: 'De ce rocher par la faveur de ses Princes, Serge de Diaghilev fit rayonner ses Ballets Russes'.

We were to film there on a Monday; I flew to Nice on the Friday, and on the Saturday evening took a train to Cannes to visit Dolin at his hotel for dinner. He knew a good deal about what I was doing, whom I had seen and what I was trying for. He was extremely frank about his own role, not aggrandizing his achievements as a dancer, and rather pouring scorn on his young self for the way he had reacted to Diaghilev. He was flattered to be admired, but not much interested in more than that. The sexual role was something no one else had mentioned before. I was naturally intrigued. Diaghilev's sexual demands, he said, were straightforward, rather adolescent, and did not involve any form of penetrative intercourse. I was, of course, not going to use this material in the film, but I felt privileged in a way, that Dolin bothered to tell me about this, without my asking. We discussed friends and colleagues, planned the outline of the interview for Monday in Monte Carlo, after which he wanted me to visit the Princesse Antoinette. After dinner he suggested a drink on the Croisette before I caught my train back to Monte Carlo. We ended up in a curiously scruffy bar, where he seemed well known, especially to a group of young men of rather dubious orientation, for whom he bought drinks fairly lavishly. I had always understood that Dolin was very fond of money, and spent most of his time in the company of rich older women who, though not exactly keeping him, certainly helped with the bills, and eventually left him quite large sums. It was a contrast to other older dancers who never had a bean to their name. Most of them lived on tiny pensions, eked out by a little teaching, occasionally writing articles or serving as examiners.

I did not much like the bar in Cannes. Dolin introduced me to a young man whom he recommended highly, and rather landed me with. After about half an hour I looked round, to find Dolin was nowhere to be seen. He had gone home, without saying goodbye. He had also not paid for the drinks he had ordered. This was a time when there was a restriction on how much currency could be taken out of the country, and I had barely enough for my rather modest needs. There was an altercation with the barman and the boys, which ended with my paying slightly more than twenty pounds for the drinks – an enormous sum at that time, when a good bed at a hotel could be had for five pounds. I had also, through the arguments, missed the last train and had to spend the night in a sleazy hotel opposite the station in Cannes, getting back to Monte Carlo the following morning unshaven and with only a few francs left. I was absolutely furious, and tempted to film the theatre in Monte Carlo and forget the interview with Dolin. Of course, by Monday I had calmed down, but it cast a cloud over our relations. The interview was more formal than I would have wished; I found him consciously acting on camera in a way that felt forced and unnatural. Although he said many useful things, the relaxed mood of our dinner never returned.

For the rest of his life Pat, as everyone called him (his real name was Patrick Healey-Kaye), was always the soul of friendliness whenever I met him. We saw each other often, on several continents, and no one was more delighted than he about his eventual knighthood. But he never referred to the night in Cannes. Perhaps it was a genuine mistake, but somehow I doubt it. Twelve years later he came to the Edinburgh Festival at my invitation, to speak about Diaghilev and visit his old friend Alicia Alonso, who was appearing with her National Ballet of Cuba. We had agreed to pay his hotel bill. When the bill arrived, it included the sum of sixty pounds for flowers for Alonso, dispatched by him, but paid for by me.

6 Critics and Observers

It was almost a relief to turn from the dancers to some of those who had merely been in the audience. Foremost among these was the critic C. W. Beaumont. Beaumont more or less single-handedly created the profession, if such it be, of ballet critic. He was knocked out by the impact of Pavlova, whom he saw in 1910, the year before Diaghilev's ballet came to London. From then on he never missed a performance. He reviewed for the *Sunday Times* for fifty years, published innumerable books and translations and ran a bookshop in Charing Cross Road that was a Mecca for all dance lovers in my youth. He looked like a suburban undertaker, always in a wing collar, with a black jacket and striped trousers, and a shock of white hair *en brosse*. He and his wife lived in a gloomy apartment off Tottenham Court Road, and it was there, surrounded by books – every book, it seemed, that had ever been published on dance – that I visited him. For someone who made his living through words, he was an uncolourful speaker. He was formal and unsmiling, with a pronounced south London accent. He always stressed the word 'interesting', his favourite word, on the third syllable – inter*est*ing. He was a curious combination of modesty and pedantry; he had seen it all, but found it hard to evoke what it had felt like in conversation. His literal descriptions of ballets on the printed page were priceless historical evidence, yet to meet, I was shocked to discover, Beaumont was frankly very dull. He was by now in his late seventies, and had perhaps said it all too often before. His books, notably *The Diaghilev Ballet in London*, had been extremely useful to me, with their accurate information, and were a necessary corrective to many people's chancy memories. But he was not going to light up the screen in interview. He wrote to me once, pointing out something he thought I might not have noticed, which was Diaghilev's extraordinary superstitiousness, yet when I asked him to tell me the story, his account of it was so much less effective than the way he had described it in the letter.

Nevertheless, he was most gracious, and he lent me one absolutely invaluable document, the *Yearbook of the Imperial Theatres* for the year 1900, the first thing Diaghilev had published connected with dance or the theatre. It caused a famous scandal. An annual report by intention, it was so opulent and magnificently illustrated, and cost so much to produce, that Diaghilev lost his job as assistant to the general director of the imperial theatres as a result. I found the yearbook riveting; it contained a complete list of not only every work danced or sung, but who had danced or sung in it, and how often they had performed. Kchessinska, I noted, had performed only a few times that season, despite her fame. It also contained beautifully illustrated essays on, for instance, the architecture of the Aleksandrinsky Theatre, the drama theatre which had been designed by Benois's grandfather, and there were odd incidental pleasures, such as finding Stravinsky's father tucked away amongst the bass singers of the chorus. The whole approach to the publication suggested the importance of the reunion of the arts, whether in opera or ballet, and here, I felt, was the first evidence of Diaghilev's belief that it was this balance between the elements which created great theatre. The old ballets had silly stories, dull sets and routine music, but often great choreography and great dancers. How much greater would the impact be if all the elements were of the finest. At least Tchaikovsky, and to a lesser extent Glazunov, had raised the musical level beyond Drigo and Minkus; but there was a long way to go before one saw more than a glimpse of what was to become the Diaghilev vision.

I had often seen Beaumont in his shop, which he ran from 1910 until 1955. I knew also of the epic rows he had with his wife, the days when quite suddenly the shop was shut – depressing for me, who lived in the country, and only had an infrequent visit to London. Algeranoff had bought for me a biograpy of Danilova there, and I had leafed through many other books that I was too poor to buy for myself, including Beaumont's own book on ballet design.

I heard about Beaumont and his habits from an occasional assistant in the shop, W. B. Morris. Monty Morris was a figure from my childhood; born in Australia, he had been taken on as a messenger boy at fifteen by the Italian Embassy in Melbourne (then the capital of Australia), and had got a taste, somehow, for music and theatre. He had come to Europe to fight in the First World War and never gone home, working for the next thirty years in the Inland Revenue as a clerk. He must have made an improbable soldier, and he hardly seemed a typical civil servant. He was very tall, very thin and extremely effeminate, with long white hands and usually a trailing scarf. During the war, almost for fun, he had started helping Beaumont out in the shop. I was riveted by Monty's eccentricities, slightly to the consternation of my mother, who had known him since the 1930s. He, in fact, adored my mother, and his interest in me was totally without risk. He lived in Belsize Road, down the hill from Swiss Cottage, in a room stuffed with theatrical memorabilia. He collected everything, and in a small back room were piles and piles of newspapers, magazines and programmes waiting to be sorted out. His hobby was making scrapbooks, with everything identified (sometimes, I am afraid, incorrectly) in green ink, in a feathery copperplate, with eucalyptus leaves added to decorate the frames he drew around the cuttings. He lived in the same bedsitter, with the same landlady, for over fifty years. On their twenty-fifth anniversary they agreed to stop being Mr Morris and Mrs Whatever, and become Monty and Lally. Lally, whom I knew, tremendously disapproved of what she called his junk. Like all indiscriminate collectors, he had, indeed, rather a large amount of junk, but there were jewels concealed among the dross. There were Dresden figurines on the mantelpiece of Karsavina in her best-known roles, signed photographs on the grand piano and good set and costume designs on the walls. And then there were the dinners, three-course meals all cooked on one gas ring and known as the 'old one and nines'. One shilling and ninepence is what he claimed you would pay for them elsewhere. But elsewhere you would not have got his enthusiastic conversation, or the often surprising drinks. On one occasion I remember him producing a case of Lanson Black Label, a gift from Sacheverell Sitwell to thank him for a huge scrapbook on the Sitwells that he had sent as a present for Christmas. He was rather deaf by the 1960s, but was still to be seen everywhere at the ballet, with his piercing blue eyes, Basque beret and high-pitched voice exclaiming with outrage or delight. He was the very model of a modern balletomane.

Monty had several great scrapbooks of the Diaghilev Ballet, which he had accumulated over the years, and when I first started to work on the project, he lent them to me. There were many pictures I had never seen reproduced elsewhere, but, of course, no indication at all of where they had come from. Some were clipped from magazines, notably the French theatrical journal *Commedia Illustré*; others from the *Sphere* or the *Sketch* or the *Tatler*. It was a desperate task to try to trace their origins. Little did I know that the great photographer E. A. Hoppé, who had produced almost all the most memorable images of Nijinsky and Karsavina in the early years, and who was well represented in Monty's scrapbooks, was not only still alive, but living, of all places, in Salisbury. By the time I found this out Hoppé had died, not before claiming his copyright. Monty was also to die during the making of the film, and his scrapbooks passed to the Theatre Museum at Leighton House. We had quite a tussle about whether I had the right to use them, and who should be paid. In the end most of the pictures I found elsewhere, but Monty's books were for some things, such as the costumes of the original *Petrushka*, invaluable. His memorial service at All Hallows by the Tower, was well attended, for he knew everyone, and everyone liked him. Dicky Buckle gave the address, and the final phrase has stayed with me: 'His ship departing, leaves a shining wake.'

Beaumont's book on ballet design, which I had known since it was published in the late 1940s, had opened my eyes to the contribution that design had made to the look of twentieth-century dance, and to the Diaghilev period in particular: from Benois's set for *Les Sylphides* to Bakst's riotous oriental colours for *Schéhérazade*, to Picasso's cubist characters in *Parade*, or his masterly backdrop to *The Three-cornered Hat*. I wondered what contemporary designers thought about Diaghilev and that period, and I set out to ask two of them, both men of real taste and distinction, Osbert Lancaster and Cecil Beaton.

Lancaster was a personal hero of mine, although I had never met him. Apart from his cartoons, which I knew from their hardback publication (we did not take the *Daily Express* at home), and many of which I can still quote, I owe to him a permanent view of the growth and development of architectural and decorative style from his two wonderful books, *Pillar to Post* and *Homes Sweet Homes*. I had always been fascinated by architecture and design, and knew my styles – Early English, Perpendicular, Gothic Revival – but through Lancaster phrases such as 'Bypass Variegated' and 'Pont Street Dutch' passed into the language. In *Homes Sweet Homes* there was a drawing, with accompanying text, entitled 'First Russian Ballet Period', which showed a studio interior, complete with harlequin figure (shades of *Carnaval*), and a piano draped with a Bakst-influenced shawl; all very familiar from the studios of my mother's arty Hampstead friends, with their love of modernism and Freud. A whole part of my childhood was full of psychoanalysts and their dirndl-skirted, befringed, harpsichord-playing wives. They were rather more Kurt Jooss than Diaghilev, but they nevertheless believed that dance rather than opera or concert music was the truest form of self-expression. No one but Lancaster and I seemed to find their stance both significant and also rather funny, grafted on to the English middle class.

We met, predictably enough, at the Garrick. He made no effort at all, and I have rarely been made to feel so tiresome and time-wasting. A pop-eyed colonel in a pepper and salt suit, with a barking voice and not a trace of humour, was how he appeared to me. He resembled the army officers of his cartoons or Maudie Littlehampton's philistine friends. Was it a pose, or did I just catch him on a bad day? In the subsequent interview he got most of the facts wrong, particularly with regard to the great 1921 production of *Sleeping Beauty*. He remembered it as *Swan Lake*, and was mistaken about both the theatre and the year. Where he became interesting was on the craft of scene painting, something that even by the 1960s was being forgotten. When it came to practical details, he changed out of recognition, and became animated and fascinating. Yet my lasting impression is one of disappointment that someone who had influenced me so strongly was so much less engaging in person than in the way he wrote or drew.

Beaton was a different matter. I had little expectation of more than a casual conversation; in fact, he took my request for an interview very seriously. My link to him was a colleague at the BBC, Hal Burton, now forgotten, but at that time a leading television director. Trained as an architect and blessed with considerable private means, Hal loved the theatre, and theatre people, and became one of the best-known television drama directors of the early years after the war. By the 1960s he was in my department making curious monologue programmes with great actresses, and interviews with leading actors and actresses about their lives. Beaton was a friend of his – his portrait by Beaton hung on the wall of his elegant flat in Kensington. He told me of an extraordinary weekend he had spent in Wiltshire with Beaton and Greta Garbo, long before the papers were full of the Garbo–Beaton affair. He had travelled back with her on the train; she was wrapped in a belted raincoat with hat pulled down over her face, and to all intents and purposes invisible, yet by some form of attraction which no one could explain, at Salisbury station people gathered outside the window of her compartment and in the corridor of the carriage, drawn to her without even knowing why. Hal, and Garbo too, were sure she had not been recognized, for it was not even known that she was in the country.

Through Hal I had spoken on the telephone to Beaton, at that time flushed with the success of *My Fair Lady* in Hollywood, following its huge triumph in the theatre. We did not meet until the filmed interview, but it was clear that he had carefully planned what he wanted to say. When we arrived at the pretty little house in Pelham Crescent, with its indigo felt walls and huge clumps of hydrangeas, my cameraman had a sudden fit of nerves. How did one light this specialist in light? Beaton was wonderfully funny and self-deprecating, claiming to have no knowledge at all of how to light for portrait photography. It could have been affected and prissy – but it was not. Then he suddenly disappeared, to reappear a few minutes later wearing a glossy silver toupee. He said to the cameraman, 'Tell me quite truthfully if it shows, and I'll take it off. It's only vanity, after all.' I liked him immensely, and he had good things to say about colour and its impact in the theatre, and Diaghilev's contribution. I never saw him again, but subsequently read his diaries with much more enjoyment than my previous expectation would have suggested.

7 National Styles and International Sounds

Another of the aspects of Diaghilev's legacy which intrigued me was its impact on young English dancers, who rather to their amazement were recruited in the early 1920s because of the lack of arrivals from Russia with its closed borders. Four of them were eventually interviewed; none made spectacular contributions, but I felt that their so English voices would somehow give a greater sense of contrast, or shock.

Ursula Moreton was the soul of gentility. By this time she was rather portly, and had grey hair done up in a bun, and a charmingly self-abnegating manner – you would not have been surprised to find her running a tea shop in the Cotswolds. Yet here she was, talking about being flung in at the deep end in 1920 as one of the harem girls in *Schéhérazade*, with its naked flesh, flashing swords and brilliant Bakst colours. Like several of the dancers, she chose to be interviewed standing up; I recall her saying she never felt like a dancer sitting in a chair. She had been a faithful and long-standing supporter of Dame Ninette, and the photos of her in Ashton's ballet *The Lord of Burleigh* look most attractive and graceful. She was at the time we met director of the Royal Ballet School, a post she held for sixteen years. Her influence on several generations of British dancers was considerable. So much has been written about the English school, and I suppose Ursula typified it. Her training was impeccably European – she was a pupil of the great Italian teacher Enrico Cecchetti, who had been ballet master in Petersburg, and who became ballet master of the Diaghilev company.

Cecchetti's influence was greatly extended by Beaumont's work with him on the translation of a handbook of Cecchetti's method, which became almost a kind of Bible for British dance. There were, of course, rival schools and rival teachers and teaching methods, several, indeed, in London: Nicolai Legat (whose brother Sergei had been thought as promising as Nijinksy, but who had killed himself after the 1905 revolution) had settled in London, and waged a fairly constant war against Cecchetti. Legat had taken over at the Mariinsky Theatre after Petipa had been got rid of. Most of what was taught in this country depended on Russian methods. These Russian techniques were themselves a mixture of French, Italian and

Danish ideas. When it came to their application to English dancers, I wondered why it always seemed to me that what was produced was, though pretty pure in technical terms, pretty pale in theatrical terms. I suspect that people such as Ursula Moreton were responsible – good, sensible, thoughtful people, but without much passion, or that feeling for the exotic which is, for me, at the heart of classical dance. Anna Russell, the Canadian comedienne who made a career out of jokes about music, spoke of the 'pure white of the English soprano'. Its dance equivalent was to be seen year after year in the graduating performances of the Royal Ballet School; excellent training and presentation, not much feeling and almost no attack. It was hard to be thrilled, as one was by even the most boring socialist rubbish at the Bolshoi. It is not just a question of jumping higher, or of a more dramatic line in arabesques; it depends on feeling internally what a movement is meant to convey, rather than just making the movement correctly. 'Cool' is the word always used about the English style, but the tomato juice of the ballet's Bloody Mary needs plenty of Worcester sauce and lemon juice, and this is what I could not find in England.

Laura Wilson, another former *corps* dancer, was even more genteel, still amazed that all this had happened to her. I felt, in some strange way, that the nearest analogy to the effect of the Russian ballet on these girls was that of the arrival of the GIs during the Second World War – nothing had prepared them for such opulence and emotion. Caryl Brahms and S. J. Simon caught the mood in their at that time famous spoof *Bullet in the Ballet*, which still makes me laugh today, with its wretched male dancer known as The Man Who Was No Nijinsky, the constant shouting matches, walk-outs and bankruptcy. 'All very Russian!' people would say, not meaning the dour, potato-faced party *apparatchiks* of the communist years, but glamorous women, dashing Cossacks, throaty, tear-jerking songs.

That was what Russia meant in my childhood. The huge émigré population that I saw in Paris and London, with their ratty old fur coats, ropes of pearls, chignons and Sobranie cigarettes, was one of the most potent images of my youth. The apartment next to ours, before the war, had been occupied by a priest of the Russian Church and his family. Russians trouped in and out at all hours. I am told the ballerina Riabouchinska pushed me round the garden in my pram, though I cannot be sure. But I remember the sound of the language from earliest childhood, and the Russian accent, in both French and English. By the 1960s few of them were still around. I had been taught Russian by teachers whose personalities seemed vast beside their English colleagues: Vladimir Koshevnikoff, who had wanted to be a dancer and had met Diaghilev in Berlin in the 1920s, used to say, with wild eyes, the Ballets Russes was 'magnificent in excitement'. Madame Alhazova, a huge woman with a jutting bosom of the kind you never see nowadays, would speak wistfully of her home town, Odessa, and the violence of storms on the Black Sea. Of the Crimean War she said, 'Your English soldiers, they could not manage, they just died.'

I loved them all, and none more than the great singer Oda Slobodskaya, who was still just performing at the very end of a magnificent career. Slobodskaya, also from Odessa, had appeared with Diaghilev in Monte Carlo in the production of Stravinsky's *Mavra* that Kochno had talked about. She hardly remembered Diaghilev, but she remembered the care taken with the rehearsals, and the insistence on the highest musical standards. She lived in a small flat off Baker Street, and taught at the Royal Academy of Music. No one knew her age, but she must have been well over seventy when I last heard her perform, in the City of London Festival of 1964. There was little voice left, but there was mastery of words. I owe to her my total love of Russian song: not only Mussorgsky, whose *Nursery Songs* she had recorded, but also the range and power of composers such as Glinka, Dargomizhsky, Borodin and, indeed, even Tchaikovsky, whose songs were hardly known. Her recording of the 'Letter' scene from *Onegin*, made in 1939, is still one of the most thrilling, even though she must have been in her late forties. Not until Vishnevskaya came along had I heard Russian sung like that. It may seem an odd analogy with dance, but I had a feeling that Slobodskaya sang like the Diaghilev Ballet danced – full-out and with an intensity that could seem almost caricatural, but for its total belief in itself. Many of my contemporaries found Slobodskaya grotesque, but she always moved me to tears. Her last years were terrible, for she endured the amputation of both legs. One or two devoted young acolytes kept her going. She did not have enough to say about Diaghilev to justify interviewing her for the film, but I will always be glad to have met her, with her rasping voice and wonderfully colourful English. I once heard her introduce a children's song by Kabalevsky in the following way: 'This is a little pig, he go he-he, Mother say, you go going he-he till you are time to go hu-hu.' Rather better than the Third Programme's solemn invocations, 'In the following song the poet speaks . . . '

Another musician who had, improbably, been a dancer in the Diaghilev Ballet was the conductor and composer Leighton Lucas. His mother had been one of the rehearsal pianists for the company, and the little Lucas, renamed Lukin, had appeared while still a child as a page in the great *Sleeping Beauty* production of 1921. He gave up dancing early on, but was very much associated with the growth of the ballet in Britain, and as late as 1974 was to orchestrate the excerpts from Massenet's music that became the score of Kenneth MacMillan's *Manon*. To a lesser extent than Constant Lambert, whose crucial influence on the development of Sadler's Wells Ballet can never be overestimated, Lucas was a valuable link between music and dance.

Why is it that so many musicians are so contemptuous of ballet? It is not that ballet does not have great scores to work on, be it the Tchaikovsky classics, or the great Stravinsky scores, and from earlier times the marvellous charm and brilliance of Delibes in *Coppélia*, *Sylvia* or *La Source*; but contemptuous they are. I remember once having a discussion with the conductor John Pritchard about bel canto opera, venturing the view that Adolphe Adam's music for *Giselle*, with its very early use of leitmotif linked to the characters of the story, seemed to me in its simple, attractive way every bit as good as many operas by Donizetti. Pritchard was flabbergasted. A former chairman of Covent Garden once asked me if any great conductors had ever conducted ballet. 'Well,' I explained patiently, 'Ansermet and Monteux, as well as Beecham and Desormière, worked for Diaghilev; Dorati for de Basil; while Rozhdestvensky started out at the Bolshoi.' He was surprised. More recently Bernard Haitink has conducted a Stravinsky triple bill with the Royal Ballet; it was greeted by music critics like the Second Coming. At last we would hear the scores as they should be played. In fact, conducting for ballet is a highly specialized skill, and any good dancer will tell you how much difference a sympathetic conductor who watches the stage can make to the realization of their interpretation. It is no good grimly grinding on at the tempo the conductor feels the composer wanted; the choreography and the needs of the individual dancer must play their part. Why do certain kinds of music work for ballet and others not at all?

Diaghilev commissioned *Daphnis et Chloé* from Ravel, but revived it only once after its first unsuccessful outing. He later turned down *La Valse* as being quite unsuitable for dance. *Daphnis* has huge tableaux, in which nothing much happens, and then crucial episodes of the narrative compressed into tiny sections, with hardly enough notes to let the action take place. *Daphnis* is a problematic score for a choreographer, but one of the greatest glories of twentieth-century music. As to *La Valse*, opinions differ. Balanchine, after all, choreographed it and linked it to the *Valses Nobles et Sentimentales* long after Diaghilev's time. But Diaghilev was notably hostile to all things Viennese, whether it was Beethoven, Schoenberg or Johann Strauss. Is there really such a difference between a Tchaikovsky waltz and a Strauss waltz? I think so, but perhaps it is familiarity that makes me feel this. Petipa and Tchaikovsky, in *Sleeping Beauty* and *Nutcracker*, conjured up some of the great waltz sequences. The New Year's Day concert in Vienna always slides into schmaltz when the dancers appear. Many ballet scores are necessarily episodic, full of short dances and divertissements, but that does not stop some of them from being great music. I know no more magical score than *The Nutcracker*. Yet it must be remembered that the core of the Diaghilev repertory involved new music. For every *Schéhérazade* or *Carnaval* there were three or four new commissions from composers as different as Richard Strauss and Poulenc. And it is Poulenc that has lasted. No one recalls *Légende de Joseph*, not even in the concert hall, but *Les Biches* is arguably the most brilliant piece of theatre music written between the wars, let alone by a boy of twenty-three.

Sadly, the conductor Ernest Ansermet's visit to London, in the summer of 1967, was cancelled because of ill-health, and he never took part in my films; but he did come to London the following year for what was to prove his final recording sessions. It was then that I met him at the old Kingsway Hall, where so many great recordings have been made. He was, appropriately, recording *The Firebird*, which he had conducted for Diaghilev on its revival after the First World War. Everyone had remembered that he conducted it from memory. I asked him why. The answer was endearing: the only score was too big to sit comfortably on the conductor's desk, so it had to be memorized.

I had been warned by John Culshaw, who produced most of Ansermet's post-war recordings, that this Swiss mathematician and philosopher, with his little goatee beard and pince-nez, could be difficult. I approached him with a good deal of diffidence, but I was completely wrong. We had two long conversations at the Waldorf Hotel, where he stayed and, incidentally, where Diaghilev had spent his first night in London. Ansermet was extraordinarily open and ready to discuss anything. He had obviously hugely enjoyed working with the Diaghilev Ballet because of the new music it presented, though he had a memorably troubled relationship with Stravinsky, who always referred to him as 'le professeur'. Ansermet was, indeed, a professor. Culshaw had told me an unforgettable story of a meeting between Stravinsky and Ansermet in about 1950. They had fallen out definitively in Paris in the 1930s, when Stravinsky was living there, and had not spoken for about fifteen years. They met in Geneva – or was it Lausanne? – I forget, but on a tram, which says a great deal about both of them. Ansermet had been recording, with his Suisse Romande Orchestra, most of the great Diaghilev scores. Had Stravinsky heard them? No. Would he like to? It was arranged that he should call on Ansermet the following day. It was at the very end of the era of 78 r.p.m. records, and through the long Swiss afternoon the shellac discs dropped inexorably every few minutes on to the turntable. Stravinsky remained totally silent. They heard *Petrushka*, *Les Noces*, *The Firebird*, *Pulcinella* and so on. At the end Ansermet said, 'Well, Igor, what do you think?' 'I think,' said Stravinsky, 'that there's something wrong with your gramophone.'

Culshaw had this story from Ansermet himself, who recounted it not in anger or in bitterness, for even he could see the joke. Though Ansermet never featured in the films, I am including our later interview in this collection, because it helps to flesh out the musical side of the story – a side quite as important as the choreography, design and the dance itself.

Another Swiss conductor who did take part was the rather younger Igor Markevich. Not only had Markevich been Diaghilev's last protégé, but he had subsequently married one of Nijinsky's two daughters, and was a link to that story too. Markevich was a slim, shy man, who looked far younger than his years. His distinguished career was at a crossroads since, worst of all fates for a musician, he had begun to go deaf. He was self-deprecating about his English, but extraordinarily courteous and charming. We filmed him at the Ritz Hotel, and he spoke with modesty about his achievements. Diaghilev had discovered Markevich in Paris in 1928 when he was only fifteen. He commissioned, of all things, a piano concerto, and presented it as a kind of musical entr'acte in the last season of the Diaghilev Ballet at Covent Garden in the summer of 1929. It was not much admired. Then, rather improbably, Diaghilev took Markevich to Munich and Salzburg – I had never thought of Diaghilev as a lover of German opera. Markevich had mislaid the score of the concerto, and wrote it off as a piece of juvenilia. But he still spoke with surprise and wonder at Diaghilev's interest in him. Markevich was an extremely handsome young man. I was too shy to ask if there had been any sexual element to the relationship. He did not volunteer, but I suspect not. Diaghilev was, after all, in his late fifties, and already ill with the diabetes that was to kill him; Markevich was still in his teens. But Massine had been a teenager when Diaghilev took up with him in 1912, so who knows? It is not important.

59

Of Nijinsky Markevich spoke with enthusiasm, though he was too young to have seen him dance. He produced an extraordinary figure for the number of rehearsals that Nijinsky had had with the company for his first essay in choreography, *L'Après-midi d'un Faune*. About 200, Markevich claimed. No one else supported this figure, but it obviously took Nijinsky a long time both to convey what he wanted – a sort of lateral movement like an Egyptian frieze – and to link the passages together. The difficulties were remembered and described in detail by Marie Rambert and Lydia Sokolova. Markevich told me a story about taking his son to Venice when he was a teenager. On the beach at the Lido one morning an elderly Italian asked if he was related to the boy playing on the sand. 'Yes, he's my son,' said Markevich. 'Very strange,' said the old man. 'There was a Russian dancer who used to come here before the First War. He was very famous. The boy reminds me of him.' 'Yes,' said Markevich, 'that was his grandfather.' Both Nijinsky's daughters and the grandchildren inherited the unmistakable features of Nijinsky's appearance, high cheekbones and the powerful, muscular neck that shows in all the photographs and in the famous bust by Una Troubridge of Nijinsky as the Faune, which was rediscovered by Sokolova in a junk shop off Charing Cross Road. The bronze cast she left me in her will sits today on the piano in my drawing room.

Markevich's reputation is today in eclipse, though I remember brilliant performances by him. He was the first Western conductor to return to Russia and perform and record *Les Noces* with a Russian choir. For the twenty-fifth anniversary of Diaghilev's death in 1954 he recorded for Decca a whole series of ballets of the 1920s, including *Le Train Bleu*, *Les Fâcheux*, *Zéphyre et Flore*, most of them quite forgotten. He was a living link, and such a nice man. His own music has been the subject of much special pleading in recent years, and there is an international committee, of which I am happy to be a member, that seeks to present his works, many of them, for example *Le Paradis Perdu*, of vast dimensions. We played *Icare*, a ballet score he wrote for Lifar in the 1930s, in the Proms in 1987, and it was admired. The musicologist David Drew thinks that Markevich provides a missing link in music between Bartók and Messiaen.

Nicholas Nabokov, the other composer who appeared in the film, was not only the author of the most photographed of later Diaghilev ballets, *Ode*, with designs by Pavel Tchelitchev, but a remote cousin of Diaghilev himself. Nabokov was also first cousin to the novelist Vladimir Nabokov, author of *Lolita*. Nicholas had written a book of reminiscences called *Old*

Friends and New Music, which I had found enchanting, ranging from childhood memories of picnics in pre-revolutionary Russia to Christmas in California with the Stravinskys, when he and Balanchine had taken the train from New York to Los Angeles, a journey of several days. There was a penetrating chapter on Prokofiev, whom Nabokov had known well in Paris, before Prokofiev had returned to the Soviet Union in the 1930s. Prokofiev does not emerge as a very likeable figure – short-tempered, and full of manic obsessions. He timed his daily lunchtime circumambulation of the Invalides with a stop-watch, and with the intensity of a contemporary believer in astrology. It was in this essay that I found the claim that Diaghilev had made Prokofiev rewrite the end of *The Prodigal Son* several times, until it was dramatically effective. Surely Nabokov of all people could talk about the depth of Diaghilev's understanding of music, something about which there was much speculation and a degree of contradictory evidence. Nabokov in the 1960s was well known for two activities: he was director of the Berlin Festival, and also of an organization called The Congress for Cultural Freedom, which provided the funds for the magazine *Encounter*, amongst other things, and was, it eventually emerged, funded by the CIA. He was a friend of Stephen Spender, and of Isaiah Berlin, and by reputation, like them, a great conversationalist. Notably uxorious, he had recently married a Frenchwoman less than half his age.

We arranged to meet in Paris, where he had a flat. By this time Nabokov had suffered the first of a number of strokes, and one side of his face was paralysed. He talked out of the corner of his mouth, in a gravelly voice, but with a dry wit, and a broader cultural perspective than any of the other survivors. He may have written only one ballet for Diaghilev, and not been close to him for long periods as others had been, yet he provided the deeper interpretation that I was so desperately seeking. In our interview, almost alone of the twenty-odd participants, he spoke not just of ballet, but of Diaghilev's life and work in terms of society and its attitudes. Much of this concerned what he called the 'scandal' of Diaghilev's homosexuality, in the sense, he added, that St Paul said the Christian religion was a scandal. Nabokov believed that the risk, and the sense of otherness, was a powerful source of Diaghilev's mystique, and he used it knowingly.

Few had written about this side of Diaghilev's life. It was well known that he had been, on two occasions, deserted by his chosen choreographer/dancer/lover – first Nijinsky, and then Massine – and that each time he had somehow risen above the personal drama to renew the work of the company. How important was Diaghilev's homosexuality, and was he, as Stravinsky is made to say in one of the conversation books with Robert Craft, surrounded by a homosexual mafia? I have always believed that the camp image of the male dancer in our time has done ballet no good in the eyes of the wider public. The image of the male dancer in Denmark or Russia is quite different, but I did not believe (and Sokolova and others reinforced this belief) that Diaghilev had liked or encouraged homosexuality amongst his dancers – quite the contrary. In his own life Diaghilev was notably monogamous; he fell for people with talent, and devoted himself single-heartedly to them. The idea that Diaghilev was a promiscuous old queen fancying the boys has no basis at all in fact, and even the dancers he loved, in most cases, eventually opted for a heterosexual existence.

Both Nijinsky and Massine had left to marry and beget children, and, as far as I could discover, the leading male dancers, especially in the early years of the Diaghilev Ballet, such as Bolm or, indeed, Fokine himself, had been entirely heterosexual. Dolin and Lifar in the 1920s had certainly been predominantly homosexual, but the image of the company was of masculinity in the men, in *Prince Igor* or *Le Tricorne*, and glamour in the women, whether in the eroticism of the final scene of *Schéhérazade* or the social commentary of *Les Biches*, where there were sly hints of lesbianism. Incidentally, Sokolova, who with Tchernicheva danced the two 'garçonnes' who perform arm in arm, said to me, 'We may have been all kinds of things, dear, but we were certainly not that!' Nijinsky was, according to many accounts, in real life almost entirely sexless, but capable of suggesting powerful erotic attraction, from the beauty of Narcisse to the strangeness of the Faune. But he could also be the violently obsessional doll in *Petrushka*, or the coolly mysterious tennis player of *Jeux*. Massine began as a vulnerable adolescent in *Joseph's Legend*, and progressed to the Miller in *Tricorne*, all fire and flamenco. Dolin as Le Beau Gosse was the very image of 1920s film-stardom, certainly in Flemming Flindt's definition, a man on-stage. Only Lifar, from the photos at least, looks too preoccupied with himself to care whether he attracts anyone. Sacheverell Sitwell told me that one day in Florence Diaghilev had commended Lifar for reading Baedeker at lunch, but on closer inspection Sachie had found that Lifar had tucked in the pages many photographs of himself. With very few exceptions, it was Diaghilev who happened to be gay, and not the Diaghilev Ballet.

Was there, however, a homosexual mafia among his non-dancing associates? Walter Nouvel, who was for many years the company secretary, was homosexual, and so was Kochno. But Benois was absolutely a family man, and Bakst constantly involved with any number of pretty Parisiennes. I do not trust Stravinsky's claim. That there was a homosexual element amongst Diaghilev's supporters is perhaps much more true: Jean Cocteau, Reynaldo Hahn before the war, and in the 1920s a group of rich society women well known for their lesbian tendencies, notably the Princesse de Polignac and the Comtesse Greffuhle, both of whom had salons of great elegance and distinction, and both of whom, of course, were married. But even so Diaghilev's closest woman friend, Misia Sert, was famous for her involvement with a whole series of rich and powerful men.

Nabokov spoke of all this from the standpoint of a much-married heterosexual, like his close friend, Diaghilev's last great choreographer, George Balanchine. He put in context something that was still, in the 1960s, difficult to discuss. It is hard today to realize with what reticence and how rarely homosexuality was mentioned. It now seems the mainspring of both biography and newspaper gossip. Nabokov's contribution was to speak of the matter with a seriousness and discretion that would not offend the other participants or, indeed, the audience of BBC1. I owe him much – his was the kind of contribution I had sought and rarely found. I became devoted to Nikki, and saw him quite often from this time on. When, ten years later, I was appointed director of the Edinburgh Festival, among the first messages of congratulation I received was one from him, facetiously headed 'Cher collègue', as one festival director to another. We worked together on a long television programme I presented about Les Noces, in 1978. He provided riveting background to the curious text, and explained a great deal of what had always been mysterious to me in that great masterpiece, which also, through Nijinska's choreography and Goncharova's design, remains one of the very greatest of all ballets – a distillation of everything Russian, and quite timeless.

Unintentionally, Nabokov gave me one of my worst experiences as an interviewer. He came to London to take part in the Noces epic. We already had Bernstein conducting, and talking about the music, Ashton on Nijinska and four pianists who included, incredibly, Martha Argerich and Krystian Zimerman. The programme was in two halves: Bernstein and Nabokov on the music followed by a concert performance conducted by Bernstein; then Ashton and film of Nijinska on the ballet, followed by a performance of her choreographed version, danced by the Royal Ballet to Bernstein's accompaniment. Nabokov was nervous, and, according to his wife, took two pep pills before the studio interview. To my consternation he was, from the beginning, very fuzzy and unclear. All our preparation seemed forgotten. He could not remember anything. It was terribly embarrassing, and then quite suddenly he fell asleep and could not be roused. It took us a while to discover that he had, in fact, taken sleeping tablets by mistake. The interview was abandoned and had to be reconvened in Paris on film a week later, with highly complex implications for the editing. We laughed about it, but not until much later. I do not think a great deal of Nikki's music will stand the test of time; he wrote, amongst other things, a full-length opera of great ingenuity, based on *Love's Labour's Lost*. But his warm intelligence and wicked sense of humour keep him fresh in my memory, many years after his death.

The search for survivors among those who had funded Diaghilev proved fruitless. They had all died, whether in Paris or London. Gabriel Astruc, the great impresario in Paris, was long dead, likewise his counterpart Oswald Stoll in London. The princesses and countesses had all gone too. In England his greatest supporter had been the Marchioness of Ripon. It was at her house, before the First World War, that Nijinsky had made almost the only remark anyone could attribute to him. They were playing a sort of charades game in which people were compared to animals. What did Lady Ripon resemble? 'Vous, Madame, chameau,' Nijinsky volunteered. Lady Ripon's daughter, Lady Juliet Duff, had raised money for Diaghilev's last two seasons in London. A great friend of Dicky Buckle, she had died in 1965. The remaining friends distanced themselves. Lydia Sokolova went to stay, from time to time, with Lady St Just at her lovely home, Wilbury, in Wiltshire. She recommended me to write, but Florrie St Just's reply disclaimed any ability to help. 'Diaghilev', she wrote, 'had very few intimate friends, and I was never a close friend of his, but knew many of the artists well. The one thing that did strike one about him was his immense knowledge of pictures and music. I don't think there is anything I could tell you about him from a personal point of view.' I fear that people such as Lady St Just thought that I would insist on talking about money or sex, which was far from my intention, but there was a kind of conspiracy of silence. Even Sacheverell Sitwell never referred to Diaghilev's homosexuality in conversation with me, and was outraged when John Pearson's book *Façades* revealed the truth about Osbert. That was the way things were. Errol Addison, last of the *corps* dancers I filmed in London, spent a good part of the time we were together briskly insisting on his heterosexuality. He cut such a crude and unattractive figure that I felt it hardly mattered either way. He had also been a page in *The Sleeping Princess*, and it was hard to believe that this tubby man with the loud cockney accent had ever been able to fit into the beautiful Bakst page's costume that was being sold by Sotheby's. His interview added little. So much of the inner workings of the Diaghilev Ballet that I was trying to describe eluded me, and I still had not got near Grigoriev. He had accepted, and then his friend Vera Bowen died and he cried off at the last minute.

8 Two *Monstres Sacrés*

Despite all we had done, and the ever-growing dossier of interviews and the picture material, there still remained the whole question of America and, most particularly, two key interviews in Europe with two of the biggest names: Léonide Massine and Serge Lifar. Both of them were to lead me quite a dance in the summer of 1967.

I now have no idea how I discovered that the way to Massine was via Lloyds Bank in Tottenham Court Road, but it was to that address that I sent my initial letter. He replied nearly a month later, saying he would certainly take part, but with no real indication of when or where. He might, he said, be in Paris in late June. Late June came, but I heard nothing. I then suggested going to Positano, where I knew him to be in July, following my planned trip to Monte Carlo to film Dolin in the Opera House. I was trying, so as to save money, to link together the travel in Europe, and had hoped that Lifar, Massine and Dolin could all be fitted into the same journey.

Massine agreed to Positano for the filming, 'subject to an appropriate business arrangement being made' with his London lawyer, who turned out to be Sir John Witt, chairman of the trustees of the National Portrait Gallery and son of the creator of the famous Witt Library and collector of old master drawings. We spoke on the phone. Sir John, for all I know, may have been a charming and cultured man, but my recollection after nearly thirty years is that I had never been spoken to with such patronizing condescension. If I had been the *News of the World* after a salacious story, he could not have been more disdainful. It may, of course, have been that Massine caused him so much trouble with his endless litigation and legendary meanness that Witt was trying to put me off getting involved in any way. I mentioned the fifty-guinea fee we were offering, and Witt said immediately that it was quite unacceptable. After much heart-searching, for I knew Massine to be rich and rapacious, while Sokolova and Karsavina were struggling to make ends meet, I agreed to double the figure to one hundred pounds. I had to make a special case to the BBC, who were far from convinced; Massine had appeared once on *Monitor* in an item produced by Margaret Dale, and had caused much trouble. The results had not been thought worth it, but I was getting desperate about the international element. However, nothing was agreed in time for me to link the visit to Italy with the Monte Carlo trip.

Silence fell again from Positano, and now a new element entered the argument. I was not able to afford to take a BBC film crew with me on these trips and had to hire locally. It was a chancy business; we never knew who or what we would get. At least in Paris the cameraman, Jean Crommelynck, had known what I was up to. His brother was the famous print maker who worked for Picasso and all the other leading French painters when they produced prints or lithographs. Monte Carlo had not been satisfactory – a news cameraman with a bad case of the zoom lens – and now we were begging a crew from Italian television, the RAI, in Rome. Hirings of this kind were done under the Eurovision exchange agreement and not considered a high priority, just a courtesy, and the BBC was notoriously uncooperative with other networks' requests. When at last Massine volunteered a date, no crew was available in Rome or Naples; when the crew was available, it was the height of the August holidays, and I could find no accommodation in Positano. It seemed an endless vicious circle.

Meanwhile, after long silences, I received a peremptory telegram from Lifar: 'Vous accorderai interview sur Diaghilev 19 août à Venise à 9 heures cimetière St Michel. Salutations, Lifar.' I knew that Lifar visited Venice every year on the anniversary of Diaghilev's death and had a service said at the grave by a Greek Orthodox priest, there being no Russian church in Venice. I found the idea attractive, since Lifar had been with Diaghilev when he died in Venice in August 1929. Eventually, after a sheaf of telegrams, the pieces fitted; Massine in Positano on the 17th, Lifar in Venice on the 19th, and each with a day before to plan the interview. Crews and travel were booked, and in desperation I asked Massine if I could stay with him – my telegram ended 'regret intrusion!' He agreed.

Massine's Positano home, three lumps of rock half a mile off the coast called the Isole dei Galli, had been purchased in the 1920s, for a sum equivalent to £5,000. They were later to be bought by Rudolf Nureyev. Massine returned every year, except during the war, and had made strenuous attempts to get some kind of arts centre going there. Everyone who knew him told me of his 'projects'. I set off on Sunday 15th, flying to Naples, from where I made my way to the Circumvesuviana Railway to get a train to Sorrento, which met a bus connection to Positano, or so the Italian travel authorities in London had assured me. Of course, nothing worked, the plane was late, the train rescheduled, and the bus was on strike. I had to take a taxi over the mountains from Sorrento to Positano, arriving an hour and a half after the time I had suggested. I had no real rendezvous point – I just went down to the waterfront and hoped I would be discovered. It was the height of Ferragosto, and half Naples seemed to be on the front at the Buca di Bacco or Chez Black. I carried my suitcase down to the end of the jetty and sat on it, hoping something would happen.

In the end, after an hour or so, just as night was falling, it did. A strapping young man in the tiniest of bathing slips came up and said, in curiously accented French, 'Êtes-vous le monsieur de la télévision?' I agreed I was, whereupon he seized my suitcase and walked into the sea, holding the case at shoulder height. Just before he and the case disappeared under the waves, he flung it into a small motor launch in which two girls were sitting. He clambered aboard and started the engine. He brought the boat alongside the quay and I jumped in. The slimmer of the two girls introduced herself in American-accented English as Massine's daughter, Tanya. The plump girl with her was a Parisian friend. We set off for the islands. It was now quite dark and we had no lights – the coastline of the Sorrento peninsula glittered behind us, ahead the shape of the larger of the three islands loomed like Böcklin's painting which inspired Rachmaninov's *Isle of the Dead*. It was in total darkness, and Tanya explained that the generator had failed. We scrambled ashore at a small harbour, and followed a steep path up the hillside to a low building on a terrace. Voices could be heard shouting inside. We continued beyond the house along a path high above the sea to a small hut. Tanya flung the door open and said, 'The guest house!' In the gloom I found a candle, and lit it. The room was about twelve feet square, with a bare tiled floor. There was a single bed, a window and a washbasin whose runaway pipe stopped a foot above the floor. No water came from the taps. I sat on the bed and wondered what on earth I was getting into. Eventually I found a jug of water, freshened up and changed from my travelling clothes.

I returned gingerly along the path to the terrace, where a group of people was sitting by two oil lamps; in the middle was a darkly attractive middle-aged woman, whom I somehow knew had been a dancer, and a Russian dancer at that. This was Massine's second wife, the mother of the girl who had met me. She had been in the de Basil company, and later became an administrator. She lived in Paris, while Massine lived in Germany, with a German companion, but obviously they still got together for holidays. Tanya, the daughter, was married to a German diplomat whose brother,

Thilo von Watzdorf, I knew since he was involved with the Diaghilev sales at Sotheby's. The Watzdorfs were very grand, and the mother of the two boys was, I believe, a member of the Luxembourg royal family. All this I pieced together that evening, with the help of the French girl, Catherine, who was, it was explained, running away from an unhappy love affair. The muscular boy who had collected my case was Belgian, a semi-literate refugee from a circus, who had been taken on to help an English puppeteer who was also staying on the island.

We sat on the terrace and talked. Everyone seemed in a high state of tension and exasperation: was it the failure of the generator, my arrival or something else? Suddenly a figure with a lit candle and a long, old-fashioned peignoir crossed the terrace behind us. No one took any notice. She was crying noisily. 'Oh, that's only Mademoiselle,' said Tanya. I nodded. It was like *La Sonnambula*. We talked and talked, and drank a very rough local white wine. Eventually some raw octopus in olive oil was produced, then a Spanish omelette. Everyone tucked in. There was still no sign of Massine. I did not dare to ask. Then at the end of the meal I looked up, aware of someone else, and behind the glare of the oil lamp I saw two dark, glowing eyes, and the unmistakable face of the great man. He was polite, even charming, apologized for the confusion, said he would see me in the morning and disappeared.

It was a perfect summer night, and now that I was used to the semi-darkness the sheer beauty and romanticism of the setting became obvious. After dinner four of us – Tanya, Catherine, the Belgian boy and I – went back down to the harbour and swam in the velvety darkness broken only by the luminous phosphorescence of the water. As we dived and splashed, a million colours glittered. I had never seen this effect before, though, of course, I remembered it from *The Ancient Mariner*. Would Massine tell me his story tomorrow? For the moment nothing could have been more romantic – Tanya was very beautiful. Voices were calling from the house in Russian, answered in French. I remembered Benois's family scrapbooks of the Crimea before the Revolution; the sense of history and continuity and Russianness was overwhelming. I can still sense the headiness of the night air and the glow of the lights on the coast as I wandered back to my curious room, and slept like a child in my narrow bed.

I was awoken by the sun streaming into the room, an easy task since it turned out to have only three and a half walls, something I had not been aware of the night before. The fourth wall extended oddly from the ceiling to within two feet of the floor, then there was a gap through which the sea flashed, a hundred feet below. I wandered over to the house, where the puppeteer produced some coffee and filled in some more details about who was who amongst this curious company. During the course of the day every one of those on the island got me alone to tell me of their troubles, and how hopeless and unstable all the others were. The puppeteer had been sent for by Massine for some reason, and was now a kind of prisoner, doing odd jobs, madly in love with the Belgian boy, though I did not think he was getting much in return. Tanya's marriage was on the rocks, and she was going to have to start again, unsure as to whether in Europe or America. Her French friend was a mass of giggles and tears. Obsessed with her appearance, she was overweight and kept collapsing in sobs or laughing hysterically. The Belgian boy seemed to have the least problems, living in a simple, semi-gestural world of his own. He could hardly read or write, and was often sent on errands and ended up in the wrong place. It was all quite dotty, and somehow quintessentially Russian. We toured the property; the main island was covered with unfinished buildings. There was part of an open-air theatre, a sort of barn – studios, I suppose. Of the other two islands, one was inhabited only by goats and the other had a boatshed.

At mid-morning Mademoiselle gave me a message: Monsieur Massine would see me at 2.30. She then proceeded to explain how awful he was to her, and how she could not go on as his unofficial secretary. At luncheon, where again Massine did not join us, there was a great deal of shouting. It appeared that Massine's current lady friend was in Positano, claiming her rights to visit. Madame Massine left the island, and was not seen until the next day. Although the generator had been fixed, no food of any kind was brought back by the boat; we once again ate raw octopus and Spanish omelette. I can still hear the slapping sound of the octopus being beaten on the steps of the terrace, to tenderize it.

Massine was formal, but very straightforward. There was much he wanted to say, and he had prepared it. In fact, the following day's interview came out so pat that I think he had almost memorized it. But how much would he say of his own relations with Diaghilev? I had always felt that because of Massine's quickness and intelligence, Diaghilev had been more in love with him even than with Nijinsky. He had been more companionable; he was also a very good musician. They had gone through the worst of times together during the war, dogged by money problems, but nevertheless creating works such as *Parade* and *Pulcinella*, *Boutique Fantasque* and *The Three-cornered Hat*. Then suddenly, in 1920, Massine had walked out on Diaghilev, without any warning, to marry the English dancer Vera Savina. It was the greatest betrayal. Diaghilev had never spoken of it to any of the people I had got to know, though Lydia Sokolova typically, staying in the same hotel as Diaghilev shortly afterwards, but on a higher floor, had overheard Diaghilev on the terrace below telling Misia Sert of his hopelessness, aimlessness and sense of loss. Yet in the end the result was creatively remarkable. Diaghilev turned back, first to the past, and staged *The Sleeping Beauty*, and then developed Nijinsky's sister Bronislava's choreography. Though she only stayed a short time, she created at least two perfect ballets, *Les Noces*, the unforgettable evocation of a timeless Russia, and *Les Biches*, which set the whole new French mood of the company in the 1920s. Massine had been closer to Diaghilev than any of his other choreographers, for example Fokine or Balanchine. How much would he say?

The following day the crew arrived from Rome; we all dutifully ate our octopus and omelette. Madame Massine returned, saying that she had invited twenty-six to lunch the next day, and we went off to film. As we walked out on to the terrace in the blazing sunlight, Massine turned to me and said, in a voice of real fierceness, 'You will ask me no questions whatever about the circumstances of my first marriage.'

Afterwards, as we made to depart, with a certain embarrassment, the puppeteer handed me a piece of paper. It was a bill, for the expenses incurred by having me to stay: £7 10s per night for the room (a good room at the Waldorf at that time cost £4 17s 6d) and 2,000 lire per meal, plus the cost of sending the boat for me and for the film crew. The battle raged between the BBC and Sir John Witt for several months, and the file is full of indignant memoranda from both sides. In the end I think we paid half – no one ever got anything free from Massine. We had a long, amiable correspondence afterwards, about his wanting me to make a whole series of television programmes about his system of choreographic notation. The BBC was, in my view quite rightly, not interested. I saw Massine for the last time a year or two later at Barons Court tube station, buying a two-shilling underground ticket with a twenty-pound note. It seemed a wonderfully appropriate image.

The film crew dropped me at Naples airport, and within a couple of hours I was in Venice. The first thing I wanted was food and a good stiff drink. I went to Harry's Bar to launch the evening with a couple of their inimitable dry Martinis and toasted sandwiches. Unusually, I found a seat at the bar; five minutes later a leathery figure, trailing a long white scarf, came in, greeted everyone effusively in French and sat down next to me. I turned and said, 'Bonsoir, Monsieur Lifar.' He thought it a good augury. 'Coïncidence,' he kept saying, 'coïncidence, à cause de Diaghilev!' He told anyone who would listen that I was making this great film of which he was the star, and how we were 'en tournage' together. The endlessly wise barmen of Harry's, who had seen everyone and heard everything, smiled patiently. (Oddly enough, they all spoke to me in French; perhaps I had first gone there with French friends, but I suspect that I had spoken French on my first visit because my Italian was not impeccable and I did not, in my snobbish way, want to be thought American. The barmen never forgot, and still greet me today in French.)

I had been a regular visitor to Venice for only about six years. My first visit was in 1961, but since then I had gone every year at least once, and sometimes two or three times. I was totally captured by its seedy grandeur, largely, I think, because of the accidental circumstances of my first arrival. I had come by train from the south of France, where I had been staying with friends. There was a rail strike in Italy and, instead of arriving in Venice in the late afternoon, I had got there at 4.30 a.m., just as it was getting light. I had no hotel reservation, and a heavy case. I hung around the station and at five o'clock the buffet opened, shortly afterwards the left-luggage office. After a coffee and a *pasticcio* I walked out into the deserted city – it was a Sunday, and there was nothing but the occasional barge with vegetables and the smell of baking bread. Following the signs for San Marco, I crossed the bridge, avoiding the touristy Lista di Spagna, and came to the Rialto through the empty markets, then on to San Marco, where there were two million pigeons, one policeman and me. As I came into the square, a church bell started tolling across the lagoon, and the sun sparkled on the water at the end of the Piazzetta. I had seen the city without people, and no crowd of tourists could ever efface that memory. It was the start of a long love affair, endangered now only by the ludicrous prices of its hotels and the awfulness of the food compared with any other Italian city. But I still go back, if only to complain, and usually spend one night or early morning walking alone in remote Sestieri to recapture that first impression.

Diaghilev had loved Venice more than anywhere in the world. This was in a sense surprising, for he was afraid of water. He had been told by a gypsy fortune-teller that he would die on water, which was the reason he had not gone to South America on the famous trip when Nijinsky had got married. He cannot have considered that Venice was on water, in the Atlantic sense, as he had gone there every summer since the early years, staying at the Grand Hôtel des Bains on the Lido. There is a photograph of him taken beside the statues of the embracing knights by the Porta della Carta of the Doge's Palace. It was somehow appropriate that he should have died there and been buried in the Greek Orthodox section of the cemetery on the island of San Michele. There had been famous scenes at the funeral, when Lifar had sought to jump into the open grave and had to be restrained. Lifar later supervised the erection of an unusual domed cenotaph with an inscription by, I think, Théophile Gautier, chosen by Benois. 'Venise inspiratrice éternelle de nos apaisements.' I had been there several times, and loved the quiet of the place, and the lapping of the water beyond the wall. Countess Moussine Pushkin lay near him, and today, a small distance away, both Igor and Vera Stravinsky are buried there.

Lifar was intrigued by how and why I had got involved in the whole Diaghilev saga. Indeed, it was a question everyone asked, and one that was hard to answer without seeming pompous or pretentious. On that evening in Harry's Bar when he asked me, I replied almost without thinking, 'Par jalousie.' It was as truthful an answer as any. I was jealous of those who had seen the company, of not having been alive during those years, and I did think, without anything more to go on than the accounts of others and the photographs, that what was achieved then far outstripped the creative work of my own time. I did not believe that innovation or creativity in the 1950s and 1960s in music and dance came within miles of what Diaghilev had achieved in the five years before the First World War, let alone over the whole twenty-year period. Lifar carried my answer all over Venice the following day. Anna-Maria Cicogna gave a lunch for him, and he told everyone. I had said the right thing. I spent the day myself sorting out the film crew and the boat hire, trying to find out how long the service at the graveside would take, and if it would be considered sacrilegious for us to film it. It was a frustrating and difficult day, but at least I ate more than octopus and omelette.

On the 19th we all met at San Michele shortly before nine. Lifar arrived with a tall bearded young Orthodox priest, who spoke very little French, only Italian and Greek. Lifar kept on saying, 'Il est beau, n'est-ce-pas? Très beau!' Even during the ceremony the attraction of the priest seemed to be his main concern. There was much incense, a final prayer, then the priest left and we began the interview. Lifar was notorious for his endless speechifying on every occasion, whether asked for or not, especially when there was a chance of upstaging anyone else. I think he thought here that he was speaking for the world. I could not do anything but stand back and let it all pour out. The closing paragraphs, describing in detail the last moments of Diaghilev's life, are, I believe, an almost total fantasy. One could never trust Lifar to tell the truth about anything; but at least we had got him, and had filmed the grave, and created a sequence suggesting the last journey to San Michele which would make a suitably solemn end to the film. The crew were the best I had yet had, and we lunched in a tiny restaurant hidden among trees at the unfashionable end of the Lido. And apart from three hours in Cologne to film Woizikowsky on the way back, that was the end of the European filming.

However, there remained pictures to be found. I was not sure how much Lifar owned – he had sold much to the Wadsworth Atheneum at Hartford, Connecticut, and I had their catalogue, but I knew he still had some things, although he was very vague when asked. I suspected he wanted money to show them to me, and this ultimately proved correct. He casually asked me if I had seen Kochno: I gave him a carefully edited version of our meeting, and explained that eventually Kochno had not taken part. Lifar was absolutely delighted. He then told me his version of how Kochno came to have a great number of Diaghilev's possessions. Diaghilev, he claimed, had in his last years rented a place in Paris to keep the books that he had collected, and many other things. It was, apparently, a sort of lock-up studio. When Kochno and Lifar returned to Paris after Diaghilev's funeral, they decided to divide the spoils between them, but the executors and the lawyers put a seal on the place. Kochno found a way in, and for several nights they went and helped themselves to anything they could carry away, taking it to Kochno's apartment. When at last the place was properly sealed, Lifar asked Kochno how they would divide what they had taken. 'What do you mean?' said Kochno. 'This is my house – prove that these things are not all mine!' That, according to Lifar, was the origin of a large part of Kochno's collection. It was being told stories like that which made it impossible for me to consider publishing my account of these meetings at that time. Today Lifar and Kochno are dead: I have no idea whether either ever told me the truth. Both had considerable collections about which they lied, and both have been sold – Kochno's, sensibly, to the French government and Lifar's in bits and pieces now scattered all over the place. In 1993, by chance watching a late-night television programme in France, I stumbled upon an interview with Roland Petit, who had just published his memoirs. Also in the studio was the Swedish woman with whom Lifar had spent his last years, the Countess Ahlefeld. She spoke of Lifar with hushed reverence – he had died in her arms, he was not only a great man but a saint. The interviewer turned to Roland Petit and asked what he thought: 'Il était un homme comme les autres' was the dry response.

It was hard not to sense a certain falling-off in the quality of Diaghilev's companions of the later years. Lifar, unlike Nijinsky or Massine, was not a great dancer. He was a sort of *monstre sacré* with a patchy record at the Opéra and a dubious role during the Occupation. Although he had been perfectly nice to me, I never liked him. Many, not I, thought him beautiful as a young man, but there was something so vain, so mindlessly self-vaunting about him that it was hard not to want to slap him down. Years later Gennadi Rozhdestvensky told me Lifar had shown him the manu-script of a section of Mussorgsky's *Khovanshchina* reorchestrated by Ravel. We tried to get hold of it for my Diaghilev Commemoration in Edinburgh in 1979; Lifar at first denied he had it, and then wanted huge sums of money even to look at it. He was a silly person.

My experience with Kochno was, perhaps, unfortunate. Others, like Dicky Buckle, were very fond of him, and found him invaluable and fascinating in his reminiscences. Some years after our meeting Kochno helped Dicky with his book on Diaghilev. Perhaps I should have persisted with him. There was something, however, in those untrusting eyes that held me back, even when he was sober. As Bob Lockyer had said, 'Poor Diaghilev.'

The cool genius of Diaghilev's later years was, meanwhile, sitting in New York, where he had almost single-handedly achieved as much as Diaghilev, establishing classical ballet as an integral part of American cultural life, and creating a string of works which extended the whole vocabulary of movement far beyond Fokine and Massine, or even Nijinska. Balanchine had still not said no, or really yes.

I had used all the right paths and people to approach him. It had taken months, and eventually I was encouraged to believe by Barbara Horgan, his administrator, that he would give me an interview: the problem was when and where. It was a fiendishly busy summer. New York City Ballet was on tour all over America – I still have all their touring details in my files – and then they were coming to Europe. Was I to go to Saratoga, or meet him in Edinburgh? I was sure that New York would be better, when he was not so busy. Then suddenly, in late August, shortly after my return from Venice, Balanchine gave a definitive no to taking part. I clung to California, endlessly trying to find a date with Stravinsky, and on 13 September I received a postcard from his secretary: 'I have just been informed by Mr

Stravinsky's doctors that he cannot participate in your film. He has in fact just been ordered to cancel all of his engagements for a period of three months. With kind regards, Yours sincerely . . . ' I have rarely been so depressed.

How much better the films would have been with Balanchine and Stravinsky I will never know. But the loss was deeply upsetting. I postponed the editing of the films for a month, to reflect and to get my enthusiasm started again. We had got so close. Today, almost thirty years later, I am sceptical. The presence of Stravinsky would, of course, have given the films an infinitely greater authority and distinction, but how much would he have said? Would he have told the truth? There are so many things in the conversation books that seem to me to be 'glosses' on what happened. Balanchine would have added a perspective on the later years, but he also was never particularly forthcoming. Surely I had enough to work on? Well, I had to and it was up to me to prove it.

The editing of the films was of extraordinary complexity. There were over thirty hours of interviews and a constant practical problem. When the interviewer is to be part of the film, he or she can intervene, cross-question, even challenge if required. When, as in my films, the interviewer (me) was to be edited out and replaced by a commentary, one had to find self-contained statements, anecdotes or judgements that would stand on their own. Throughout the filming I so often wanted to intervene, to ask why, to say, 'Explain that again', to go into things more deeply; but it would not have worked. There is only one moment in the two films when my voice can be heard off camera. Karsavina was talking about the experimental version of *Romeo and Juliet* that she danced in 1926 to music by Constant Lambert and designs by Miró. She had not been impressed – she thought it was 'The Emperor's New Clothes'. 'I couldn't see anything in it, but Diaghilev thought that it was wonderful . . . Perhaps intellectual people could see it.' She shrugged. 'Do you really think they could?' my disembodied voice is heard to say. 'They said they did.' Time and again in the editing we had to drop stories that were too long, too detailed or too hard to place in a context for which there were no pictures. We also had to include the necessary narrative, and the musical sequences as well. Hardly a thirtieth part of what I recorded in interviews was used in the films. A few more fragments emerged in a long radio programme a few years later about Diaghilev, but the bulk of it was never used. For several years afterwards I guarded the negatives and the soundtracks of the interviews, moving them from place to place with the help of a benevolent film organizer at Ealing

Studios. There were dozens of cans of film; hours of Karsavina, Sokolova, Massine and the rest. The BBC was not only unwilling to catalogue it all and put it in the film library, but also quite unprepared, for contractual reasons, to make it available to anyone else, like the Dance Collection in the New York Public Library. Then one weekend there was a clear-out of the cutting rooms and everything disappeared. I had taken the sound tapes home with me, and still have them. When I left the BBC in 1977, against the rules, I took the programme files as well, and these are the basis of this account. But that moment in the interview when Karsavina speaks of *Spectre de la Rose*, and extends her hand, fifty-five years later in a Hampstead garden in the identical gesture to the famous photograph, that moment is lost, I suspect, for ever.

The biggest problem in the editing was to make the dance sequences live, with sometimes only three or four still photographs to represent a whole ballet. The Americans thought it impossible, and so, I regret, did the film editor with whom I was working – a notably successful and experienced man. I think the project would have failed totally if it had not been for his assistant, a young red-haired enthusiast called Mick Jackson, who now has Hollywood director credits to his name. He shared my vision, and found a way to animate the photographs, cut to very brief sequences of music. Occasionally I had been obliged to find abstract images – the dawn sequence from *Daphnis* used no pictures of the ballet at all and was shot on a summer afternoon on Wimbledon Common. The can-can from *Boutique Fantasque* was based on eight photographs from the *Illustrated London News* and really danced before your eyes. The response of the dancers to the films was almost always to these images. They felt that I had somehow 'caught the spirit'. Karsavina wrote: 'What I found a distinguished feature was the way you used stills, flashing them up in rapid succession, so giving the *élan* of movement. The whole programme was remarkably well executed. What an amount of research must have gone into it.'

Looking back today, the films seem full of awkward corners, messy photography, and, as they are in black and white, the sense of colour and exoticism has to be imagined. But whenever they are shown, they somehow seem to impress. I think it is because there is something so patently genuine and emotionally truthful in many of the contributions. Since all but three of the participants are now dead, and since so little of what they said to me was ever heard, it seems, out of gratitude to them, worth seeking a wider audience.

PART 2

The Interviews

Tamara Karsavina

1885 ST PETERSBURG–1976 GERRARDS CROSS

Tamara Karsavina studied at the Imperial School and made her début at the Imperial theatres in 1903. Closely associated with the dancer and choreographer Mikhail Fokine, she became the prima ballerina of the Diaghilev company and created leading roles in a large number of works, including The Firebird, Petrushka, Narcisse, Thamar, Le Dieu Bleu, Carnaval, Salome *and* Jeux. *Her partnership with Vaslav Nijinsky became a legend, typified by the ballet* Le Spectre de la Rose. *She rejoined Diaghilev in London after the First World War for the première of* Le Tricorne, *and subsequently made regular guest appearances with the company.*

Can you recall the first time you ever noticed Diaghilev?

Oh, very well indeed, I never forgot it. I had a glimpse of him before I knew anything about him or who he was, and that was at a rehearsal of the *Nutcracker* in the Mariinsky in 1900. We danced in the performance, the pupils, and then in between were taken to a box with the governess, and there we sat. And I remember the stalls were quite empty because everybody was on the stage, an unusual thing. And in walked Diaghilev. I didn't know who he was, but it gave me a terrific thrill. Of course, he was very good-looking with that white streak in his hair, he looked absolutely fatalistic. I was only a girl of fifteen, very romantic, so I thought I would fall in love with him.

When did you meet him?

I met him two years later after I graduated, my first year on the stage. That was at a banquet. There usually was a yearly banquet given by balletomanes to the company, and I actually sat next to him. I remember everything about it. He made me some compliments on the way I pinned a rose to my corsage. It was very much like the way I wore the rose afterwards in the *Spectre de la Rose*, and I thought him a charmer. And then he saw me home, and so his victory was complete. And I must tell you, I think I blurted out that I was in love with him. But what makes me proud now is that my first impression was of something unusual in the man, a man of not ordinary calibre. So it wasn't only the crush of a young girl, but his direct magnetism. I guessed that he was a great man, and then it was justified.

Tell me about the standard of dancing in the Imperial theatres at that time. Who were the principal dancers?

Well, it stood really very high under Petipa. The technique was excellent, and there was an absolute constellation of stars, wonderful dancers, Kchessinska, Preobrajenska, Trefilova, then Pavlova came, all before me. But it was static; the only medium of dancing was toe dancing, and they never went beyond that. Also the Imperial Ballet stood isolated from her sister arts. Petipa created wonderful masterpieces, but they were done on very mediocre music. There were two sorts of hack musicians attached to the theatre, Minkus and Pugni. The décor too was very ingenious, with most wonderful theatre devices, fountains on the stage, wonderful traps and appearances, transformations and all that, but it had no artistic value whatsoever.

But nevertheless you had a tradition in Russia which nowhere else in the world had at that time?

That is true, because in Western Europe the ballet had degenerated into a kind of revue, like those mammoth revues at the Alhambra.

Did you feel what you were doing in the Imperial theatres was better than that?

Oh yes, we believed it. But even when I was wholeheartedly devoted to Diaghilev and all that group under Fokine and the new artistic orientation, I still cherished the academic art. But I had the best of both worlds, because in winter I danced in the Mariinsky Theatre and in the summer I usually joined Diaghilev.

How did it feel to belong to the Diaghilev company in those early years? How strong was the contrast?

It was very noticeable. There was a new horizon. Diaghilev had all the best that there was in the artistic world around him, especially in the first years, all those who belonged to that group of *Mir Isskustvo*. As you know, there was a great renaissance of art in Russia headed by Benois, and Diaghilev made something whole out of the performance, wonderful artistic décor and music and everything. It wasn't just patched together, it was a complete performance.

You saw the great exhibition of historical portraits in St Petersburg in 1905.

Yes, it was quite magical. It was displayed in the Tauride Palace, with its magnificent rooms, and it was open in the evening, which gave it some kind of special enchantment. I remember the people used to keep quite silent, there was a sort of hush. It was the first exhibition where all the gems of our portrait art were collected. And Diaghilev took very great care in collecting everything. He travelled up and down Russia in all the little provinces and would find some priceless portraits sometimes in the attic. In my family there were some historical portraits, perhaps not of great artistic value, but one represented the first Russian actor in the first Russian play and then his wife and his daughter with a little spaniel in her lap. These portraits were used to cover the water troughs, so they had rings around. So we had them cleaned and gave them to the museum.

What was Benois like at that time?

When he was young, he was rather prone to take umbrage. Sometimes very peppery. But with age he mellowed a little bit, but his knowledge, apart from his genius, was something remarkable. He was very often called to make the attribution of a picture which might have been discovered somewhere, and the artist not known.

Did you feel there was a new atmosphere in the arts in St Petersburg in the early years of this century?

Oh yes, indeed. It was rightly called the renaissance of Russian art. And it would be fair to say that it was led by Benois. He collected his friends round him – you remember in his autobiography he talks about the little red room where they used to gather and discuss matters of art. He could teach others without really being professorial, just like that, spontaneously. And then they started their journal [*Mir Isskustvo*] and at that time Diaghilev was only a provincial youngster. When he came to them, they thought he was rather indolent and lazy. But then he proved his mettle, because when they started the journal, he became the editor and did marvels. But it was all round, not only in painting, but it spread into music. You know there was that 'mighty heap' of composers headed by Rimsky-Korsakov, and so on. It was everywhere.

What were the reasons why you decided to join the Diaghilev company in 1909?

These new horizons that opened. There was so much that was fascinating and new, so many new productions, all different in style, so it was like leading so many different lives.

Tell me about the preparations for the first season in Paris. Diaghilev did a great deal to alter the Châtelet Theatre.

Oh yes, very much so. He attended to details; in that way he was rather like Napoleon, who had a wonderful gift for detail. I must say, it was hectic; we seemed always to be in a hurry and none the worse for it. Diaghilev did everything on a big scale. In the Châtelet the orchestra pit was too small for our orchestra, so he just ordered several rows of stalls to be swept away. And as we rehearsed, all very tense, very nervous, there was an awful din going on in the auditorium. Fokine would, now and then, turn and shout into the auditorium, 'Sergei Pavlovich, stop this something something noise.' At times we couldn't hear the piano. And at noon suddenly hush fell, everything was deserted except for us, and Diaghilev looked at his watch, and said, 'Of course, noon, *tout Paris bouffe.*' They all liked to have a good fill at noon, but we didn't, because that was our chance to go on. And then a marvellous thing happened. We were all on the stage rehearsing, and then, like the fairy's magic wand, all of a sudden, big trestles appeared, and the waiters from Larue, if you please, spread a most delicious meal and there we had a wonderful picnic with the background of *Armide*'s enchanted garden, sitting on the rostrum and the floor. He did everything in a big way, he was a very lavish man, so he was never secure financially. In the first year he brought all our choruses, which made a great impression on Paris because they were very good, and he also brought with him the master of all these stage devices, an absolute wizard with trap doors and everything.

Attention to detail, enormous expenditure. This was part of the success?

Well, it answered. And anyway, Diaghilev, at that time at least, never thought of financial success. The first priority with him was to give good things. He would never give anything second-rate. Once when we discussed some future production, I said, 'Do you think it will be a success?' and he said, 'Can't tell, one can never tell, but we want it to be good. I believe in it.'

What about the impact of that first night? It had the most incredible success, didn't it?

It was fantastic. We couldn't believe our ears or our senses. I remember it also because I became a casualty, and it attracted all the attention. All the intelligentsia of Paris, the artistic world and the beau monde were allowed on the stage at the end, crowds. It so happened that the first performance finished with a divertissement which Diaghilev called *Le Festin*, when Nijinsky and I danced what is called now the Blue Bird, a *pas de deux* from *Sleeping Beauty*. But Diaghilev transformed it. He made me the bird and him the Prince. And there were some wonderful costumes that Bakst designed, rather Asiatic, like in a Persian miniature. I remember I had big feathers curling up here, and then a tiara with plumes, and he had a tunic, and we had big bangles with jewellery. And you know what stage jewellery is, very spiky. So somehow my hands got caught in his bracelets, and I got quite lacerated, there was blood everywhere. I remember all the crowds, all these ladies with their silk handkerchiefs, stopping the bleeding.

Overnight Paris talked about nothing else but the Russian ballet. And you found yourself suddenly famous.

You try my modesty very much. But I was astonished. I was young, of course, then, I was quite simple, unsophisticated. Next morning I was sitting in my room, darning my stockings. There was an old friend with me and he said, 'You mustn't do that.' I said, 'Why not?' 'But you are a celebrity now.' And he brought me the papers, and for the first time I learned I was La Karsavina.

Do you remember the influence the ballet had on fashion and design?

Oh, very well. The ladies appeared in turbans. Misia Edwards, afterwards Misia Sert, was very much a leader of fashion. And once after visiting me and Nijinsky in our dressing room, as she was coming out, the crowd said, 'It is a princess', and another quick-witted Frenchman said, 'An empress'. She was so glamorous. And then in interior decoration there was what they called Bleu Bakst in fashion, the blue that he used in *Schéhérazade*. The leading couturier Paul Poiret made me a dress which was a sort of variation on the Polovtsian Maidens, with a hat absolutely like a Kalmuck hat.

Who were Diaghilev's friends at this time? Who did he spend time with when he was not working?

He brought absolutely loads of friends, not only the artists who were concerned in it, but all his friends who had an understanding of art, for instance Walter Nouvel – he might have been a professional musician if he wasn't so lazy – and then Prince Argutinsky Dolgorukov, who was a great friend of ballet; he even brought an old general who really did know about technique. And he surrounded himself with all the brilliant minds, like Cocteau and Reynaldo Hahn. They were constantly on-stage.

Diaghilev was a very demanding person, wasn't he?

Oh yes. Sometimes he could be quite ruthless and work his artists to the limits of their power.

How did Diaghilev get people to work so hard?

He had a tremendous gift of persuasion, very great charm and wonderful tenacity. He would talk one into everything, even against one's better judgement.

Did he do that to you, ever?

Did he not! He really made me miserable for a time. He persuaded me to sign a contract with him for Paris on top of a previous one with the London Coliseum, and then when I was with the Coliseum, telegrams started to arrive from Diaghilev, several a day. I dreaded the yellow envelope. At breakfast it was on the tray, at supper it was on my table and absolutely ruined my appetite. He sent his emissaries to talk about it, I went daily to see Mr Stoll, asking him to give me leave of absence, and he was adamant and so tears were my only weapon. And probably Mr Stoll was warned off by my tears and finally gave me two weeks' leave. So after all Diaghilev got what he wanted. He usually did.

Did his presence make a difference to the company?

Oh yes, that's the key word. Presence, he had presence, he had personal magnetism. He would appear at a rehearsal even for a brief time, and however jaded the artists were, he sort of galvanized them, and when he left, there was a blank – an anticlimax.

Many people have said it was difficult to be on friendly terms with him. But you were very friendly, weren't you?

Oh yes, we had great affection for each other. He sometimes used my confession of the crush to make me do anything that he wanted. But he really didn't have to because I liked him so much and he was very, very affectionate to me.

Tell me about the time you were together in Rome during rehearsals of Petrushka.

There, I remember, that was when the classes were introduced with Maestro Cecchetti, it was in 1911. There was a big exhibition there. There were fewer social contacts than in Paris, so Diaghilev, with Nijinsky in tow, of course, used to call for me every morning and took us to a lesson with the maestro. There were general classes, but Nijinsky and I worked together separately. And Diaghilev would usually sit in the auditorium and watch. And once he said to me, 'I would make a bad husband, but I could make a very good father.' He called us 'taking his children to school'.

What about all the travelling? You rushed about all over Europe during those years.

Well, we did it in comfort. They were long travels – it's not like now, going by aeroplane. We had the express train and it took about two days from Petersburg to Monte Carlo. All Russians regarded going abroad (I mean old-fashioned Russians) as a great adventure. So there was a terrific ceremony of seeing off. All the balletomanes would appear with flowers, and one old man, I remember, brought me an icon to bless me for the journey, and also a bucket of caviare. Diaghilev happened to travel on the same train and we polished off this quite big bucket of caviare!

Did you feel a part of some exciting new venture, capturing the attention of the world?

That's exactly what I felt. Diaghilev sometimes shared his ideas. Once, it was in Petersburg, he rang me up and said, 'Listen, I have got a most wonderful new ballet for you.' And he told me the story of *Le Spectre de la Rose*. That was a very happy production.

Was it a happy company?

I think yes. There were always some complaints and grievances, but Diaghilev could smooth it all and his authority was very much respected.

Was there firm discipline?

Yes, very good. Not by stringency – we had no fines – it was the authority of Diaghilev, and his magnetism. I wasn't the only one who was absolutely for a time under his thumb, but a much older person than I, a ballerina of the Moscow Theatre, Catherine Geltzer, she had some grievances she wanted to talk over. There was no end to her militant spirit, she wanted really to have it out with him. And she said, 'Well, I went to talk to him, he started talking, and all was forgiven.' Oh, he had great charm.

What did he look like?

He was very good-looking. Perhaps in a man of lesser calibre it would be called too good looks. But he also had some peculiarities, funny things about him which in other men might be considered faults. For instance, he walked with that sort of funny rolling gait, rolling his head from side to side. He reminded me very much of a sea lion. They look awkward, but when you look at them, they have perfect grace. I wasn't the only one to have that impression. Lady Ripon, a great patroness and personal friend of ours, she would usually call him Le Phoque, rather tenderly.

Did you feel there was an artistic policy, or did things happen very much hand to mouth?

Oh no, definitely not. Everything was worked out; he had usually gathered friends – it was like that the first year – who all discussed. It was in his flat, they all sat round, along the great table. Vassily, his servant, brought the relays of samovars, the tea went round, and everybody discussed or drew in one room, with Stravinsky playing the piano and Fokine listening. And then what they called a committee meeting took place in the middle room, and when Diaghilev wanted to make me do something, he would take me to his little bedroom. He only had a bachelor flat, with all the icons there.

What was Fokine like as a man?

He had terrific tempers. Sometimes he would even throw chairs about. But withal very lovable. We were devoted to him, because he took the artists with him. He gave them insight into the part. Just to watch him dance in front of us. He was a magnificent dancer himself, and he would, as he danced in front, give a sort of running commentary on it. When he was angry, he would say, 'It's putrid, tatty', but he could also admire the artists as he worked with them. He could stand back and say, 'That's wonderful.' And from my knowledge of him, working with him (as you know, I had all the leading parts in his ballets), I got to know him, and in a way anticipate what he wanted, and sometimes I would take a pose and he would say, 'That's it, that's what I wanted.'

What was his method of working? Did he come prepared, or work it out as he went along?

No, it was inspiration, the inspiration of the artists he had at hand. In a way he was like a sculptor. Sometimes he wanted a pose, he wouldn't explain very much, he would show it and then he would come and arrange the pose, the arm and so on, and then look at it, and either be content or change it.

What do you think he brought to choreography that was new?

He was the first man to see that ballet as it stood then couldn't develop any more. And he guessed from the great possibilities that were in the academic technique that it could develop, evolve. He created different styles of ballet, because he believed that every subject must have its own treatment and its own style, but they were all on the basis of the academic technique, only he went further without breaking with it.

The best-loved Fokine ballets seem to have been very romantic ones, like Les Sylphides, *or* Carnaval. *Did you enjoy dancing them?*

I simply adored it, especially *Carnaval.* It was very gay, and very mischievous, in the old tradition of *commedia dell'arte.* It is, incidentally, the only ballet in which Fokine used conventional gestures.

What about the dramatic ballets he made mostly for you, like Thamar?

Oh, I also loved them. In fact, I loved every new part because it was so fascinating, in spite of all his tempers. I liked *Thamar,* but at first I couldn't quite understand, and then Diaghilev helped me. I must have been very melodramatic in the beginning with big gestures. Then Diaghilev took me aside and said, 'Listen, you are just lazy and indolent, and all that fire there is from inside.' He also looked at me and said, 'You know, what I would advise you, have a straight line of eyebrows to give you that look.' And I did it, and it helped. It just gave me the key to the part.

Do you think part of the effectiveness of the Fokine ballets is that there were no longer set divertissements and passages of mime, but the action became drama?

Oh yes, that was a part of his artistic credo, his conviction. He thought that the introduction of mime scenes would reduce the ballet. It had to be direct action. We didn't do it the old way, with artists coming on and miming what happened, and reproducing the action. Perhaps in a very wonderful way if the artist was a good mime, but it was an insertion. Fokine made the action direct, and the acting in his ballets was a natural reaction to the situation.

Did you find the new music you had to dance to difficult? For instance, Firebird *was the first modern score. Did you find that hard?*

At the beginning very, because we used to dance to very simple music really, you might call it square, all divided in so many bars. When I met with the music of Stravinsky, I loved it, I loved the sound of it. I was fascinated, but it was difficult. I was never one to count, because it deflected my attention. I never counted the bars. And, I must say, Stravinsky was very kind; he would come before the rehearsal and play the piano for me to explain all the different parts, and I learned to visualize the musical line. It helped very much in Ravel's ballet, *Daphnis*, where every bar has a different count to it.

Perhaps the most successful of all the dramatic ballets was Petrushka. *Did you enjoy working on that?*

Oh yes. I liked the Moor part most especially, with the Carnival Butter Week, because I remember as a child it was a great excitement to be taken to it, and, of course, Benois remembered it well. It was so very colourful. The ballerina was highly mechanical, especially in the first part where we danced as puppets, before we came to life. I think it was fascinating. And the music gave me terrific nostalgia when I left Russia, particularly in the last act with that dance of the Coachmen, which they used to do in real life to keep warm as they waited, and the snow falling. All that reminded me of my country, made me feel very nostalgic.

What about the Greek idea that one saw in ballets like Narcisse *or* Daphnis? *Were you interested in the idea of free movement?*

Yes, we were. When Isadora Duncan came to Petersburg, we loved it, and it first showed us how free movements can be. We usually had set positions, but then from Duncan we learned that the arms can move much more freely and have patterns and be more expressive without transgressing the line of the classical dance.

Many of Fokine's ballets are still known today. Les Sylphides, Firebird, Petruskha. *Do you think revivals capture the same spirit as the original productions?*

Well, perhaps not all. *Les Sylphides* was part of our upbringing in the romantic tradition. It will never be outdated. It's not topical, it's pure art, and never can be stale from custom, but I think, excellent as dancers are today, they haven't got that same feeling of style as we had engrained in us.

Now let's talk about Nijinsky. What was he like as a man, as a person to talk to?

I knew him when he came from the school; when he made his début, I sponsored him because I was four or five years older, and his teacher asked me to dance a *pas de deux* with him, and the reaction of the company was a pretty good thermometer of his success. It was quite an ovation. Well, he was a modest, shy person. He started in leading parts dancing with all the stars, but, of course, leading parts for a man weren't the same as they were with Diaghilev, or under Fokine; they were very secondary to the ballerina. And therefore he wasn't the same Nijinsky that Europe knew. I think much is due to Diaghilev, who saw qualities in him which perhaps Nijinsky didn't even know or suspect were there.

What were those qualities?

There was a kind of incorporeal lightness. I give you an instance – in *Le Spectre de la Rose*. People who never knew Nijinsky but revered his legend asked me what was the height of his jump, as if that was the most important. No, all the dancers had great elevation. It was part of our teaching. But what he really did was the way that he used it. In *Le Spectre de la Rose* you couldn't say that he jumped, he just floated over the stage, he was incorporeal. He had a wonderful quality of feline grace, which was also guessed by Fokine, who made parts for him in which he could show his artistic quality. Like *Schéhérazade*. And I remember when we waited to go on the stage, he used to pad up and down, like an animal in a cage.

Was he a good actor?

Yes, perhaps not in the same way that Fokine was. Fokine portrayed human passions beautifully, but Nijinsky was detached. He was in a class of his own; he was more of a sylph than a man, perhaps.

What about as a partner?

On the stage very good, very good. He was very musical and we felt . . . I should say we were tuned together, knowing each other, never bothering, sometimes even slightly improvising the movement. But off-stage he was uncommunicative, and not very articulate. I remember we had once a misunderstanding and that was in *Giselle* when we revived it on the stage of the Paris Opéra, where it hadn't been given for a very long time, and Diaghilev attached very great importance to it. I remember he came to fetch me in my dressing room and, as Russians do, made the sign of the cross on me and led me from my dressing room on to the stage, and said, 'Let's go and re-create *Giselle* in the Paris Opéra.' At rehearsals I did it as others did it before me, taking the style in which the gestures were not quite conventional but the old kind of pantomime. And when we rehearsed, Nijinsky just stood and did nothing and it was very disconcerting, it put me off. So I talked to Diaghilev about it and he said to me, 'Now leave him, he will get it right, you will come to understand each other. He doesn't talk much, but he writes reams and reams of paper just on that part. He thinks it. He was just thinking the part in his head.' And finally at the performance it did come together very well, in harmony.

Do you think it was partly the influence of Nijinsky, and his relationship with Diaghilev, which led to the renewal of the position of the male dancer?

Oh yes, very much so, and also the choreography of Fokine, which always looked with disfavour on the male dancer playing second fiddle to the ballerina. The structure of Fokine's ballets wanted different highlights.

Tell me about Nijinsky as choreographer, particularly about Jeux.

Oh, *Jeux.* I think he had difficulties in that. He seemed a bit confused at first, and I rather missed the method of Fokine, who usually explained what he wanted. For instance, once I asked him what style there should be in *Armide* and he said, 'The baroque style', just like that. But I couldn't understand what Nijinsky wanted, and he couldn't or wouldn't explain, and got very upset about it. I didn't take part in the *Rite of Spring*, and there he worked with Marie Rambert, who was a Dalcroze pupil, because of the difficulty of the music. I think he always found difficulty in that; he was essentially a dancer.

Jeux *was not a success, was it? Nor* Narcisse *or* Salome?

No, they soon went out of the repertoire.

Do you think the failure of these ballets was because they were not very Russian, and what the public wanted was Russian *ballet?*

You are right there. In the first season we built all our hopes on *Pavillon d'Armide*, and it was really a marvellous production. Benois knew how to give it a kind of sorcery, and the only reason it's not given now is that it was a terribly difficult production, with all the stage machinery and complicated costumes, most expensive, of course. But what really brought the new note, showed the originality, were the purely Russian things like *Polovtsian Dances.* The great success of Nijinsky's and my *pas de deux* was because it had that oriental style. *Le Spectre de la Rose* was not Russian, but it was a huge success.

Was it just the dancing of you and Nijinsky?

No, it was a perfect ballet of its kind and a very happy production. Fokine

94

had absolute spurts of imagination. He did it all in one rehearsal; and it was perfectly conceived, and those little scenes at the beginning and the end, for me, were quite a new approach to mime. You had hardly any gestures. I would pick a rose and put it on my neck like that and look towards the window before he disappeared, and then realize it was all a dream. But, as gestures, I might be just sitting on that chair and talking to you.

Looking back on those seasons before the war, what do you remember with most pleasure?

I loved practically every new part because it said something new. You had to dig out something in you that you didn't know of before, and create it. But I can only reverse the question. There are very few ballets that I didn't feel happy in.

Diaghilev had a very difficult time during the war years. Did you think the Diaghilev company would survive?

Well, it is a wonder that it survived, because those were very lean years for him. As you know, he could only dance in the neutral countries, and there weren't so many; mostly it was in Spain. King Alfonso was a very generous patron, but Spain was a small country, after all, not very rich. It couldn't pay for it. Diaghilev really fought for the survival of his Ballets. But I think that those difficult times showed how great he was. He always liked to overcome difficulties, I think he enjoyed it, but that showed his mettle because during all the difficult time he thought of the future. It was there in Spain that he had the idea of *Le Tricorne*; it was a genuine Spanish ballet. On our stage, in the Mariinsky, we had a lot of ballets on Spanish themes, but with a quite different approach. There they were made into ballet dancing, sort of balletized, but here it was the genuine article and he used that time in Spain to extend his artists. He told them all to go anywhere, nightclubs, fairs, cabarets, just to learn the dancing.

I only knew about all that afterwards when I rejoined Diaghilev. I was in Russia during the war and when I rejoined, he used to talk about it. And one thing particularly struck me. He said, 'I never knew what blow would fall on me, whether I would be still a free man tonight. And every morning I made my bed myself and patted it and thought, there, there, my dear, shall I sleep on you tonight?' And that coming from Diaghilev, who was accustomed to being waited on hand and foot by his faithful Vassily, his valet. That showed you that he really began appreciating things which are taken for granted, but now they became precious.

Did you feel there was a very different atmosphere in the ballet during the 1920s?

Oh yes, I did. I felt nostalgia for all these people I missed, all the early collaborators and advisers, Benois and Bakst, Stravinsky and all that, and, of course, there was a different choreographer, Massine.

What did you feel about Massine's choreography?

I admired his choreography very much, and I think he had a wonderful quality of bringing the action and dancing together. You remember in the *Boutique Fantasque* where these ladies, non-dancing characters, come. He gave them a special walk and a sway of crinolines, and I don't know anybody else who did it before, to bring it all together. But working with him was not as exhilarating as with Fokine, because Massine never took us all into his confidence as Fokine did. I felt I was an instrument more than an artist.

You did have a succession of very entertaining parts with him – Le Tricorne, Pulcinella, Good-humoured Ladies, Boutique Fantasque, *many of them comedy roles.*

Oh yes, and I liked the comedy. I always thought that I hadn't enough chance to do it, I simply revelled in it. You know, all my life I admired clowns. I think it's the greatest artistry there can be.

Did you feel that Diaghilev became less interested in Russia during the 1920s, and more interested in France?

Well, partly it was circumstances. In his first period he was inspired by all the Russians with European outlook, and then naturally he was cut off from this connection, but also I think he got very much under the influence of the avant-garde, the French avant-garde, and it became much more sophisticated and there was even, I think, an awareness of the box office. More sophistication and much less spontaneity.

What about his flirtation with surrealism?

That, yes, it drove him on and on. Somebody asked me if Diaghilev was a snob. Not in social life, because he had no need to be, but he was an artistic snob in a way, or became one. And as that was new and took attention, he went to the surrealists. And I wouldn't like to tell you my impression. I thought that it was nothing. Can I say what I think? What you saw in

Romeo and Juliet was the expanse of the backcloth, sort of faded blue, wishy-washy, and then the yellow disc on it. And I couldn't see anything in it, but Diaghilev thought that it was wonderful. It was like the King's new clothes, that tale of Andersen. And I felt I was a child who said that the King was naked. But, of course, perhaps intellectual people could see it.

Do you really think they could?

They said they did.

What about Constant Lambert? You had a lot of trouble about him, didn't you?

Oh yes, there was terrific drama there, and there you can see the power of Diaghilev's persuasion. The thing was originally called *Adam and Eve*. And I came to Monte Carlo to join Diaghilev and create that part and he told me the whole story. He had tried to persuade Lambert to change things and it was very difficult. Then Diaghilev used a very absurd argument, but he could get away with it. He said, 'Adam and Eve for Madame Karsavina – but she's a married lady, she won't hear of it.' And so he finally changed it to *Romeo and Juliet*, and there was high drama there. One day Diaghilev made some cuts in the score in the morning. That same afternoon Constant Lambert came to me, in a terrible state. He said, 'I won't have the music cut, because I respect Bronislava Nijinska's choreography so much. I won't have a single step cut out. Will you persuade Diaghilev not to make the cuts? Or if he does, I am going to the theatre and will take all the parts away.' So when he left, I called Diaghilev. We were staying in the same hotel, and he came to my room and I said this is the situation. So Diaghilev went straight to the theatre and ordered the score to be locked away. Then he met Constant Lambert and they had a terrific tiff. But Lambert was very penitent after it. At the memorial service for Diaghilev he said to me that he couldn't think, without his heart breaking, that they had had that quarrel. And I said that, after all, it didn't do any harm. He seemed to be comforted.

Tell me something about Bakst.

Bakst, he was a most good-natured person, and always the butt of everybody else. This particular sort of nucleus of Russian artists of the *Mir Isskustvo* were all extremely good friends, but they always took Bakst on, and he took it all very good-naturedly. He was rather a dandy, very carefully dressed, with an eyeglass and so on.

And did you know Cocteau?

Oh, Cocteau, very amusing in conversation. Very brilliant, terribly spontaneous. He simply spurted out the very brilliant sayings.

And Picasso?

Picasso was very reserved. He wasn't like Cocteau, who was extremely talkative. He usually sat in the corner during the rehearsals of *The Three-cornered Hat* and made drawings. He was very silent, very reserved, I would say. Always scribbling something. But there was that kind of smile on his face as if he sized everybody up, and I think mentally he liked to pull everybody's leg. During the rehearsals of *Le Tricorne* he used to sketch my costume, and I looked over his shoulder and said, 'How are you going to make the costume for me?' I expected something magnificent with spangles. 'Oh,' he said, 'very, very simple.' And he said, 'I am going to make it round you.' And that's why he did it at the rehearsal, because he wanted to watch the dance, and know how the costume would move with the dance. You know that wonderful compelling line of his; he really knew movement.

What did you think of the conductors you had, like Monteux, or Ansermet or Beecham?

Monteux I liked very much and Ansermet too. But I think I liked Monteux most because he usually took into account our part. Sometimes the music is played in different tempo and the steps wouldn't fit into it. Sir Thomas Beecham, of course, went absolutely on his own. He produced a marvellous sound, though.

Looking back on the twenty years you spent with Diaghilev, what for you seems the most important influence he had on the history of ballet?

He gave it an absolutely new orientation. He *made* modern ballet, and the ballet as spectacle with the other arts, possible. He was the first man to gather together all the wonderful elements that make a ballet.

How do you remember him personally?

With great affection. We had our tiffs, of course, but great affection. And when he was a very ill man and spent most of the time in bed – it was the last season at Covent Garden, I believe it was in 1929. I was a guest performer with him then and he got out of bed and came to see me, and he said, 'Now you see that I love you because I got out of bed.' But what rather astonished me was that his whole life he was rather a hypochondriac and was afraid of everything. If he sneezed, he thought he would die the next day. But this time he was seriously ill, but it didn't seem to depress him, because he made plans all the time. He talked to me about the new ballet he was going to commission from Hindemith, and I asked what his new music would be like and he described it like this: 'Don't look for melody in the new music, it will be more of an orchestral sound. It will be like the transmutation from one precious stone, ruby into diamond, diamond into sapphire.'

Do you think your own career would have been different without him?

Oh, very much. He played a very great part in my artistic education. He was a very great influence. I think it would certainly have been different.

Anne Benois-Tcherkessova

1896 ST PETERSBURG–1984 PARIS

Daughter of Alexandre Benois, designer of Le
Pavillon d'Armide *and* Petrushka, *Anne Benois
knew Diaghilev from her childhood as a familiar
figure in the family circle.*

Could you tell me what your father told you about his early meetings with Diaghilev? – the period of the Mir Isskustvo, *and the first years of the Diaghilev Ballet.*

They met when they were quite young, and, of course, still in Russia. Diaghilev came from the provinces. It was his cousin Filosofov who introduced him to his other friends, and in this little circle my father really was the leader – if you like, the principal animator. Diaghilev's appearance made quite a stir; he was a big boy, very jovial, very enthusiastic. At that time he was principally interested in music and he loved song, and as there were also small musical evenings in this little circle, Diaghilev used to sing, accompanied by Walter Nouvel, who was also a great friend and a very good musician, and from that time on inseparable from Diaghilev. He accompanied him on all his journeys. Gradually, as the whole group of friends became closer, they embarked on new ideas. They had little meetings where each one prepared a theme, and little by little the thing evolved, to the point when they decided to create a society, which would concern itself with all kinds of questions of art – what really was art? – without taking account of nationalist tendencies, so that *everything* that was art could be taken into consideration, studied and commented on. It continued like this until the idea came to them to create a magazine, and that was because of Princess Tenischeva. Well, you know the rest of the story. The paper went on for several years, and it led to magnificent articles, which gave many people of high culture the possibility to write and demonstrate their opinions. In the magazine there were articles on art, on philosophy, on literature, on music. It was a very complete world.

Was it popular?

At that period, no, not yet. I can't say that their ideas were popular at that time. It had something of the feeling of an élite, among which even members of the imperial family participated. But, to tell the truth, the wider public thought it all a manifestation of decadence. They were so imprisoned in conservative ideas, from the artistic point of view.

What are your personal memories of Diaghilev?

They go back a very long way, from the very first time that Diaghilev started coming to our house, and for us as children, the appearance of a sort of genie was a little worrying. He had a very big laugh. He had a laugh like an ogre. When he opened his mouth, it was enormous, and the sound was like thunder rolling round.

Did he laugh a lot?

He laughed a very great deal, and, I must say, one of the general particularities of this circle of friends was that they loved laughter. They had a great sense of wit and of humour, and they dealt with things from their point of view very light-heartedly. That, of course, was part of their charm.

Your father wasn't, as I understand it, entirely in favour of the direction Diaghilev took towards the end of his life.

Well, it was in the early years a total and complete union of ideas with Diaghilev, both in the theatre and also regarding the first years of their friendship. But then, after the war, Diaghilev turned very much towards the painters of the left, if one can say that. Sometimes even to painters of extreme tendencies, and he rather left his former friends to one side.

Did your father resent this?

My father resented it, I'm afraid, very painfully, because he loved Diaghilev very much and he had a great deal of admiration for him, and he couldn't accept the idea that the great epoch we lived through had been some sort of distraction, valid just for a moment. One has to say that in the later years there were extremely interesting productions, where my father appreciated some things about them, the décor or the costumes. He remained eclectic and very just in his judgements. It wasn't a question of principle, it was a question of trying to find real value, to try to find what would last.

Tell me why everybody was so interested in the Ballets Russes. What had Diaghilev done during these years to cause people to care so much?

I think it was a kind of overturning of existing taste, and the effect is still felt in our time. There was nothing like it when the Ballets Russes came for the first time to Paris, and nothing comparable anywhere in art. One simply can't speak of the theatre, it was just routine. But the Ballets Russes brought with them a breath of art, of new ideas, young ideas, if you like, 'picturesque' art, because there were real painters who took part. They weren't just decorators, they were real painters who were at the heart of this great work. It overturned everything, even fashion.

Marie Rambert

1888 WARSAW–1982 LONDON

*After abandoning medical studies in France,
Marie Rambert went to work with Émile Jacques
Dalcroze at the Institute for the Study of
Eurhythmics at Hellerau, near Dresden. It was
here that she met Diaghilev, who subsequently
asked her to assist Nijinsky in the preparation of
the choreography for the* Rite of Spring. *She later
joined the company and was on the South
American tour when Nijinsky married. After the
First World War she settled in London and
founded a school and a company that still bear
her name.*

How did you first come into contact with Diaghilev?

I think it must have been at the beginning of 1912. I was then studying with Dalcroze, having turned my back on ballet. I had studied ballet as a child. Then I had seen Isadora Duncan and I was carried away by her. To me, she and Pavlova are the two great goddesses of the dance. One day there were two visitors in class, but we were quite used to it because very many distinguished conductors used to come and watch the eurhythmic classes of Dalcroze; it was a completely new movement. And then these two men came in, one tall and portly and the other very small, very neat, with a pale face. However, I didn't look much at them that day. It didn't produce any impression on me because I was very absorbed by the class – Dalcroze giving classes was always exciting. And then I was terribly surprised when next day I was told that Diaghilev wanted to see me. It was in Berlin, I think at the Adlon Hotel. We had a talk, went to the theatre and saw a performance of *Cléopâtre*, *Carnaval* and *Faune*, I think. And afterwards we went to supper to have a really good conversation, and Nijinsky came a little later. And Diaghilev kept asking me what were my impressions. I am surprised how stupid I was, or how I could just say the things, how daring, how impertinent. I said, 'Oh, I didn't like *Cléopâtre*. I thought that the procession came in out of time.' 'Unmusical,' he said. I don't know why Diaghilev should try to please me. He said, 'Yes, they did walk rather like cooks.' But actually I was wrong, and Fokine was right, because it was much nicer for them to walk in *through* the music than to march in like a march. Then we talked further; we talked also about *Faune*, and he asked me whether I thought I could help Nijinsky with *Sacre*, and I said, 'Yes, I think that I could.' So we arranged the date when I was going to join the company. All this happened terribly quickly. I was absolutely staggered at all that.

The place where I had to meet them was Budapest, a lovely, exotic city. I arrived during a rehearsal of *Firebird*. Karsavina was away and her place was taken by Piltz, who was wearing a yellow, terribly worn-out tutu. I remember that perfectly well. And, of course, there was this benevolent giant, Grigoriev, there, leading the rehearsal, magnificently, and I watched it, and went to performances. But it seemed some time before we could start work. You want to know about the lessons and so on? At the beginning it was a question of giving them lessons in eurhythmics, so that they should get used to listening to the music and interpreting the rhythm. Up to then the ballet in Moscow used to dance in general to the music of Pugni or Minkus, it was 'ektata ektata'. It was even called 'ektata'. That is quite obvious rhythms. And here came the score of *Sacre* before them, where you have to count two against three or three against four, and then suddenly a crotchet equalled a quaver, and all sorts of things like that. It was necessary to prepare. I started giving them lessons, but they didn't like the lessons at all, and I don't wonder. They had already had a very difficult lesson in the morning with Cecchetti, and then lots of rehearsals. The only time was to try to give it half an hour or so before the show. So Grigoriev had this splendid idea. He said perhaps much better than lessons would be to teach them whatever Nijinsky arranges, worked out at rehearsals with Nijinsky, and then teach every artist his part from the musical point of view he'd arranged. That worked very well.

So Nijinsky started rehearsals. Now Nijinsky was a very silent person. Some people thought him inarticulate, because he had absolutely no small talk, but I talked to him at the rehearsals, at preparatory rehearsals, because every day we used to stay in the afternoon, Nijinsky and I with the pianist who played Stravinsky's score, and then I had to analyse. I had to say we will do eight bars, or we will do seven and a half bars, and let's stop here. That would be a phrase. It was very difficult to divide, because that music was so new. However, we managed to do these rehearsals. At that time when we started rehearsals Diaghilev was in Paris. We were rehearsing chiefly in Monte Carlo. During the rehearsals Diaghilev wasn't there, but there was a perpetual surveillance by Diaghilev's valet, Vassily, the famous Vassily, who perhaps every twenty minutes or certainly every half an hour would come in and say, 'Vaslav Fomich' – that's how he addressed Nijinsky – 'perhaps we had better shut the windows, it's draughty.' And then he would go out. And twenty minutes later he would come in and say, 'Vaslav Fomich, I really think you should put on a scarf or a jersey or something.' And half an hour later he would come in and say, 'I think it's rather too hot.' I mean, it was so obvious that Diaghilev had told him, 'You have got to be there and see how he behaves with that woman.' But Nijinsky didn't take the slightest notice of me. I can tell you there wasn't the beginning of love, on his part in any case. But Diaghilev wanted to make doubly sure, so we had this Vassily. And then the following day we had the rehearsal with the company, and Nijinsky arranged the steps as he thought it should be.

I forgot to tell you that before the very first rehearsal of *Sacre* Diaghilev addressed the company. He knew full well that they wouldn't like Nijinsky's choreography. They had already hated with all their might *L'Après-midi d'un Faune*, Nijinsky's first masterpiece, and it was necessary to prepare them a little. And Diaghilev tried to say to them how beautiful this music is, and how expressive, and how Nijinsky was full of new ideas, and so on. He tried to prepare them. It didn't work very well. I think they hated it till the last day, to the last rehearsal, to the last performance.

Nijinsky, in the way he composed it, was struck with eurhythmics, and he wanted very much to translate every note of the music. And I knew that even Dalcroze didn't want to always translate every note, but to have what he called 'contrepoint plastique', leave certain notes of music, but Diaghilev insisted absolutely that every note of the music should be done by a step, or a movement of the arms, and so on. In the end I think he was right, because the music was so powerful, and its rhythmic impact so tremendous, that when it was all done by a company of magnificent dancers as they were, that practically doubled the impact of what Stravinsky had written. It really did. Since that production of *Sacre*, I should say, the next most powerful thing I saw was his sister's production of *Noces*, which happened in 1923. That was the nearest. Otherwise I can't see a masterpiece of equal dimensions.

We rehearsed, then, in Monte Carlo. Oh, before that, in Budapest, Stravinsky arrived. And he sat down at the piano. I think he watched a rehearsal first; he was appalled. He said, 'This is not at all the tempo, this has got to be quicker, this has got to be slower.' Nijinsky said, 'I know what dancers can do.' There was an epic battle between them. Stravinsky sat at the piano and tried to make an orchestra. He stamped with his feet and banged with his hands on the piano, and shouted and sang and so on, and, do you know, I can't remember who won. It is well over half a century ago. So I am allowed to have forgotten that.

Then we came to Paris, where we were to open at the Théâtre des Champs-Élysées, which is beautifully decorated by Maurice Denis and Bourdelle and various sculptors, but it wasn't finished when we arrived. And we had to rehearse on top of the building, and very often workmen had to go through that particular room to get on to the roof or something, and Nijinsky was furious. Had I known what was going to happen, perhaps I would have tied the door, because he lost his temper, and he said that the next time that man crosses, I am going to kill him. And, indeed, the next time the man came he raised a chair. Well, of course, people stopped him, but it looked as though he was going to. That was sort of a very violent temper. And another time too he behaved very badly to Karsavina during a rehearsal of *Jeux*. And she – like the incomparable person she was, and absolutely there is no one existing like her today – she knew how to behave, how to calm him. Anyhow, Diaghilev came and insulted Nijinsky, and said, 'How dare you speak to that goddess, and you, why you are an urchin compared to her.'

Finally the first night came. We had rehearsed. We had beautiful costumes and scenery by Roerich, who was a great connoisseur of prehistoric Russia. In this ballet, like in *Faune*, Nijinsky invented a special basic position. In *Faune* the position was that the feet, both parallel, were going in one direction, and the body was facing the audience, and the arms were facing the audience too, but you walked on one line. The whole action was from one wing to the other, like on a bas-relief. It was a very, very difficult position to hold, because nowadays we study so many techniques in addition to ballet, all contemporary work which stems from Isadora Duncan and Ruth St Denis and Martha Graham and so on, but at that time one only had learned the classical technique. And so it's the more astonishing that Nijinsky should have been able to think out a new position in which he wanted to do the movements and move in them. Not merely reproduce. It would already have been an achievement to have reproduced a bas-relief, but he produced a complete ballet. And I say about that ballet that, although it is very beautiful music, Debussy is impressionist and the ballet itself abstract, there is a sort of plot. Nevertheless, it's this *abstraction* that Nijinsky managed to convey, and when you think that that was in 1913. And already he had invented a completely new way of progressing. That is an important point about him.

When it came to *Sacre*, the feet, instead of being parallel, were with the toes turned in, like primitive people who don't know how to walk. In short, a complete reversal of the classical ballet technique. But he kept it up right through the ballet. He didn't think of inventing particular jumps; it was stamping the ground because the idea was to stamp the ground and make the earth fertile for the spring. And then in the second tableau, the sacrifice of the chosen maiden, he demonstrated a dance. When he was showing it, I was absolutely *bouleversée*. Really it was something so extraordinary. It was the most tragic dance that I have seen, either then or ever since. And Piltz was doing a very pale, sort of picture-postcard reproduction of it, and yet people found her extraordinary in that part, because the part was so great, and even when you took away the whole of Nijinsky from it, you were left with his choreography and that was something incredibly eloquent.

Then when the first notes of the music started on the first night, the shouts in the audience, hisses, terrible. The Parisian audience did not expect that from Nijinsky, their beautiful man from *Spectre de la Rose*, or *Sylphides* or something like that. To see that and to hear this music. Today when we listen to *Sacre du Printemps*, it's almost like listening to a lovely prelude by Bach, but at that time it seemed all to them such dreadful dissonances. But we went on, because Diaghilev had said in advance, whatever happens, the conductor must go on playing, and we go on dancing. It was terribly difficult to hear the orchestra because of all that noise in the audience. Nijinsky stood in the wings counting out one, two, three, one, two, one two, three, one, two, three, four, etc. Then we started the Second Act, second tableau, the sacrifice of the maiden. She had to stand for some seventeen and a half bars, or thirteen and a quarter bars, on the spot with her feet turned in, her hands under her chin and trembling like that. So somebody in the audience, from the gallery, shouted, 'Un docteur', and somebody else shouted 'Un dentiste', and somebody else shouted, 'Deux dentistes', and, of course, lots of people laughed, others shrieked. The pandemonium was absolutely terrible. At the end Nijinsky in the wings said, 'What an idiot the public is. *Dura publika, dura publika*.' And we only gave perhaps three performances of it in Paris. Most people hated it, but there were a few people who realized the greatness of it, and then in London we gave about three performances, and then that masterpiece was never seen again, not a trace of it is left, not a film, not a recording.

Romola Nijinska, Nijinsky's wife, says that she has got it all written down, but I don't know who will be able to decipher it, because it's only Nijinsky, it was entirely personal to him, and to write down dancing is jolly difficult, even today, to read it back still more difficult. So I am afraid that masterpiece is lost.

We also rehearsed *Jeux*, which was only for three people, himself with Karsavina and Schollar. Here again he made a discovery. Here the gestures were from sports. From the first time he introduced on the stage a contemporary trio. Three people in contemporary clothes. He was dressed more or less like a sportsman of his time playing tennis in white trousers, only they were caught at the ankle like his ballet trousers. And the girls wore short pleated skirts with jerseys. At the dress rehearsal of *Jeux*, by the way, the first costume that Bakst designed for Nijinsky was so utterly hideous. Sort of shorts which showed his overgrown thighs. Diaghilev always knew very well how to dress Nijinsky, and he always looked harmonious and marvellous. But this in some way underlined all the bulges there are in the calves, and he wore a red tie, and, I think, red braces. It was something hideous. Diaghilev said, 'He is not going to wear that costume.' And Lyovushka Bakst, who was on the left, said, 'What, what, he is not going to wear that costume? He is.' There was an epic battle between Lyovushka and Seryozha. They had a dreadful battle. In the end Diaghilev said, 'I don't care what you say.' He sent them all to Paquin, who was the greatest dressmaker of that time, who made very elegant dresses for the girls. The man's trousers were copied from his practice clothes and it made a very good costume, and it was the first time that a contemporary man appeared in a ballet. The movements were sort of stylized sport move-ments. All the time they had the fists closed, not tightly, but a little bit as though they were holding a tennis racket or a golf club; it was mixed up, all that sort of thing.

But all this . . . When one thinks, I always wonder how, what made him do that? Because there was a very visible transition from Petipa to Fokine, but there was absolutely no link between Fokine and Nijinsky. Absolutely everything he invented from the beginning, and everything that he invented was contrary to everything he had learned. But here came in the greatness of Diaghilev. He knew when he loved those young people, say Nijinsky or Massine or Lifar, he made them into gods. They couldn't sustain it after his death. Not the height at which they were with him, because it was too high for anyone.

What about Nijinsky as a dancer?

There you ask me a question. To begin with I can say definitely that I have never seen anybody like him, or anybody who made that tremendous impression that he made. Often people say, did he really jump so high? And I always say I don't know how far it was from the ground, but I know it was near the stars. He had that extraordinary personality, you followed his eyes; all his soul was in his eyes when he danced, like all dancers of genius. My two ideals are Pavlova and Isadora Duncan. Those are artists of the stage who can transcend the stage, who can speak to the audience directly by their personality, who are completely independent of their technique. It didn't matter what Pavlova danced at all; anybody else dancing these dances, it wouldn't even matter what you were looking at. It meant nothing, most of the dances that she did. But those were only means. She could go and speak direct to the audience about her own ecstasy, and made you share that ecstasy with her; and the same thing can be said about Isadora Duncan. She too, she did very simple movements, but there are millions of people who try to do simple movements like her, and nothing comes of it. But in her case her soul revealed itself immediately, and she had the same quality of ecstasy.

Well, about Nijinsky. I sat once in the stalls during a rehearsal with Diaghilev – it was a rehearsal of *Faune* – and I said, 'Oh, do you know, I think this is his most marvellous part', and Diaghilev said, 'Yes, and what about *Petrushka*?' 'Yes, of course.' 'What about *Sylphides*?' And he went on. And, indeed, I could say that when he danced *Spectre*, he was the very perfume of the rose, because in everything he extracted the essence. In *Sylphides* he was the very soul of Chopin, in *Petrushka* he was the pain of every man weighed down by fate, by cruel fate. Then again *Narcisse*. It wasn't an important ballet, but he looked like a Greek marble, it was Greek youth, and when he did *Faune*, he was a completely dehumanized creature, half animal, but not so much animal as nature in general. And that picture that he did in *L'Après-midi d'un Faune* is to my mind a stronger evocation of the Greek mood of that moment than anything he painted. And when he was showing the *Sacre* movements to Piltz, he did the most tragic movements that I have ever seen.

Did Nijinsky talk much to you?

Légende de Joseph, written by Strauss and with a libretto by Hofmannsthal, was originally conceived for Nijinsky. And he talked to me about it when we were in Monte Carlo, when I had a chance, when Diaghilev was away. We used to walk out together from rehearsals, and have wonderful talks. He could talk if you asked him questions. He didn't talk spontaneously, but if you asked him questions, he always gave very good replies. I asked him, for instance, about Nelidova, the girl who was brought from Moscow, chiefly for *Faune*, *Cléopâtre* and, I think, a goddess in *Dieu Bleu*. And she had rather a long nose, at that time one called it a Greek nose; everybody else had slightly turned-up noses, and she was not what people at that time called a beauty. But when she danced *Faune*, Nijinsky, thanks to these 150 rehearsals, managed to transform her to such a degree that she looked like Pallas Athene. And I said to Nijinsky, 'Surely she must be very grateful to you for having turned her into a goddess?' And he said, 'She grateful? – she has never heard that word. What she would really like is that I should write for her a Spanish dance with a carnation in her teeth and a rose behind her ear.' And he did, sort of Spanish movements which were quite extraordinary. And it was true, the woman was really quite foolish. She could only talk about a sailor whom she had left in Petersburg or something. Quite a silly woman.

What about Karsavina, was she a match for Nijinsky?

Ah, Karsavina. Karsavina, I think she remains, with her incredible charm and beauty today – you know her as well as I do. That woman, every year she perfected herself, every year she went on, and at that time one had never seen a dancer who had that extraordinary sensitivity she had. She responded to music, she responded to the choreographer, she responded to her partner. Whatever Nijinsky did, she was always in harmony with everything that surrounded her. Even in a ballet like *Narcisse*, which was not an important ballet, with very inferior music by Tcherepnin, nevertheless she created a complete character of Echo, with that sadness, and all she had to do was to repeat the voice. It was very beautiful. And then *Spectre*, which one could have thought, there is this terrific part written for a man, but you always saw she was there, and in her own right, a magnificent, incomparable artist.

What about rehearsals, and the influence of Grigoriev?

Oh, Grigoriev also is a person I love so much. The memory of that man, the memory of movements and everything is quite extraordinary. He was a very exacting regisseur. He never let people do as they wanted. He got from them what he wanted, what was necessary for the ballet, and at the same time he had the most charming, adorable manner, very kind. And consider, above all, what he has saved – an enormous repertoire for us, as though we had it photographed in a way. Unfortunately he alone cannot do the whole of *Sacre du Printemps*. But his wife, Lubov Tchernicheva, that great beauty and wonderful artist, she remembers a lot. The two of them together can reproduce practically everything. *Faune*, of course, they could reproduce; unfortunately of *Sacre* nothing is left.

Can you describe Diaghilev? What did he look like when you first met him?

He was a tall, portly man with a very leisurely way of moving. He had that famous white strand in his black hair. I think he started dyeing it very young, I was told. I don't know whether he dyed it white, or whether it went white and then he dyed the rest black. Anyway, a very imposing personality. At the beginning, after being rather impertinent at our first meeting, I became afterwards very humble with him, because I admired him from day to day more and more, because I realized the incredible courage he had, and the incredible inspiration. He radiated it absolutely, it all came from him. Everybody around him was alive. I met him again in Paris in 1914; they were doing that season *Légende de Joseph*. The Paris public called it *Les Jambes de Joseph*, because Massine had terrific thighs, but he was beautiful as Joseph, ideal. And I was angry with Diaghilev, who tried to explain to me that Nijinsky could not have done that part. 'It's very lucky that he is away, and that we have now Massine.' I thought it was real treachery.

Did Diaghilev change over the years?

To me, not. No, I always remember him the same. After all, I met him in early 1912, and then I didn't see him at all during the war, but when I saw him again, he was to me exactly the same as he was before.

You saw him towards the end of his life?

Yes, he came in 1928 to my studio. That was a wonderful, wonderful occasion, because I had Frederick Ashton in my school, and in 1926 he did his first ballet, *Tragedy of Fashion*, with décor by Sophie Fedorovich, and then he continued to study with me. And in 1928 he did a new ballet, *Leda and the Swan*, which was going to be included in a play by my husband. And we did a sort of preview of it in the studio. We had just acquired the Mercury Theatre and transformed it, and we gave two parties, one perhaps from four to six and one from six to eight, I can't remember. Anyway, there was a lot of people. And after the second party I rushed to His Majesty's Theatre to see a performance of *Noces*. And everybody was already in because I was late, and in the foyer stood Diaghilev, talking to Courtauld, who had been at our party, and who was obviously telling Diaghilev what a lovely ballet it was, and what a beautiful girl Diana Gould was, and so on. And Diaghilev said, 'Why don't you show me that, why don't you invite me?' I said, 'Sergei Pavlovich, you are always invited, all you have to do is say the date.' Finally we agreed on a day.

He came an hour late. We had already done the barre and the centre, we were coming to the adagio. I said to him, 'What would you like to see?' He said, 'Go on with the lesson.' And I gave them an adagio and an allegro. He said, 'Why do you put that girl at the back? Bring her forward.' That was a little pupil of mine who was very charming and very witty, so he wanted her in front. No, I put in front my boys, Ashton, Turner and Billy Chappell, but he was not interested. He wanted that particular girl, because she was witty only. And then he began to look at Diana, and I said, 'What would you like?' He said, 'Just continue the lesson as you usually do.' I finished the lesson, and he said, 'Well, that's quite good, that's our good old master Cecchetti.' Then we showed him a bit of *Leda*, a *pas de deux*, Ashton with Diana Gould, and Diaghilev became very attentive. And when they went to change, he said, 'I would like to talk to that girl.' Diana was then sixteen. I brought her out, and Diaghilev said to her, 'Voulez-vous venir chez moi?' And she said, 'Je viens ce soir avec Maman.' And he said, 'Non, non, je veux dire, voulez-vous venir danser chez moi?' and she said, 'Oh.' That was all she could say, of course. Breathless.

That was in 1928. After that I saw him in 1929. At Easter I was in Monte Carlo, and we had lunch together, with Lady St Just, who was a very great friend of his and Kochno. And Diaghilev was full of the *Swan Lake* in which he was going to show Spessivtseva with Lifar, which was really one of the great events of his last season. And then the last time I saw him was in London at a party, I think, the day before the last night. I know he was going away immediately. And I knew by that time he was very ill. I didn't know it was diabetes, although I remember at that luncheon with Florrie St Just she said, 'You oughtn't to eat this.' He said, 'Never mind, never mind.' He never took any notice of that very dangerous illness. And when I saw him at that party, he was completely transformed. All traces of power had left his face, only helplessness and kindness remained. And he talked to me with such closeness as I have never heard from him before. He really was kind and good. And I said, 'Sergei Pavlovich, you must look after yourself. You are going to have a big long holiday.' Well, you know what happened.

How much do you think dance might have developed without him?

In ballet it's always difficult to assess how much these artists could have done without him. He has created for them an ambience. He has fertilized the ground, as it were. All was prepared for them if they had talent. He dragged it out of them, he put it in conjunction with all the circumstances that were necessary for creation, and in that way we had choreographers like Fokine to begin with. It's true that Fokine started before him, but he reached his height with Diaghilev. I don't think anybody will contradict that, although Fokine himself does in his book. Then came Nijinsky, then came Massine, all terrific choreographers. People forget now how much

Massine has created of great beauty, and he continued to create even after Diaghilev. Then came Lifar, but in between times there was Balanchine and there was Nijinska. All choreographers of the first rank. And then think of the people who painted for him, who did for the first time décor. He put them together with the stage, with the ballet, with music, that was something Diaghilev could do. He was a fertilizer of genius, I would say, and he dragged the best out of every artist around him. There was Benois, there was Bakst, afterwards Larionov, Goncharova, afterwards the French Derain and Braque and Pruna and Picasso. All of these people who perhaps never would have thought. It is true that it was a tremendous advantage and tremendous honour to work for Diaghilev, but it was also an incredible joy, and they did more for him than they could have done for anybody else. It was interesting. It was made great for them by the presence of that giant, God rest his soul.

C. W. Beaumont

1891 LONDON–1976 LONDON

*Critic and author of many books on ballet,
including* Mikhail Fokine and his Ballets *(1935)
and* The Diaghilev Ballet in London *(1940), from
1910 to 1955 Beaumont ran a shop in London
which specialized in books about dance.*

What impact did Russian ballet make on you when you first saw it?

It made a very considerable impact, because we had never seen anything like that before. There was another company, which was a sort of herald of the Diaghilev one. That was the company that came in 1908, I think, speaking from memory, with Koslov, and Karsavina made her first appearance there. That was a company of about eight or ten, and they were at the Coliseum. My wife saw them and when Pavlova came in 1910, she insisted on my going to see them.

Were you excited by what you saw?

I was never really interested in dancing. I was always interested in the theatre, but my wife persuaded me to go, and I was quite carried away with it. And, of course, a year or so afterwards the Diaghilev Ballet appeared at Covent Garden and that completed the attraction.

Tell me about the first things you saw.

I remember seeing *Carnaval* and was tremendously impressed by both the dancing and the setting. There was something quite homogeneous, which one had not seen before.

What about Fokine's choreography? Do you remember The Firebird?

I was very impressed by *Firebird*, especially the music and the costumes. Of course, it was the magical effect of the setting and costumes, which I didn't think the later version achieved. The original one had a palisade running across the background, and then there was a sort of practical tree in the middle, different from what they have now, which was loaded with apples, which all glittered gold in a sort of amber light. And then there was the suggestion of curious fantastic trees above the palisade. But you really saw nothing but the tree. The gates were placed facing the audience, and not at the side as now, where you can't see them. And when the Prince pulled the gates in an endeavour to follow the Princess, suddenly the whole of the background lit up, which was a very exciting effect. I think it's better to keep the original design if possible, because that has generally been conceived working with the original choreographer, and so more probably represents his ideas.

What about the actual steps? Have they changed much over the years?

Well, I should say basically it is the same, although it's very difficult to preserve these things, even though we now have systems of notation which are said to preserve them. Though you can transfer the actual steps and movements, by passing them on verbally or by demonstration, you don't always get the quality. You're told, 'We do so and so, and so and so, on certain bars', but you don't get the quality, which the choreographer has infused. That depends on the ability and skill and artistry of the person conveying it, which may vary considerably at times.

Did you feel that the Fokine ballets were as well danced in the later years of the Diaghilev Ballet?

I think they were always well danced, but naturally I think they were never quite so good as when they were done by the original interpreters. I have seen many, many Polovtsian Chiefs, but I have never seen anybody to equal Bolm in it.

Why was it so special?

The whole savagery of the thing was very exciting. They danced as if they were something from the Mongolian Steppes.

We are always told how important music was to Diaghilev, but in the early years there were ballets like Cléopâtre *when the music was a pot-pourri by several different composers. Did* Cléopâtre *make a strong impression?*

I found *Cléopâtre*, parts of it, very dramatic. I saw Fedorova do the main role, the lover of Tahor. Her lover is killed and then she comes and sees this dead corpse of Tahor on the stage, just covered with a black cloth, and then she goes and removes the black cloth rather apprehensively, wondering what lies beneath it, when she sees it's her dead lover. The impact is tremendous, and Fedorova was a really great artist.

Did you see the ballets with Nijinsky's choreography?

Yes, I saw *Jeux*, and I saw *Sacre du Printemps*.

What did you think of his ability as a choreographer?

It's difficult to say on those two particular ones. I didn't care very much for *Jeux*, which seemed to me rather static. It's very modern for its period; I don't think one's got used to that yet . . . *Sacre* was very impressive, very impressive indeed. Much more earthy, in a sense, and primitive than something one sometimes gets later. Because there wasn't any love element like has been reproduced in some later versions by other choreographers, it was really like a tribal rite that was being carried out. And the dance which Piltz did when she danced to kill herself by sheer exhaustion was frightening to watch.

What was the public reaction to Sacre?

Well, I should say the audience was staggered, because the music was so unlike anything one had heard. One had been prepared, for instance, by *Firebird*, and even *Petrushka*, but in *Sacre du Printemps* . . . At that time people had perhaps just come in from a choice dinner; suddenly to be assailed by *Sacre du Printemps* was highly disturbing.

Did they applaud?

I think they did applaud, but for a moment they were rather staggered, and then afterwards the more musical in the audience would have appreciated what was being done. I think the ordinary ballet-goer was certainly rather shaken.

Who were the audience at that time?

In the stalls they were mostly intelligentsia. Perhaps that's not the right word. Intelligentsia and fashionable people who were up in the social world, these were mostly the people who filled the stalls. But, of course, there were a number of enthusiasts who were in the gallery and amphitheatre who were very carried away, and there were tremendous arguments about these things up there, much more even than I have ever seen since. I went up there myself, both in the amphitheatre and in the gallery sometimes, to see what it was like, and there were really quite fanatical arguments about things.

Did the ballets have an effect on design, on clothes and fashion?

Oh, they had a tremendous impact. I remember going to Paris soon after I had seen one or two of the seasons and there you could see books brought out by well-known fashion designers like Poiret, obviously inspired by some of the costumes. Even little things: in *Pavillon d'Armide* you may remember that Nijinsky is a sort of Negro slave, and he has a little neckband of black velvet. You can see it in a drawing by Sargent of his head, and this became very fashionable. Ladies wore this little narrow neckband, with perhaps a little diamond ornament on it.

What was the secret of Nijinsky's impact on the audience? Was it just the dancing?

No, I don't think it was only the dancing. I think it was primarily because he was a very great artist, and every role that he created was quite different from the other ones. You see some dancers who have very considerable talents technically, perhaps even mimetically, but on the other hand you can see it's just the same dancer wearing a different costume. But with Nijinsky that wasn't the case at all. He was a completely different person and I never have honestly seen anyone, or seen very few people that have really that same achievement. In *Schéhérazade* he was rather gross and seemed to broaden his body, and when you saw him in *Carnaval* as Harlequin, he was very slim and mercurial and something quite different. Again when you saw him in *Sylphides*, there he was a wonderful romantic person. He seemed to epitomize the romantic movement.

What about Karsavina?

A very beautiful dancer, and also equally good at both comedy and drama. Really dramatic in *Thamar*, for instance, and yet you couldn't imagine anybody more charming than Columbine in *Carnaval*.

What was the secret of their impact on the audience? Was it just the innovations?

I don't think you could say that as a whole. From the classical point of view, what about *Sleeping Beauty*? That's one of the best classical productions, probably the best production I have ever seen. One will never see a cast like that again.

Did you feel that after the war the company changed from being very Russian to something much more Western?

Oh, undoubtedly. Specially musically. But I think that was influenced by the war, because, of course, at that time Diaghilev was in Switzerland, Italy and Spain. Italy produced the Goldoni *Good-humoured Ladies*, just as Spain produced the *Three-cornered Hat*. They were there with the local atmosphere and were able to recapture it. Massine did it in a wonderful way.

Did the audience change very much over the years? Was it much wider?

I don't think so. I think quite a large proportion of general public went, if even only out of curiosity, and by that time Diaghilev had had a very widespread influence and reputation, so everybody was anxious to see anything new.

Could you describe Diaghilev?

The first time I saw him he was pointed out to me when I went to some of the early seasons of the Diaghilev Ballet, and I should say the most noticeable thing about him was a really enormous head, which stood out quite remarkably from the general heads of the audience. I noticed him during the interval going to greet some friends in the stalls, and he was very immaculately dressed in white tie, and full evening dress, and had this beautiful head; I even think he wore white gloves, or carried white gloves. Very immaculate during the early seasons. I think I saw him more about 1918, when I met him personally. Then one was impressed again by this enormous head; he seemed to have more a head and shoulders, and one never looked below that because one was so impressed by this body, looming out at you. I don't know if you know the statue of Peter the Great, by Rastrelli? There's quite a considerable resemblance, I should say, both in appearance and also in manner. I think Diaghilev was rather a mixture, very ruthless at times; on the other hand nobody could be more charming. When he came to see me, in the shop, he would sometimes want things, and ask me to look out for this or the other, some document, or something he needed, and then he would just brush your arm with his hand, which was rather plump and warm, and it was impossible to resist this caressing gesture. On the other hand he could be quite different if he was annoyed about anything. He usually sat in the stalls, generally his favourite place, and I saw him under many different conditions.

One of the things, though, that most interested me was when I was invited to attend a costume rehearsal, which was held actually on the stage. Diaghilev sat in a chair, and Grigoriev stood near him, or sat also on a chair. Then there were one or two persons assisting, and they had the costume designs preserved under a talc sheet, and each dancer came on as he was called. They began with the principals, and Diaghilev compared the costume design with the actual costume realized. And after he had examined this very closely and had approved, he then asked the dancer to do a variation, or some of the steps that he was going to do. And often the dancer found – especially, I remember, in the *Sleeping Beauty*, they were very heavy costumes with gold braid on them, and he started saying, 'Oh, this will have to go, the skirt will have to be reduced, this trimming will have to come off', and kept trying different things while the costumier was in despair at seeing his creation, as he thought, ruined.

Describe his features.

His features were very authoritative and varied rather considerably according to circumstances. They were alert and sharp at dress rehearsals, but sometimes he would relax and you would see the eyelids close down, and then he would look rather oriental, almost with a touch of a Buddha in a state of meditation. It was this curious oriental touch. I didn't mention anything about his rather thick, wavy hair with a strand that was either bleached or natural, which earned him the nickname of Chinchilla, as you probably know. One thing rather interesting was that I noticed that he was addicted to almond perfume. Whenever you went into a room where he had been, there always lingered in the air a certain touch of almond essence, which was unusual.

And his voice?

His voice could be short and sharp, but on the other hand it could be, as I said before, so caressing that it was very difficult to resist. I never heard him speak English, but he was said to know English or understand it. But I never heard him; he usually spoke French, as far as I was concerned.

What was his manner like at class or rehearsals?

He sat down very quietly at rehearsals, and sometimes he would clap his hands and stop something, and ask Grigoriev to go and rearrange something. But, of course, a lot of his time was spent in lighting. He used to like washed colours with a certain white light, and he could spend hours, practically all day, getting what he felt to be the correct lighting effect.

He would generally come to see me in later years at the shop, and very seldom arrive alone, always with a kind of group of attachés – his secretary, Kochno, and perhaps one or two dancers – and he would arrive like a general with his aides-de-camp, and fill the place up; you couldn't get in or out.

You saw him one night at the Savoy?

I saw him at the Savoy under rather strange conditions. He was supposed to be trained originally to be a singer, and he took a great interest in music and studied music. I never heard him play the piano, though. But I used to be friendly with Lopokova and her then husband Barocchi, who was the business manager of the company, and when the performance was over, I used to go back to the Savoy with them and we used to talk about ballet and things of that kind. One evening I was just leaving, and coming down the stairs. To my surprise there was a door open on one of the landings, and Diaghilev was there in the half-light, sitting at a piano, and on the piano were piles of scores, and he was sitting there playing, and I saw his rather plump fingers going over the keys. And I didn't like to stay there too long and intrude on the situation, but I always remember that picture of him in the half-light with his enormous big head, and he was just playing, oblivious of anybody passing.

What was his secret – perfectionism, an eye for detail?

I should say all of those things. He was a great perfectionist, trying to have the best of everything, and he wanted the best dancers, and the best designers and the best composers, and he wanted the whole thing presented as well as it could possibly be.

How did he persuade people to work together?

Well, he did. I don't know how he did it, but he certainly persuaded everybody to work together by the same caressing tone he used to use, I imagine, on everybody he wanted to influence.

Tell me about the famous production of the Sleeping Beauty.

That was done in 1921. I think I would regard that as the most beautiful production I had ever seen. I saw many of the rehearsals. Diaghilev was in the stalls with Stravinsky and Bakst and Grigoriev. I don't think there were many other people beyond myself. One saw only pieces that he wanted to examine. Of course, Sergeyev arranged the production largely, but there were many other dances that were done by Nijinska. I was very impressed by the production.

Why do you think it failed with the public?

I think the answer is very simple: because previously Diaghilev had concentrated on short one-act ballets. The public were used to that, and they were used to having three different ballets in one evening, and they were not ready for a classical ballet that took a whole evening. They had never done anything like that before. They had done the *Swan Lake*, but only the Second Act, and they had done another version I saw with Nijinsky, that was very condensed. They had never done a full-length classical ballet before, and it was rather interesting, because it was in a sense a complete volte-face for Diaghilev, because he went right back to the beginning, but he always had a great affection for this ballet and I think he was always hoping an opportunity would occur to present it.

It seems so strange. The public had followed all his previous changes of direction. Was it just the length?

I think it must have been the length and the similarity of the technique, although, of course, there were character dances in it. There were some ideas about introducing a certain modest, modern touch in it. For instance, I was told that there was going to be a boy and girl who were going to take part between the acts and talk about it in some fairy-like way; and I was asked what I thought about it, and I said I didn't approve of that. But whether that carried any weight, I couldn't say. But at any rate they didn't do it.

Tell me about the disasters of the first night.

The disasters resulted from the scenery not working as had been planned. Bakst had designed a wonderful creeping lilac which came both from the bottom of the stage, came up from underneath, and also from the flies. I saw it at rehearsal and it jammed once there. It just stopped, and the same thing happened on the first night. Another thing was in the hunting scene, where they had a mist suggested by dropping gauzes. The gauzes hung on a piece of projecting scenery, and Diaghilev tore his hair practically, watching this, and as soon as the interval came, he went storming behind there, and there was the devil of a row.

In the mid-1920s there were ballets like Chout, Pas d'Acier *and* Train Bleu. *Did you enjoy them?*

I didn't enjoy *Chout* because it didn't seem to me very effective choreographically. And another thing, Larionov had designed the costumes very much in the cubist style, and the costumes and the setting, one rather outshadowed the other. You could hardly see the costumes because of these extraordinary patterns which clashed with the background. I am sorry Diaghilev didn't seem to alter that.

What about Parade?

I didn't enjoy *Parade* as a whole, but there are some very nice solos by Massine as the Chinese conjuror blowing fire out of his mouth.

What about Balanchine's ballets? Did you like them?

Yes, the *Prodigal Son* was extremely impressive, and especially Lifar in it. And I think on the first night Diaghilev had quarrelled with Lifar, and Lifar was in a great state of nerves and very upset indeed. He gave the performance really as though he were performing himself as the Prodigal Son. And he drags himself to his father across the stage, and, as far as I remember, he had very little on his shins, and you could see his knees were cut with the floor of the stage. It was a very impressive performance. And he came up to his father and begged forgiveness and was received back into the family, and I think Diaghilev appreciated this. And then he went behind and they both fell in each other's arms, and he congratulated him for the performance and they made it up. So the *Prodigal Son* had a special double meaning.

Was the company as strong at the end of twenty years as at the beginning?

Well, I think it was always pretty strong. I don't think it was ever so strong as it was in the early days, or in the *Sleeping Beauty*, when they had wonderful stars and all the fairies were principal dancers. It was Spessivtseva one night, and Trefilova another, and Lopokova another and Nijinska another and so on. I was very impressed with that performance, and I also liked the way the fairies were dressed, because they had a suggestion of being something not belonging to the world of mortals, not like we have now, where you get dancers very nicely costumed, but you don't have the impression that they are something different from the courtiers. But in the Diaghilev one you did, because they had this curious make-up with rather elongated eyes and it gave them a sort of insect appearance, especially with these long antennae which were attached to the little crowns they wore.

Looking back thirty-eight years since their final performance, what do you remember most of the Diaghilev Ballet?

I probably remember *Sleeping Beauty* very much, because I saw it every night for about three months, not to mention the rehearsals. I don't know whether Diaghilev regarded me as a very inferior mascot or what, but he used to come and see me, and he insisted on my coming to see the performance. I don't think he attached any particular importance to what I might say, to be honest, but Russians being very superstitious, and Diaghilev in particular, perhaps he thought he ought to have me there in case. And he came in once, because we kept open then quite late, at seven, I think, at night, and said, 'You must come along and see the new production. We are opening tonight.' And I said, 'Oh, I'm not dressed to come', and he said, 'You can come and share my box.' And I said, 'Well, I don't think I can go like this dressed as I am.' 'Oh yes you can,' he said. 'Dans la nuit, tous les chats sont gris.' That's a Pushkin phrase. So I suppose he thought that being in the dark I could just stand back in the box and it wouldn't make any difference. But he was very kind to me, I must say, Diaghilev.

But after 1918 I had a special pass which enabled me to go and watch any performance, and if there were seats I was allowed to go and sit there, and in the interval Grigoriev gave me access to the backstage, so, of course, I went backstage, and made all sorts of notes that I wanted for describing some of the ballets, which were very useful. It was very interesting to see the ballet from both sides. The only other person I know who had this privilege was Laura Knight.

Lydia Sokolova

1896 LONDON–1974 SEVENOAKS

Born Hilda Munnings, Sokolova was one of the longest-serving members of the company, joining in 1913 and, apart from a short break in 1922, remaining until the end. Massine created many roles for her, including the Chosen Virgin in his version of The Rite of Spring. *Her memoirs* Dancing for Diaghilev *(1960) give the most animated account of life in the Ballets Russes.*

Tell me about the first time you auditioned for Diaghilev? What happened?

I was dancing at the Coliseum with the company of Theodor Koslov and his brother, and there were a certain number of Russian people and a certain number of English. When the Diaghilev company came to London, they were needing about four or five dancers, and to our amazement there were just a few of us chosen to go and give an audition at Covent Garden. When we arrived there, of course, we were desperately nervous. There were two men and three girls – three English girls, and both the men were Russian. We could see nobody, because the front of the house was dark, but we knew that Diaghilev was sitting there with Nijinsky, Maestro Cecchetti and Madame Cecchetti, and I think there were two or three others; we couldn't see who they were. Maestro Cecchetti came up on to the stage and stood us in our line and gave us some exercises to do. Everybody seemed to be doing extremely well, particularly the Russians, because they were used to this, conversation being in Russian. But we English girls were absolutely petrified. I had been extremely stupid. I thought it was the right sort of thing to do, so I put on a new pair of ballet shoes, which was fatal. And, gracious me, before I knew where I was I was down on the ground. Tripped over those new ballet shoes. And whack! Down I went. So I picked myself up and carried on with some more exercises, and down I went again. And by this time I was absolutely shaking, and thought that was the end of my future engagement with the Diaghilev company. We were dismissed and sent away and went back to our own Coliseum Theatre. The following day we had news that we had been accepted and I had been accepted, having fallen down and disgraced myself. But it was most exciting. So then we had to tell Theodor Koslov and his brother and the whole company that we were leaving. I had already been dancing with Theodor Koslov for nine months, although I was then only sixteen years old.

Finally we arrived in Monte Carlo, looking like a lot of school kids, particularly us English girls. The men, they were accepted any place, but I was very plump, and just at that sort of age when you are losing your puppy fat. And it was all very, very frightening, because there were about seventy-five dancers in the company, all of them extremely glamorous. There were more Polish than Russian girls. The men were mostly Russian. And these Polish girls were beautiful, all Polish girls were in those days exquisitely beautiful. Lovely hair, beautiful eyes and lovely pale complexions. And they looked at us and thought, well, these are not going to last very long. Where did they find that little crowd? You know how they could be.

We soon discovered the clothes we were wearing – the practice dresses which were quite all right in London, and in a company like the Koslov company – they were accepted, but certainly had no glamour. The costumes that the girls wore in those days were like a great bouquet of flowers, because they were made, just like the Grecian things that Pavlova wore with elastic under here, and elastic round there. They were crêpe de Chine, and everybody got themselves a different colour. When you saw all these girls dancing together, they looked just like a great bouquet of flowers. And so we had to find out ourselves how they were made and scramble round as fast as we could into Nice and buy crêpe de Chine and make ourselves dresses like theirs. In later years, just before the war broke out, I thought how nice it would be to have something entirely different to all this colour, which I realized was very confusing for any choreographer or ballet master. It must have been awful to see patterns in all these vivid colours. It must have been a problem. So I made myself a black one, and this caused quite a sensation. And Diaghilev approved, which to me was really rather extraordinary, because it was so entirely different to anything else. It stood out. But he approved. He didn't say very much, but he didn't tell me to take it off.

Tell me about your first impressions of Diaghilev.

Well, he was really very frightening. I always felt that it would be like talking politics with Churchill. You would feel that you just knew nothing, you just didn't count. He didn't converse with you, he didn't talk to anybody. He was a very quiet man. People seemed to think that he was noisy and rampaged about. He did not do that. He spoke very little. If he met you on the stage, he might just give you a little smile and pass by. He did not praise you, and he did not criticize you. There were one or two things that aggravated him tremendously. And that was when you had a large head. He himself having such an enormous head, he had a horror, I think, of anyone else appearing with one. And I remember when I was already a principal dancer dancing in *Petrushka*, and I had put a lot of curls around because I remembered Madame Karsavina had had some very pretty curls in one of her old pictures. So I had some with my fluffy hair and the little bonnet hat. And he saw me in the distance and came over straight away, and he said, 'You go straight back to your dressing room, and take out all that hair. I can't bear the sight of your head. It must be made smaller.' That was the sort of thing. If it were personal to you, he would correct you.

He disliked a woman's thighs. You will notice that in our day you never saw short tutus. They were all just above the knee. It was only Pavlova, with her beautiful, slender, lovely legs, who could wear those tiny tutus which were created on crinolines. But we didn't wear crinolines, we had just tarlatans, and nets and things. And the reason for that was that Diaghilev could not bear the sight of a woman's thighs, until later years when it became a modern fashion, and people had thinned down and their bodies changed, and then he put you in tights. For instance, people like Doubrovska, who was long and thin and slender, well, he enjoyed looking at her in all-over tights. But from that point of view he was very, very strict. As a man – what shall I say? One only heard things by rumour. And rumours came from the outside. Nothing ever petered through from Diaghilev himself.

What about his personality? What was he like as a person?

I thought he was terribly nice myself. I loved him very much. Most people thought he was really rather horrid, from the way they said, 'Oh, he's always so fussy' and 'He just doesn't talk to anybody.' But I thought he was a delightful person. Very, very seldom did one know of him being angry. If he was angry, he just pursed his lips, and went very pale, and would keep perfectly silent, turn round and walk away. He did get into one or two very angry rampages and that was at a very important rehearsal we had one day. One of our young men, Slavinsky by name, wasn't there to open this picture. And the whole company was waiting and waiting, and finally he said, 'This is too much.' And he walked up and down like a lion in a cage and he thumped his stick and he shouted at Grigoriev, 'If you know where that boy is, go out and get him.' We all had our own idea where he was, because we knew he was an amorous young man, and he probably had forgotten the time, and Grigoriev also had an idea where he might be found [i.e. with his wife], and went off and brought him back. And we thought they were going to come to blows, because he shouted at Slavinksy in such a way that Slavinsky lost his temper also, but finally they quietened down.

That was the only time I ever saw him really thoroughly angry.

He never went anywhere alone. You never saw him alone. He always had two or three people, a sort of entourage, with him. If by chance he had to come out of the stage door, say, in Monte Carlo, where we spent our home life, he had to walk the whole way round the terrace, and under an arch, and through round the front of the house, and you saw him walking alone. It was so odd. It looked as though he had lost something. He was wandering along, he never walked quickly. He was never a man that you could say, 'Oh, there goes Diaghilev.' He always walked in the same rhythm, the same pace. And he always had his malacca cane with the silver top, and in the evening, when he was dressed, then he became immaculate. Then he was in the theatre as theatre is. Perfumed, powdered, his hair all re-dyed up. It was always dyed, because he had his white streak, but the white streak was his natural hair, and the other part was the tinting and the dyeing. And then his white shirt, and tails and tie and everything, and his cuff-links. He looked absolutely terrific. And he knew, of course. He knew the sensation he created when he entered. He was the sort of person that it was just the same to him if he were talking to royalty, or to the stage-hands. It made no difference. He was always a regal gentleman. Perfectly lovely. He was very conservative in the way he dressed. His clothes mostly, I would say, were dark grey, not pale grey; he never wore that, never wore any blues or browns or any colour that would attract attention to himself. And in the evenings he always had his ebony stick with him, and he was a picture. Absolutely lovely to look at.

And I thought that on the whole he was very kind to us; he was fair; he was one of those people who didn't have any favourites. If he felt that somebody was losing their head a little through success – you know how we are when we are young, we get excited when we have tremendous applause – he would watch very, very carefully about this. And he knew exactly what was going on, and you were getting just a little beyond yourself, and he sat as though he were a spider in a web and he had you all on strings. And as each one had a period of success and admiration and invitations and so on, he'd let that string go and he'd let you out just so far until he realized that that was enough, you were going over the traces. Back you came and you stayed in the *corps de ballet* right down there and somebody else would go off. You never got away from those strings. He held you absolutely tight. He wouldn't let you go.

We were rather like white elephants. He would never let us go to parties or go visiting without his permission. Lunches yes, that was all right, but if there were parties to be attended, either in the Paris seasons or the London seasons, where there were always masses of invitations, he would receive the invitations himself, and allot certain numbers of us to go to that house and let certain other ones go to that house. And he knew where we were, and he knew what time we came home. He was very, very strict to see that we were not overtired or that we didn't allow ourselves to let out secrets or behave badly. That's why people used to say in those early days, 'Have you ever seen any of the Russian ballet? Do you know any of the Russian ballet?' And people would shake their heads and say, 'No, I don't know them. We only see them walk about, all looking very glamorous.' Because the girls and boys, they dressed most magnificently. The women with ospreys in their hats, and beautiful shoes, and tailored suits, and dresses, and in Monte Carlo you had three changes of clothes on the terrace every day, and we were expected to do the same.

For instance, in the mornings you didn't wear suits as one wears a suit in the morning now. You wore spectacular frocks, rather like, almost like tea gowns, pretty hats, and tilted hats with flowers and things, particularly when Bakst was around, because he designed, and we wore those dresses with panniers and hats tilted in the front with flowers all at the back. He designed a dress for Madame Karsavina and this dress was so beautiful, it was all pinks and blues, and it was made of pure silk with taffeta bows, and the little hat was tilted in the front and she had all the beautiful dark curly hair underneath. And so it was; the Aga Khan was around, and one had to be really smart. Then in the afternoon one wore suits, so after rehearsals when we came out on to the terrace, then we would walk up and down like the others did, taking the air and being looked at, admired if possible; and then in the evening, if we had an evening rehearsal, not performances, we really dressed ourselves up, and put on our prettiest clothes to attend rehearsals, because big rehearsals in those days were spectacular things. People came to watch and look at all these lovely girls and boys.

We had two different sorts of men. The girls were . . . I wouldn't say there was much difference, there were tall girls and smaller girls like myself, but the men were definitely segregated. There were what we called Malchiki, which were the boys, who were five feet three, five feet two, five feet four, and then there were the big strong men, tall six-footers, who danced things like the Negroes in *Schéhérazade*. They had to look tremendous, and they were magnificent dancers, of course, beautifully trained.

All through this time it was most exciting, really, because Maestro

Cecchetti was in charge. It was very thrilling for us, because to be trained by this maestro who had trained all the biggest ballet dancers in that era anywhere, Madame Pavlova as well as Madame Karsavina, Trefilova, Kchessinska, the whole lot of them were all trained by him, and also Nijinsky, and we were being trained by him too. Well, I was most enthusiastic, even though I couldn't speak Russian at all in those days.

Tell me about Cecchetti and his method.

He had a very strict method of certain exercises for each day of the week, and those exercises built up towards the end of the week. There were certain days when one had sort of what we called *terre à terre*, little things, *entrechats* and technical things. Other days the jumps got bigger and bigger and bigger. I was in my element when it got to the jumps, because the one thing I really could do, if I could do anything at all, was jump, because I had naturally a good elevation. And I enjoyed these classes. I loved them. What with standing on the stage, watching Madame Karsavina, and being spellbound and almost forgetting my cues to start, by watching her and becoming so enthralled in this marvellous exhibition of dancing . . . These things made my life complete; I didn't want anything else at all.

We had a Paris season after Monte Carlo. We then got to our London season and we were rehearsing and practising in Chenies Street at the big drill hall there, which belonged to the army. And the day came when it was the end of the season, and it was a sort of Cecchetti examination. He set steps and sequences for little groups of us, and amidst were some most wonderful jumping exercises, huge jumps. Of course, I was having the time of my life. I enjoyed every minute of it. And at the end of it he went up on to the little stage, which there was in those days in the drill hall, to award prizes and to my complete amazement, almost shock, he awarded me the first prize of the whole company, for the most progress. And I had only been with the company eight months, nine months, to be exact. And I still have a photograph of himself as he signed it. He always called me Eeda, he couldn't say anything else. He spoke in a language of Russian and French and Italian all mixed up, and the date is on it, 1913, and it, I really must say, is a thing I prize most in my life. It's still in the silver frame, just as he gave it to me. I must admit, I wasn't very popular for a long time to come after that, amongst the company. Still, they soon forgot it.

Did you get much support? Were the company generous to newcomers?

No, they were not. They were not. By nature they were rather jealous people. It was a little difficult for them as far as I was concerned, because there were small solo parts, little solos, little comings-out to do things. And one of those girls was a Polish girl, and she was just about the first, other than Madame Tchernicheva, to have a baby. And when I arrived in Monte Carlo, she was just about due to give up, and to go back to Poland to have this child. I had gone into the whole repertoire, and in a month I learned one ballet after another. Anna Bronova, she couldn't take the pace at that time. She left us – I can't remember exactly how long she was with us, but not terribly long. Doris Faithful, she stayed longer. She left and came back. She was one of those people who are rather inclined to drift. She was very pretty, and very useful, and was always given nice parts. I don't know, I suppose I had a very, very quick brain or something, and I was pushed into all this Polish girl's parts, and I hadn't been in the company more than a few weeks before I was popping out doing something all by myself, to the horror of all these girls that had been in the company, well, for two or three years anyway. So maybe it was a good thing that I didn't understand much Russian in those days. I only learned to speak later.

Did Diaghilev ever praise you?

I can't remember him having done so. No, I can't remember. He never gave anybody presents except on very, very rare occasions. He had this idea, as he told me, and told us all, for that matter, that his ballet was full of soloists; there was no *corps de ballet*, there were no parts where you could say that is a star, or that is a star, except for people like Madame Karsavina or any of the great dancers that came as guest artists. We had to have a figurehead naturally, but the nucleus of the thing was all on a par. There were a few of us that had more ability, I suppose, than others, or were able to give character, shall I say, to various roles. Therefore we were typecast, or we were given these parts to play, as I was. That's how I found myself galloping ahead.

The only time I ever remember being completely rebuffed by him, it was an awkward moment. We had a new ballet called *Cimarosiana*, and Leon Woizikowski and myself, we were both character dancers, and everywhere we were paired up whenever possible. And we were given a tarantella to dance. Our costumes were absolutely hideous, couldn't have been uglier. They were shocking things. Leon had a sort of pouch and a pompon hanging right in front of him, sort of Pulcinella. And at rehearsals at the Paris Opéra, I remember upstairs in the rehearsal room when he and I danced this dance when the company was collected together, quite suddenly the company applauded. If that happened, which happened very, very rarely, I assure you, it was obvious that there was a winning thing there. So we thought we had got a winning little number to come out and dance. A sort of divertissement, it was.

And when we did it that night at the performance, and we went off together in our funny little odd movements, there was thunderous applause. It was absolutely spontaneous, it burst like thunder. And we were so excited; we thought, this is marvellous. To cross over from the Opéra, there was about three minutes' walk, I would say. That's exaggerating, but it's a very, very long walk from one side of the Opéra stage to the other, and if you really want to do it, you go through the corridors at the back. I had to get to that other side of the stage for my next ballet, so instead of walking on the stage, I walked through the corridor, and to my horror, when I got halfway across, I could just see Diaghilev all by himself coming towards me, which was a terrifying thing to happen, to come face to face with him. What could you do? You didn't know what to say, you didn't know how to behave, you didn't know whether to smile or look serious, or not look at all, because he was quite a frightening person to meet like that. And I go along, and I was still rather pleased with myself about this performance that we had just given. So as I met him, I didn't know what to say. I said, 'Well, that was good, wasn't it?' It could have meant anything, the dance or the applause or anything. And he just looked at me as he passed, and he said, 'It could have been better.' And that was that. So it would have been better to have said nothing at all than to be snubbed that way. He could be terrifying.

But he was kind when you had problems?

Well, he was sweet. He had no patience for ailments. He just couldn't register slight illness at all. He would drive you if you were ill right to the extreme moment before you completely gave up. And he had at one time when I was in trouble called me, and said that he would like to speak to me. I had been having a lot of family trouble, and worries and illness and home troubles, and he could see, he always knew when things were going wrong with his artists, he sensed without asking questions. He had also heard rumours, probably, about one's private life. And he gave me orders to go and see him at the Savoy, which was a very frightening thing, because you never knew whether you were going to be reprimanded about something, which he wouldn't do in public. And when I got there, I was very scared and shaky, and he put me in a corner, right in the corner, I remember it so well, in one of the downstairs rooms of the Savoy, and he sat in front of me, and he asked me a few questions which I tried to avoid answering in detail. And then he said, 'Now, I want you to remember that I can be as a father to you, and when you are at any time in trouble, real trouble, either in the day or in the night, and you send for me, I will come.' And I am perfectly sure in my mind that he never said that to anybody before, and did not say so to anybody afterwards.

Later, when I was desperately ill, and it wasn't known whether I would live or not, having had very serious operations, he came to visit me in the nursing home, and the company had to leave the next day for the south of France. He phoned through to that nursing home twice during the journey to Monte Carlo to see whether I had survived or not. So how could I not love anybody like that? Of course I loved him.

Did he like children?

He was very sweet with children. He was embarrassed by them, as a lot of men are. If he saw children in the street, he wouldn't stop and talk to them, but he would frequently tap them on the head and tap them under the chin and so on. During the war when we had such very sad trouble, no money or anything, and we were stranded in Madrid, my husband and baby and I stranded with no money whatsoever, we used to meet him every evening in the park. We had no money to go to cafés, neither he nor we. But we would sit on the bench, or walk up and down, and he would nurse her. She was then only about ten months old and he would nurse her, and she would play with his monocle, and touch his cheek, and he was amused and so sweet with her. And later when we came to London, he always enquired how she was, because she had been desperately ill. That was the time when I went to him and said, 'I don't think that child's going to live. She's dying, there's no doubt about that.' I had got no money for doctors, and he said, 'Well, I have no money either, but let's go upstairs and see what we can find.' We went up to his tiny little bedroom, couldn't afford anything better, and he opened his standing wardrobe trunk – you know those American wardrobe trunks – and he opened one of the drawers, and he pulled out a little sack, a little leather thing about so big that was full of coins that had come from all the leftovers from all the visits to various countries. And he turned this out on the bed, and there was an awful lot of tiny little centimes and so on, which weren't any good to anybody. But any coin that was of any value whatsoever, sort of two-shilling piece, or five pesetas or so on, he picked all those out and he said, 'There you are. Go and change those into pesetas, and get a doctor for Natasha.' That was very sweet of him. He was a dear.

Did he like animals?

He had a rather cruel streak where animals were concerned. He had a little dog once, a tiny griffon, and they were very naughty, he and Massine. They used to get this little dog drunk so that they could be amused watching it wobble about on the table, and it developed eczema, and they used to leave it to be looked after in some kennels or other. But finally he gave it to me because he couldn't cope with it, with its baskets and its medicines and, I don't know, brushes and everything. I had that dog for a very long time, but I had to have it put to sleep, in the end. He hadn't any horror of dogs, but he was rather cruel, to them.

But cats, now there he did have a horror. I remember once when we had a dress rehearsal, the fatal season we had at the Prince's Theatre, which did go wrong. It was a bad season, it wasn't a happy season at all. Anyway, it's not a happy theatre. It's built over a plague pit, and in those days the rats used to be running about so much they played the harp. They used to run up and down the harp strings. But at the dress rehearsal a black cat came along and walked across the stage, and Diaghilev screamed and shook his head and held his face and ran about and said, 'There's the omen, there's the omen.' He really had a horror of cats. Particularly black ones. That's just superstition. Many Russian people are rather superstitious. Mustn't put a hat on the table, or a pair of shoes here or there. They are like that.

What did you call him when you had to address him?

Always by his two Russian names, Sergei Pavlovich. I think there were one or two people who privately had nicknames for him, but Lydia Lopokova was the only public one; she always referred to him as Big Serge. And as she was a sort of little comic, he took it all in very good part. But outwardly to us he never seemed to have a sort of sense of humour that meant you could play around with his name. One would feel lack of respect, which, of course, he had from every angle. We always knew as soon as we were on the stage or in the theatre if he was in the front of the house. It went round like a grapevine. Diaghilev's here, everybody knew. Ping, up, you had to be, as he was in the house. But I don't think you could have played around and given him any nicknames.

What about your own name?

Well, I had a horror to begin with of the name I was christened with. Hilda Munnings. I just couldn't radiate anything. I couldn't demonstrate that name, I just never did like it, even as a child. So I was very grateful when Diaghilev himself decided that something had got to be done about me, because I was already dancing principal parts, and becoming a soloist right through from those early days. In 1915, when the company was recalled, I was this one and only English girl with this rather ghastly name. Munningsova. And he called me over one day. We had all given in photographs that we had, to be sent to North America for our first tour in the States. And he said, 'I have signed all your photographs last night.' I thought, this is extraordinary. How could he sign all my photographs with that awful name? He said, 'I have christened you Lydia Sokolova. You are the namesake of a very famous ballerina.' So I did my party piece. I kissed him and said, 'Thank you very much. I will be Russian from now on.' And I have never manifested, or felt any other way, other than Russian. I have lived a Russian life for so long. When I came back to England, I couldn't speak English. I could speak Spanish and French and I found English awfully difficult, until I had been here a little while and acclimatized myself again. But even so, even now, when I wish to say something that I can't find words for in English, I speak them in Russian. I feel part of it . . .

When you first joined the company, Fokine had left and Nijinsky was in charge. How did you feel about that? What was his personality like?

That is a very difficult question to answer, because one never really registered any personality. It was a remote personality. He made no contact at all with any of the dancers. He never spoke to anybody. He walked about, up and down, picking his fingers and fussing with his face and his eyes; he'd look at you for a very long time, and then he'd turn and go away. So it was impossible to know him as a person. As a dancer, of course, he was supreme, and again completely remote. You couldn't talk to him about his dancing. You wouldn't be able to say to him, 'Were you sure at such and such a time, or were you nervous?' He wasn't there. He was way out. As a choreographer, well, I don't know how I can tell you because it was just something he brought with him and showed you and you could either do it or you couldn't do it. Then he would start again, and he would do a little bit of this and a little bit of that. Our opinion about him as a company was that it was never instant inspiration, that it was mostly worked out at home with Diaghilev and his advisers and musicians and the composers, and that it came almost on a platter, and we were then taught to do this.

I came racing straight in to Nijinsky, which was a most terrifying thing, because Grigoriev took all the rehearsals for all the old ballets, the actual existing programmes that were to be given. And apart from that there were the Cecchetti classes in the morning and then these rehearsals for the *Sacre du Printemps*. Luckily for me I had been studying music quite seriously for quite a long time and the music part of it didn't frighten me, as it did most of them, because they had no knowledge. They played to sounds, to melodies, to the Rimsky-Korsakov and the Borodin, and so on. But to work out a terribly difficult thing like the *Sacre du Printemps*, it was really terrifying. It was at this time that Madame Rambert saved lives – at least, she saved the lives of many people. And we used to run around with little pieces of paper with all the accents, and stamp and run and stamp again. And she was always there to interpret, a sort of go-between, between the composer Stravinsky, the pianist and Nijinsky, and so this thing was worked out. Well, that was completely remote. It was a mechanical calculation, and nothing more nor less. I still remember, for instance, some of the steps of that first *Sacre du Printemps*.

Then my next experience was when this friend of mine, or she became a friend later, had left to have her baby, Klementovich by name, I was told to dance in the *Faune*, *L'Après-midi d'un Faune*, which was very, very scarifying, may I tell you. Because there were so few of us. And he would explain, or try to explain, that you danced and you moved between the bars of music. He coudn't explain, nobody seemed to explain it to me, that one just danced not between the bars of music, but through melodies, through and over. I understood that because, understanding music, I knew where you had these sounds which continued on. And so everybody was trying to walk as though the music didn't belong. But once you mastered it, and you could hear yourself, or feel yourself dancing in sound, it was the most delightful thing to dance in that you could possibly imagine. There was one thing that you had to learn. It was all done one way, absolutely flat. If you could learn straight away that by pushing your wrists forward, your hands forward from the wrist, they would stay. What people tried to do was push the hand back flat. It doesn't work that way. If you just tilt the wrist forward, you can just do it completely relaxed, whichever way you wish to do it.

Tell me about Nijinsky's wedding.

Oh well, that is another very long story, isn't it? Shall I sit down? Shall I tell you from the time on the boat? When we left on the steam ship, the *Avon*,

Diaghilev stayed behind because he had a fear of water and we were somewhat concerned because this young lady, Romola, as we knew her, was always with Nijinsky. We had seen this at rehearsal rooms, and she used to come and sit with me in my dressing room and talk English, but never disclosed that there was a secret going on. As soon as we left, she would go upstairs on the top deck, and we watched this. Three weeks' journey, not like now, a couple of hours or so. And so we stayed together. We used to go practising. Madame Rambert and I shared the same cabin, so we did our exercises in the cabin, hanging on to our bunks. And when we got to Rio, they went off the boat, and came back in the evening and announced their engagement, and the captain gave us a dinner party. This was the most horrifying thing that we could imagine, because we knew as a company, apart from the private life of Romola and Vaslav Nijinsky himself, that it couldn't work, it just would not work. Diaghilev just would not permit it. After all, he could not permit it because they were so near; he couldn't have a woman in the party, so to speak. He couldn't get down to tacks and so on. So we were pretty scared about this and thought it would never go through.

When we got to Buenos Aires, there the invitations went out and we went to this rather dreary wedding. In fact, if I remember rightly, I didn't go. I don't remember having gone, but I did go to the reception afterwards. I don't think many of us did go. We were so shocked and so worried, because we had heard straight away that Diaghilev had telegraphed to say that Nijinsky was out. And that to all of us was the most terrible thing, terrible thing. Our whole world collapsed under us when he told us he was out. Then on the way back – how can I explain this to you? He had many contracts, obviously. The managements of these big theatres, like the Colon and other places, they paid Diaghilev big moneys because of Nijinsky. Now Nijinsky had those contracts in writing, but they didn't mean a thing. Diaghilev didn't pay Nijinsky thousands and thousands of francs, dollars, pounds, what have you. And so when they married, they naturally had these documents. She felt he was entitled to that money and if Diaghilev was going to push him out, the only thing they could do was to claim his salary. And so we got back to Rio and they went to stay at a hotel. I can't remember which place it was actually, it was such a long time ago. They sent a note down to the management to say that some of these moneys must be paid, otherwise he wouldn't dance. And so the tragedy started. And, of course, there was no money like that sort of money to pay him. And then we were all shipped back, and he refused to dance. When we arrived back, he wasn't allowed to come anywhere near us, and that was the end of Nijinsky for the time being.

Talk about Fokine, his style and its originality.

It was varied. It demonstrated absolutely clearly the character of the ballet that it was interpreting. Individual, completely individual, easy, very, very easy to dance, because you dance to sounds, you dance to melodies. Whatever it was – if it was *Schéhérazade*, you dance to the movement of *Schéhérazade*. If you wanted to go down, you went down and you got up, and all the music said do that, and you did that. And then he had this wonderful feeling of working things up to an orgy without it being an orgy, if you know what I mean. It was just a lot of tremendous excitement that gradually built. It didn't go just straight into the finales, the thing built and built and built, and, of course, that is what held the public so.

Schéhérazade was the thing that made the biggest impact anywhere, because it had a story running through it, and there was the tragedy at the end, and the fights with the supers, and the wonderful staircase. The boys were trained to fall down this staircase backwards, and stop halfway dead, and they did it superbly. Oh, it was a moment when the scenery and curtain went up, and you saw these vivid reds and blues and greens, and the Bakst thing that came at you. Oh no, from the spectacle point of view, there really was nobody like Fokine to produce those things. *Narcisse* was so charming; it came away from all this colour and glamour into something very delicate and beautiful. And it was so typical for Nijinsky. He was able so easily to do this lovely movement with water, and stroke his hair, and pose and drape himself, which he loved doing, of course. And *Daphnis, Daphnis and Chloe* was a most beautiful thing to do, and it was so enjoyable to dance in those. Fulfilment there always was. When I first joined the company, you were not allowed to dance *Sylphides*. You had to stand in the wings for six months before you were allowed even to dance in the *corps de ballet*. That was the rule. And so it was a complete picture. There was no question of the *corps de ballet* popping up on this foot or that foot. Anyway, *Sylphides* is considerably altered. Things don't quite fit these days as they used . . . then *Carnaval*! Charming. I danced every part in *Carnaval*, right from the Valse through to Estrella, then through Chiarina, and finally Columbine, which I danced for years and years, with Idzikowski and various other people too.

The one thing that thrilled me, of course – it thrilled everybody, not only me – was to watch Fokine and Karsavina dance *Spectre de la Rose*, because although Nijinsky had this strange power, and was the dream, when Fokine was the partner of the girl that he loved, he did it with full understanding. He got exactly what he wanted out of that ballet. Nijinsky made it into a feat of dancing, all the great jumps, and the strangeness that he put into it. Fokine did it with Madame Karsavina just as he intended it, just like a story out of a book. They were beautiful together.

Then, of course, when Nijinsky started to do it, there was this tremendous idea that he jumped through the window. As a matter of fact, when he did jump through the window, it looked far higher than it was, because the opening of the window was only three inches, four inches or so from the floor. And when he jumped out, he fell straight into the arms of Vassily, who held him up for about three or four minutes until the end of the ballet, and this procedure went on all the time. But I was a very lucky girl, really, because later on when he was near his final collapse – and there was trouble in North America before the final collapse and we were sent home without any money, and the contracts were all washed up – he taught me to dance *Spectre de la Rose*. And I danced it with him two or three times, and that was quite wonderful. I had the dress that I wore – I had this dress specially made, copied, of course – and all his hand marks and the red marks of his make-up were on that dress, and I carried it with me everywhere. And a girlfriend wanted to dance it with Anton Dolin, and she asked me if I would loan her this costume, which I did. I was sorry afterwards, because she wore it so many times that it became very dirty, and she sent it to the cleaners, and it just fell to pieces, and so Nijinsky's hands were gone.

Why do you think Fokine's ballets have stayed in the repertory longer than anything else?

I think, as I have said, that they are simple, they are spectacular, they are musical. If you are in the audience, you can sit back and watch them without having to make any effort whatsoever. They satisfy, where the others, a lot of them are an effort; you have to think hard, you have to exert yourself without being able to sit back and let the dancers do it, and entertain you.

Tell me about the time of your desperate situation in Madrid and how the company was finally saved.

Yes, that was really a very tragic time, but had a happy ending. It was the time that Diaghilev gave me the money, the last money that he had. And there were telegrams flying backwards and forwards to try to arrange an engagement in London with the then Oswald Stoll, later Sir Oswald. And they couldn't get it fixed up. You couldn't move companies, you couldn't move people, you couldn't move freight. You couldn't do anything. You were stuck right in the war. And we had this wonderful offer to come to London, to stay as long as we could. We had King Alfonso on our side. He would move heaven and earth to help us, because he loved us and he knew us, and we knew him, and these telegrams kept going backwards and forwards with Eric Wollheim, who was then the agent working between the two. The telegrams – I read them, and they were so vague they may have been censored and put into bad wording, but you could not understand what was going on. They seemed to contradict themselves each time. But the greatest thing was that we could go, the company could go, but they couldn't make arrangements for the baggage, the scenery and all the freight; and they were begging the King to put in his word to help us. One night it became very desperate, and Diaghilev thought, this is the end, it will never work, we can't do it. And I wrote out a telegram for Diaghilev to be sent to London to Eric Wollheim for Oswald Stoll. And he waited and waited all day long for a reply for this thing, and we kept meeting and nothing happened, and in the middle of the night, it was about the first night only we had had rest from this child of mine who was practically dying, and I had managed to fall off to sleep having walked for nights with this child, and suddenly I heard his voice shouting, 'Ilda, Ilda, Ilda, wake up. Ilda, wake up.' And I thought it was one of my nightmares. And I opened my eyes, and standing at the bottom of my bed – how he got in I don't know – there was Diaghilev, saying, 'Read this, read this, read this telegram.' And I jumped out of bed in my nightie, just as I was, and this telegram said, 'Everything is arranged. Just work from your end, the freight can go through', or words to that effect. I can't remember at the moment exactly the wording, and we were freed. Well, we embraced, we cried and he went off, and the whole thing worked out in that one night. When we arrived back in London finally, and he had been sweet to my child and I had helped him with this telegram, I thought, now I am really going to know Diaghilev. I have seen him in this awful moment in my nightie, and I did play an important part. I met him on the stage of the Coliseum, and I went up to him, and he was quite distant.

Tell me about the Massine period. How did he work?

He worked quite differently to any of the other choreographers, though I hadn't known many before Massine, but it was certainly a different method. There were certain of us that responded very easily, others found his work very difficult. I think the main thing that one felt was everything was worked out in the opposite direction to what any other choreographer would have done. You would feel that with Massine you would go that way, where with somebody else you would go that way. If you were working with Fokine, you would lean that way; if you were working with Massine, you had to turn your body over this way. All his movements were odd. You had to respond quickly to that, because his work was difficult to remember because it was odd. He worked for the first few years that we had him as choreographer with a wonderful book that Diaghilev had found him that was all notation. It was a very old book, but a lot of work that was written down there he interpreted and it was exactly what he wanted. And that, I think, is how he found the foundation of his ideas.

He had a tremendous sense of humour that was hidden. He never expressed a sense of humour himself, but he could bring it out from others. He never laughed, he never enjoyed working at rehearsals; he was heavy and dire, and would walk in with his hat tilted on the front of his head and his papers under his arms. And go in and change and come out and start straight away. There was no feeling of relaxation or even happiness, until one struck ballets that he himself thoroughly enjoyed, for instance in *Pulcinella*. He adored *Pulcinella*, and so did we. It was gay, and he had Leon [Woizikowski] as his opposite, who was also one of his creations. In fact, except for their height – Massine was slightly taller than Leon – you could hardly tell the difference. In later years, when Leon took over all Massine's parts, some of the things he danced better than Massine. Others he hadn't the body, the flexibility, the slenderness that Massine had, but nevertheless he created Leon as he created me, shall I say. I shouldn't say that, but he created me as an artist. He did the same with Lydia Lopokova, I feel, although she was more of a classical dancer than I ever was. But nevertheless he was able to bring out the comedy of Lydia and the fun. In *Femmes de Bonne Humeur* he just made all those people bubble. Idzikowski also. He got all that fun out of Idzikowski, that no other choreographer has ever been able to do.

Pulcinella was the most delightful ballet to dance, it was one of those things that you looked forward to. Well, there are not many ballets that you can say that about, because a lot of them are worrying and you are frightened, and you feel that you may forget, or you have too many repetitions of the same thing, so you feel that you have to count them down on your hands. But *Pulcinella* absolutely went with a bang from the moment the curtain opened. It was pretty, it was gay, and the girls, Lydia, Lyubov Tchernicheva, looked so magnificent, beautiful, and Vera Nemchinova, and the boys were all dressed up in their pretty clothes. And then I came out of the main door, just in a simple red tutu thing, a chiffon skirt and a black thing with a little green ribbon on my head, and went straight into a very difficult classical variation. But once that was over then the fun began, and we used to laugh and talk and shout with the music at the end, and had a lovely time. We were always sorry when that was over.

But some of his other ballets, they could be very difficult. *Boutique*, for instance. We each had, as you know, our allotted position, and each one worked hard to make that position the best you could get out of yourself. And the Second Act, when the dolls were dancing in the night with Danilova or Nemchinova, whoever was the ballerina, it was just one of the most beautiful moments you could imagine. Such a contrast in all the dances, the tarantella, the mazurka and all the things that went in the beginning. That was a tremendous success, *Boutique Fantasque*. That was a grand season.

What about Tricorne?

Tricorne had to be worked for. *Tricorne* you had to study. All the time we were in Spain, during our rather trying tour when we were faced with disaster, we went to see all the gypsies. And that was when Diaghilev picked Felix Fernandez, having seen all the gypsies he could possibly see. He finally decided that this boy was the one. But he was not really stable-minded, and he thought Diaghilev was going to make him into a star. They got out of him every single movement that he could learn, or do or think, and he taught Massine and myself, and we worked together for hours and hours in London, here at the Alhambra and in class, on Spanish dancing. So when Massine finally produced *Tricorne*, we had got it at our fingertips. I could dance Spanish dancing in those days just as I could speak Russian. It was perfectly natural for me because it was a training that I had done and loved doing, of course. And so it was a great excitement to do *Tricorne*, and it was something so entirely different from anything Diaghilev had ever done before. And the scenery was hot, and you felt the sense of the sun and the traditional dances that were in the villages and so on. I loved it myself, I thought it was a tremendous ballet. I think it was far more fun to dance than to watch, in many ways.

Tell me about Nijinska and the classes she gave when she was in charge.

Well, I found her very difficult, not as a person, but I found her training very difficult. I suppose I was of the old tradition; she was getting on in modern terms. And although she danced herself exactly like Nijinsky – in fact, she danced *Spectre de la Rose* once dressed as Nijinsky, she danced it quite frequently. She had these odd manners that he had, and in her classes she tried to train you that way. Everything was out sideways, and tremendous jumps from side to side, things that went backwards and forwards. There wasn't any foundation, there was no sort of collective education like there was with Cecchetti, for instance, or Legat, who trained us also for a long time – Nicolai Legat, who was one of the famous choreographers and teachers in Russia. But Bronia was odd. I think about the only person I can remember, and that's going back some time, that really excelled in her classes was Ninette de Valois. She loved them, and she could do it as easily as ABC. In fact, she took over these variations in *Sleeping Princess*, which was all this way and that way, which Bronia used to do, and running and jumping and back to do the thing again terribly fast. The only person that could do it after Bronia was Ninette, and she did it equally as well. It was terribly difficult to follow her, to dance in one of her ballets after her.

When we did *Les Biches*, and she created the hostess for herself, she improvised mostly. That was the trouble with Bronia. If she suddenly felt she wanted to pull her face this way or that way, and her arms this way or that way, she'd do it. She wouldn't leave it as the dance was arranged, she would put in this extra thing, or a little thing with her feet. When she decided to leave the ballet, when she quarrelled with Diaghilev over the new creation of Lifar – Lifar was going to be made choreographer – she quarrelled with Diaghilev about this because Lifar was her baby, her student, and she felt it was an insult to make him a choreographer. So she left.

Tell me what happened after you were picked for the role of the Chosen Virgin in Massine's version of the Rite of Spring.

I think the picking of me was the biggest shock I have ever had. Having danced in the Nijinsky one, and having known all the scandal and all the scenes that went on in the theatre, it was really rather a shock to be chosen, as you can well imagine. Two or three people were tried out for it, but, as I told you, I was one of Massine's sort of own products, and I learned his first few steps quite quickly. He decided, I suppose, that I was the one he could work on and get the thing done as quickly as possible, and probably I would be quite capable of interpreting this thing. Of course, I didn't realize at that time – otherwise I should have got extremely nervous and frightened about the whole thing – the length of the dance and the fierceness of it, the exhaustion that it created. It really was one of the most frightening things that any dancer ever could undertake. Because you were alone, completely and utterly alone. When you started, he said, 'You had better write some of this down.' I hadn't got anything to write it down on, but in my handbag I had this wee little penny book, which Hilda Bewicke, who was one of our soloists, had given me the night before, because in it she had drawn the shape of a little frock she had made, and I had said, 'If you let me have the pattern, I'll see if I can make one like that.' So that's all I had. I got this little book out, and I started scribbling down the various numbers with accents on, and then when I turned the page, Massine would grab this little book and there he's written a few things down, and I have put underneath in Russian, Massine himself wrote this.

After about four days of this caper we were going through in this rehearsal room in Liverpool he decided that he couldn't cope with it with the company all round, so Diaghilev gave us permission to go to London by ourselves, which was really quite a feat, I might explain, and practise there. And with us went Vera Savina, who was then taking over the part of the principal dancer in *Sylphides*. And so we started rehearsing seriously in this dirty little place in Maiden Lane, down in the basement, down dirty little steps with all the lino torn. A horrible place it was. And there was a tiny little dressing room where forty of us scrambled in so that we practically hardly could get our clothes off. Anyway, that is where that dance, the most important part, was created. First I would practise and write down my various notes, and while I studied that Vera would dance her piece of *Sylphides*. The two ballets were so completely different, *Sylphides* and *Sacre du Printemps*; the difference between Chopin and Stravinsky was so fantastic, it was almost historical that these two composers should conflict with two English girls doing it. That's what amazed me. Anyway, halfway through he said to me, 'Well, I don't see that it's possible to carry on trying to do this with a piano. The thing to do is to do it by metronome, at such and such rhythms.' That's how we created the whole dance. And it wasn't until we finally got to Paris that I realized the stupendous thing I had undertaken. I didn't think that any female could really dance to such extent such tremendous jumps. And halfway through, of course, I couldn't count myself any more. It was impossible. I was hammering my way round the stage, throwing my head and my hair backwards and forwards, trying to keep not only the counts of my steps, but to know that I wasn't galloping in front of the orchestra. I had to be with the orchestra, and recognize it as well. So when it got to this pitch, Leon Woizikowski, who was leading the *corps de ballet,* he was given permission to count the number of steps. He would say, 'Fifteen, sixteen, seventeenth, eighteenth, change.' And then I'd go to the next one and the next one and the next one. That's how that worked.

They gave me one of the original Nijinsky costumes. They were flannel, painted flannel, very heavy sort of chemises; and my own red wig from *Narcisse,* in the Bacchanale. And I tried. I only got halfway through. It was impossible in a thing like that, and this red-hot wig over my own hair, which was down to my knees anyway. I just gave up. I couldn't. So they decided then that I must leave the lightest thing on my body that it was possible to have. And they made me a silk chemise, and allowed me to dance with my own hair, which really was quite exciting, because it was very blond, and against all these terrible wigs that people wore, this one blond-haired girl, with it right down practically to my thighs anyway. My hair was very thick. And it was stitched. I had to have it stitched all the way in and out with threads to keep it from falling in my face so that it stayed more or less put right to the end.

Was Stravinsky a help to you?

No. At the dress rehearsal he was frightening. He walked up and down the centre aisle with his yellow scarf flying, and shouting to the orchestra, and trying to interfere with the orchestra, and Ansermet turned to him and said, 'Either you go or I go.' You couldn't do it with two. Either one had got to conduct; the other one mustn't interfere anyhow. And when we got to the end of that performance, the first night, I really thought I'd die. I was so frightened. I wasn't frightened of dancing. I was frightened of forgetting. It was so long. I thought that with the tremendous effort that I was undertaking, I didn't think that I would be able to remember how many I had done, so I invented myself the idea of each step that I did, not the rhythms, but each step. Suppose that the first was five times, the next fourteen times, the next ten times. I pressed a finger down, although I was dancing all the time I was doing all these things. I was all the time counting, *raz, dva, tri* and so on, and pressing my fingers down at the same time, and dancing, so you can imagine it wasn't easy.

It was your biggest triumph, wasn't it?

Oh yes. I am very grateful indeed that in all my experience of the ballet I was given the opportunity to do it. A satisfying feeling, for the rest of one's life to know that you have achieved, and I think my greatest joy was when the curtain finally closed, and it went up again and Stravinsky came up on to the stage, and took my hands and kissed them, and for a young girl, that was just something, very exciting.

Did you enjoy the modern ballets of the 1920s? Things like Chout *and* Train Bleu?

Some I did, and some I thought were not worth the effort. Some I felt were just an experiment. Diaghilev had to move with the times. He had discovered all these young painters and composers, and he realized their ability, and he realized their talent. And the only way he could bring them into the artistic world and into the creative world was by giving them small ballets to write and design. *Train Bleu*, for instance, was very topical. It was great fun while it lasted. It was just a ballet of the sort of things people did on the beach in the south of France and, of course, there was no train in it. Every day the *Train Bleu*, which was the express, went to the south of France, taking people down there. I think that was really the beginning of people wanting to go to the south of France in the summer, because they never did, in those days. But it didn't last, it was a gimmick.

What about Les Noces?

Ah, *Les Noces*, now that is a big question. Nijinska has just revived it, and I might tell you that she has revived it superbly. She has done it exactly as it was. I think it's the only ballet that has survived in revival, really survived. With the others one feels that so much is lost, because they were ballets that were typecast, and they were something to do all the time with the choreographers, where *Les Noces* is an episode, a Russian episode, full of sadness and full of emotion that only the Russian can give. No, that is a very, very fine work, and a work, I feel, like many of Fokine's works, that will live for a very long time.

Tell me about Balanchine.

Balanchine was a strange chap. He has a most extraordinary sense of humour. He's a very fine musician. He can sit down at the piano and entertain you for hours, just the same as he can tell funny stories for hours.

He can tell stories for hours and hours and hours and not be tired. And the same with his work; it bubbles. And if he felt you had a sense of humour, and could bring it over without being comic, if you know what I mean, he didn't try to make it funny. He would allow the comedy to come through you if he felt you had got it naturally. He did not try to make people amusing if they were not amusing anyway. I loved his work, but it wasn't easy. It was a new experience, and at the time he was also doing small ballets. For instance, *Barabau* was the greatest fun you ever, ever knew, but again it was a ballet that couldn't last. It was only just a gay little episode in a village, and there were a lot of tipsy soldiers. I was an absolute horror, my hat on top of my head; Leon danced on top of a barrel. But it was fun. I think one of the most delightful ballets of the modern time was *Les Matelots*. Now each artist in that that Massine created was absolutely correct. They were typecast, Lifar as a French sailor – nobody ever repeated that – Leon as the Spanish fisherman. I was just a Spanish fishwife, Vera Nemchinova was just a young wife, pretty in a simple dress. We had tremendous fun with that. That was another ballet we really enjoyed, like *Pulcinella*. But, of course, he could turn them out.

Tell me about the time Balanchine made a dance for you in half an hour for Triumph of Neptune.

Oh, that was tremendous fun. Lord Berners wrote the *Triumph of Neptune* and naturally we never interfered, we never asked for parts. I asked several times to be let off parts, but I never asked for one to be given to me. It was just not done. You were snubbed, and that was that, if you dared to do such a thing. But I waited very, very patiently, shall I say, till the end of the ballet, and discovered that I had got nothing. One tiny little quarter of a minute entrance for the whole of this ballet, thoroughly English, absolutely couldn't be more so, and so gay, typical of all our penny-plain and tuppence-coloured things. And so I went to Diaghilev at the end of rehearsals, and I said, 'Do you know, I really am most unhappy. The ballet rehearsals have come to an end, this great big thing, about seventeen different tableaux, and I haven't anything to do. After all, Lord Berners is English, I am English. I really should have been given something.' He was so angry, so annoyed. He said, 'The best thing you can do is to go to Grigoriev.' So I went to Grigoriev, who I knew couldn't do a thing about it. After all, he was only Diaghilev's mouthpiece, you may put it that way. He said, 'You go to Lord Berners', so I trotted off to Lord Berners, almost in tears, and thought, I'm not going to get anywhere. He was quite horrified, and said, 'But I naturally thought you were going to be given one of the principal parts. There are so many to choose from.' And he said, 'Something's got to be done about this.' I said, 'I don't know, I'm so unhappy.' So he said, 'Never mind. Come straight back after lunch.' Diaghilev and Lifar, Lord Berners and Grigoriev came back after about an hour and a half and said, 'Oh, you're all right. We have discovered something for you.' And Lord Berners said, 'Well, you know this hornpipe that's the interlude music with the curtain down showing one of the exotic tuppence-coloured things, you can have that, if you can get George to fix you a dance fast enough.'

So we went down into the depths of the theatre, underneath the stage. We had no piano whatsoever, but he had the piano score, and he said, 'Come on, show me some Scotch reel steps.' So I did a few things that I knew, that I had done as a child at Scotch dancing, sword dancing and so on. And with the music, he singing it and counting it out, we had rattled off this beautiful little dance. It was a gem. And we must have been down there, I suppose, half an hour, twenty minutes, and then somebody thumped on the top for us to go upstairs. And I had never heard the music, I hadn't an idea what it was. And when it came to the last four counts, four, three, two, one, on, George pushed me on, and off I went; I could dance it for you now. And it just went across the stage like that, and came to an end. With a stop. And, of course, we didn't know, but the orchestra, who knew that there wasn't a dance there five minutes ago, they all beat on their stands, and gave me a bit of encouragement. Well, then it came to putting on a costume, and there was no costume; so they all rushed off to Fox – the old theatrical place – and they found two costumes. They said they hadn't been out of the shop in 150 years; they didn't know where they came from. And this little thing, it was a tunic, all covered with metal containers, blazing with stones, and it weighed sixteen pounds. They weighed it. I took it to a butcher's shop and had it weighed; it was sixteen pounds. It was solid metal with stones, and they used to put it on in the prompt corner as I went on that side, and it rattled all the time. I finished up on the other side, and my dresser used to run round there, and rip it off as I went off into the wings. But the fun of the whole thing was that I finished it up. I had a tremendous ovation with this dance and it became one of the things of the ballet in the end. And I ran off, and I thought, well, how do I take a call? I don't know. And I ran back on, and I took this last position, and this went on. The more I did it, the more I got called back. And the curtain was hardly down when Diaghilev came tearing round. That was another time when he really reprimanded me. And he said, 'Don't you ever dare do that again.' I said, 'What have I done?' He said, 'This is no music hall, and don't ever let me see that again.'

What about the musical standards? The orchestras and the conductors, were they helpful?

Some of them, certain ones. I think the thing that impressed us more than anything about the orchestras is that composers don't make good conductors, for dancing. I don't think they make good conductors really even for opera, because they understand their music as they want it understood. Where dancers are concerned, there's no flexibility. You have got to stick to your routine, you can't give way one way or the other. But there were certain conductors that one felt completely relaxed with. For instance, Ansermet and Eugene Goossens were the two conductors that I had no fear of whatsoever in the *Sacre du Printemps*. I knew that they knew that I understood what they were doing, and once they had given me the upbeat and they would know my rhythms, they would keep their orchestra to their rhythm and we would meet on the two beats of the music twice during the whole of the dance, and I never missed it. I relied entirely on those conductors.

You were with the company sixteen years, longer than almost everyone else. What did it mean to you?

It was gigantic. What else can I say? I still hardly believed that it really happened. To me it was a strange destiny. When Mordkin gave me lessons before I joined the company, the only thing he taught me was a dance to the waltz 'Destiny'. And I never realized till later that that had significance; that is quite true, that is all he taught me. My father paid him five guineas a lesson; even in those days, that was in 1910, 1911. And so as this thing happened to me, I think the thing that counted was that I dropped the English notion. Once I had dropped anything to do with being English and became Russian, one of this little village that moved about, to think in Russian, to dream in Russian – I always dreamt in Russian – to pray in Russian. Everything I did was always completely Russian, still is frequently. I think that was when it grew into reality. And I think that is why I was so very grateful to Diaghilev, to realize that my work was worthy of having that position.

What was the secret of Diaghilev's success?

His tremendous understanding of the artistic world. I think in all senses. His complete understanding. He was able to switch away from things material. He could think. His understanding of pictures, old pictures; he could tell you where any famous picture was, in which museum it was, he could tell you where the duplications or copies were. His knowledge of music was quite fantastic. In fact, when he died, he had decided to give up working with ballet, and completely take up opera. I am glad it didn't happen, because he felt he was past the creative time, he was sick and ill. It was a myth, I think, a desire, a tremendous ambition which may not have happened, may not have worked out. But there's no doubt about it, he's one of these people who had it all. He wasn't only a man that understood music. He understood dancing, he understood painting, understood all these young people and the hidden talents that they had, and he was able to discriminate. How he knew that Picasso was going to be a Picasso, or any of them, for that matter. After all, I grew up with all these young people. I knew Picasso as well as I know you. When he was a young man, if only I had thought to buy one of his pictures or his drawings then for about twenty or twenty-five pesetas, which he would have been extremely glad to have, I should have been a rich woman today. But, of course, one took it all for granted. They were just part of us, all those composers. Look at all the fun we had with Poulenc. He used to sit down at the piano and entertain us for an hour at a time. All those people were just part of our existence, and, had it not been for Diaghilev, the world would not have this vast wealth of art that it has today, of this I am quite sure. Had he not existed, what would have happened to these people?

Can you recall how you heard of this death?

Oh dear. We were at Le Lavandou having our summer holiday. We knew he was ill, we knew he was in a very, very bad way, and he went to Venice and we were all very worried and frightened. We had an awful feeling that he wouldn't be able to carry on afterwards. But we didn't think he was going to die. We thought he would give the whole thing over to somebody else. And that he would watch it, and the ballet would carry on. But I went round to this little kiosk where we bought the papers. And, you know, French papers are folded, not like ours are, in two like that. They are longways and then folded over. And I used to buy the continental *Daily Mail* every day and read it to Leon in Russian, as I do books, many books. I translated like that, reading to him in Russian, from the English. And I picked hold of this paper out of the rack, and right at the side in big black letters I saw 'Death Of'. And I just stopped in my tracks and I gave one terrible sob, because I knew what I was going to see. I couldn't turn it over. And I went back to the beach, and I just handed it to Leon and said, 'Diaghilev', And then I collapsed a bit and he walked away. When I came to from lying down there hidden in the sand, I looked up to see where Leon had gone and I saw him walking right the way along the sand, just kicking the sea with his foot like that, as though that is the end of everything. And then we were faced with pretty well disaster for a long time. However. It was a very, very wonderful experience and God granted me the ability to receive it and make use of it.

Léonide Massine

1895 MOSCOW–1979 WESEKE, GERMANY

Trained as an actor as well as a dancer, Massine joined the Ballets Russes in 1914. During the war he made his first choreographic experiments; he became principal choreographer and Diaghilev's companion, but left the company to marry in 1921. He returned in 1925 and continued to create new works until 1928.

Tell me about the first time you met Diaghilev.

It was in Moscow in December 1913. One evening I was dancing at the Bolshoi and some friends of mine in the ballet told me that Diaghilev was in the audience. Naturally I had heard his name before and I heard a lot of wonderful things about his company and I was intrigued by this news. Later on I heard again from my friends that he would like to meet me after the performance and speak to me. I was, of course, thrilled about that and the meeting was arranged, the next day at the Hotel Metropole in Moscow where he stayed.

So I came there and, of course, I was bewildered by all these rows of bowing waiters, some of them in gold uniforms, and finally I was told that I can go up, and there I was knocking at his door. Then a young Italian man appeared, which was his valet, by the name of Beppe, and he said to me, 'What do you want?' 'I have come here to meet Mr Diaghilev.' He disappeared for a moment and then he returned, saying, 'Signor Diaghilev will see you in a moment.' That moment seemed to be very long to me and many things passed through my thoughts. Then finally I came into the room and I saw Diaghilev. At first I thought he was very tall and then I realized he was a medium-sized man and I noticed at once that he had a white lock of hair on his forehead. Then he said, 'I have seen your performance yesterday at the Bolshoi and I rather like it, and I would like to tell you that I have come to Moscow in search of somebody to take the title role in *Legend of Joseph*.' Then he said, 'Of course, this is only my first acquaintance with you, but if my choreographer, Mikhail Fokine, will approve my choice, then you will be engaged in the company.'

I was at the same time delighted and bewildered, because at that time I was hesitating whether I should make a career in dancing, as a choreographer and dancer, or be at the dramatic theatre, which I loved. However, this hesitation was for me rather a crucial point. I asked my friends what they thought of this. I went to the school, and I told them of this proposition. They said, 'You are very foolish, because you are bound to make a career in dramatic art, and there you are leaving for a year.' The more I talked, the more I was convinced I should remain in Moscow. However, Diaghilev told me he was only two days in Moscow and I must make a quick decision.

So next day I came back with the firm idea that I would reject this engagement and I would stay in Moscow. The more I approached the hotel this idea was very definite indeed. I therefore came to his room and the moment I was supposed to tell him that I thanked him for his proposition but I had decided to stay in Moscow, I heard myself saying, 'Yes, I accept your proposition. I am going to leave Moscow for Europe.'

So then you left with Diaghilev. Did he explain to you his ideas about choreography and dance?

At first we went to St Petersburg, where he said I am to be auditioned, and on the way he talked a little about Fokine's new methods, and of his new approach to choreography, of his great evolution compared to academic art, and that already made me understand that I am amongst something very wonderful, which was, of course, completely new to me. Now in St Petersburg Fokine auditioned me. I came to his place. He had a very beautiful apartment all in white, and on the wall the only painting I saw was Giulio Romano's *The Nine Muses*. Fokine was not very talkative to me, a very formal man, and he said, 'Do you see that painting of Giulio Romano? Would you like to take the positions of some of these muses?' I tried my best, and I have shown what I could grasp from this. Then he was again silent, and he said, 'Would you like to do some movements?' I looked round the room; the room was rather small. I said it was rather a small place to make big jumps, so I said, 'Would you please put one of the chairs in the middle of the room?' He was rather amused by this idea. I moved the chair, which was about three feet high. I looked at it. I stood one foot back and I jumped over clear to the other side. He didn't show any reaction. He said, 'Our audition is over.' The next day I heard from Diaghilev, strangely enough, that Fokine approved of his choice and I am to join the company. Then he went to a photographer in St Petersburg; Bakst was at that time there. He suggested certain costumes and I made the first photograph for the *Legend of Joseph* part without knowing what it was going to be.

Then we left for Cologne, and on the way Diaghilev talked to me more like a friend than as a director of his ideas of the approach to the whole theme. He said it is a biblical theme, the *Legend of Joseph*, which was treated many, many times in more splendid ways, but mostly the period that interested him was the Renaissance, the Renaissance artists. The strange word 'Renaissance' was new to me. I didn't know what it is all about. He said it means that it will be conceived in the style of Veronese, Titian and Tintoretto. Then again these three names intrigued me. I said, 'I hope to see their works later on.' And so we went on, and arriving in Cologne – Hotel Excelsior, as far as I remember – I saw again the same atmosphere of waiters and all kinds of servants, which was rather strange, and, I must say, I didn't like very much that luxury. Diaghilev was quite at home. He talked to the musicians, to the artists, to the regisseur of the company, and made telephone calls, long-distance telephone calls and so forth and so on.

Then first rehearsals started and Fokine was showing me his steps. At first, of course, it was extremely strange to me, because I quickly realized that he had completely left the academic positions and his composition was more in a free style with natural movements of arms and body. At first I thought that the easiest part for me was the plastic part, by which I mean the movement of arms and body. I think I could master that to a certain extent, but when it comes to technique – I was completely lacking in technique, since I learned very little at that time in Moscow. Diaghilev soon understood that and he asked Maestro Cecchetti to give me tuition in the real technique as required. I loved Cecchetti lessons, and I thought they were wonderful and I still think so. And I made, I think, fairly good progress in them. However, I couldn't in a few months do what other people do in three or four years and therefore I felt I was unprepared technically for that part.

Tell me about the rehearsals for Joseph *and Richard Strauss's visit.*

In the first stage Hofmannsthal and Count Kessler discussed what is really the meaning of this work and while Hofmannsthal was saying this is a biblical story, von Kessler thought it was much more than that, it was a struggle between good and evil. Then the rehearsals started and the composition was fairly advanced. Richard Strauss came once and he would like to see what has been done to the music. So I danced a few passages, and he looked at it and he said, 'Well' – I think at a certain moment he actually sang the music – 'a big leap there.' And to our astonishment, and particularly that of Fokine, who didn't like that kind of interference, he got up from his chair, he made a big leap and he ended on one knee. Fokine was silent and the rehearsal was over. Then further on at the rehearsals, there were discussions between Diaghilev, José Maria Sert, who made the scenery, and Bakst, who did the costume sketches, and I think there was quite an agreement between them. The very imposing scenery of Sert with the columns and black background with a lot of gold on it matched well the elaborate costumes which Bakst designed for Rubinstein and the others.

Tell me about your beginnings as a choreographer. When did you first attempt to stage something?

During the First War Diaghilev lost most of his company and he lost his chief choreographer, Mikhail Fokine, who remained first in Russia and then in Sweden. And it was a rather serious situation, because his ideas were going ahead, but he couldn't realize them. In Florence he took me to visit the Uffizi Museum and through rooms full of most remarkable things. We stopped at the medieval paintings, the primitives of Simone Martini and Pietro Lorenzetti, and he then asked me during that visit whether I thought I could do a ballet. I sharply answered, 'No.' Then a moment later I looked at Simone Martini's *The Annunciation*, a most remarkable painting, with the archangel and Maria in a very dramatic pose. I thought for one second, and something came to me which I couldn't explain even now. I turned round to him and I said, 'Yes, I think I can do not one, but a hundred ballets for you.' That was the beginning.

After that we went to Ouchy in Switzerland and Diaghilev was starting to get artists from Poland and from everywhere, and after this study of Italian primitives he suggested that I should try to compose something in that very style and he said, 'Why couldn't it be a liturgy with an Orthodox chant?' Larionov and Goncharova were around, and he asked them to help with the scenic part. Well, I was all for it. I was full of Byzantine and primitive-style things, because between other things we went to Ravenna; we saw the most marvellous Byzantine things there. And we worked in Ouchy, outside Lausanne, in a large room, and everything seemed to be shaping very well. The difficulty came when Stravinsky, whom Diaghilev asked to compose this thing, could not get the chants from Kiev. Kiev was bombarded heavily and it was not possible to go there. So he abandoned that idea, unfortunately for me, and he turned towards Rimsky-Korsakov Russian-type themes. Since he was deeply Russian himself, he loved all his life Russian art. He picked up as a first sort of music the Rimsky-Korsakov Midnight Sun, part of the *Snow Maiden* opera. So I composed that and on that occasion Larionov was most helpful. He often got up and showed me some steps and he gave me an impulse to do this work. So that was the first production.

Then after that there was *Las Meninas*, which was sort of a suggestion by

José Maria Sert after Velázquez's infantas on a very delightful Fauré pavane. And that was the real start for me, my first works. They were given for charity performances for the Red Cross in Paris and in Geneva. Then finally we came to the composition of *Contes Russes*. First it was only one tale, which was called *Kikimora*. Again Larionov was very helpful and Diaghilev, who thought Liadov not a first-rank composer but a very good Russian composer, decided to make a series of legends, and that's how the *Russian Tales* were born.

When you first came to choreograph, did it all come easily?

Once I felt that I could do choreography, I had like a bombshell of invention in me and I was overwhelmed with ideas of all kinds, but without the slightest knowledge of how to use them.

How did Diaghilev help you realize your ideas?

Well, often discussing with Diaghilev that very idea, how to master choreography, he used to speak a lot about Nijinsky and *Sacre du Printemps*. And he told me how Nijinsky had such an *idée fixe* of the Dalcroze system, and how he went that way and how he made a gross error by applying it to the Stravinsky score. That very error made me think that there must be something that would be a counterpoint to the music danced, the texturally rhythmic structure of a score translated into the rhythmic, texturally rhythmic score of choreography.

From the start you were interested in ballet as drama.

I must say that since I didn't possess anything as sensational as Nijinsky had in his elevation, I thought that instinctively the point which is nearest to me was drama, introducing a dramatic element into existing technique. And I thought that was the right road for me, and that's how I started to direct my thoughts.

Meanwhile you had become a very proficient dancer.

I had got a certain amount of technique, but it was never my strong point. Where I thought I really could do something more than the others was exactly that dramatic quality which probably was a happy fusion between technique and the character of the role which I was supposed to create.

Tell me about Diaghilev's musical abilities and his musical taste.

I think his abilities and his tastes are somewhat in common. One couldn't be without the other. He had sort of organic feeling for music, that is, he would at once understand whether it is an empty subject or something really worth listening to. On one occasion, for instance, in the case of *The Good-humoured Ladies* it is he who played 500 Domenico Scarlatti sonatas to pick out 15. And there I must say too he disliked Alessandro Scarlatti. He took Domenico Scarlatti because Alessandro Scarlatti was much more academic, much more cold. Now another occasion was with Pergolesi's music, which he found unedited in this famous Italian conservatory, San Pietro a Majella, or at the oldest conservatoire of Cimarosa, Pergolesi and Paisiello. And there again he played at the piano many, many Pergolesi pieces. I had already found this *commedia dell'arte* scenario which was Pulcinella, and he quickly found exactly what was required, with the sort of quality that only he was able to say. Then he asked Stravinsky to orchestrate it, and he said to him, 'Igor, I would like you to do for me this style of Pergolesi, and not Stravinsky', which Stravinsky very well understood, and, as you know, he did it. The third occasion was *Boutique Fantasque*. Once in Rome during a Rome season Respighi brought some pieces of music by Rossini entitled *Péchés de Vieillesse* and he gave them to Diaghilev, who played them and made a sort of piano score of them. Not that he was a virtuoso musician, but he could play the scores, the orchestra scores, not only piano scores. So there was no question music for him was one of the elements in which he was absolutely at home.

You also felt that painters had an influence. Didn't Toulouse-Lautrec influence Boutique Fantasque?

Once we touched that subject, you could see it was about the Lautrec period, so I at once tried to associate this with the same style and I found that Lautrec had marvellous ideas, he and Seurat, and I at once started to work in that direction and I made my principal character quite Lautrec-like.

Tell me about the origins of Tricorne.

We were performing in Barcelona and Falla, who was then at the beginning of his career, invited Diaghilev and myself to see his production which was entitled *El Corregidor y La Molinera*. It was orchestrated for eleven instruments, brass instruments. And the story is extremely amusing and we sat right through it, and afterwards Diaghilev said, 'I think it is a very good thing for a ballet.' For dancing I was at once taken by flamenco and by all these kinds of things, and I gladly accepted his proposition. Then there was a long period when he commissioned Falla and his music, and he said, 'Mon cher Falla, à seule condition que vous écrivez un grand finale.' He wanted a very big, dancing finale. Falla was very willing to do that and he said, 'What about jota?' And Diaghilev said, 'That is a most splendid thing.' That accounts for the very huge finale which Diaghilev planned to have.

Then we went to Madrid and now it was my part. I had to study flamenco thoroughly and I met a very extraordinary young man called Felix Fernandez, who was by his craft a printer. He came often to rehearsal, and I made his acquaintance and he said to me very strange things. He said, 'You know, I like so much flamenco that when I do my printing and put my articles together, my feet are dancing.' I said, 'That must be a very extraordinary passion', a vocation for dance. So I worked with him a long time, and little by little mastered, since I had a fairly good ear, the flamenco rhythm. That, of course, was the ground work for *Tricorne*. It's full of zapateado. Then Diaghilev listened to every bit of music Falla wrote, and he made only one objection, which I think was a right one. It arose from the minuetto by the Corregidor which was part of the ballet. He said, 'My dear Falla, this is more like a pastiche of seventeenth century and it really doesn't belong to the story. We want the Molinera, the Miller's Wife, and the Miller to have prominence, but the Corregidor is a mock figure. Let it be like that; we won't give him more room.' So he quickly crossed that out and Falla was very consenting, he understood. Then came the part of Picasso. Picasso was a very important part of the production, and he gave to it the real spirit as far as production. All his advice, all his suggestions were marvellous. Whatever he said was deep in me and I must say that if I ever considered this production of Falla, I owe a lot of it to Picasso.

I believe you had the idea for the farruca.

Well, farruca was, of course, a phenomenal dance, danced by that young man Fernandez and many others at that time. I thought it was half bullfight, half dance. I thought it was a beautifully interpreted bullfight without killing the bull, and it puzzled me. However, I can get into that trance feeling that extraordinary thing that emanates from a dancer of the farruca. And I was still hesitating, and finally once I was dining in the Savoy Hotel Grill in London; suddenly in the middle of it an idea struck me. I said, 'I've got it', and there it was. And so the farruca was created and I think I haven't missed the main point of it.

Does it remain one of your favourite ballets?

Probably as performed, yes. Because of that dramatic feeling in it.

Have you ever changed it when you revive it?

No, no. I have a film of it. I was one of the earliest film lovers. I filmed all my productions, and there might be small details which are not important to the body of the choreography to be changed, but on the whole it remains exactly the same. I am extremely careful when I do my work, and even more careful when I do the work of another. I wouldn't allow Fokine to be changed a bit.

Did Diaghilev have an artistic policy?

I don't know whether one can call this a sort of artistic policy, but he certainly felt very strongly one thing, that ballet is not only what you see on the stage, dancers, but ballet is part of a very complex spectacle. That is, for him it was poetry, literature, painting, music and choreography. And without it he never saw anything that would be an expression of his ideas.

What do you think was the secret of his success?

I think the secret of his success was *son goût impeccable*, his taste. He knew as much about poetry as about music, about choreography, as much about other elements. For him it was all one. He never divided that and because of his marvellous taste he succeeded to find the right collaborators, to have the fusion of people who really understood each other, suitable for the theme, and suitable for the rendering of the whole thing.

Did he rely on his own judgement or did he ask the views of other people?

He often asked advice, mostly of the people who were involved in the work, but most often he relied on his own judgement.

Did he ever become discouraged? Did it ever occur to him to give it all up?

Not that I know. The hardest time obviously was the years in Spain when there was a fierce period of war, all frontiers closed, no engagements, and then he had a slight hesitation. He asked his good friend Misia Sert. Of course, she said at once, 'Serge, je pense que tu dois arrêter.' Instead of following what she said, instead of stopping, he increased his strength. He got out of Spain, he got visas and engagements with dogs and elephants and the comedian Grock, but he got out, he insisted on it, and he saved his ballet at that time. No, he was too convinced a man to give up in any situation.

How did he manage for money? How did Diaghilev find the necessary funds?

Well, that was really an extraordinary part of him. We had no supporters, he had no subsidies of any kind, and if people gave him a few centimes in his life, they would speak all their life about it. But his incredible way of doing it, living on the engagements which he had no difficulty to have and supporting his company to the next engagement always.

How high was the standard of dancing?

I would say the dancers were below today's efficiency in technique, but they were probably much more aware of the higher artistic standards. They knew what Diaghilev wanted to do and they felt his ideas, they were enclosed with him in what he was about to do. What is nowadays probably the most extraordinary virtuosity and efficient technique, somehow it's lacking that very element.

How important will Diaghilev's place be in the history of ballet?

History is a very mischievous thing. I don't know how it will turn, but I do hope that it will be at all times recognized that the Diaghilev era was the most brilliant era in ballet of all times.

Was there a degree of Diaghilev following fashion or did he create it?

Diaghilev was extremely flexible, and sensible to any evolution in the art world. When he saw there was quality. Whether it is Russian art, Russian painting or further advanced art, such as cubism, when he felt that there is a quality, the form of art didn't frighten him. He was always following the ideas of the day as long as they were the valuable ones.

Is there a legacy of the Diaghilev Ballet which still influences us today, which changed the way we look at ballet?

I do think certainly he turned the wheel of the history of ballet. No question. Fokine's aesthetic and Nijinsky's aesthetic, all these things are certainly left, and even his principle of fusion of arts. Unfortunately it's not living in all today's producers, but some of them picked up enough to know that the ballet is a component art, and unless all the four sister arts are on the same level the work will be on one leg.

How much do you feel you owe personally to Diaghilev?

Well, to say briefly, I owe everything to Diaghilev. When he took me as a young boy from the school, I knew really nothing about ballet, nothing about aesthetics, nothing about paintings, and I owe to him all the education that I now possess, however little it is, to him, to his effort.

What do you hope we can do in the future to keep his memory and example fresh?

I have a sort of persistent idea in me, that sooner or later, rather sooner than later, we must film all the early Diaghilev ballets. All the Fokine era, and Nijinsky era, with the best symphony orchestras, in the original setting, and with its original choreography, because now it can be done, but it will not be possible much longer. And that is what I think would be the next logical step ahead in what you are doing in your field.

Leon Woizikowski

1897 WARSAW–1975 WARSAW

*The Polish dancer Woizikowski joined the Ballets
Russes in 1915 and, but for a short break in
1922, was with them until the end. An
outstanding character artist, his partnership with
Sokolova was much admired in the 1920s.
Massine, Nijinska and Balanchine all created roles
for him.*

Tell me about your first meeting with Diaghilev.

It was in 1915. I travelled from Warsaw to Lausanne to join the Diaghilev company, this great Russian ballet company. Two days after I arrived Diaghilev sent for me, to have a look at me. I said to him straight away, 'You know, Sergei Pavlovich, I've come here to dance for 600 marks a month and I've found the rest of the company are getting 720 marks a month.' He looked at me and said, 'Well, what do you want?' and I said, 'The same as everybody else.' He said, 'What, are you a communist?' And then he paused for a minute and said, 'Oh, all right, I'll give you 720 marks, but you'll have to work for it.'

We had a period of four months rehearsing in Lausanne and then we were going to go to America. So we all went to Bordeaux and then we were eleven days on the steamer *Lafayette* crossing to America. It was ghastly, everybody was ill, absolutely everybody. And then we did a tour right across America for several months. We travelled and travelled and travelled and then we had to come back to Italy. We came back on a ship called the *Dante Alighieri*. We didn't know much about this ship, but I noticed that the sailors were carrying on board enormous boxes. I happened by chance to ask one of the sailors what they consisted of and the sailor replied, 'Oh, macaroni, macaroni.' Once we got to sea I learned that what the ship consisted of was over 300 cases of ammunition and the Diaghilev Ballet. We crossed the Atlantic to Spain and went to Cádiz, and then we were several months touring in Spain. After that tour we ended in Barcelona and from there we went to South America. Montevideo, São Paulo, Buenos Aires, Rio. In Rio I can remember we were giving a performance and Diaghilev got incredibly angry. After that we went back to Spain. We did a tour, a very big tour. Then we went to Portugal, to Lisbon. We gave a few performances, but unfortunately revolution broke out. For twenty days we never went out of the hotel, we couldn't set foot on the pavement, we just looked out of the windows. We couldn't go out because people were shooting at each other. But nobody seemed to get hurt much. We found out actually that it was a revolution between the students and sailors. Then things quietened down again and we gave some more performances and then we went back to Spain and once more to Barcelona.

There was a real problem here. We did a tour in Spain, but then there wasn't anything to do because we couldn't travel; we couldn't go to France, we couldn't go to England because of the war. Luckily the King of Spain, Alfonso XIII, helped us. But nevertheless for three months in Barcelona we never worked; in fact, we practically starved. But after three months of near starvation we were set free because they agreed to take us in England, so we left for London, where we did a season lasting over seven months at the Coliseum. Diaghilev used the opportunity to try to get the company back into shape again and to check the costumes and the scenery and try to renew everything. And then once again we went on tour, Manchester, Sheffield, Edinburgh. Then we went back to France and a tour there and then we came back to England again. And we were there in England until the end of the war – that was in 1918. Then, of course, it was possible to travel again, to Italy or to go back to America, whatever we wanted. So we travelled a great deal and we performed a great deal.

Tell me about the time in Madrid when the King of Spain danced with the company.

Oh, it was in the Royal Theatre. After a performance the King organized a banquet for the company and ourselves, of course. He really liked it and Diaghilev was there too. And everybody drank champagne and ate frightfully well. Then the King of Spain told us that he knew how to dance as well and he seized a bowl of fruit and danced in and out round the chairs with this bowl of fruit. And he said, 'Voilà.' We laughed a great deal. Of course, he came to a lot of performances and he knew *Schéhérazade* extremely well and he started doing the movements that the young boys did in *Schéhérazade*. I must say that he may not have been a dancer, but he was jolly good.

Tell me about the time in Saragossa when you danced Schéhérazade *without any sets or costumes.*

Well, *Schéhérazade* had very heavy designs by Bakst and wonderful costumes for the Odalisques and for the Slaves and very brilliant and beautiful scenery. But we were giving performances in Saragossa and when we got there, it said on the bill that we were doing *Les Sylphides*, *Prince Igor* and, I think, *Thamar*. When the performance finished, the Spanish public refused to leave the theatre and we couldn't understand it. Then the

Spanish impresario came and said to Grigoriev, 'They are not going to leave until they've seen you dance *Schéhérazade*. That's what they came to see, they want to see *Schéhérazade*.' Grigoriev didn't know what to do. By chance we happened to have the music of *Schéhérazade* with us, the orchestral parts, but we didn't have the décor or the costumes. So Grigoriev said, 'We'd better do what we can.' The young boys used the costumes from *Prince Igor* and the girls did what they could, put on turbans and things. Grigoriev didn't have the Shah's costume either, so you can imagine it looked pretty ridiculous, but nevertheless it happened, we did it. Of course, nobody had any swords or anything, so at the end Grigoriev just shouted at everybody, 'Don't bother about the swords. Just kill yourselves anyhow, just kill yourselves.' That all finished and then the public left the theatre.

Weren't all these journeys, all this travelling, wasn't it all very difficult for the company?

Yes, it was not comfortable, it wasn't easy. But on the other hand we were young, that was the important thing. Nobody thought about the war or was afraid of going on the ship. And I get back to the *Dante Alighieri* for a moment. When we got to sea, an Italian officer came into the saloon and said there was going to be a drill, a lifeboat drill, just a rehearsal. Everybody rushed to their cabins, grabbed their lifebelts, found out what number boat they were supposed to be in and went to the lifeboats. So when it happened again two days later, everybody knew what to do: they grabbed their lifebelts and went to the boats and they all just came and said that's fine, you all know the drill. But the one person who didn't take part was Diaghilev. He was never seen at these rehearsals. He never took his coat off, he just sat on a chair on deck with two lifebelts wrapped round him. He was really afraid. He was afraid of dying because a gypsy reading his hand had told him he would die on water. So he just sat there waiting for the end. But luckily nothing of that kind happened. Then one day there was an alarm at five o'clock in the morning and everybody thought, is it a real alarm or is it just a test? So everybody dressed and grabbed their lifebelts and rushed up on deck and went to their lifeboats, and the officers came and counted it out, but they found that there was somebody missing. Of course, it was Diaghilev who was still in his cabin. I don't think Diaghilev ever took his tie off the whole of that journey.

It took us eleven days to get to Cádiz. On the last night the captain gave a banquet for all the dancers on board and he read out a signal confirming that shortly after we'd left America we'd actually sunk a German submarine. There were, in fact, guns both fore and aft, and it was an Italian ship and we were at war. Two days later we arrived at Cádiz and started out again on tour.

Tell me something about the atmosphere in London at the end of the war, when you were there.

We opened with *Tricorne* in 1918, but work had begun on this before, in Spain. Massine had been working on it for some time. It was a marvellous thing, the music was tremendous. Karsavina was the Miller's Wife and Massine himself the Miller; they were both splendid. I danced the Governor. I was really a bit young for the role – the Governor should be an old man – but still I came on-stage and trembled and shook a bit and hoped for the best. On the first night I got so carried away that I forgot I was meant to be an old man and I started dancing energetically. On the following day Diaghilev called me on one side and said, 'Listen, Woizikowski, you really must remember you are meant to be an old man. You were dancing like a young man.' And I said, 'I'm terribly sorry, Sergei Pavlovich. This role really isn't for me, you know. I feel these Spanish rhythms and I want to dance, so there it is.'

Tell me what Diaghilev was like at this time.

Diaghilev was rather a strange man, you could say he was rather heavy. He didn't really have much heart, especially not for the dancers. If you dropped dead on the stage dancing, he wouldn't really have been surprised. I was dancing *Petrushka* one night. The first scene went very well and in the second scene I damaged my leg. I was practically reduced to dancing *Petrushka* on one leg. And after the performance I asked to see a doctor. The doctor came and examined me and Diaghilev said, 'Yes, I noticed that you danced the last scene as if you only had one leg. What's the matter?' I said, 'I've hurt myself. It's really very painful', and Diaghilev said, 'Well, what are we going to do? We still have a performance of *Boutique Fantasque* to put on now.' And I looked at Diaghilev and Diaghilev just turned and walked away. It was strange. It was also very painful, because he knew that I was a good dancer, and how could I dance on one leg, particularly in the tarantella of *Boutique Fantasque*? But anyhow my leg got better and I was well enough to dance the opening night in London.

*Can you tell me something about the atmosphere in Monte Carlo in the
1920s?*

Diaghilev had a contract in Monte Carlo for five years, for the six months
of the season. There were four months of opera and two months of ballet.
Of course, there were also operas in which we danced, like *Prince Igor*,
Aida, where Balanchine arranged some dances for the men, and *Turandot*
was also in the repertory, where there was a small dance arranged for me
with Balanchine, who danced himself also with Tchernicheva and
Doubrovska. And then there were parties. I remember one night Diaghilev
asked all the soloists to a kind of club, with cabaret, and we really didn't
know what to expect when we got there. In fact, we found Lord
Rothermere. And it turned out that it was Lord Rothermere who had
invited everybody. Diaghilev was rather offended that everybody was
drinking a great deal, litres of champagne, and when we'd all had a bit to
drink, Diaghilev asked one of the dancers to dance with Lord Rothermere.
There were toasts and all the rest that you could imagine and all the
dancers danced with him.

So when he was thoroughly exhausted with dancing, he sat down and
Diaghilev sent for his secretary. 'Would you translate, please?' And he said
to Lord Rothermere, 'Now, you know what I most want to do is to put on a
new production of *Sleeping Beauty*, the one-act verson called *Aurora's
Wedding*. It has wonderful sets and costumes by Bakst.' So the secretary
translated and there was a long and rather thoughtful pause. Then after a
while, 'Tell me, please, how much is this new production going to cost?' So
Diaghilev said, 'It's going to be £20,000 and, of course, it will be fantastic.
It will look marvellous and the stage will be packed with extras and all the
rest of it.' This the secretary translated. Rothermere reflected for a moment
and then said, 'OK, 15,000, but not a penny more.' But Diaghilev was
naturally pleased. 'Give me the money. I agree 15,000.' Then somebody
appeared – we didn't quite know who it was, but it appeared to be Lord
Rothermere's secretary – and Rothermere said, 'Write out a cheque for
£15,000.' So he did this and handed it to Diaghilev. Diaghilev inspected it
very carefully and put it in his pocket, and we all started drinking again and
it was all very successful.

Did you like Train Bleu?

I liked *Train Bleu*. I had a really quiet role in it. Lydia Sokolova had a
marvellous role as a tennis-playing sportswoman. It was amusing, it was

very modern, it had a certain success, there's no doubt about it. The best of them all was *Les Biches*; that had a real success. It was very good, a beautiful production, very nice set and costumes. We played four young sportsmen.

What did you think about Fokine's ballets at this time?

Of course, the Fokine ballets had been very good, but you felt that Sergei Pavlovich was always looking for something new. There were some Fokine ballets, like *Cléopâtre*, which really seemed much less interesting by this time. It was the new ones that were interesting, like the Balanchine ones. The *Prodigal Son* was extremely interesting. Lifar had the principal role in that. There was the *Triumph of Neptune* – that was his first big ballet. It was quite interesting, but it was terribly long; there was very little dancing in it. It was a big production, but somehow there was not much going on in it, but it was the first thing he tried to do on a large scale. I also liked *Apollo* very much. *Le Bal* was a marvellous ballet. *Barabau* had a very big success wherever we did it. Balanchine's works weren't as good to dance, but they had a very big success everywhere. We did them in France and England and everywhere, *partout*.

What was the technical standard of the company like at that time?

The technical side was good. Everybody worked very hard, everybody was very strong. That was the situation up till about 1925. After then Diaghilev was forced to take on a lot more French dancers and perhaps it wasn't quite so good. He couldn't just depend on dancers who left their homeland, but it never was anything dreadful.

What about discipline in the company?

Oh, it was very strong. Everybody turned up for everything, all rehearsals, all classes. You simply couldn't afford to be ill. Nobody let you. Of course, if somebody was really injured, they couldn't dance, but nevertheless . . .

What about Diaghilev? He came to rehearsals, didn't he?

Yes, he was very quiet. He sat and listened most of the time. He did occasionally query the tempo of things. He would sometimes say to Grigoriev, 'I don't think this passage is working very well', but he really didn't interfere, he just looked. But he looked and kept on looking.

Did he ever get angry?

Yes, he did, yes, he did, very angry indeed. He would absolutely bellow. He would get the whole company standing up there and he'd shout and say we were dreadful dancers and it was embarrassing. Oh yes, that happened from time to time.

What about money? Do you think you were reasonably well treated?

As I said at the beginning, it wasn't particularly good, but as time went by after a while I got 900 francs and then later 1,500 francs a month and eventually 3,000 and then by the later stages 8,000 francs. It was possible to live and not die.

What was the atmosphere in the company like?

It was very good. We lived like a family; people helped each other, taught each other roles. There was absolutely no sense of jealousy. When you first joined, Diaghilev used to say, 'Of course, this is my company and I must ask you one thing, you really simply mustn't drink.' You know I really like to drink vodka, but there wasn't any drunkenness. During the day everybody was very sober and straightforward. Of course, after performances we used to go to restaurants and have supper parties and that was different, but even then nobody ever got drunk, absolutely not, never.

The company had a very big repertory at this time, didn't it? How many ballets in all were you doing?

It was enormous, absolutely enormous. I never tried to work out how many. But he produced over the years more than fifty ballets. I must have danced in thirty ballets myself. Some of them we didn't dance very often, that I only danced very occasionally. There were ones like *Apollo* or *The Prodigal Son* or *La Chatte* where Lifar took the principal role or occasionally I would do those roles when he wasn't doing it. But even though one didn't dance these roles very often, you still worked on them. I've quite often danced four different ballets in an evening. I don't know where I got such energy and health from. With Massine and Nijinska you really never did more than two ballets in an evening. But later on it was more than that, and I quite often did four.

Tell me about your last meeting with Diaghilev.

My last real meeting with him, I remember, was rather tragic. It was in Paris after a performance. Lifar had danced Renard and Diaghilev invited all those who'd danced that evening and it was very cheerful. But I noticed he drank rather a lot. We all drank a bit, but we weren't used to seeing him drink to that extent. He was already unwell. He would eat all kinds of things he shouldn't have eaten, like *blinis* with sour cream. He shouldn't have eaten that. Caviare was all right, but there were sweet things he shouldn't have eaten. People told him about it, but he took absolutely no notice at all. He was very nice to us that evening, I remember. We said goodbye to him because we were all going on holiday. Then we were on holiday in St Maxime and we read in the newspaper that Diaghilev had died in Venice. It was absolutely dreadful. We really couldn't believe that he was dead. We would like to have gone to Venice for the funeral, but there wasn't time to get Italian visas, so we couldn't do anything and that was that.

Ursula Moreton

1903 SOUTHSEA–1973 LONDON

A member of the corps de ballet *from 1920 to 1922, Ursula Moreton went on to work closely with Ninette de Valois from 1926. She was a founding figure of the Sadler's Wells Ballet and director of the Royal Ballet School from 1952 to 1968.*

How did you come to join the Diaghilev Ballet?

I was a pupil of Cecchetti, one of the earliest English pupils he had over here in 1918, and Diaghilev used to come to watch the students' classes and asked whether I would join the company about a year before I actually did so. And I was finally sent a telegram the night before their Prince's season in 1920, to know whether I would join them that night when they arrived, and dance the following day.

Did you do so?

I did. We had a rehearsal for three ballets and I danced in all three the following night.

How could you possibly do that?

I can't remember. I only know I prayed and hoped for the best.

What was the atmosphere of the company like when you joined?

It was very much a family concern. The whole of the group of people were naturally wandering about Europe together and had at that time, in fact, been doing so rather more because of the war years. They were really very happily welded together, so that in a way the English felt a little outside it. But on the whole they were kind to one. One had to put up with certain sorts of bricks, of jealousy and so on, but on the whole awfully helpful, awfully kind.

Tell me about the repertory at that time.

Oh, the repertoire at that time was the three-ballet system, the known works – *Schéhérazade*, *Cléopâtre*, *Thamar*, *Carnaval*, *Papillons*, all those old things which had made such a stir. *Petrushka*, and then in addition, which was fascinating to me as I was such a newcomer, an entirely new ballet, *Chout*, and also Stravinsky's *Rite of Spring*, Massine's production. I didn't know any more than trying to count and keep my head above water. One was terribly interested, none the less, and fascinated by the strength of that particular production.

Tell me about Massine's choreography and method. How did he work?

He worked from a book very much. Very, very detailed before he ever got to you, terribly precise. He demanded absolute precision from his dancers, absolute understanding of his characterization, as his choreography concerned expression through the body. He was one of the first people who gave mime through every part of the body, stylized. This was a terribly important factor; and very interesting to work with because it was so different. Not that the whole thing wasn't different for me, because I was absolutely new.

Chout *hardly had a choreographer.*

Well, it was Slavinsky, a Polish dancer. It was actually choreographed before that season, so that one just fell into it. It was an old ballet; I can't really remember much about it, and I didn't like it, whereas I loved the *Rite of Spring.*

Were there strong feelings in the company about the new works as opposed to the old pre-war repertory?

Oh, tremendously. The company themselves loathed anything new. They couldn't bear anything except the things that they knew, and they were sticklers for keeping the status quo in every single step, which was very valuable, of course, because one felt that the Fokine productions were reproduced with love and dedication, especially on the part of Grigoriev, the regisseur, who did all the rehearsals.

Tell me about the quality of the dancing.

Strong in principals. I would say that the standard of the *corps de ballet* was not high, not by modern standards, anyhow.

Was this a temporary phase?

Yes, inevitably so. Because it was the dregs of the company that he came away with before the war years, and there had been no rejuvenation of younger people at that time. In fact, they did not come until later with the more modern ballets when Lifar joined the company. That was new, fresh blood. Balanchine.

Tell me about the company style. Did you feel you were part of something that had a unity of approach, music, design and steps?

Oh, enormously so. One was fascinated by this. And the integrity of the whole approach to a work. The work, the energy, the marvellous interest that Diaghilev always had at all times, day and night, to see that everything was perfectly done. Even the works that were still there, the dresses were renewed, and the style of wearing the costume was absolutely as the designer wanted. Bakst and Derain and the other designers were also always present, or very frequently present. The conductors also had a very strong say on how the thing was being carried out. Even in the older ballets, each actual rehearsal aimed for perfection. It was marvellous.

Do you think today's dancers have the same acting ability, musicality and maturity they seem to have had then.

I think that they were more mature as artists . . . the Russians have a more dramatic sense. I happened, myself, to like the dramatic work, but many English dancers prefer the more classical, abstract approach. In fact, perhaps it is our forte. I think that they were brought up amongst ballets where drama was the first thing. *Schéhérazade* and *Thamar*, all these things required this particular facet, rather more than the strict classical technique. This was Fokine's breakaway from the old regime. That, I think, is why they were a more dramatic company than we are now. Something that one shouldn't emulate. They were absolutely Russian.

Do you think one can now revive ballets like Schéhérazade?

Yes, I think one could revive *Schéhérazade*. Whether it would quite have the same impact, I don't know. And many companies have; the Festival Ballet has done a production of it. I find myself that they do lose without the touch of possibly Diaghilev, and Grigoriev, in charge. The spirit to some extent, however careful – perhaps because one is so careful – is apt to be a little lost.

Perhaps the most surprising thing in this period was the revival of Sleeping Beauty. *What did you think of it?*

Well, this was staggering, really. We were told at the end of our season at the Prince's that this was in hand. Sergeyev had arrived from Russia with quite a number of refugees, plus his books of notation, or what was the equivalent to a notation, to rehearse it. We were terribly interested, of course, because of having read a lot about it. The company talked about it;

they had a very great knowledge of it, many of them having danced in it. We looked forward so very much to this. Madame Brianza was taking classes, who had danced Aurora in the first *Sleeping Beauty*; Cecchetti, who had been the old Carabosse, was naturally there; and Nijinska was doing any refurbishing that Diaghilev felt was required. And so the whole time, which was about two months of rehearsal, was absolutely fascinating. And we thought that it was going to be such an enormous success. The costumes and décor of Bakst were fabulous, really beautiful. And to our utter astonishment the whole thing fell flat. One couldn't forgive the English public. I couldn't at that time. It seems extraordinary. But one couldn't convince people. The British public is conservative; they had been used to seeing *Schéhérazade*, *Thamar* and *Carnaval*, and that is what they wanted. They were not prepared for this at all, and we had never seen anything like it since, at least not within the living memory.

Did you enjoy dancing in it?

I enjoyed it enormously. I was very busy all the time – I was in every act – and thrilled because of far more classical dancing, which always pleases dancers, than I had experienced in the company's work before.

Of the rotating ballerinas, who impressed you most?

Oh, Spessivtseva, without question. She was absolutely beautiful, and it was a great experience to have been able to have seen her dance that. As a virtuoso artist, Trefilova was interesting; Egorova was lyrical, and Lydia Lopokova was amusing.

What about the costumes everyone talks about – were they easy to dance in?

No, very difficult. They were beautiful, the designs were very, very elaborate. Bakst always had appliqué work on appliqué work, outlined in silver and gold, and with the heaviest gold and silver and satins imaginable, so every costume weighed a ton. Mine, I remember, you could scarcely lift with one hand, and we did this very quick little dance in the last act, Hilda Bewicke and I, the Porcelain Princesses, and it really was quite an effort to get around in them. But still, you felt they were so beautiful, one put up with it.

How were conditions in the company? Were you well paid?

Very badly paid indeed, as Diaghilev obviously had very few funds. He was good to his dancers and treated them like a family, but actual remuneration was poor. In fact, that was why I didn't join them the first year, because I simply couldn't afford to tour the continent on the money offered.

Did you have contact with Diaghilev?

Oh, very little, but one did see him, and one was conscious he was at all performances. He actually came up to me after my first performance, when I had had to learn the Red and White Waltz in *Boutique Fantasque*, an Eastern slave woman in *Prince Igor* and *Sylphides* from Wednesday night to Thursday morning, and he came up after the performance, and said that I had only made one mistake in *Prince Igor*, and he congratulated me. Now, to have taken that much interest in one wretched *corps de ballet* dancer is quite something . . . I was very, very impressed by that, but, of course, I was much too junior in the company to have any real contact with him.

Were you afraid of him?

No, no, I wasn't. I think I had a great awe for him, the whole company did. He was a father to them, but father in the Russian sense. Very conscious of his power, and also conscious of his great integrity and dedication to the whole thing. He really felt to his heart if anything went wrong, and one was conscious that the important thing was the great welding of the company, which worked like a team.

How much do we owe today to Diaghilev's influence?

Everything, I would say, literally everything. We had no idea of what ballet meant in this sense in this country at all before that.

Why was it not possible for anyone to carry on after he died?

Well, because nothing was ready. The British public wouldn't accept it, and, indeed, how young Dame Ninette was, and I was, at that time. We had the courage, the temerity to start something, but it was years before we could build anything that would be even considered seriously. We just had to take our courage in our hands and hope that in time we would produce something.

What matters today? What is the most important legacy?

The legacy, I think, is the artistic unity and integrity of ballet with all its component arts. But the dancing itself, of course, is the core of the matter.

The perfection must be absolute. But, none the less, it is not the only thing. The surrounding factors must be as perfect and must be completely harmonious to bring the effect, the expression, the whole thing to some culminating point.

Laura Wilson

SYDNEY, AUSTRALIA 1901–

Laura Wilson was a member of the corps de ballet
in 1918 and 1919.

How did you come to work with the Diaghilev Ballet?

I had just gone away on my summer holidays in 1918 when I received a letter saying, 'Return at once, an important audition.' So I rushed back to London and we went up – there were about fifty of us, I suppose – to the auditorium, and we discovered to our horror that practically the entire company was there, sitting around and watching us, some of them very strange-looking to us. There was a very exotic-looking young man in the most extraordinary flowered shirt and those ballet breeches they used to wear in those days, which I had never seen before. We all had our little dances which we did, and then there was a pause, and he came and gave us a sort of class, using all sorts of technical terms that I had never heard of before. So it was just a matter of keeping our eyes open and copying what he did as quickly as you could. And then there was a lot of excitement around the door, and in came this burly, rather shabby, shabbily dressed man, and everybody stood up, and I thought, I don't stand up for anybody except the King, so I sat firmly down. Then we had to do it all over again, starting with the dances.

The awful thing for me, and I always say this is why I was taken into the company, was that my music was one of Chaminade's things, miles and miles of music, enormous cuts, and the pianist forgot all about it when it came to the point, so I went on improvising and improvising until I couldn't think of anything more to do, and I just sat on the floor at his feet and listened to the music. And he laughed about that, and, I must say, he had a charming smile and I always think that was why he took me, he thought it was very funny. Also, I was the youngest, and I think he was a bit sentimental, like most Russians who like young people.

Then, of course, we started rehearsing straight away, and up to that time I had never really done anything more, shall we say, 'characteristic' than the hornpipe and the sword dance in my extreme youth, and a tarantella. Otherwise everything had been very, very academic ballet. The first ballets we did were *Cléopâtre*, *Schéhérazade* and *Igor*, and this was quite a plunge for us, all these extraordinary movements we had never done before, but very exciting. But the thing that was difficult was that nobody explained what we were supposed to be, what we were supposed to be doing, and when we huddled together with expressions of horror, I don't know what we were being horrified about. All this was very difficult. There were one or two older members of the company who had been with them a long time who were English or spoke English, and if you asked, they said, 'Oh, do what the others do, dear.' It was not very helpful.

What language did you all talk in?

A smattering of all sorts of things. One picked up a little Russian. At that time there were some Spaniards and some Italians, of course, Poles and Russians. Polish one never picked up, it was very difficult. There's a sort of language one gets. But really it was a matter of using your eyes more than anything.

You were involved in Tricorne *and* Boutique *in your first season. What was Massine like to work with?*

Oh, very, very interesting. Very quiet, which was a great relief, but while you were working on a thing, you were just a yard of material, you had no feelings, nothing at all. You were just something he used. But it was wonderful to work with him; I learned a tremendous amount from that. He had a curious way of working things out, his groups and things. He would get hold of people and, as though they were just yards of material, would walk about until he'd got something that he wanted, and then we would have to remember that.

Were you conscious of being involved in something that was going to be of importance in the history of ballet?

Yes, I think I was, because although I had never seen any ballet, I had heard about this ballet and it had been my great ambition to get into the company, principally because of what I had heard about Karsavina and Nijinsky. I don't think one realized its implications fully at that time, but certainly it opened up the most enormous field of movement and possibilities to me.

Tell me about Cecchetti's classes – what were they like?

Oh, again a tremendous eye-opener to me, because I had had a lot of problems from my early bad training, and he just seemed to be the answer to all these things. He was very terrifying to work with. He had this old-

1 Diaghilev in New York, 1916

2 Tamara Karsavina in *The Firebird*, 1910
3 Anne-Benois Tcherkessova with her father, Alexandre Benois,
in St Petersburg, *c.* 1903

4 Dame Marie Rambert, 1976,   5 C. W. Beaumont, 1920s
6 Lydia Sokolova in *The Rite of Spring*, 1920,   7 Léonide Massine in *Le Tricorne*, 1919

8 Left to right: Lydia Sokolova, Anton Dolin, Jean Cocteau, Leon Woizikowski, Bronislava Nijinska in *Le Train Bleu*, 1924
9 Ursula Moreton in *The Sleeping Princess*, 1921   10 Laura Wilson, 1917

11 Errol Addison at the Royal Ballet School, c. 1960   12 Leighton Lucas, 1940s
13 Ernest Ansermet, 1960   14 Ninette de Valois, 1923

15 Henri Sauguet, 1927   16 Igor Stravinsky with Nicolas Nabokov, 1956
17 Alicia Markova, 1928   18 Osbert Lancaster, 1940s

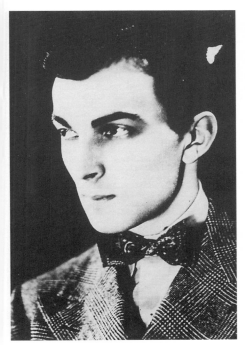

19 Cecil Beaton, 1925   20 Sacheverell Sitwell with his wife, 1929
21 Igor Markevitch, 1928   22 Serge Lifar in *The Prodigal Son*, 1929

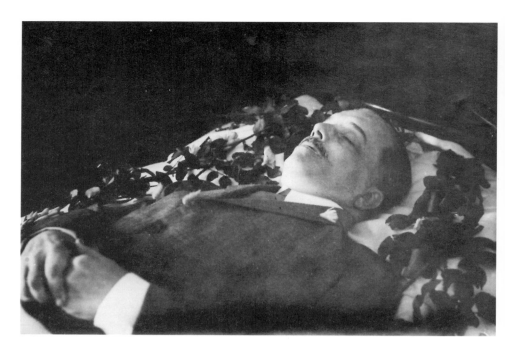

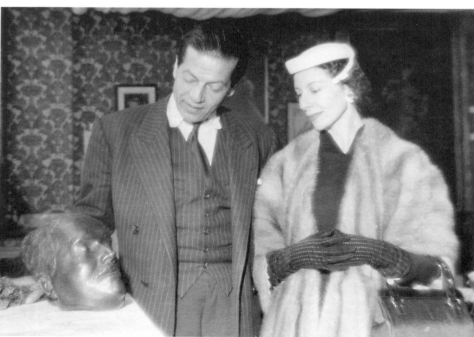

23 Diaghilev on his deathbed, Venice, August 1929
24 Serge Lifar and Dame Alicia Markova with Diaghilev's death mask, 1954

fashioned continental way of teaching; he shouted and screamed. He had this little stick which he walked round the room with while we were doing our exercises, tapping, and you knew he was going to go wham, not actually hitting you. I was too young and silly to realize what he was getting at, and that he didn't hit the people who didn't like being hit. Some people do. They were terrifically hard work, but the great value of them, I think, to a company was that it was a well-balanced diet of exercises for every day of the week from which, if you came regularly, you got all that you needed as a professional dancer.

Was the company technically as strong as companies today?

It's awfully difficult to know. I think probably not, but I think also they were better dancers.

What was Karsavina like?

Lovely. One of the loveliest things ever. She never put on any airs at all. She would get dressed in the corner of this big horrible studio we used to work in, in Shaftesbury Avenue. She was very untidy, bless her heart; she came in and grabbed a tutu from under a bench, and another bit of something from somewhere else, but just so simple, kind and dignified and altogether just as she still is, the most lovely person.

Did you have much contact with Diaghilev himself?

No, no, very occasionally, not conversational. No, he rather liked to pretend he couldn't speak English. Of course he could. He was very autocratic.

How much were you conscious of his presence?

One was conscious of his presence in the company always, and very conscious of him out front. He didn't appear at rehearsals very often, but it was interesting to see how the whole company got on its toes most when he did.

What about his appearance?

When he first came to England at that time, he practically only had what he stood up in, because during this period, when the company was out of work in Spain, he sold all his personal belongings to keep them alive. But there was a wonderful occasion when he arrived just after an orchestral rehearsal at the Coliseum in a complete new rig-out of clothes, and all the old members of the company, the Russians and Poles and so on, clustered round him just like a family of children with Father coming home in something awfully grand. They felt the material and tried on his hat, and they used his umbrella and so forth, and he just sort of stood and beamed at them. It was very charming, and that was the first time I really felt he was a human being.

How long did you stay with the company?

I was with them a year the first time, and then about six months the second time. I didn't have very much stamina, unfortunately, and I finished up my first year having scarlet fever very badly, and for a time I thought I wasn't going to be ale to dance at all.

Did it affect your life, working with them?

Well, in all sorts of ways. I think for a long time it did affect my health, if you mean that, but I think it has coloured one's whole life tremendously. It opened up such visions, such perspectives of dance and its possibilities that one had never realized before. I really think that all our lives have been affected by the Diaghilev company, whether we know it or not. Because one of the first things that I remember from as far back as I can was when we first came to England; I came from India. Clothes were so grey, everybody's clothes were awfully grey and dull, and I think that décor of rooms, everything had been tremendously affected. One's outlook on dancing, of course, was enormously affected too, and I think a great many people began to very much despise technical dancing, not realizing that you can't do the other without a technique.

Do you think ballet today would be the same without Diaghilev?

I shouldn't think so. It's difficult to say, but I shouldn't think so. I think it was enormously far-reaching, it created an appetite. Of course, I suppose Pavlova also did that by going round the world, but it certainly opened the eyes of the British public, France and so forth, very, very much.

Errol Addison

1907 HEATON, YORKSHIRE–1983 HASTINGS

Errol Addison was a corps de ballet *member from 1918 to 1921.*

How did you come to join the Diaghilev Ballet?

I came to join the Diaghilev Ballet because when I was fourteen years of age I was taken to do classes with Maestro Enrico Cecchetti, who at that time, of course, was ballet master of the Diaghilev Ballet. He became extremely interested in me, and English boys at that time were very few and far between. At that time the only other one was Leighton Lucas, who was already in the Russian ballet under the name of Lukin, and he was there mainly to study his music. When it came time for the Diaghilev Ballet to go back on the continent, Cecchetti didn't want to lose me, so he asked Mr Diaghilev if I could join the Russian ballet, and Mr Diaghilev was quite cooperative, and that was how I came to join the Diaghilev Russian ballet, but I still kept my English name.

You were about fifteen.

I was fifteen, just over fifteen, yes.

Rather young?

To start with my mother came with me. My mother was not a very worldly woman, and she thought that the pitfalls and dangers were terrible for a young boy, and she warned me against the terrible women there were in Paris who at that time congregated on the streets. We lived in a pension in the Rue Lafayette. When I used to come home from the theatre, these young ladies eventually found out that I was terribly scared, and so they used to have a wonderful game every night and chase me up the Rue Lafayette. I used to run like hell because my mother had told me such terrible stories. I was scared stiff of them.

How long did you stay?

I stayed with the Diaghilev Ballet altogether about three and a half years. I joined them at the end of 1918 and I left them after the finish of *Sleeping Princess.*

You were there for both the London seasons at the end of the war when

Tricorne *and* Boutique Fantasque *were created.*

Well, *Tricorne*. I was in the original, in at the start of it. I was one of the Policemen. *Boutique Fantasque* was already created before I joined them, and I eventually did the chief Cossack in that.

Did the company prefer these new Massine ballets or the old Fokine ones that had come earlier?

There didn't seem to be any particular worries about that. They seemed to be happy dancing in anything. No great conversations about 'I detest so-and-so' or 'I like that'. They seemed to cooperate with everything, and all was quite happy.

What was the daily routine? You worked quite hard.

Yes, we had a class every morning and we would then rehearse very strongly, but we always used to get a break in the afternoon so that we could get a rest before the show, unless there was something terribly important coming up. I mean to say, when we were putting on *Sacre du Printemps* in Paris for the first time, we rehearsed like hell. I always remember that, because Stravinsky used to play the piano for rehearsals, and he broke four pianos in one week.

Did you all find the music very difficult?

It all used to be done with a system of counting. That is where I learned to count so well in Russian. It was all *raz*, *dva*, *tri*, *chtire*, *pyat*, and there were odd numbers, and once you learned the counting, you found you could cope all right. You couldn't very well listen to the melody because in *Chant du Rossignol* there wasn't much melody to listen to.

Was it a happy company?

It's difficult to remember exactly. You always find people who are not happy, but taken by and large, I should say it's happier than the ballet companies of today. There wasn't that feeling all the time that I could do it better than she could. Ballerinas were much less – how do you say? – friendly in those days, they were a thing apart. It really was a case of drinking champagne out of the ballerinas' slippers and they were looked upon with reverence. Whereas today the standard of training has improved so much that there are so many girls standing round in the *corps de ballet* who look and say, 'I could do it as well as that.' 'I could do three pirouettes, she can only do two.' They forget it's more than just sheer technique that makes a ballerina.

What was Massine like to work with as a choreographer?

Oh, excellent, excellent. He was very, very hard-working, he was kind, and my memories of him are very nice, funny in one way. I know that in one of his ballets, *Sacre du Printemps*, he flogged me in one of the principal places, and I was tickled pink, and then just before the ballet was due to go on, I was told, 'Thank you very much, you have been rehearsing in Mr Massine's position.' But he had given me one or two tricky poses on elbows and knees that had taken me hours of practice to get, and, of course, he couldn't quite make it, so I went on anyway.

What about the revival of Sleeping Beauty? *Did you think it worth doing?*

I was very sorry it was a failure, because I thought that, as events subsequently proved, he had got the right idea. But the first night was positively tragic. The transformation scene just completely went to pieces, and it raised laughs, rather more than anything else. Pieces getting stuck, the lights going all wrong, and the critics were absolutely merciless, and the whole thing was queered, I suppose, which was rather a pity.

Did the idea of different Auroras every night work?

Spessivtseva was, of course, beautiful, graceful, everything you could possibly desire about a ballerina. And Egorova was fantastically strong on pointes, but she was the original ballerina with flat feet. She had such feet, they were so flat, that with the physical qualifications required today, she would never even get a job in the *corps de ballet*. They would say, 'Oh, her feet. Oh, the poor thing. No, she's finished.' Trefilova was petite, brilliant, very flashy. One rather amusing incident: as you know, at the end of the Rose Adage with the four princes – I was the English prince – we do the promenades round and the attitude at the end. By that time the ballerina is rather out of breath, and breathing rather hard, and Trefilova suffered from shocking halitosis, so we used to walk round at very great arm's length to keep out of the way. The event that sticks in everyone's memory was Cecchetti's Carabosse. He played it with an impish roguishness. You knew he was a wicked fairy, but you weren't really quite sure he was going to be a wicked fairy until the time came for the cursing.

Did you see much of Diaghilev?

Very little indeed. My only real contact with him was when he agreed that I should join the Diaghilev Ballet. I was taken to see him – he was staying at the Savoy at the time – and when he said, 'Yes, most definitely, you can', and I got up and shook hands with him, one of the most vivid memories of my life was shaking hands with him. It was just like shaking hands with a pillow. It was the softest, flabbiest hand I have ever shaken; you seemed to disappear in it. It was actually quite revolting. It's a memory that I have of him that I wouldn't say was all that pleasant. I didn't have all that much to do with him. He was quite apart from the company. He was looked upon as a god, and certainly his presence was magnificent, both in appearance and everything else.

Do you think Diaghilev in any way had a bad influence on ballet?

Yes, I do think there are certain ways in which he had a bad influence on ballet, but I don't think this is a question that I would like to say any more about. I think we are beginning to get rid of it, thanks to a few boys like Mr David Wall and a few others like myself, who stuck it out. All right, and good luck to him.

How much does the Diaghilev legacy matter?

I think it matters quite a bit, because quite obviously Diaghilev was the man who really brought to public notice the popularity that ballet could achieve.

Was your time with Diaghilev important to you?

Most definitely it was. After my experience in the Diaghilev Ballet I think I discovered that ballet wasn't exactly the career for me. I went on the music halls for twenty-five years. I was in the Royal Command Performance at the Palladium in May 1932, I was on the opening bill at Radio City, New York, and achieved a certain amount of fame in the music-hall world, and after twenty-five years I came back to ballet again because I realized that having made a fortune and spent a fortune, I had got to do something for my old age, so I came back to try to remake my name in ballet, and set up as a teacher of ballet in my old age, which I have done.

Leighton Lucas

1903 LONDON–1982 LONDON

A corps de ballet member from 1918 to 1921, Lucas subsequently became well known as a conductor, composer and arranger.

How did you first come to be involved with the Diaghilev Ballet?

I had been dancing for some years as a child all over the country, and my mother was a pianist, and became a rehearsal pianist for the Diaghilev company. She invited me down to the Cecchetti studio to watch this company rehearse, and I was absolutely fascinated, as you can well imagine, and I was asked then to give an audition. I gave an audition to Massine, and, I must say, I think it was one of the most frightening experiences of my life. I was terribly young and very shy, and this formidable company of fantastic dancers all sitting round and watching me dance, and I was then sixteen, and I really was very frightened. But they were enormously polite, delightfully polite, and I remember going into the little cubby-hole afterwards to change, and there was a neat, tiny, beautifully built little dancer there who spoke to me very politely, and in beautiful English, and I afterwards discovered this was the great Idzikowski and I am very happy to say that Stas and I are still the warmest friends today. Anyway, I gave my audition and bowed my way off the floor, and went home.

Three days later I had a telegram: 'Come immediately to the rehearsal room.' Somebody in the company had broken or hurt his foot, and they were one man short in the Bacchanale of *Cléopâtre*. I went down that morning and I rehearsed solidly from eleven till one, this one dance which lasts about three minutes, I think, and that afternoon I went on at the Coliseum. It was an enormous moment in my life. I had never seen a theatre as big as that to begin with, and fantastic lights; you were surrounded by these enormous lights blinding you. I could just see the orchestra pit and the conductor and behind that this enormous blackness which was the audience. I was too involved actually remembering the dance to bother much about the audience or anything else. My friends in the company were shouting at me in various languages, directing me, pushing me round to the right places, and I got through very successfully, thank goodness. That evening we repeated it, and the next day I was on again, and then I started rehearsing. And I had to learn the whole of the repertoire, because there was a very large repertoire at the time, and I slowly took my part in these different ballets: *Sadko, Oiseau de Feu, Petrushka*. And then suddenly it was 1918. November. I went to the rehearsal room. I was met by Kremnev, a little dancer, and he said, 'Lukin, no repetizki aujourd'hui. Peace come', which was the most fantastic phrase I have ever heard in my life. I got so used to this polyglot language that eventually I found myself talking it too. One spoke French, Russian, Italian, Spanish, words of anything. I think there were three English people in the company at that time; there was my dear friend Lydia Sokolova, and who else? Later on Errol Addison joined us; you remember him, a wonderful dancer. As peace had come, Diaghilev's first idea was to get across to Paris again, and so I was invited to go with the company. I stayed with them all over the continent, and back to London again, for the next three and a half years.

What were these tours like?

They were jolly hard work, because on the continent you play on Sundays. In fact, it was our gala day, you always got a gala performance on Sundays. Every morning, whatever you had been doing the night before, you were on the barre in the morning for a class with Cecchetti at nine o'clock, and you had a two-hour class. And then at eleven you started your rehearsal, your current rehearsal, and then in the afternoon you were more or less free until the evening performance. Of course, if there was a matinée as well, it was pretty well non-stop. And when we went to Spain, for example, we were there in the summertime and it was so terribly hot we never started our performance until ten o'clock at night, finishing about half past twelve or one, and we used to go and call up – what do they call the guard that keeps the keys for all the hotels? You had to go and call him up to let you into the hotel at night. It was a fascinating life, of course. I found it invaluable, because, as I say, I was terribly young at the time and it's a very liberal education, not only in travel, but in life itself and in the arts. Because if you think that my associates were Ernest Ansermet, the conductor, there was Picasso, there was Derain, Prokofiev, Stravinsky – it's fantastic to be surrounded by people of that calibre at that age in life. One becomes awfully accustomed to living with foreign people. To this day I never feel a stranger anywhere. Maybe you don't know the language, but you soon find your way about, and it's remarkable how quickly you acclimatize yourself.

Tell me about discipline in the company. Was it strict?

Oh, very strict, very strict indeed. There was one thing that always amused me very much. I noticed that when after a rehearsal or a class we'd all change, the last man out always bowed to the room before we shut the door. This I liked very much. It's a formal gesture. Every time Diaghilev came in to visit a rehearsal or a class, we all had to stand up, and mistakes were not only frowned upon, they were *verboten*. We were not allowed to make mistakes, although I must quote an example of this. *Pulcinella*, Stravinsky–Pergolesi. The most beautiful, beautiful work. We did the first performance of that at the Paris Opéra and we had been rehearsing, as the ballet used to rehearse for months and months on this one work. There were four little Pulcinelli, of whom I was one, and we were all dressed in huge white gowns with black wooden masks over our faces, so we were completely anonymous, and little red hats designed by Picasso. By the first performance of this work we knew it, we were bored, we knew it so well, and came the moment we four little Pulcinelli were doing our dance, and for the briefest second I hesitated. My mind wandered – is it right or left turn – and before I had thought about it I had done it the right way and forgotten it. And when I left the theatre that night, my name was on the board. Lukin rehearsal tomorrow morning, *Pulcinella*. And for two hours the next morning I had to go through this dance until I went screaming mad, to make perfectly sure I never did such a thing again. Diaghilev was in front of every performance, and he had seen this and his ire worked to such an extent to think that anybody in *his* company could make a mistake. This was the sort of standard we were set.

How were you paid? Was it enough?

We were paid very poorly. It wasn't a very big salary, I forget what it was. But we used to have this pay parade every fortnight. A fortnight seemed a long time. I remember we were always very broke by the time pay-day came. On the 1st and 15th of every month we used to go down to Grigoriev's office in the morning and queue up outside. And Grigoriev used to recite a list of fines. He would deduct fines if you were late for rehearsal. Once I actually missed an entrance in the *Sleeping Princess*, which upset everybody very much. I had got careless about it, and forgot I was on, and I heard the music start and I ran all the way downstairs, kicked on with great vigour by Grigoriev, and I was fined, I think, half a crown for that. That was the sort of thing. And, as I say, it was highly disciplined. It was not unlike being in the air force, when I was there, except it was less agreeable in the air force.

Tell me about the orchestras and the conductors.

The first conductor I came across there at the Coliseum was a man called Henri Défosse, who was a very good conductor. I don't know where he is, I've not seen him since. He came over from Paris and even at that time I was really making music, I was composing even then. And I used to talk to him about the scores, about the music, and he was interested. He saw that I was keen on music and he actually gave me a little job to do. For one of the 'Kikimora' dances in the *Contes Russes* there was no piano part for rehearsals and my mother couldn't cope with this enormous full orchestral score, and so I was told to make a transcription for piano of this thing, which I did, and I was paid the princely sum of two pounds for it. But it was invaluable as experience. It's a a very difficult thing to do, and I sometimes make my students at the Academy do the same sort of thing to find out how far you can go. That was my first introduction to music, and Diaghilev always teased me about music. I used to go about without a hat on, I never wore a hat, and he was permanently hatted, his famous bowler hat; and I would bow to him and he would raise his hat. And he said to me once, rather arrogantly, 'Lucas, do you not wear a hat so that you can let musical ideas fall down from heaven straight into the brain?'

How much contact did you have with Diaghilev?

Frankly I was rather frightened of him. He was a rather formidable person, and naturally I was only a very humble member of the company in the ninth row of the *corps de ballet*, but he was really very charming, most intelligent, but I had very little to do with him. I say frankly he was a rather formidable person and, of course, when he was angry, the voice, I couldn't follow him at all. I couldn't speak much Russian. But sometimes he would have a riot meeting with the company and it was terrifying. And, of course, the man who could outdo him at that was Grigoriev. Grigoriev, he has a very large voice, and they used to have these strike meetings. I never quite found out what they were all about, but I imagine somebody wanted more money or something, or a bit more time off, and they used to have these riot meetings, and the screaming, the yelling, the shouting, I was absolutely terrified. I didn't know what was going on, I expected murder any minute. But it all passed over quite amicably eventually, and they all decided pro or anti. That went on quite frequently.

Would you say it was a happy company?

Oh very, yes. I think they were actually too busy. When you are as busy as that, you can't be discontented, but one got bored with certain ballets if repeated too often. And, of course, there was trouble from the permanent travelling. You never stayed anywhere more than – well, three months was a long stay. We would do that in Paris, but most places it was a matter of weeks.

Did you feel you were involved in something important, not just any old job?

To me it was enormously important. It was opening my life and my mind, really. You see I must remind you again, I am stressing this, that I was terribly young at the time. I hadn't had this enormous cultural background so it was an entirely new world. I was absolutely fascinated. And, of course, I was fascinated too that when we were on tour, I used to be able to go to all sorts of odd concerts in odd towns that I would never have seen otherwise. I saw a lot of opera when we shared with the Opera at the Costanza in Rome. We used to go and see performances when we were not dancing. The same at the Opéra in Paris. I saw performances of *Samson and Delilah* from the grid at the top, from the lighting grid. I put an overall on, went up and watched it all from up there, which is a fascinating view of an opera.

What was reaction later to the Diaghilev Ballet?

Fantastic, absolutely fantastic. It was a religion. Of course, when the Ballets Russes first arrived here, I thought London had gone mad. A friend of mine, a queer little balletomane, he used to have a little photograph of Lopokova, and built a little shrine to it, and burnt candles in front of it every day. This was the intensity of the devotion to this art. And I saw a girl at Charing Cross Road fall down on her knees and try to kiss Idzikowski's hand as he went down the road towards the Coliseum. It was an intense embarrassment to him, I assure you. You know how formal he can be.

It was quite fantastic. It revolutionized indoor decoration, everything was Bakst at that time. A friend of mine in Chelsea, she built a whole salon which looked like *Schéhérazade*, and she used to sit cross-legged with a turban on in Turkish trousers and smoke long cigarettes in a holder. They thought this was absolutely the thing. The *dernier cri* was the Diaghilev Ballet. It really was fantastic.

How did you get your name?

Well, my name is Lucas, and they didn't have any English names in the company and I wasn't asked. Suddenly my name was called Lukin. I didn't choose it. We never chose anything, we just did what we were told.

Ernest Ansermet

1883 VEVEY–1969 GENEVA

Conductor for the Ballets Russes from 1915,
Ansermet was closely associated with Stravinsky.
He founded the Suisse Romande Orchestra and
made many recordings of ballets he had
conducted for Diaghilev.

Have there been changes in your lifetime, in the whole approach to conducting?

Yes, yes, there is really a great difference. Whereas at the beginning of the century even very difficult works, like *Heldenleben* of Strauss, or *Also sprach Zarathustra*, or *Elektra* or Debussy, were always written in 4/4 time, 3/4 or 2/4, I mean full numbers, but just after the First World War, or even a little before, Stravinsky began writing music changing the bar all the time, making an irregular cadence: 5/8, 2/8 and so on. It was necessary to invent, for this kind of new rhythm, a new conducting technique. That is why, before my time and until my time, conductors never had lessons in conducting. They had models – for instance, for me Nikisch or Weingartner, for Klemperer Mahler and so on – models, but they had not received lessons. They studied conducting by seeing how the great conductors conducted. But with this new technique it was necessary to have lessons. Since this time have begun conducting classes, which were not existing before my time.

Did you yourself ever have any lessons in conducting?

No, I followed a number of great conductors as models, and that was all. I had a few discussions with Weingartner; he gave me some *conseil* – how do you say *conseil*?

Advice.

Yes, he gave me some advice. Not lessons.

What was the first music you conducted?

Oh, it was rather light music, conducting what was called the Kursaal de Montreux. I had to make the afternoon concerts for the English ladies living in Montreux, and taking teas, and in these concerts I conducted waltzes by Strauss, marches by Souza, fantasies on operas and so on. But it is excellent practice, because, of course, we do all that without rehearsal. We must give exactly what is necessary to the orchestra. Then already in that time I had once a week a symphony concert with all kinds of classical, romantic and modern music. That is to say that at this time in Montreux before the First World War I conducted the First Symphony of Stravinsky, and I invited him to conduct the scherzo of this symphony in the following concert. So I made many experiments of that kind. Then I was called to Geneva to take direction of what was called the Abonnement Concerts. There I had all the repertory of symphonic concerts. That's how the Suisse Romande Orchestra began, and the way forward to the new music of France and Russia. Debussy, Ravel and the Russians.

Their music wasn't well known at that time, was it?

No, because my predecessors in Switzerland were all Germans, and they were making concerts of classical and romantic music of Strauss and Mahler, not one page from Debussy or Ravel. I had to reveal all this to our public.

What was it about Russian music? What drew you first to Russian music?

It was a personal taste. When I was young, my musical taste was rather for rhythmical music, so I was very fond of Rimsky-Korsakov, Borodin and Mussorgsky, the Russians of the north. And it's also true that I knew the music of Stravinsky.

How did you get to know this music, as there weren't copies of it? Did you find it, did you buy it? Did people show it to you?

No, I met Stravinsky in Montreux and we became friends. He has shown me his music and he has given me his scores, and we played four hands at the piano of *The Rite of Spring*, so I learned the music of Stravinsky from Stravinsky himself. This is why I'm still true to the Stravinsky of this time, because it is precisely the Stravinsky of this time who has given me his music.

What was he like as a person at that time?

He was an attractive man, always very lively, full of spirit, temperament, and working very hard. I have seen him at that time composing *Le Rossignol, The Nightingale*; finishing the opera and also finishing *The Rite of Spring*.

The first work that you conducted for Diaghilev was, I think, Fireworks, wasn't it?

Yes, the *Fireworks*, and then *Firebird* and *Petrushka*.

What was the musical standard of the Diaghilev company orchestras of that time? They were, after all, playing very difficult modern music. Was the orchestra up to it?

Well, in Paris he had excellent orchestras. In London also, and I must say even at the Alhambra Theatre – where I began to conduct for Diaghilev in 1919, where we gave the first performances of the *Three-cornered Hat* and *Boutique Fantasque* – the orchestra was excellent. It is simple, I had John Barbirolli in my cello section.

Did you have enough rehearsal time also?

Yes, sufficient. Diaghilev was very careful about that. Of course, it was not very much, but it was sufficient.

Is there a fundamental difference in conducting a work like Petrushka *or the* Rite of Spring *in the theatre or the concert hall?*

For me, no. I know that there are people who believe it should be so, but for me, no. When I used to conduct the *Rite of Spring* or *Petrushka* for Diaghilev, it was exactly the same as if I had to conduct those works for the concert hall, or for a gramophone recording.

You were very popular with the dancers in the company.

It is perhaps for one quality that I have from birth, that is my musical feeling of time as cadential time, not metric time. Of course, the cadence is divided by the metre, in three or two, and so on, but the cadence is a unity, and it is because musical time is cadential time, that it is the time of movement. Not of the steps, but the dynamic, that is the difference. I am sorry to say, I observe that many young interpreters have lost this cadential feeling. They consider that musical time is metric. They are metrically absolutely exact, but there is no impression of movement, of dynamic, and this cadential feeling I developed immensely in conducting the Russian ballet. For instance, with Nijinsky. Nijinsky was a wonderful dancer in this aspect. When he was dancing *La Spectre de la Rose*, he was jumping from behind the stage, and I had to be with him exactly, but I couldn't see when he was beginning the jump. So I had to feel this movement, and I made the movement with him in order to be exactly with him. In the beginning I was sometimes not quite right, it came a little late, or a little before, and I told Nijinsky, 'But I follow you exactly', and he told me, 'But you must not follow me, you must be with me, not follow.' And, of course, it was exactly the point. You have to feel the movement of the dancer, and the same movement musically. I think that has given me a great security in the constancy of the movement.

I tell you, once I had to record *Boléro* of Ravel to make a film soundtrack, but when we made the recording, at a point two-thirds of the way through the score, a telephone bell was heard, and we had to stop and begin again. We began again and we did the whole, and afterwards I received a letter from the film company telling me, 'What is surprising is that we can edit together the two recordings because they are perfectly synchronized in terms of the tempo.' That is not because my beat is right but because my cadence is right. That is the point. If you take the value of one beat, you can vary it very easily, but not the cadence, as the cadence is the movement.

Tell me about Ravel, because you knew him very well. Was he a difficult man?

He was very eccentric, very original, and also – how do you say? – secret. He would not externally express his feelings at all. He was discreet, but so musical. He came very often in the first years of my orchestra to Geneva, where he had an uncle, and sometimes he would bring part of a score with him, and try it out, to improve how it was sounding.

You worked a great deal with composers in terms of their first performances. You have probably done more first performances than any other living conductor. How have you found working with composers in the creation of their works? Do they understand the problems of the conductor?

Yes, yes, but the conductor must not be a slave, and not have too much respect for the composer. He must have his own opinion and his own conviction, and expose this conviction to the composer. Often the composer will understand at the moment of the performance things he had not foreseen before. I had this experience very often, especially with Frank Martin and with Honegger. I said you could do this or that, and they would say, 'Oh yes, you are so right.' Of course, the composer has written it and he knows what he wants, but he has not the distance from his work. The conductor has that distance, so we can sometimes give to the composer some ideas which are to him useful.

What about your interpretations? Do you look back over fifty years' conducting now, and find that some of your interpretations have changed over the years?

I hope they've improved. I say that because at the beginning we all have some technical difficulties, and then we learn with time to dominate these difficulties, and then find the right way of realizing the passage. I am sure that I conduct *La Mer* better today than twenty years ago.

Did you know Debussy?

Yes, I've known Debussy. I had the chance of meeting him. He invited me to his home one day and we had the chance of examining together some of his scores, and he gave me good advice. He was very liberal, very liberal-minded. For instance, looking at the score of the *Nocturnes*, I said to him, 'For the "Nuages", you write here *assez modéré*. What do you mean by *assez modéré*? Is it the crotchet or is it the bar?' 'No,' he said, 'it's the crotchet, more or less.' He was not like Stravinsky, who would have given me metronome marking 120.

Was Stravinsky always very precise about things?

Oh, always, and very authoritarian, but he is less so today, I know. With age, he has also learned that the musical tempo is not metronomic.

Looking back on your early years, do you think that the ferment of that time represented a real turning point in music?

Oh yes, the days after the First World War were a turning point. We had passed through a period in which music was always conceived in a determined tonality, D major, C major and so on, to a music which coordinated several tonalities together in the simultaneity, something we call polytonality. It was never a question of polytonality in the school of Schoenberg. With Schoenberg the music had to be tonal or atonal. But polytonal, he wouldn't have known what that was. Polytonality was begun by Debussy in our time, though we find, if we want, polytonal passages by Bach, and it was always in the music also of Beethoven. In the finale of the Ninth Symphony there's a moment when we have a major third in one voice and a minor third in another. So it is polytonal. Of course, this polytonal music was very difficult to understand for the public, and that made for the difficulty we had to impose this music after the First World War, when came the atonal music. Because I know that when you hear polytonal music several times, you finish by understanding it. If you hear atonal music, you will never understand it, not better after twenty times than at the first hearing. So it is very different. But for the public it is rather embarrassing, because they see no difference between a music which is difficult to understand and a music which is difficult to understand because there is nothing there to understand.

Can we now talk, Monsieur Ansermet, about the Firebird? *Stravinsky has been quite dismissive of this work in recent years, calling it on one occasion 'Rimsky-Korsakov with pepper'. I don't know what he means by this, but do you retain your affection for it?*

Yes, of course, but it is very much Rimsky-Korsakov. There are many parts where the technique is similar to Rimsky-Korsakov. When he adds 'with pepper' it is because it is much more refined, with much more complicated combinations, but I think it is absolutely fantastic to have written such a work, with basically only two chords, the association of a minor third and a major third. On the basis of these two chords he has really built the whole score. Melodically and harmonically, you find it is always the same thing, with a variety of result which is absolutely astonishing. He was young then and, I must say, from the point of view of scoring there is not one fault. Everything sounds well, and magnificent, but it is practically difficult, because he divided everything, and so you have three flutes, for instance. This is very difficult, and also in the strings there are some difficult passages, but it's an excellent score and I like it immensely. It's the first score of Stravinsky that I had to study profoundly. When I joined the Diaghilev company, it was the first score I had to conduct in the Opéra de Paris, and then in America. It was for me difficult to lay it down, because the only score at the disposition of Diaghilev was the manuscript, an immense manuscript, so big that it was impossible to place it on the stand. And so in order to conduct I had to learn by memory the whole ballet already for my first performance, because I could not use the score. But I did it. I was young enough in those days. Since then, with Stravinsky's new ideas about scoring and writing . . . You know that in 1919 he made a suite for small orchestra. The suite is perfect in its way, but it doesn't suppress the value of the original. What is regrettable is that he has made a new version of the whole ballet where he has all simplified, like he has done in the suite, and to my mind that is terrible. It takes out much of the colour and the value. After all, the *Firebird* was conceived as impressionistic music. You cannot put that in classical terms so easily, and doing that you are forced to make some changes, which are not good.

Ninette de Valois

1898 BALTIBOYS, IRELAND–

After a great deal of varied experience de Valois joined the Ballets Russes as a soloist in 1923. She stayed for two years and occasionally returned as a guest artist. She later went on to found the Vic-Wells Ballet, which became the Sadler's Wells Ballet and eventually the Royal Ballet.

How did you come to join the Diaghilev Ballet?

Well, the same way all the other English dancers joined it. There was no company in England, there was nothing for us to do. You received a good training with various great teachers that were in the country and then you went into musical comedy. I was lucky enough to get into the opera ballet at Covent Garden during the international season, but there was nothing else. And so straight from Cecchetti's studio, who recommended me to Diaghilev; when he was short of dancers, I joined them.

How did the atmosphere of the company strike you when you first met it?

Oh, a little terrifying, of course. I had never been in a repertory ballet company before and it was so different to shows in London, where you did the same thing every night for nine months or a year. And this tremendous repertoire to learn and the various styles. I came in 1923 at a rather interesting time, when it wasn't very big. It was just after, about eighteen months after, his smash at the Alhambra, and so it was a small company and economically run at that time. But I did come in when they still had all the traditional ballets going of the pre-1914 repertoire, and then all the new innovations of Massine and Nijinska.

How did you react to the contrast between the two schools, the Fokine ballets and the Massine and Nijinska ones?

I was very much of my age, and I was terribly interested in Nijinska's ballets, and the Balanchine ballets. I was there for Balanchine's very first work for the company. I was naturally, as I say, of my age and I got a great thrill out of the really modern works. Next to that I preferred the Fokine ones, and I'm afraid I held *Lac des Cygnes* in great contempt. I think we did it pretty badly and it was rather badly put on, a rushed performance, and I thought it was dreadful. I learned to change my mind about it, but it seemed terribly old-fashioned to us at that moment against the other music scores and things. I got a tremendous thrill out of *Les Noces* and things like that, and I loved the Massine repertoire also.

Was Massine easy to work with as a choreographer?

Oh yes. I had already had a little experience with him in London because he had left Diaghilev and had been running a small company in London with Lydia Lopokova, and I had been a member of that. I knew a little bit of his style, but, of course, I didn't learn his repertoire until I got into the Diaghilev company. Nijinska was in sole control when I joined them. She was not only our choreographer, but she was also our teacher. She insisted on giving classes because she felt that the style of her choreography was not understood completely by the company, and so we had our daily lesson from her, as well as all her new works mounted on us.

Was she a good teacher?

Very interesting teacher. Not the traditional, orthodox work that you have got to have in your background, which I had already had for years. She was wonderful for me because it was semi-choreographic classes. Some of them disliked it for that reason. But I had had so much traditional training by then that I found it a joy. And, of course, for a newcomer it was a great lead towards the style of her choreography.

Tell me about the début of Balanchine as a choreographer with the company.

I can remember him. He and Danilova joined the company with Gevergeva and Efimov, who later went to the Paris Opéra. The four of them joined. Diaghilev saw them at the Empire in London; they had come out of Russia to do some dancing on their own. He was a young man, and came with us for the first season in Monte Carlo. Nijinska was very busy, and they gave him the opera ballets to do. She simply couldn't face another season of opera ballets. He danced in the company, somewhat indifferently, but we all adored him. I can remember him so well, though I can't remember the opera just now, the first time he ever arranged anything. It was a *pas de trois* in some opera for myself, Doubrovska and Danilova. And I remember coming into the dressing room after, and saying, 'I think he's a genius.' It was such a lovely dance. Just for an opera ballet, which is very hard.

It showed right from the start, his quality?

Oh, right from the start, because the quality he could put into an opera ballet was absolutely extraordinary. But he was always very funny. He took it all as a huge joke, took all the opera ballets as a huge joke; he wasn't the least bit pompous, but he was obviously going to be the coming one when Nijinska left. We knew he was going to take over.

Looking at a ballet like Train Bleu, *do you think there was a tendency for Diaghilev to go for novelty at any price during this period?*

Definitely. I think there was a phase of novelty at any price. He lost Massine at the height of Massine's strength, which was a very serious blow to them. He took on Nijinska then, who, I think, he always felt, from his angle anyway, would have certain limitations of repertoire. She only stayed with us fifteen or eighteen months. He really was very much at sea when he first lost Massine. She did some lovely things for him, Nijinska. Of course, I think *Les Noces* is one of the greatest ballets still that has ever been produced. I owe so much to her as a professor, as a teacher, and I have the greatest admiration for her. But I don't think she ever fulfilled everything Diaghilev was looking for, and even the ballets she did for him, *Train Bleu* and things like that, they are very experimental. I don't think they are important, not really. They were amusing, some of them were interesting, some lovely choreography, but I think the beginning of the Balanchine era, from the modern angle, is more important.

Do you think there was a tendency for design to overshadow the choreography?

Well, not necessarily overshadow. I think it was the efforts they were making to show how important design was. But then again Diaghilev had always done that. It had been the same before the war. In the big ballets he produced before the 1914 War Bakst practically outshone everything else. No, he has always had this thing that the décor and the ballet itself, the choreography, were of equal importance. In fact, at times he slightly sacrificed us to some of the designs.

What was the atmosphere of the company like at the time you were with them? Was it a happy company?

I was very fond of them all, I got on with them awfully well. We were all so hideously overworked. An uncomfortable hard life which the dancers had, and the travelling was terrible. We took these long journeys, eight in second-class carriages, you couldn't sleep or anything. No, no, it was very different from today. No hotels were found for you. You had to arrive anywhere and find your hotel, whatever happened to you. It was a pretty rough, hard life, and the work was hard.

You weren't very well paid, were you?

No, we weren't well paid, but we weren't too badly paid. I was never short of money. You had to be careful, but we were not particularly badly paid. You were better paid than the English ballet was when it started, far better.

Can I ask you now about the technical standards of the company at that time?

Purely technically, I wouldn't say that it could compare with the standards of today. I am talking about the rank and file, I'm not talking about great names. Of course, they are the same; through any generations you have great stars. There's always that sense of equality, according to the period of work. But the ballet, the *corps de ballet*, were nothing technically to touch what you see today. This I really do emphasize. People have forgotten. And, of course, technically speaking, I don't think the same difficulties were asked of us. It was all-round style, musicality and interpretation. Perhaps the artistic side of it was extremely high and very high standards were asked of you and expected of you. But technically, no, the *corps de ballet* dancer of today is very much stronger; much more is asked of them than was asked of a dancer in those days.

And yet the Cecchetti method is still taught?

The Cecchetti method is very fine, but it is the school of an individualist, a very specialized branch, even of the Italian school. I think it's a wonderful system, but it's not the beginning and end, and I learned just as much from other teachers. Though I greatly appreciate the years I spent with him, it was by no means the start or the finish of my own technical development. It was a part of it. It was extremely appropriate to that particular period of Diaghilev works, because his big repertoire then was very much for the males. It's interesting – people don't realize that when I was in the company, there were more men than women. That's unheard of in any company today. I think we had about twelve more men in the company than we had women. That shows you that the emphasis was very much on demi-character work, and here again, I think the Cecchetti system, springing as it does very much from the Bournonville school, the Danish school, was particularly apt and good for this sort of work. Quite a lot of the old ballerinas in Russia – and I met a good many in the company there – didn't like it, didn't like his work. They preferred their own pure school, but all of them admitted how much he had added and given them. But it's not a school that you can completely finish in; in my opinion you have to go on to other teachers.

What about Diaghilev himself? What impression did he make on you when you first met him?

Well, I was really always too scared of him to say that I had looked him straight in the face. He was the most extraordinarily frightening man, at least to me; I don't think to everybody. There were members of the company who had no sense of fear of him at all, and I simply couldn't understand it. I can remember this extremely big head, a wonderfully shaped head, but it was an enormous head. And he – it was a frightening personality, and strange anyway to a humble member of his company. A strange sense of aloofness. You just felt he came into the room, and there you all were, and you were just a fly on the wall, and if he did see you, and remembered you, he was very polite and nice, but you felt perhaps that even then he was just thinking of something else. I never really got anywhere with him at all.

Looking back, what you do think of his achievement in holding the company together?

Oh, extraordinary. One doesn't quite realize it, of course. No subsidy of any sort, though he got help. As I said, we were very well looked after. If you were ill, you were paid. Nobody thought of stopping money if you were ill, it went on. I don't know how he did it. Mind you, life was much cheaper then, it was a much easier thing to do, but we didn't dance every night. Going round the opera houses in Europe, the most you might give would be perhaps three or four performances a week. Only when we came to London did we dance every night, or in Paris. And think of the expense of this company. But, of course, we were a small company.

Was he a good businessman?

Not really a good businessman, but I think he had quite good business advice. He could be pretty extravagant from time to time. No, I don't suppose he was a businessman at all. But he had no competition. He was the one and only during the time, and what ballet public there was was pro-Diaghilev on all possible occasions, and that's all I can say about it. He just managed to keep us going in the most remarkable way.

Do you think he had an artistic policy?

Oh, quite definitely. It was a progressive policy, but he had a great respect for tradition, which, of course, is right. There was nothing revolutionary about Diaghilev. It was evolution always. And he adored, when we were in the south of France, collecting the old ballerinas. Trefilova came along there to dance *Lac des Cygnes*, and this sort of thing he was marvellous about. You never lost touch, or your respect as a young dancer, with traditional roots, and this was wonderful, because the company consisted of young people like myself with very advanced ideas, and strong opinions about everything. Really traditional ballerinas from the Imperial Ballet, and men the same, thought everything was frightful, but the balance was very good. He was very, very firm that tradition was what he wanted, and that he wasn't going to lose it.

I remember his excitement when he was asked to bring the ballet to La Scala in Italy. This just shows his strong traditional feeling. I had left the company then, and he said would I come to the Scala to dance in *Aurora's Wedding*, the Third Act of *Sleeping Beauty*. He wanted me to do the Pizzicato and the Finger Variation. He had already had lots of people doing it since I had left, but he was so keen on the season, he wanted who he thought, or they thought, perhaps, most suited to this dance to do it on that occasion. And I think they considered I had proved to be among the ones most suited to these two particular dances. They were very quick dances and easy for me to do – I was a quick dancer – and he wanted me to go all the way to La Scala to do these two variations. And I said I really didn't think I could. I had just taken up production work, and I was at the Festival Theatre, Cambridge, and he said, 'But think, think, you will be able to say you have danced at La Scala.' It was extraordinary. I didn't care a bit, but to him it meant an awful lot.

Do you think the experience you had with the company stood you in good stead when you came to run a company yourself?

Oh, I owe everything I know to that company. If you chose to sit around and watch, you could learn, as I say, the tradition, the importance of tradition, you could learn all the modern tendencies, you could see the organization as a whole, you got used to the criticisms, the attitude, the spacing of rehearsal sheets. All that side was very well done. I have learned everything I know. I don't know what I would have done without it.

I think he came at a time when it was extremely important for anyone who was going to do anything to see the thing in the making, and, of course, he had round him real enthusiasts. The start of his company, after all, what was it? Something that will probably happen one day in the Royal Ballet. A group of brilliant but rather disgruntled dancers felt they were a new generation and wanted things to move on a bit, and they broke away, really to come under his guidance, from the establishment. Well, you must have an establishment, and he was the first person to recognize that, and you must have these healthy breakaways. We are quite a way off that yet, but he was a very shining example of a healthy breakaway, which shook Paris, and shook every country in Europe that had a sort of static establishment. We hadn't got one here at all, but it was the basis, the start of ours, which meant that our establishment wasn't quite as static even from the very beginning as some of those which were already in existence.

Henri Sauguet

1901 BORDEAUX–1989 PARIS

French composer Henri Sauguet was a member of the circle around Satie and a friend of Cocteau. His score for Diaghilev, La Chatte (1926), was the first of more than thirty ballets he was to write for various companies.

Can I ask you first about the circumstances in which you received the commission for the score of La Chatte?

My goodness, it's already forty years ago. Serge Diaghilev, for the return to the company of the celebrated dancer Olga Spessivtseva, wanted to create a new ballet for her, and he asked me to write a ballet on a scenario which was signed Sobeika, which, of course, was Boris Kochno's pseudonym, and this scenario was *La Chatte*. It fulfilled many of my wishes, first of all the great hope I'd had just at that time – I was twenty-six – to enter into this famous company by writing a ballet, and in doing so to become one of those musicians who people noticed, because the musicians chosen by Diaghilev were always very happy as a result of it. And so I accepted this plot about a cat. I've always actually loved cats, and I've lived with cats, and the idea of putting into music the story of a cat which is transformed into a woman was for me a double pleasure.

He made me come to the Hôtel de Paris, where he lived when he was in Paris, and with this extraordinary sense of hierarchy which he had, because he was a prince, Diaghilev received me as if I was already one of the great composers. In fact, you almost became one of the great composers by working for his company, and he asked me to write *La Chatte*. That gave me the pleasure, for the first time in my life, of going with him to the south of France, which I didn't know. I was in effect invited to write the ballet in Monte Carlo, where it was going to be presented, and where the company was going to be for rehearsals. So I spent two months in Monte Carlo, during which time I wrote the ballet. It was first given, if I remember rightly, in 1927 at the Opéra in Monte Carlo, with Spessivtseva and Serge Lifar.

How did you work during rehearsals?

It was something which had been extremely well organized. I worked during the day and in the evening I went to the casino. I met there the company pianist and Balanchine, who was going to be the choreographer, and I showed him the music I had written. The following day it was put into rehearsal. Every day towards noon Diaghilev would come by and members of royalty or important people or artists would come and listen to what I had done. Then I came back and got on with the work. This way the ballet was born little by little from a very close collaboration between Balanchine and myself.

The one thing which had been left unknown to me was that I had not had a chance of seeing the full décor until the first rehearsal on-stage, the décor and costumes of Antoine Pevsner and Naum Gabo. Diaghilev, as you know, was really involved in all the new movements and very much influenced by what was happening in terms of innovation. The sort of return to Delibes, which one can find in my music, a sort of re-creation of that mood, I think it might have shocked him a little bit. But he wanted at the same time to show spectators that he hadn't abandoned the avant-garde. So he asked that the décor should be done by two Russian constructivists, who had just come to the West, Pevsner and Gabo. It was, I think, the first ballet which had an abstract décor, with these costumes made of cellophane, very synthetic, which admirably incorporated the choreography of Balanchine, which he must have understood in advance, as well as a transparency that reflected the limpidity of the music.

Almost by chance?

Well, you can't really say it was chance. Diaghilev had thought about it. The risk was rather more for me, or for Pevsner and Gabo. I was very afraid when I saw the sets, and I thought, my goodness, he's going to have an absolute horror of this sort of limpid, clear, simple music that I've written. But not at all, he understood extremely well, and I think the great success of the ballet – because it was so, within a few months it had reached a hundred performances – came just from this successful blend of dance, choreography, décor and music. This was what Diaghilev succeeded with better than anyone else, because this man had in his hands the reins and he was so powerful that he could control all the different elements of the spectacle and of the ballet.

How did you find Diaghilev himself?

The man was extremely impressive. I had actually already met him some years before, because at an earlier date he had wanted to have a ballet from me. I was introduced to him by Erik Satie. He had asked to meet me, having heard a little of my music. Satie brought us together in 1924, that is to say three years earlier. Even at that time I was extremely impressed by him. I must say that contacts with him were always of great courtesy; he avoided anything which could be hurtful, even though during the rehearsals he didn't lack force and at times violence, as everything went through his hands and in front of his eyes.

Nevertheless, he had a manner with his composers which was quite extraordinary. I remember, for example, he invited me to lunch with him at the Café de Paris in Monte Carlo, and during the lunch he spoke of his experiences with Rimsky-Korsakov, with Stravinsky, with Debussy, with Ravel, with other musicians whom he had had attached to his company, and I was asking myself where this was all leading. He began to explain to me that he had actually had to ask these great musicians at times to make either cuts or modifications to their work. It turned out that it was a way of telling me that in the finale of my ballet, perhaps certain bars could either be replaced or cut. It simply knocked me sideways. I absolutely wasn't used to manners of this kind, and I must tell you that he's the only one who ever took that tone in asking for cuts. I've written twenty-four ballets since that time, and I've seen them – how can I put it? – *de toutes les couleurs*, but never in such beautiful colours as Diaghilev showed that day.

And how did you find the atmosphere of the Ballets Russes?

Oh, it was riveting. You didn't join a company, it was like going into a house, or perhaps a court, if you wish, where you became one of the musicians of the prince during the time. It was continual work; everything was concentrated on the ballet, on the performance that day, and on the future, and there was an extraordinary and very exhilarating atmosphere. I must say, for me it is an unforgettable memory, which marked me for the rest of my life. I have not always found that atmosphere in the work that I've done for the ballet. I was really very spoilt, and when you think about it, it was prodigious, and Diaghilev was the absolute master, the man who did everything and saw everything. Nothing escaped him. I have never since seen a man with such an understanding or such a sense of the science of it all, such capacity for work and at the same time a sort of grandeur and magnetism. He was a man of extraordinary allure, absolutely unique in his way.

Anton Dolin

1904 SLINFOLD–1983 PARIS

Patrick Healey-Kaye first appeared with the Ballets Russes as Patrikeyeff in the Sleeping Princess *in 1921. He rejoined the company in 1923 and was renamed Dolin. For a time Diaghilev's chosen companion, he appeared regularly in leading roles until the last season. He founded the Markova-Dolin Ballet after Diaghilev's death and later directed London Festival Ballet for ten years.*

What was the atmosphere like when you joined the company in November 1923?

It was a wonderful atmosphere, because it was an atmosphere of work, it was a dedication to the dance. Very hard: classes every morning at nine o'clock, rehearsals that went on immediately afterwards. Most of the afternoon we'd be rehearsing, and if we were not performing in the theatre at night, there'd be another rehearsal in the evening. It was a wonderful atmosphere to work in, the studio was marvellous. I first arrived here in November 1923. Believe it or not, I was a shy and timid young man. But suddenly arriving from London via Paris into the midst of all these very great dancers. I didn't speak French, I didn't speak Russian. I must say, the first few days I was here I felt miserable. In fact, I think if I'd had the money, I'd have got on the first train and gone home.

What was the Monte Carlo Opera House like to dance in?

Lovely theatre to dance in, lovely stage. When you think of all the many ballets that we created in this theatre: Nijinsky danced with Karsavina *Spectre de la Rose* for the first time in this theatre. The theatre is a perfect size. If I had the money and could build a theatre, I'd copy the theatre in Monte Carlo. The stage and the audience, it's a perfect combination.

Tell me about the company's repertory at the time you joined.

It was a very large repertoire, and you mustn't forget that if we are going back to 1923, '24, the repertoire still consisted of *Schéhérazade, Sylphides, Thamar, Igor*. In fact, I think the very first ballet I danced in was in the *corps de ballet* in *Prince Igor*. And the next one was *Schéhérazade*. I hated them both, I might say. But in 1924, the beginning of '24, already the new repertoire was being rehearsed by the choreographer who was with us then, Nijinska. She was a marvellous person, Nijinska. I was absolutely devoted to her. I suppose the teachers I owe most in my life were Astafieva in London and then Nijinska. The ballet she was preparing at that time was *Les Biches. Les Noces* was also being performed in Monte Carlo when I arrived, *Les Biches* was being rehearsed, and at that time Diaghilev was preparing a rather interesting season of the Gounod operas, *Médecin Malgré Lui*, *La Colombe* and one other, I've forgotten its name [*Philémon et Baucis*]. Anyway, there were three Gounod operas, and there was a ballet in two of them. I danced in the *Médecin Malgré Lui* with Lubov Tchernicheva. I should say it was my first almost leading role, but it was an opera ballet, not actually one of the ballets. My first great role.

My début was an exciting event, because everybody was hoping that they were going to get the role of Daphnis in *Daphnis and Chloe*. I remember when the rehearsals were going to begin for this great revival, because it hadn't been revived since Nijinsky. And they saw the names Lydia Sokolova and Anton Dolin up on the board. I think it caused quite a lot of consternation in the company. I was delighted that I was going to have Lydia Sokolova to dance with me, not only because by that time we had become fairly good friends. At the beginning I don't think she liked me a bit. She thought I was a bit cocky and conceited, which really I wasn't. It was much more a defence that I was putting on. I don't think I was conceited. I thought I was a pretty good dancer. I must have been quite a good dancer at that time, otherwise I wouldn't have had the roles that I got, but I was delighted to get them, believe me. But I was delighted that it was Hilda, as we called her, because first she was English and it was much easier for me from the point of view of rehearsals. The ballet was being revived with the memory of what they remembered of Fokine and then Nijinska was going to rechoreograph, or choreograph in her own way, certain of the scenes. I know that my solo was completely choreographed by her, and the *pas de deux* that we eventually did also. Later, of course, came the *Train Bleu*, which was a great ballet for me. That was Jean Cocteau's work. He wrote it, Nijinska choreographed it, and I danced it for the first time a few months later in Spain, where it was first done, and then in Paris.

It was an interesting period, I think, for me in the Diaghilev Ballet, because when Nijinska left the company, much to my regret, Balanchine arrived. So I was there for the first advent of Balanchine and his choreography, and before he was ready to create ballets for the Diaghilev Ballet, Massine was brought back to the company. And Massine came principally to create a ballet for Alicia Nikitina, myself and Serge Lifar. It was Lifar's first leading role, that of Flore. The ballet was *Zéphyre et Flore*. I had a tremendous admiration for Massine as a choreographer and a person, but I found working with him terribly difficult. I think I was so imbued with the work I had done with Nijinska, she had done a tremendous thing for me and my career, I didn't suddenly want to switch. But it was a wonderful period from my point of view, that period of the Diaghilev Ballet from '24 to '29, to have worked with three great choreographers, Nijinska, then Massine and later Balanchine. The last two ballets that were done by Diaghilev in London were the *Fils Prodigue* – Lifar, and myself, Doubrovska – and *Le Bal*, which I danced with Danilova, and both of these were done by Balanchine.

What was Balanchine like?

George was very quiet. In fact, I don't think I have ever known George otherwise. He's a quiet person, never loses his temper, unlike me, because I lose my temper very easily. I was very interested to work with him. I found him again difficult to work with, or I think most dancers find him difficult in the beginning. He's got a special style. There's no question of it. I don't like the words 'Balanchine dancer', but I do agree that there is such a thing as a style of choreography which is typically Balanchine. His ballets then were more story-wise, whereas today they become more abstract. *Fils Prodigue* was a story; *Le Bal*, that was more or less abstract. It was Chirico who did the designs for that.

How did the Fokine ballets seem when they were revived?

Some of the new ballets of my period have not lived, whereas most of the Fokine ballets have lived.

Did the company enjoy revivals?

I think the company liked revivals, yes. I naturally, when I first joined the company, was delighted to dance in those ballets. I had never danced in them. Learning them perhaps was not as difficult as learning some of the more modern ballets we were to do later. Whereas the modern ballets we did in that period 1924–29, few of them really have lived. *Fils Prodigue* has lived, *Les Biches* and *Les Noces* have been revived, as you know, whereas the Fokine ballets, the great ballets of Mikhail Fokine, have lived and will go on living, and exist in practically every repertoire of every ballet company today.

Why is that?

Why, I don't know. How can I tell you? Why does a Raphael and Tintoretto and Rubens live, whereas a lot of modern painters – well, they are very expensive, but will they live for ever?

But didn't everyone have something like Cléopâtre *by this time?*

I think the last time *Cléopâtre* was danced probably was in Barcelona in 1925 or '26. But when Diaghilev was in London in 1929, there was a very good season at the Royal Opera House. But I remember distinctly that Eric Wollheim, who was Diaghilev's manager for many years, tried in vain, completely in vain, to get Diaghilev to revive *Schéhérazade* and *Cléopâtre* for the 1929 season. Diaghilev said *no*, he could not. Diaghilev always contended that they had seen those great ballets danced by great artists, and the artists were no longer there to dance them, and he didn't want to see them. He said, 'After all, this is my ballet company. I have to see the performance every night, and I want to see the ballets that I like, and not the ballets that the public want to see. I'm selfish, but that's my way.'

Did Diaghilev consider what the public wanted?

Yes, I think, a little. I'll tell you one in particular, which was *Aurora's Wedding*, which was really a one-act version of the *Sleeping Beauty*. It was a popular favourite with the company, and that Diaghilev did revive every year. Another ballet that was a very great favourite with the public – not so much, I think, with Diaghilev – was the ballet that Beecham arranged the music for, *Les Dieux Mendiants*. It was a charming ballet, very popular, beautifully danced by Woizikowski, I remember. I wasn't in it, but I always loved watching it. That was Balanchine. That was a great favourite; I don't think Diaghilev cared for it, but the public demanded it. *Sylphides* was always a popular ballet, *Petrushka* he revived for the last season in London. I remember Karsavina dancing the doll, I was the Moor and Leon Woizikowski danced Petrushka. That was very exciting to me.

Was Diaghilev still interested in the nineteenth-century classical works?

I think he would have done more. In fact, there was no question that had Diaghilev lived . . . And it affected me and my career to a great extent. It affected, incidentally, also Markova's career, because Diaghilev was going to revive in 1930 *Giselle*. When I went back to the company in 1928, one of the chief reasons, one of the incentives for me to go back was the promised revival of *Giselle* with Olga Spessivtseva. He talked to me a great deal about it in the last season in Monte Carlo. He talked about it in London, he talked about it when Spessivtseva came to dance with Lifar, myself, Doubrovska, Danilova, in *Swan Lake* during the last season. He would have revived *Giselle*, and I often wonder what that revival would have been. A great many things that I have put into my various revivals and restagings of *Giselle* are various things that Diaghilev told me in 1929.

Some people have suggested he lost interest in ballet in his later years.

Nonsense, he never lost interest in anything. He was always madly keen on the ballet, madly keen on his dancers, a friend to his dancers to the very end. He was a sick man during the last year of his life, unfortunately. He was even spoilt, he was spoilt by his friends. He was told by his doctors not to drink much champagne, not to eat sweet foods, he was diabetic, and he just wouldn't listen. He enjoyed good food. Who doesn't enjoy good food, let's face it. But had he taken a little more care of himself, perhaps he would have lived a few more years. There were a great many more things that he was out to accomplish. He had not lost interest in the ballet, I know.

Was the general level of dancing higher than now?

No, I think not. I think technically there's no question that the ballet companies today are stronger. Artistically perhaps not.

What do you mean?

I think we matured a little later. We had to learn our roles and know our roles better than young dancers do today. I think they mature a little too quickly. With Diaghilev we had an education. We would go on these tours to Barcelona, we'd go to Italy, to Germany. We were told to go and see good paintings, go to the museums. Diaghilev himself was an inveterate museum-goer. The first time I went to Italy it was nothing but museums and churches. I only seemed to spend more time on the beach when we were in Venice on the Lido. But now, looking back, I realize what a wonderful education it was. And I feel pretty proud, as a young English boy longing to be a great dancer, that this man had this great interest in me and undoubtedly did help me tremendously. I would never have become the dancer that I hope I became if it hadn't been for the tremendous help and knowledge of everything that Diaghilev gave me.

Can you describe Diaghilev?

Diaghilev was a very large person, I would say, in more ways than one, with a great brain. He was a big man. To describe him is difficult. I suppose he ambled gracefully along. I remember he was very conscious of people walking. One of the first things he said to me when I arrived in Monte Carlo was, 'You walk very badly. You must learn to walk, not only to dance.' I think I have been conscious of people walking ever since. He had tremendous charm. There was nothing he couldn't get out of you, get from his dancers, because he had all that charm. But we also knew with that charm that Diaghilev had more, a tremendous knowledge, a great artistic culture. I loathe the word 'artistic' as a rule. This man had everything at his fingertips. He knew music, he knew painting, he knew dancing, he knew dancers and he knew people. A lot of people here referred to Diaghilev as a snob. I don't think he was a snob. I believe Madame Karsavina referred to him in the same words as I would, as an artistic snob. I think that's a very good description of Diaghilev. He loved to be surrounded by the right people, he hated second-raters. He couldn't stand anything that wasn't absolutely first-class. He liked to live in the best hotels. As he said, 'I have the best ballet in the world. I can take it anywhere I want, and if I am going to take it to the best opera houses, I am also going to live in the best hotels.'

Could he be amusing?

When he wanted to be. When he wanted to be entertaining, he could be very entertaining. He had a marvellous flow of language; he spoke French beautifully, he hated speaking English. With me he had to speak English in the beginning because I, as I say, didn't understand a word of French or Russian. Both languages I learned fairly well later. But he could be a very entertaining person. He played the piano well, he had a charming, very high alto tenor singing voice. A lot of people think of Diaghilev as being a person who only cared for the modern works and the modern composers. I can assure you I have sat with Diaghilev on the Piazza in Venice, and he practically had tears in his eyes as he listened to the arias of Puccini, *Bohème* and *Madame Butterfly*. He adored Puccini, absolutely worshipped him.

What did you talk about?

We talked about music, painting, we talked about the theatre. Diaghilev was extremely interested in the theatre and theatre artists apart from the ballet. Of course, all the dancers I got to know through Diaghilev naturally, but I first knew Madame Elvira Popesco, I knew the Guitrys through Diaghilev. Popesco was one of his favourite actresses. The first thing I saw in Paris was *Revue de Cuisine*. We talked about modern art. There were times, I'll be perfectly honest, when it got a bit boring, because I like to do a few other things. And if I dared mention that I'd like to go off and play a game of tennis, it was completely alien to Diaghilev. The word 'tennis' didn't enter his vocabulary. I like to play tennis and I like to go off and swim and dive too. But partly that was the revolt in me to a certain extent. I knew that this was a great education for me when I was young and I am grateful for it, but on the other hand always traipsing around and always having to go to museums – I would like at times to go off and play tennis or go to a good movie.

Did you have rows?

I have always been argumentative. We both have that in common, Ninette de Valois and I, we both love to argue, both love to win our point. I'm afraid I did not often win my point with Diaghilev, but we'd argue with him sometimes, much to my shame, as I say now, perhaps.

What is the main legacy of your years with Diaghilev?

It was the whole influence of that company that has remained with me for the rest of my life. And anything good that I have achieved I think has been done because of the wonderful education and the wonderful chance that I had mixing with these great artists at a very impressionable and young age.

Tell me about the party in your studio in London that Diaghilev came to in the summer of 1929.

That was a great occasion, but I remember it as a rather sad occasion. I had asked Diaghilev three days beforehand, before the première of *Le Bal* in the summer of 1929, if he would come to a party that I was going to give in my studio. He said he would if he felt well enough. And I remember speaking to Lady Juliet Duff, and I said, 'Juliet, please try and bring Mr Diaghilev with you.' They were great friends. I knew instinctively what I must do. I had a very ordinary upright piano in my studio – I hadn't really been able to afford a good one – and three days before the party I went to Harrods, where I bought myself a very good Blüthner piano, a three-quarter grand. I knew that that would be the first thing, when Diaghilev came into my studio, he would look at. And it was, funnily enough, when he did arrive, looking rather ill on the arm of Lady Juliet, the first thing. He went over and he looked at the piano, and he said, 'You know, you have very good taste, because Blüthner is a very good make.' And it is one of those things you instinctively think he would have thought about. And he stayed about an hour.

But historically it's interesting because it was the last party Diaghilev ever went to in his life. Four days later the season was to end. And two days before the season actually ended in London, all were gathered together on the stage and Diaghilev came to wish us all goodbye, and we wished him a happy holiday. He was supposed to have gone off for a good cure. Unfortunately he didn't go for that cure, he went off and had a good time in Venice, where he died, as we all know, on 19 August 1929. I was making a film at the time, the first talkie made in England, called *Dark Red Roses*, and I was sitting in the garden resting between takes. Balanchine choreographed that ballet with Lydia Lopokova and myself; we were doing the dance sequence in it. The *Evening News* came out, and I saw on the poster 'Death of a Great Impresario'. And I knew instinctively somehow this was Diaghilev. And we were very sad that night. We had to dance, we had to make the film. I don't think any of us felt like it, but we did.

Alicia Markova

1910 LONDON–

*At fourteen, Markova was the youngest dancer
ever engaged by the Ballets Russes, and she had
an unusually affectionate relationship with
Diaghilev. She was to become the first great
classical ballerina from Great Britain.*

When did you first see Diaghilev?

The first time I ever saw Diaghilev I was ten years of age at Princess Astafieva's, where I went to class. I didn't know that Diaghilev was coming in to look for some extra dancers for the *corps* of the *Sleeping Princess*. So I did my class, and then this very great man came in, and he saw the older dancers. After the lesson there was a little whispering, and Astafieva asked me if I would dance. My usual dance at that time was Rubinstein's Waltz Caprice, so I danced. And that was the very first time he saw me. Apparently I impressed him; I didn't realize it at the time, but it was all arranged that I was to go into the *Sleeping Princess* as the tiniest fairy in the world. I was being written in as the Fairy Dewdrop or something, and Nijinska was to do a new variation for me, but unfortunately I went down with diphtheria, so that was all out. Anyway, I had to wait months to recover. And while I was recovering, he sent a message that he knew how disappointed I was, but that I could come to the performances of the *Sleeping Princess*. That's how I was so fortunate in seeing all those very great dancers. Diaghilev said I was to continue working very hard with Astafieva, and when he returned, he would see me dance again, and perhaps I would go into the *corps*. Even that was fantastic to think about and work for.

Then suddenly, later that year, Diaghilev brought the company back to the Coliseum with Sir Oswald Stoll, and first thing sent word, 'How is the little one?', as he used to call me apparently. Astafieva reported that I had been working very hard and progressing well. He said, all right, he would see me dance. I was still only thirteen. I was whisked round by taxi, and Diaghilev arrived with Dolin (Pat, as he was to me – we had been trained in the school together) and Nijinska. I had an audition. Two hours it lasted, until it was time for them to return for the evening show at the Coliseum. I was put through everything. So I thought that was that. I hoped I had done well. Two or three days later the phone went again. Mr Diaghilev. They were coming along to audition me again; this time with Diaghilev were Madame Nijinska and Boris Kochno. So I had another two hours' audition, when I was put through God knows what, and I still didn't hear anything. Then the next day when I went to class Astafieva said it was more or less decided that I would join the company. But, of course, it was such a problem. They didn't know what to do with a child. I think Nijinska had children, and it was decided that I would be put in her care and we would board with her, my governess and myself, and she would be responsible for feeding me and everything, and also for my classes, to watch my artistic training. Then within a few days suddenly Nijinska was out. Something happened. So I thought, here we go again! This is the end.

About a week later we got a phone call again. Mr Diaghilev is coming to audition me, again. Thank God, I didn't have any nerves. I was, I suppose, the only person that had never been afraid of Diaghilev. It was strange, he never instilled fear into me. So for this audition Diaghilev arrived with Kochno again and George Balanchine, and Pat Dolin. That audition lasted for three hours. Balanchine, I don't know the different things he asked me to do. I was doing double turns in the air, and *fouettés* from one end of the room to the other, which I could do, and I didn't realize at that time that nobody else could do them. Only the men did double turns in the air. And Dolin partnered me for all the partnering work, and so after three hours they left. Then on my fourteenth birthday the news came through. Diaghilev had decided he would take me. So that was it. I was in the great Diaghilev company at fourteen. On New Year's Eve there was a big party at Astafieva's studio after the show that night and Diaghilev asked me to dance my Waltz Caprice, and I was introduced as the baby of the company. So I left for Monte Carlo later in January in the care of Ninette de Valois, and that was when we were first brought together.

The first ballet you did was a new version of Le Rossignol *by Balanchine. What was it like working with him? Difficult?*

Oh, it was terribly difficult, but so interesting, I must say. I adored it. First of all, I suppose, it was a different world, because that time, musically, I had been brought up on Rubinstein's Waltz Caprice and the Pizzicato from *Sylvia*. That was my musical education. And then suddenly to be thrown into Stravinsky's *Nightingale*, which at that time couldn't be played at rehearsal by the pianist. We had to have the pianola, on the rolls. My rehearsals would be called late in the evening with Balanchine, or on Sundays, when the company were more or less resting and quiet. In the morning I would have my classes with Cecchetti and he would be instilling me to turn out, and then I would have to come in the evenings with

Balanchine, and all these wonderful modern things he was giving me, all turned in. I found that rather confusing. In which direction do I go? And I think that was the first time it was explained to me that this is the difference between being a dancer and when you start being an artist. To dance you just turn out, but to be an artist, you have got to go in any direction.

Tell me about the costume.

Diaghilev said that Matisse would do a new costume for me. You can imagine, at fourteen, having a new costume designed by Matisse. It was all-over white silk tights, with large diamond bracelets on my ankles, and my arms, my wrists, and with a little white chiffon bonnet rimmed with white ospreys. It was all very modern, something to do with the Chinese legend of white being associated with death, so again confusion. That was perfect for the Paris opening, because nobody had any objections to a female appearing on-stage in all-over tights. But two years later, for the London première at the Prince's Theatre, suddenly the London manager was in a panic because of the Lord Chamberlain. At that time it wasn't permitted to appear like that. So there was this terrible situation where I was allowed to appear at the Paris Opéra in the tights only, but before we came to London, we had to find Matisse to have the costume adjusted. That was when he designed those little white chiffon trousers to go over the tights, studded with rhinestone, and this little tunic that went over that also to make me decent. But today, to think about these things! It was very strange.

Let's talk about La Chatte, *the next ballet you were to be associated with.*

Oh, yes. Today, somehow, in the younger ballet student's mind I am always associated with *Giselle* and the little wings, and the Victorian era, but I was so lucky that I was in all the most modern productions and I always adored that. But with *La Chatte*, of course, we had all that mica. I didn't go into it when it was created, because Spessivtseva created it and had an accident, and then Nikitina took over and she hurt her foot, and then I went in, I think I was the third Cat. I was only sixteen at the time, but I was very observant. I had noticed that they complained so much about the floor because it was black, American cloth, terribly slippery in certain areas. And other areas, because of the very modern design, were like cotton, two surfaces, and I figured out that was causing the accidents. So when I took over, Balanchine put in the most difficult things, adding to what he had already choreographed, and I thought, I don't want to hurt my foot, I don't want to be put out, because it was such a wonderful ballet, marvellous role.

I had to solve this problem somehow, with this slippery floor, because otherwise I wasn't going to be able to do all these double turns in the air that Balanchine had given me, and all these pirouettes on pointe which he had added, so I suddenly remembered when I danced on a ballroom floor, I used to have rubbers put on my ballet shoes. So I thought, I am not going to say anything to anybody, I'm going to have my ballet shoes rubbered and see what happens. And that was the solution to the problem for me, I just wore rubbers. Nobody ever discovered, and I never had an accident.

Diaghilev gave you lots of tips about costume and make-up. Tell me about the time you danced Swan Lake.

Diaghilev decided he wanted me to be as simple as possible – no crowns and feathers. So I was to have a band with little diamonds and pearls just to keep my hair in place. For the first performance everything was fine. Then suddenly in the second performance, in the middle of the White Swan adagio, I don't know whether I was doing extra pirouettes, but suddenly down came the band and I finished with it round my neck. You can imagine how I felt. Because somehow with Diaghilev one always wanted everything to be just right, so I was mortified. I thought, now I'll never be allowed to dance it again. Afterwards he came on-stage, so I apologized. I called him Sergipops. I'd heard the Russian, and Sergei Pavlovich I couldn't get my tongue around, so to me he became Sergipop. I apologized, so he said these were things I would have to learn. 'For the next performance you will have to stick it on.' 'But what with?' He said, 'I don't mind. You stick your headdress, you stick your hair, you stick your wig, you stick your shoes, everything must be stuck on, because the audience must only ever see perfection. I don't mind how you do it, or what you do, but it has to be stuck on.' I went to the dressing room, and I thought, stick, stick, what do you use to stick? So I suppose my English upbringing came to the fore. I thought, seccotine. So from that day seccotine was always with me. And the next performance I had this little band stuck on with seccotine; my hair was seccotined. And I still have the little band today. And if you turn it on the other side, it still has the skin and the hair and everything where it had to be ripped off after the performance.

Professionalism as usual! Didn't Diaghilev ask you to find some bird of paradise feathers in Manchester?

Can you imagine! That to me explains Diaghilev. It was my first performance in the Blue Bird in *Aurora's Wedding*, and I had a new costume, and it was all ostrich feathers on the headdress and felt wonderful, so grown-up, so glamorous. And after the rehearsal he came on-stage and he said to the wardrobe mistress, 'Off with the headdress.' I wondered what was happening. Then he turned to Kochno and said, 'She must never wear ostrich feathers, ostrich feathers are vulgar. Now always remember, you must never wear ostrich feathers.' That was lesson number, I don't know how many. I said, 'Yes, Sergipop, but what am I going to wear for the performance tonight?' He said, 'You must always wear birds of paradise. They're elegant and graceful and they move beautifully, because you are small and light.' He turned to Kochno and said, 'She must have the headdress for tonight.' Kochno said, 'But, Sergei Pavlovich, in Manchester, how are we to find blue birds of paradise in Manchester on a Wednesday morning?' He said, 'I don't mind. I want the headdress for tonight.' And so, of course, Kochno thought of a way out. He said, 'And what about the money? Do you know what blue birds of paradise will cost?' Diaghilev said, 'Are they expensive?' So he said, 'My goodness me', threw up his hands in horror. With that he said, 'Impossible', and Kochno left.

But Diaghilev put his hands in his pocket, which, as you know, was very ample, and brought out two five-pound notes, the old kind. My mother was with me, and he handed the two five-pound notes to my mother. He said, 'Take her and go shopping, and get the blue birds of paradise for the headdress tonight.' We had the money, but we went all over Manchester, but couldn't find blue, but we found the natural bird of paradise, which we bought, and we fixed it. I was on that night. I made the headdress myself with the diamonds, which he wanted, the turban and the birds of paradise. I still have them in my collection. This to me was Diaghilev: blue birds of paradise in Manchester on a Wednesday morning, ready for the show that night.

He was always very kind to you.

To me he was wonderful, yes. I don't know whether it was being a child, but I had this affection, and also always thinking of my welfare, which, I suppose, the older members of the company just couldn't understand. Now, of course, when I think back, it must have been very strange.

You were ill one day and he gave you advice.

Oh, he came to a rehearsal, I think of *Nightingale*, and I wasn't there. I had a bad cold. And next day at rehearsal – he would always go like this [beckons] and call you over. He said, 'Why weren't you at rehearsal yesterday?' I said, 'I am very sorry, but I had a bad cold.' He said, 'Don't you rub down after work when you get very hot?' I said no, I didn't. He said, 'Don't you have cologne?' I said, 'I am very sorry, I can't afford it on £2.10 a week.' So again the hand went in the pocket . . .

He took an almost fatherly interest in you.

Yes, yes, he did. A little later I remember him saying to my mother if he had been a wealthy man, he would have adopted me. That he had never had a child, and it was the first time that he felt that he would have liked a child.

Tell me about your conversations with Diaghilev. What language did you speak?

Most people had the impression that he never spoke English. I believe he understood very well, and I didn't speak anything but English. Somehow we communicated. I think I was fourteen and I still had my English governess with me, and I was at rehearsal one morning, and suddenly Diaghilev went like this [beckons] and I went over. He looked at me and said, 'Afternoon', and I nodded. 'Four.' I said, 'Yes.' 'My hotel. You, Guggy governess, hotel, go, drive, flamenco, tea, chocolates.' I thought, I can't be hearing correctly. Anyway, I gave a big nod and went back and finished my rehearsal with Grigoriev, and, of course, four o'clock to me wasn't coming soon enough. I wanted to get there by three o'clock in case we lost the way and were late. We arrived in the lobby of his hotel. Four o'clock, no Mr Diaghilev. Five o'clock, still no Mr Diaghilev, and we sat. And hours are much later in Spain, and I kept saying to Guggy, my governess, maybe we made a mistake in the time. Then six o'clock came and she started saying, 'I'm sorry. Diaghilev or no Diaghilev' – she was being very English then – 'an appointment is an appointment. The appointment was for four o'clock. It is now gone six and we are going home.' Because my bedtime was 6.30. I didn't know what to do. I thought, this is terrible. I tried every excuse with her to delay things. Well, I delayed until about 6.15 and then I was dragged by the hand out of the hotel and home to bed.

I went to rehearsal next morning as usual, and Diaghilev walked in, and suddenly I see [beckons] again and I trot over. And he looks at me and he says, 'Where were you yesterday? You had an appointment, your rendezvous four o'clock.' I suppose it must have been the very first time the company, all the older members, had heard about this appointment, and they all said my governess was so wrong. 'For Diaghilev you wait all night. Nobody ever goes home.' But I said she was being a real English governess. They said, 'But you can't do this to Diaghilev.' So I thought, oh, this will probably be the end of my career, of my life, everything. So when he called me over, he said, 'You had a rendezvous.' I was this big in socks still, and Diaghilev, as you know, was very tall. And all the company could see was me saying, 'Yes, but you said four o'clock and I waited until 6.30 and you weren't there so I left.' This little thing talking to Diaghilev like this. Apparently, it was the first time in the whole history of the whole company that ever anybody had spoken back. Then he informed me that it was a great pity that I wasn't there because he was taking me to tea outside the city to see these wonderful Spanish dancers, and this was to begin my education and my knowledge.

Has the example of the company stayed with you, throughout your career?

Definitely. I have everything to thank him for. The artistic training, the knowledge, but not only that. When you think I was a little girl in her teens and whenever I didn't have a rehearsal of my own, I attended every orchestra rehearsal, every lighting rehearsal, anything that was going on. I wouldn't miss a thing. That, as I realized later, was what gave me the knowledge that I have been fortunate enough to have. And that's why I feel, with younger people, this is so important. With Diaghilev it wasn't only our work; he would always encourage you to take an interest in other artists, and what they were doing. At the Coliseum when we were in the variety bill, he'd say, 'Go down, there's a wonderful Chinese juggler on. Go down, don't miss them, go down, and stand in the wings and watch.' Or with somebody else he would say, 'Now watch the way they take their call.' The artistry, this was the marvellous thing. He made you aware of other artists, and to have an appreciation of other artists and other arts.

Osbert Lancaster

1908 LONDON–1986 LONDON

*Cartoonist and writer, Lancaster saw the Ballets
Russes in his youth. He later designed several
ballets for the Sadler's Wells and Royal Ballet
companies.*

Looking back on the Diaghilev Ballet, what particular things stay in your mind?

The first time I went I was very small. I was taken by my mother to the first season in 1919 at the Alhambra, and then later I was taken to see the *Sleeping Beauty*, with the sets by Bakst. And it was really quite extraordinary, because one never had seen anything like it before at all. The most glamorous spectacle, up to that moment, had been *Chu Chin Chow*. *Sleeping Beauty* was something absolutely out of this world. It was extraordinary, the impression it made, the visual impression. I can remember very, very little about the dancing, and practically nothing about the music, but I remember Lopokova as the Lilac Fairy. That and the sets were what remained in my mind.

People have suggested that in the 1920s the scenery became too prominent and outshone the dancers. Do you agree?

I don't think people made that criticism then, in the early ballets. I think that certain of the dancers did, and I have heard Ninette say we must always avoid what happened in the later period of Diaghilev, when the sets, particularly by Picasso or Chirico, or whoever it was, really became in her view more important than the dancers or the music. I don't think it was wholly true. But I think the best were what the Germans called *Gesamtkunstwerk*. It all fitted in.

Diaghilev did involve major painters, and that was new.

I think this is where he was so brilliant, the extraordinary sensitivity to change in the artistic atmosphere. Because in the early ballets – and Bakst, it boils down to, is a nineties artist – it is the end of art nouveau or *Jugendstil*, all that period. And, of course, Diaghilev himself edited what was an art nouveau magazine in Moscow. And then he realized, when the war was over, that the whole of this atmosphere had changed and that he must get hold of a totally different, new generation, represented by Braque and Picasso among his designers and Les Six of the new composers. Which

I think alienated quite a few of his original supporters, who longed for the early days of *Petrushka* and the *Lac*.

Has time justified their fears?

No, I don't think so. I think it is different. I think it is excellent to have great artists who are not prima facie stage designers brought into the theatre, because it is jolly good for the theatre. But they don't always turn out better designs. Where Benois and Bakst were tremendously important is not, as everybody thinks, the brilliance of the colour they used, particularly Bakst, but certainly, as with Benois in the *Pavillon d'Armide*, they were tremendously scholarly. It revived the style of stage design that had disappeared throughout the nineteenth century, the great painted perspectives that arise from the Bibiena school in the eighteenth century. And certainly the last act of *Sleeping Beauty* was completely architectural, with its great vistas and pillars and things going through. I think that was their great contribution, that they knew about architecture in which everything works visually, which with so many designers it does not.

Do you think we are still feeling the effects of this change?

Yes, I think so. In the world of ballet, certainly. I don't know whether in the theatre generally, because I think there has come a great reversal to the very solid built-up realistic sets, I mean Visconti, Zeffirelli, classic examples which are really representative examples of exactly the sort of thing against which Diaghilev or his designers reacted.

Who made up the audience at this time?

Well, an enormous number of my contemporaries at Oxford used to dash up and stand in the gallery. In those days, of course, the stalls were packed with smart London rather; then also what I think in those days was the Chelsea set, which is a very different thing from what the Chelsea set is now. High-minded artistic publishers and their wives, who played harpsichords. They were there in full force.

There was already a cult – the balletomane had arrived?

Yes, that, I think, from the 1920s onwards. I strongly suspect even before that, even before the war, that had started, almost contemporaneously with the first Paris season.

What effect did design for the ballet have on interior decoration or costume?

I think you can see that almost at once. Chiefly due to Bakst, and, I think, probably chiefly due to *Schéhérazade*, which was the one that caught the interior decorator's eye. Everywhere there were orange cushions, and that sort of dark purple, puce and aubergine colour and very sharp emerald greens, and a great deal of black was used to show these up. Then, of course, there was a great dress designer called Poiret, who was very much in the Diaghilev world, and he started those trouser suits, you know, harem suits, all of which stem from *Schéhérazade*.

Do you think Diaghilev courted this kind of influence, a bit of showmanship alongside the dedicated artist?

Oh well, that is why he was so important. Those two don't invariably go together. He was as ruthless as any American impresario, or any of the big tycoons of the theatre, but at the same time he had enormous taste. That was the really odd thing about him.

You saw him once, didn't you?

I saw him once. That was in Monte Carlo. I was very young, and I just remember in the foyer of that wonderful Garnier Opera House a crowd of people going to and fro through the rooms and back again, and I suddenly saw this dynamic figure, a big heavy man, white *mèche* and monocle, a very pale face charging through with a whole flutter of aides-de-camp and assistant publicity men, just following in his wake.

You worked with Oleg Polunin, who painted scenery for Diaghilev. Tell me about his methods.

It was the method prevailing very largely all over the continent, whereby you pin the canvas, the backcloth or whatever it is, on to the floor, and then you square it up, and walk about drawing with a piece of charcoal on the end of a bamboo stick, and then paint with long brushes. It has the enormous advantage that you don't have to use anywhere near so much size, you can put the paint on very liquid. If you are painting on a vertical paint frame, then, of course, unless it's fairly thickened up, the thing just drips down like that. Whereas if you paint on the ground, you can adopt a technique of washes and watercolour, which is an enormous advantage in interpreting something which is rather watercoloury in effect, say Laurencin's sets for *Les Biches*, that sort of thing, or some of Derain's sets. But it has a further advantage from the commercial point of view, from the company's point of view, in that owing to the fact that there is so little size you can just roll the thing up, just fold it, put it in the basket. It will come out almost like a handkerchief, whereas something painted on a paint frame, as most things are here, if you have got to roll it up very carefully, then ten to one, if it has remained rolled up for very long, it will start cracking, because of the size.

What do you think of revivals of Diaghilev ballets?

I thought the revival of *Petrushka*, which Benois redid the sets for, visually worked 100 per cent. I am not certain that choreographically it worked; the crowd scenes to me seemed to lack something from what I remembered of them as a young man. The revival of *Les Biches*, I think, worked visually pretty well, but I thought musically not at all. It didn't seem to me that the orchestra or conductor really understood what Poulenc was getting at. All the snap had gone out of that side of it.

Do you think ballet would exist today without the contribution of Diaghilev?

No, I imagine not. I imagine that the sort of ballets would be like Kurt Jooss and that rather, to me, intimidating Central European school of ballet. And, quite apart from anything else, having trained people like Ninette and others, who carried it on, there simply wouldn't have been the audience for it. What he did was to create an audience so that when he died, and the thing folded up, there was a tremendous void which people wanted filled. That is the real importance, that there was an audience to be satisfied, which was prepared to pay to be satisfied.

Were you influenced by what you saw?

Oh yes, enormously. I think the whole idea of abandoning three-dimensional sets altogether, and relying on the paint shop to produce the effect. And the far greater freedom. One got the idea that one could do things you would never have dreamt could have been done successfully, and you could get away with them. But, of course, you knew that Diaghilev had done them, or somebody in his company, and had got away with them. Therefore it was worth trying.

Cecil Beaton

1904 LONDON–1980 BROAD CHALKE, WILTSHIRE

Cecil Beaton, photographer and designer,
regularly saw the Ballets Russes in the 1920s.

As a designer yourself and someone who saw the Diaghilev Ballet, can I ask you what influence it had on theatre design in general?

Oh, tremendous. It can't be exaggerated, because people didn't pay much attention to design in the theatre. Drawing-room comedies and those sort of serious plays just had ordinary badly painted scenery. But the ballet influence infiltrated itself into musical comedy and then the theatre in general. One can't overestimate the importance of Diaghilev.

Was it basically a sense of colour that Diaghilev brought to the theatre?

Yes, I think it was mostly. For instance, when I first saw the ballet, it was interspersed with all the variety turns at the Coliseum. I was staggered, because I was accustomed to the sort of pastel colours of musical comedy. I don't think they went in for designers. They wrote at the bottom of the programme 'colour schemes by Comelli', whoever he was, but it was nearly always very, very vague, and indefinite. Suddenly you had this terrific impact of bright orange, bright emerald green, all the colours you had seen used sparingly, filling a whole stage.

Did it affect society as well, costume or interior decoration?

I think so. In the 1914–18 period there was this futuristic oriental fashion, tasselled cushions and black and white strange wallpaper. I think it did have a tremendous influence on Poiret. People like Ida Rubinstein, of course, were great influences, although they were rather laughed at at that time.

Is it still influential today?

I think it has been absorbed. I think that all ballet today has learned a great deal from all the various artists that Diaghilev was the first to employ.

Looking back on your experience of seeing ballet then, was it novelty that gave it success. Was it for a wide audience?

No, it was very special to begin with. There weren't balletomanes, there weren't great fans. It was a limited audience that appreciated it. That's why, I think, the poor troupe had to share the bill with the sea lions, and clowns and performing dogs. I think the Sitwells and a little group like that were very appreciative of it in London, but it's nothing like it is today. There weren't great ballet fans.

Did it make you want to get involved, even want to work with the Diaghilev Ballet?

I was too in awe. I don't think I ever felt I would reach that position. I suppose maybe I would like to have, but I was perfectly content to just go and see and watch and absorb.

Have any particular productions stayed in your mind?

Oh yes, I could describe all of them in detail. I don't know of any particular one. It's rather sad when you see these things disinterred after thirty years or whatever it is. *The Good-humoured Ladies* was one of the very first I ever saw, and the colours that Bakst created in those rather heavy rich costumes against a very dark background were absolutely staggering at the time.

What about the Goncharova designs for Firebird?

I never really liked the *Firebird* from the visual point of view. It was one of the few I wasn't terribly impressed by. I realize that of its sort it's good, but it just isn't my idiom.

What about Sleeping Princess?

I thought it was too much of a good thing. It was too sacchariny, too pretty. If you had just a slight moment of it, I think it would have been very interesting, but I couldn't absorb it. It was too much of a sugar cake for me.

And for the rest of the audience?

It was a great failure. I believe Diaghilev lost an enormous amount of money, and never recovered from it, but that's just beside the point.

Tell me about your own encounter with Diaghilev in Venice.

It was very pathetic, in a way. I had tremendous awe of him and when he appeared on the Piazza in Venice, he looked so magnificent, and I felt so sweaty and hot and insecure. It's awfully difficult to drag a great portfolio around and I had self-consciously brought this bulging portfolio from the place that I was living in and I was terribly keen that he should give me encouragement, and he was extremely polite and showed a great interest in all my activities. Then he started to look at all the pictures. One by one he turned the pages and I'm afraid one by one he saw copies, very poor ones, of all of the designs that he had commissioned. One was Marie Laurencin's *Les Biches*, another was *Petrushka*, another one was *Schéhérazade*. I had very little original talent in me at that time, but I was so enthusiastic that, I suppose, misguidedly I thought he might see some sort of germ here. But he was very polite, and then in my nervousness I spilt the whole portfolio on the ground like a flutter of pigeons and as I picked some of these things up, he was more interested in retrieving the photographs which he suddenly saw and spread out. They were my first experimental photographs, that I had taken of my sisters. One head one way, the other the other, and upside-down, all freakish, all stuntish, and these really rather excited him, and although I should have been grateful for that encouragement, I think it was rather wasted on me, because I wanted just a little dewdrop about my designs.

What was his manner like?

Very grandiose. Very *grand seigneur*. Immaculate. He moved slowly. He had to turn his whole head round, his whole body round, if he wanted to look over his shoulder. He spoke quietly. He was rather like a sort of chinchilla. He was pale, grey, and had marvellous pale-grey hair, pale-grey suit with pearl-grey stud. He had a mouth rather like a shark, and a marvellous poreless complexion, and was extremely suave. I don't know how anybody in the heat of the day in Venice could retain such serenity.

Did you like him?

I was much too much in admiration of him to like him. I was frightened of him because I was in such awe.

Sacheverell Sitwell

1897 SCARBOROUGH–1988 WESTON, NORTHAMPTONSHIRE

*Poet, critic, biographer and essayist, the youngest
of the three Sitwells, Sacheverell wrote the
scenario for Diaghilev's only English ballet,*
The Triumph of Neptune, *in 1926.*

Tell me about Diaghilev's appearance.

You mean, what was he like to look at? Well, he was always immaculately dressed, at night, that is to say, in a wonderful white waistcoat with white tie and top hat. Always the last word in elegance from that point of view. He had this very large head, as I expect you have been told, and this lock of white hair. I think he always prided himself on being like Peter the Great. In fact, I think he had some remote kind of descent from Peter the Great, and certainly the death mask of Peter the Great is remarkably like the death mask of poor Diaghilev himself. Have you ever seen his death mask? There is a very strong look. It's this kind of shaped moustache he had, and the way his hair was cut.

How was he dressed during the day? People have said he was rather shabby.

He was generally muffled up in a heavy, rather untidy-looking old overcoat; I remember that very well. But on gala nights, on first nights, he would appear in a magnificent impresario's real fur coat. He had a monocle, and he had a funny way, when he was thinking, of making a sort of face as if he was chewing something; this was while he was reflecting, or ruminating, whatever you like to call it, on any subject. And then I remember him sitting in the stalls at rehearsals, and shouting very loudly when anything went wrong. And I remember one conductor, whose name I will not mention, at a rehearsal, who didn't seem to be conducting awfully well, and I remember Diaghilev tearing like a mad bull down the aisle and seizing the conductor's hand, and conducting the piece for him. That obviously was quite a sensation on that particular afternoon.

Was he always surrounded by people when you met, or did you meet him alone?

I met him alone in the sense that if I had luncheon or supper with him, there would probably only be one or two other people there, but, of course, generally in the theatre he was surrounded by a sort of real gang. He would have fifteen or twenty people around him.

When you went out to lunch or supper, what did you talk about?

What did we talk about? We talked largely about books, which he was very interested in, and then we talked about paintings. In Florence, of course, we talked largely about paintings in the Uffizi and Pitti, that sort of thing. And then I used to ask him about interesting people he had known. I remember, for instance, asking him about Aubrey Beardsley, about his meeting him in Dieppe. And he was a mine of information on all sorts of subjects which were very fascinating, and interesting from that point of view.

Do you think he had a really deep knowledge of music?

He had a very profound and deep musical knowledge, and had been a very good pianist. He had an extraordinary knowledge of music, and an extraordinary and abnormal instinct about it, I think, as, indeed, he had about painting too. Especially when he took that remarkable and revolutionary turn in his career, and gave up the Russian side of the Russian ballet, and adopted the leading French painters for a time, like Picasso and Matisse, and Braque and Derain.

Why do you think that happened?

I think that was his instinct for success which made him do that, and also he felt that he was exiled from Russia, and he couldn't go on being exclusively Russian.

You talked with him always in French?

My French isn't awfully good; and he talked French to me and I talked English to him, so I seem to remember most.

Did he speak English?

I never heard him speak more than a word or two of English. I remember on one occasion going to a friend's house to luncheon with him, and I remember him, to everybody's surprise, suddenly saying, 'More chocolate pudding.' But that's almost the only time I ever remember him talking English. No, generally he talked French, and we managed to carry on some kind of conversation like that.

When did you first meet him?

I think I do remember being introduced to him in 1914 when I came up from school, a long leave, and I was taken by my brother to hear

Khovanshchina, which made the most marvellous and wonderful impression. I think the brass instruments in *Khovanshchina* are something really quite extraordinary and exceptional, such as at that time one had never heard before. But I got to know him when he came to England, when his season opened at the Coliseum about two months before the war ended. His company only appeared for about half a minute. I remember always walking seriously out of the Coliseum at the beginning of Grock's act, and it was only after I must have walked out about twenty times that I realized what I was missing. You probably never saw Grock, but his partner used to come on first and play the violin, and that seemed awfully boring, and I didn't know how wonderful it was going to be a minute or two later, so unfortunately I missed seeing Grock on numerous occasions. And when eventually I did stay on, I can't tell you how enjoyable it was.

I think you were still in the army at that time.

I was in the army at the time at Aldershot, at a frightful place called Albufeira Barracks, and I remember in the evenings always having to rush back by the milk train from Waterloo, and arriving at Aldershot at a quarter to two in the morning. I remember on one occasion saying that I must go off, I had to go back to Aldershot, and Diaghilev saying, 'Alors, qu'est-ce que c'est, cette Aldershot; c'est le nom de votre maîtresse?' Unfortunately he was wrong there. It was not anything of the sort; it was just this dreary military centre which I had to get back to as soon as possible.

What was the first impression the company made on you? Was it colour, or music, or the choreography?

I think at first it was the wonderful dancing and the music, and as those impressions faded, one became interested more in the painting side, and in the *mise en scène*. And I remember being a fanatical admirer of Bakst at the time; and I remember thinking, during the war, what a fearful waste of everybody's time it was not being able to do that sort of thing, instead of having to do these ridiculous exercises on Aldershot Plain in which I was then engaged.

The personality of the company changed very much after the war – did you think for the better?

There were a few marvellous years after the war, for there was a kind of *annus mirabilis* in 1919. When you come to think of it, it was the next year after the war, in fact. It was only about six months after war had ended when he was able to produce the *Tricorne*, and also the *Boutique Fantasque*, and when Picasso and Derain, who in those days we thought to be as great an artist as Picasso, were both in London. And that was followed in the winter of 1921 by the wonderful revival of the *Sleeping Princess*, at the Alhambra.

Tell me about that, for you saw it often?

I must have gone nearly every night, yes. And it was certainly the most sensational first night I have ever seen in my life. I believe Bakst did all the scenery, and 300 dresses for it in six weeks, or something incredible like that. The music, in a sense, I was familiar with, because I remember my grandmother had it on the pianola, and I remember playing that ferociously when I was only eight or nine years old, and it was wonderful to hear all that again. I still think the entr'acte, the Panorama, is one of the most beautiful pieces of music. But in any case I am a tremendous admirer of Tchaikovsky. I remember one or two quite well-known people making complete idiots of themselves on the first night, saying that never again could music such as that, banality such as that, be performed again, and they little realized that it was the supreme masterpiece of all music of that description.

Do you think this was one of the reasons for its failure? Ironically, it was out of joint with the fashion of the time.

No, I think the main reason it failed was owing to ferocious attacks by Ernest Newman, who attacked everything he did, and really wrecked the prospects. The other reason was that after the very startling modernity of the previous season's productions, a lot of people thought that it was extremely old-fashioned. It was the kind of music which they weren't used to any longer. Of course, the wonderful feature of it was the extraordinary number of first-rate dancers in it. The part of the Princess Aurora was taken alternately by Trefilova and Egorova and Spessivtseva, and, of course, Lopokova appeared as the Lilac Fairy. And Carlotta Brianza, who had been the original Princess Aurora, took the part of Carabosse. And then I remember the gala performance, which I think was in January 1922, when Cecchetti appeared as Carabosse. Cecchetti had been the original Prince Charming, of I don't know how long before. I suppose about thirty years before. And then he was presented with an illuminated address and carried off the stage by the company afterwards.

What was the audience like at that time?

Well, as I'm such an admirer, partisan of his, one of the only things that can be said against Diaghilev was that he had a rather snobbish side to his character. But in order to gain the sort of support that he had to have, it was absolutely necessary for him to recruit rich people who were interested in that sort of thing. And therefore the audience was very much like it might be now on a gala night at Covent Garden. Of course, there were a large number of artists and also any number of people who were mad devotees and who couldn't afford to go any lower down than the gallery.

Did the audience change? Did he lose the most influential people when he became very modern?

I think a few people found it difficult, yes. A certain number of people found *Les Noces* difficult to swallow. One person who was a great admirer of *Les Noces*, rather unexpectedly, was H. G. Wells. Largely by that time, of course, he had tacked on a number of avant-garde characters who would stand for almost anything which was produced in that sort of way.

Do you think the work of the later years was as good as the earlier works?

I think it died off to some extent because he lost interest in it himself, owing to the impossibility of getting any fresh dancers from Russia, and because by that time, except for one or two very young English dancers, like Ninette de Valois or Ursula Moreton, I felt there was no reserve for him to fall back upon.

Tell me about your own involvement. How did you come to work with Diaghilev?

I first came to work with him because I used to help choose the entr'actes. In those days he performed lots of pieces of music in the entr'acte, which have now become quite familiar, but in those days they hadn't been heard, such as Gounod's Wind Symphony, the Fête Polonaise by Chabrier out of *Le Roi Malgré Lui* and one or two Rossini overtures, things of that sort. And I used to help. On various occasions I wrote the programme notes for those, and later on I wrote a book for him called *The Triumph of Neptune*. *Roméo et Juliette* had music by Constant Lambert, who was an Englishman, but apart from that *The Triumph of Neptune*, which had music by Lord Berners, and for which I wrote the book, was the only English thing that he ever produced. That was taken, as I think you know, from the old toy shop at Hoxton, and from the prints there.

This was a very different world, Pollock's Toy Theatre, from the world of Les Noces *or* Train Bleu.

Yes, it was, but it was one which he took to at once. I remember his delight on being taken down to see the shop in Hoxton. I remember very vividly the delight of dear old Mr Pollock, who was a great friend of mine, who ran the shop, and who was a kind of Dickensian character. I remember his joy on being given tickets for the theatre, and seeing all these effects that he had only seen in a very small space reproduced large. A lot of people, I suppose, might have been rather irritated by that, but not Pollock, who absolutely loved every moment of it.

Tell me about Lord Berners.

Lord Berners was a person of very considerable talents, in different directions, because he wrote amusingly, he painted well and he wrote music. He was also a great humorist. Somebody was telling me the other day of a typical sort of joke of his, that in the country where he lived there were a lot of steamrollers outside the house, outside the gate. And he spent an enormous amount of time painting a new notice, which he put up next morning: 'Streamrollers at play.' That was very typical of him. He would take almost any amount of time and trouble to play a joke.

What was his music like for The Triumph of Neptune?

It's rather difficult to describe. It was really quite individual. I can't think of anything else quite like it. There was a kind of tipsy rendering of the 'Last Rose of Summer' at one moment, which was interestingly done and a very good finale, but it wasn't an enormous success. I think the scenery was the best part of it. The scenery was taken from these old prints and Diaghilev sat up the whole of the two nights before the first night, helping. I remember seeing him paint the scenery. I don't think he got any sleep at all, and then eventually, on the critical night, he appeared in his wonderful fur coat, and his eyeglass and white waistcoat, and all the rest of it.

Did Diaghilev take an interest in other areas of the arts? Did he go to exhibitions?

He certainly went to every exhibition and everything of that sort, and yes, took an enormous interest. He was also very anxious when his company were on holiday, for instance, in Florence, that they should be taken to the Uffizi and the Pitti Gallery, and see all the works of art. He was insistent on that. I remember having lunch with him at Fiesole with Lifar, and Lifar was consistently reading his Baedeker, and I said how very industrious he was, and Diaghilev said 'Not at all', and he opened the Baedeker and Lifar was looking at a lot of photographs of himself. I remember that. That seemed to be his chief interest.

How did Diaghilev discover young artists? Were you ever with him? I believe he went to a performance of Façade?

Yes, he did. He certainly went to the first performance of *Façade* at the Chenil Galleries, but then he was always on the lookout for talent. It was one of the great things about him. And in the last years of his life he worked a lot with those French composers, Les Six, not with Honegger, but with Auric, Poulenc and Satie, of course. I remember the performance of *Mercure* by Satie, with a drop scene and costumes by Picasso. That met with very little response, so he asked my brother and me to collect all the weird characters we could think of and fill as many of the stalls as we could, and so we went to the Café Royal, and other purlieus. I should think we managed to get about seventy to eighty characters to come to the first night. I think I mentioned this somewhere in something I wrote, and I had a very angry letter from poor Evelyn Waugh, who was a great friend of ours and had been among the people we had collected, saying that he wasn't one of the people with long hair down to his waist or anything of that sort.

You met Picasso very often in those days. What was he like?

When I met him at that time, he was almost exactly like Napoleon to look at. He was a real kind of Mediterranean type. He certainly is the most prodigious and wonderful genius, the genius of the age. He may not be a very nice one, but he is the genius of it. And at that moment he was painting the huge drop scene for the Spanish ballet of de Falla, in a studio somewhere behind Leicester Square, and I remember going there to see it and to see him, and the curtain was, of course, flat on the floor, and he was lunching on the floor himself with a bottle of wine. It was standing on a table where there was a painted bottle of wine on the curtain. The curtain is now in the Seagram Building in New York, hanging outside the Four Seasons restaurant, and very magnificent it looks too.

I've been told that when in London, Picasso went off and had a lot of clothes made for himself.

Oh, did he really? I don't remember the tailor thing, but I think that's very like him. He's always had a passion for dressing up. He always likes wearing masks and that sort of thing. He was probably trying to disguise himself as a basic Englishman, which is a thing which I think would not come off, because he is such a very Spanish-looking person.

Do you remember Diaghilev's cousin?

That was in later days when it wasn't going so well, and when they appeared at the Prince's Theatre and the Lyceum and places like that. And then Mr Wollheim would always station me and my wife in an empty box at one side of the stage, and opposite us would be Diaghilev's old cousin, called Korybut Kobytovich, who looked like a very distinguished retired ambassador. And I learned the art of applause from him – how you needn't bother to do anything until the curtain has come down for the second time, and then you applaud frantically, you applaud vigorously, and the curtain goes up again, and so on. Like that you can get eight or ten curtains. He was a dear old man who was unmercifully teased by Diaghilev; I think he was his cousin.

Diaghilev had an enormous appetite, didn't he?

He certainly had a glorious appetite, and it was quite an inspiring moment when he put his eyeglass in his eye and began looking at the menu. But I was always under the impression at Kettner's Restaurant, where I often used to have luncheon with him, that he was allowed double helpings at single price. I also remember having supper with him at the Savoy in the Grill Room. I think there's a plaque under the table where he used to sit. But unfortunately his appetite in later days was rather curtailed by his having diabetes. And I suppose what killed him, poor thing, was that he wouldn't keep to the rules about diet or about the horrible injections of insulin that he had to take.

How much do we owe to the legacy of Diaghilev?

I think that anybody who is fond of the theatre or of music owes more than it's possible to express to him. Because it has now become the pastime of tens of thousands of people in England, the United States and everywhere else, and that is entirely due to him and to the two women who took up from him when he was dead: Madame Rambert and Dame Ninette de Valois.

Igor Markevich

1912 KIEV–1983 ANTIBES

The last of Diaghilev's protégés, the young composer was to become one of the leading conductors of his generation. He married one of Nijinsky's daughters and for the twenty-fifth anniversary of Diaghilev's death made gramophone recordings of many of the ballets of the 1920s.

How did you meet Diaghilev?

I will try to tell you in my limited English. It was in 1928. Diaghilev had heard about me as a composer and he wanted to listen to my works. Of course, they were very childish works, but Diaghilev was interested even in very childish works. Then I met him several times. One time is a historic one because it was the evening in December '28 during a Russian ballet performance when they brought Nijinsky to see if maybe the dance would impress him and perhaps awaken something in him; there is a famous photograph of this evening and I was present. Everyone was, of course, very moved seeing this famous and legendary man, and I was too, but I would have been much more so if I had known that several years later he would become my father-in-law. I could not know all that, everything was so new to me, but in that time I saw Diaghilev several times, and it is in that moment that he had the idea to ask me to compose a ballet for him.

But the commission from Diaghilev was a piano concerto.

Yes, and it was just because Diaghilev thought that at sixteen I could not be experienced enough to compose a ballet. He wanted to know if I was able to orchestrate it, how I was able to develop a musical piece, so he asked me to compose a piano concerto, and then he asked Vittorio Rieti to give me lessons in instrumentation, and these lessons were given about the piano concerto that I played here in London in the summer of 1929.

Tell me about the rehearsals: were conditions adequate, did you find it difficult?

Oh yes, because when Diaghilev wanted to do a new experiment, and I was a new experiment, everything, all the power of the Russian ballet and of his means, was concentrated on that. So I remember that for several months it was one of his first interests, and during the rehearsals I had all the possibility to get accustomed to play; I never played a piano concerto, it was my first time with an orchestra. It was conducted by Roger

Desormière, who became a friend of mine after that. And we had the possibility to prepare it very well.

Looking back, do you think it was a good work?

Yes, I think it was not bad. I think it was probably good for the age I was. In itself I think it was much too marked by a certain tendency to what has been called a 'retour à Bach', but I think the work is still valid.

After that London season, you went to Germany with Diaghilev. Where did you go?

When Diaghilev wanted to help an artist, he wanted also to give him every possibility to be stimulated, and also to discover in himself all his possibilities. And the little journey, very short, I had with him was typical of this kind of thing because he wanted me to hear modern music. We went to Baden-Baden to listen to pieces of Hindemith, Milhaud, and he wanted me also to hear Wagner or Mozart opera, which I had never heard before. I was a boy of sixteen, so we went there and it was interesting all the time because he was showing me museums, and I met Richard Strauss, I met Milhaud, I met Hindemith, very interesting people. But, of course, for me it was a discovery of a completely new world. He has been always like that with all the people he has tried to help; even with Stravinsky, with Nijinsky, when he decided that he would make choreography for the first time, which was *Prélude a l'Après-midi d'un Faune*. You have no idea, it's nearly unbelievable. Nijinsky was certainly extraordinarily gifted, as we know after what he had done with *L'Après-midi d'un Faune*, with the classical choreography, and with the *Rite of Spring*, which has been absolutely revolutionary, also in the choreography field. But who could know that before? Nijinsky was completely inexperienced. So Diaghilev first gave him about 200 rehearsals of this piece which lasts ten minutes, something of a luxury today, which is nearly unbelievable. But he also brought him to see the bas-reliefs, to see the sculpture, to see all these things, which later gave the idea to Nijinsky to make all the choreography in profile.

That is typical, the kind of thing Diaghilev did which makes me say that he has been the most extraordinary *agent provocateur* of history. Of course, it had nothing to do with politics, but he was an *agent provocateur* of genius, of talent, of ideas, and he had something really extraordinary. He had the way to provoke in the artist the best of himself, very often a thing they wouldn't have discovered in themselves without him. It was even difficult, sometimes, to know who was the real composer. I remember that when I was composing my piano concerto, sometimes I got even – I wouldn't say angry, but I was in despair, because he told me, here you should compose like that, here you should put the piano, here the orchestra should play and not the piano, things like that. I said, 'But I am the composer.' It was very difficult to know exactly who was the creator. Because sometimes you had the impression that he was creating, by what we say in French, *par personne interposée.*

Your time with him was within a few months of his death. What were his manner and appearance like at this time?

I think it was difficult to know, especially for a young man like me who had no experience of life and who had not known him before, that he was so ill. And I don't know if any one of us guessed that. We were so near to his death. He was joking, he was full of enthusiasm, interested in the future. His appearance, his manner, was something quite special, because he was a very old-fashioned gentleman, which is strange, because we have the impression also that he was a kind of *révolutionnaire*, by all what he has done, by all the scandal of the premières he had, and not only the *Rite of Spring*, but *Parade*, with many other things. The *Roméo et Juliette* of Constant Lambert was a scandal as tremendous as *Rite of Spring*, for instance. But his appearance was the appearance of a very old-fashioned gentleman, he was of another dimension from the other people you see. He looked more important than all the other people. He was tall and rather fat. He had fur coats and monocles, a stick, gloves, a silk *cache-col*, all things which gave him great importance, and the way he was walking, entering a restaurant or a theatre, was something like a ship entering a harbour, with little, little ships around him, which were all of us. I think he had a beautiful appearance. He used to say that by his mother he was a descendant of Peter the Great, which is probably right, and he looked like him. His mouth looked astonishingly like Emperor Peter's.

What were your conversations about? Music all the time, or pictures?

Oh, about everything, because especially with young artists he was interested to open the mind of the artist with whom he had to work. We used to speak about everything. But all the day long we had the impression always to be working on something, and it was an extraordinarily creative and stimulating atmosphere.

What do you think is the importance of his work today?

I think it is of very great importance for the simple reason that he had this capacity to stimulate the artist to give the best of themselves. For this reason those from whom he commissioned work – and not only in music, but also let's think of Picasso, or Massine, Lifar, Fokine, all these choreographers too – have given their best works for him. For this reason the importance is absolutely outstanding.

His support for the young French school of the 1920s has been much criticized. Was it, for you, better or worse than what had gone before?

It's not a question of good or bad. It's difficult to answer that. What is certain is that it's very important too. *Les Fâcheux, Les Biches* have certainly been important in their time. And *Parade*. Musically, *Parade* remains a monument of new music, only because it was the first piece of *musique concrète*, with the typewriter, the sirens, and all that. As with very many things of Diaghilev, now we understand how he has seen for a long time in advance, for instance, with the score of *Parade*. No, I consider they are very important and I consider also that it's sometimes too early to know what is really important. One needs more time to be able to judge. But I think, for instance, *Parade* is as important as *Le Pas d'Acier*, which was the first ballet on a mechanical theme.

What do you think makes good ballet music?

My answer would seem to be a joke, but I think that good ballet music is a thing you can listen to without ballet.

How important was Diaghilev's influence on music?

If we consider the thing on the positive side, it's fantastic that just one man has been able to create so many things, and to have such an enormous influence on the course of the whole of the history of music. After all, the *Rite of Spring* has had as much importance as the Ninth Symphony of Beethoven or the *Tristan* of Wagner in the course of music. But there is one negative thing we must also consider, in that Diaghilev took absolutely no interest in the school of Vienna; in Schoenberg, in Berg and Webern. I remember when I talked about these composers to him, he told me that he considered that the experiment was already finished and over. Certainly he made a mistake, because now, considering how things are going on, it's probably the most important current of today's music. Certainly this has been one of the very few areas where he has been, I won't say blind, but not interested. But certainly, if you consider the positive side, his influence was enormous.

Serge Lifar

1905 KIEV–1986 LAUSANNE

*Lifar joined the Ballets Russes in 1923 and
became a principal dancer two years later.
Diaghilev's closest companion in his later years,
Lifar created many roles in the ballets of Massine
and Balanchine. He later became director of the
Paris Opéra Ballet and a prolific choreographer.*

Tell me about the last days of Diaghilev's life.

Well, it was exactly thirty-eight years ago today, on 19 August 1929, that Diaghilev died, here in Venice on the Lido, more exactly in the huge room of the Hôtel des Bains. At his deathbed there were three people present. He practically died in my arms, and by my side there was Madame Sert and Boris Kochno. There was a Russian priest and a nurse, but of his friends there were just three of us. It was an unforgettable moment, almost Shakespearian, as he died at dawn, and his last breaths were at the moment when the sun rose, and the first ray of sunlight fell on Diaghilev's face, and there was an enormous tear which ran down his cheek. That was the end. It was, of course, a very moving scene, but we were so on edge that we simply weren't prepared for this. I pushed Kochno away, Kochno wanted to push me away; eventually we were both told to go away. The body was prepared and when I came back into the room, I was extremely calm and with a great sense of calm I made him up and dressed him, even acted as barber. I did it rather theatrically. I brought also a tuber rose, which I placed in his buttonhole. I arranged his Peter the Great moustache, I brought out the different colours of his hair. He always had that vision of colours of one side darker, and this other part of his head was grey. It was a part of his charm, he was a terrific charmer. He very much liked perfume, he was a man of extreme refinement. I was really there all day until the arrival of Diaghilev's uncle, who came from Paris, Korybut Kobytovich.

We brought Diaghilev here to this island of San Michele. Why? Because Diaghilev adored Venice. That's why on this tomb I had inscribed the phrase in Russian, which he had written in one of my notebooks from lessons with Cecchetti. He began the book, which he offered me, which was very pretty Venetian paper, with this phrase that 'Venice is an everlastingly calming inspiration'. I wanted to make sure that his death mask was taken, and I asked some Italian artists immediately to take a death mask, and I have still got it in my museum, beside the death mask of Chaliapin, as I was also at his deathbed. I have also the death mask of Pavlova, and those are my most precious possessions. But Diaghilev always had a presentiment that he would die on water, and it's for that reason that going to London with Diaghilev, going across the Channel to Dover, was an enormous affair. Diaghilev was afraid, he was afraid of dying on water, he was afraid of crossing from Naples to Capri – that was even another great business, and because of that he never accepted, after 1918, going to the United States of America. He simply wouldn't cross the Atlantic, particularly after the crossing in 1917 when he was terrified of the sea. He always had a dreadful fear of being drowned. He was frightened of water and he was frightened of death. It was a tragedy, and I have always kept his photograph, showing how Diaghilev spent ten days not in his cabin at all, but on the deck of this ship, wrapped in a cape, wearing lifebelts. He spent ten days like this, drinking whisky; it was a dreadful tragedy.

But, of course, he adored Italy, Florence, but particularly every year he loved coming to Venice, to get inspiration from this calm, and then he died here. So it was providence, really, and I wanted him to be buried here in this Greek cemetery, and for thirty-five years I have done the same thing, had the same service said, an Orthodox service which keeps the memory fresh, and to pay homage, if you like, to his spirit and his soul. This Greek priest, he comes every 19 August and we pay homage to this man who overturned the artistic aesthetic of the twentieth century; a man of great style who wrote an immortal page in the history of art. I often say that it is the same kind of grandeur as one had during the Florence of the Medicis, or continued afterwards by Louis XIV, with all that grandeur, all that refinement, all those ennobling qualities. Through him the twentieth century revealed one of the most extraordinary pages in the history of the arts and I was part of that.

You could say that I am his spiritual heir; it's true and, I suppose, in another way not true. We're all Diaghilev's spiritual heirs, even those artists who never knew him. But I had the privilege to know him during this time, and that's the great thing, and also it was thanks to this man, who was everything and nothing, who was not an artist, but who wished to be an artist in his youth. He finished the conservatoire in two different classes. He was a pianist and also he was in the class of composition. He had rows with Rimsky-Korsakov and they finished by having a row in which Diaghilev wanted to make an opera on the subject of Boris Godunov, even though an opera of genius was already in existence, but Diaghilev wanted to do a new version. Naturally Rimsky rejected it. Diaghilev was so furious he said to Rimsky, '*Maître*, you'll see which of us will be the most famous.' And, of course, Diaghilev succeeded. He has become immortal.

Where did his impeccable taste come from, the thing that everybody has commented on?

It came first from the atmosphere of his youth and his childhood. He came from an aristocratic family, but at the same time a progressive family, very artistic. Diaghilev's stepmother was a pianist, a singer, a remarkable one, and there were always at the home of his cousin Filosofov, musical evenings, literary evenings, and right from his youth Diaghilev got a taste for music, from all these discussions that he heard. He was born to feel, and he developed not just his spirit, but his instinct, and then there were extraordinary meetings in his family, because Mussorgsky came to accompany his stepmother. You see the atmosphere of this small provincial town. He was born near Pskov [incorrect]. His father was in the army, but it was still the provinces.

Then, of course, they went to St Petersburg, into a very extraordinary milieu, and immediately he made the acquaintance of a group of the most advanced artists, and found his master, who was soon overtaken by Diaghilev's ideas. This master was Alexandre Benois. He then met painters and musicians, he met Walter Nouvel, who was concerned with the most advanced ideas of music, almost modern, and the first things he did – well, he created an artistic magazine in Russia, which was called *The World of Art*, and then through this magazine, which lasted for almost five years, Diaghilev revealed Russia to the Russians, at the same time showing the importance of all the Western schools. He had even for the wider public rediscovered the Renaissance, and this was considered one of Diaghilev's first miracles.

He went to work for the imperial family as an attaché to the ministerial court. A young and handsome aesthete, he was placed in the department responsible for the Imperial theatres, and immediately, with his knowledge of painters, he wanted at any cost to renew the whole theatrical aesthetic, and the theatrical aesthetic at that time was very heavy from the point of view of decoration. He decided to ask some of the painters he knew to work in the theatre, so he asked for the ballet *Sylvia* of Delibes. Instead of having traditional, heavy, dusty décor, Diaghilev asked for something new and fresh, but, of course, this decision outraged the functionaries, because it was undermining tradition, and he was obliged to be sacked. Diaghilev then left the Imperial theatres, where the Emperor himself had signed his dismissal. It went sixteen times backwards and forwards, dismissed, rescinded, dismissed, rescinded. It was already a battle of wills and of influence.

Do you think that Diaghilev kept all his life this feeling of being Russian, even when he spent fifteen years abroad?

Yes, yes, I'll get to that if you let me. But I was saying that for the first time it's an extraordinary fact that Diaghilev had ideas, not just artistic ideas, but social ideas. Diaghilev made an exhibition of historical Russian portraits – it was done at the Tauride Palace – a huge exhibition, extraordinary. It was the year 1905, the year of the first revolution, the year I was born, in fact. On returning to Moscow afterwards Diaghilev foretold the Revolution, he foretold the social changes in politics in my country, and I think, basically, he was in favour of these changes, to renew things – I'd say not just artistically but in the sense of society. He had something in common with the ideology of Lenin, because I have these documents, which are extraordinarily valuable, a transcript of a speech which Diaghilev gave, in which he said, 'I have made this exhibition. I have visited the whole of Russia to gather it. I have seen the whole national treasure, and I can tell you that we live in the dawn of the new epoch, and I salute all these changes, not just artistic and social. I celebrate the end of the epoch of the palaces, and I hope this is a revolution that will succeed. Russia is in the course of getting involved in a revolution which I hope will not be bloody, but will certainly have passion. It will be beautiful, the body of aesthetics, and the new aesthetics in front of us.' After saying things like that, I'm astonished that Diaghilev wasn't sent to Siberia, but he continued, and in 1906 he had already begun to make a mark in the West. He brought an exhibition to Paris, and he showed Russian painters with great success: Benois, Bakst, Roerich, all the young Russian painters, and this new school was presented in Paris.

The following year, 1907, he decided to present the treasures of Russian culture in historical concerts of Russian music with Rimsky, Tchaikovsky and Mussorgsky, with excerpts from *Boris Godunov* with Chaliapin, which was certainly a historic event in Paris. The following year was really the greatest revolution, artistically speaking, for the West, for he brought the whole of *Boris Godunov* with Chaliapin to the Paris Opéra. From the eyewitness accounts of the friends of Diaghilev who were present at this performance it seems something which nobody could understand, the extent of the enthusiasm, and it was the following year, 1909, the year of the famous Ballets Russes, which came together with the opera, that was a revelation of the new art. The new art which Diaghilev brought with him was an extraordinary fund of talent. With Fokine's work he presented

Pavlova, Karsavina and Nijinsky. I'm just mentioning the most important names. But it was a revolution also, and naturally, as a result of it, he became the artistic master of Europe, and in the course of it he revealed Russia.

Could you explain to me this question of the synthesis of the arts which was Diaghilev's policy?

The ballets already in themselves are a synthesis of all the arts. But Diaghilev made the synthesis of all the arts by applying equal importance to music, décor and choreography, and having interpreters on the same level. But particularly what he probably for the first time revealed, in the history of this art, the choreographic art, is the creation of movement, which up till Diaghilev's time was unknown. Up till the time of Fokine, choreography was of very much an academic vocabulary. This school progressed through the nineteenth century, from Vestris to Taglioni, up to Pavlova and Nijinsky, but the ideas of Diaghilev's colleagues discovered quite a new form of art, which was the choreography of the twentieth century. It meant that each choreographer would have his own personal language based on tradition. One could say that there are seven names to retain, who have totally revolutionized the choreography of the whole world, except sadly until today in Russia, as Russia has remained with what one might call the vocabulary of Petipa. That doesn't amount to much, because Petipa is still scholastic, just school, school, school, just academic. Diaghilev was an admirable organizer, but, of course, he wasn't a creator. The creative names were Fokine, Nijinsky, Massine, Romanov, Nijinska, Balanchine and the youngest, the smallest of them, was me. For Diaghilev I just did one small piece of choreography the year of his death.

That was how, in general, Diaghilev conceived art, and one must say immediately that on the musical level it was an absolute revolution. One can't forget that without Diaghilev one wouldn't have had *Daphnis and Chloe*, or *The Rite of Spring*, or *Petrushka*, or the *Firebird* of Stravinsky, and he presented over forty different composers in his twenty years. It's immense. And the same thing with the painters. Without Diaghilev one wouldn't have seen *Schéhérazade*, with its amazing oriental décor, something totally new for the West. One wouldn't have seen the brilliant décors of Picasso for *Parade*, one wouldn't have seen Matisse's work for *Rossignol*, or the work of Derain, Braque, Utrillo, just right up until the end when it was Chirico and the marvellous French painter Rouault, who did an absolute masterpiece for Prokofiev's *Prodigal Son*. I interpreted this admirable work, and I was proud that I had the opportunity to create Stravinsky's *Apollo*, which was a masterpiece of this great genius of the twentieth century, who was very much the child of Diaghilev. The *Prodigal Son* was by Diaghilev's other child, Prokofiev. We all belonged to the family of this seigneur, this magician, Diaghilev. All the dancers, all the choreographers, the whole of choreography around the world has evolved thanks to Diaghilev, thanks to us, but above all thanks to Diaghilev. I must say that he had this gift of a magician, because I repeat, after his death all these great artists, all these great creators, they wanted to push Diaghilev aside, saying that his shadow was too heavy. We had our genius as well. But I repeat, without Diaghilev, they would perhaps never have had the occasion to express themselves.

As a personality, Diaghilev was a magnificent bear. He was heavy, he was handsome, he was gentle. He was a child, a kind of big grown-up child, with no defences. I knew him first at the age of fifty; he died at the age of fifty-seven, so I knew Diaghilev through this time and I can say that through all my friendship with him, right up until his death, he was like a big baby. He never aged during this time. The terrible thing is Diaghilev died young. He was five years younger than I am now, and that's appalling, because I feel even at my age, trying to live the life of a creative artist, I've hardly started. So Diaghilev left this world very young, and I repeat that in his life he was a man without any defences. There were dramas with telephonists, because he lived always in a room in a hotel, practically a maid's room. He spent millions and millions on his artists, but practically nothing on himself. He had two suits, one grey and one blue, a dinner jacket, a full evening dress, a summer coat and a heavy winter coat, which had been eaten by moths. That's what he called his baggage, the treasure of his life, and he died poor. He had 50,000 francs in the bank, which was an advance received for the coming season in Monte Carlo. But for artists he was generous. He paid, no matter what sum, to create these possibilities, to allow the creators to be free to concentrate on their work.

Relations with telephonists at times were extremely difficult. There were no automatic telephones, so it took ten minutes, fifteen minutes to get hold of anybody. Then there were dramas. He was always provoking theatre directors, waiting ten minutes to come on the line. But he also loved cheerfulness around him, and the person whom he really liked was his cousin, whom they called his uncle, Korybut Kobytovich. He left Russia the same time as I did, in 1923. Diaghilev liked fooling around in private, and, especially when Uncle was reading the paper peacefully and quietly,

Diaghilev would take his slippers and throw them at the paper, and terrify poor old Uncle Paul. Then he had to be comforted, he had to have a drink of water, and then to calm him down Diaghilev would say to Uncle Paul, 'My dear, do you want to make a telephone call?' Paul didn't reply. 'Go on, get me so-and-so on the telephone, would you?' KK didn't move. Suddenly Diaghilev insists. Poor Uncle gets up, goes to the telephone and says to Diaghilev, 'Wouldn't it be better if I went to see them and took a taxi? I could go there and back.' Then there was another drama. 'Imbecile, you could take the whole day doing that, it is just a matter of a phone call.' That was a matter of the generations, because KK had a terror of technical things, and the telephone for him was absolute hell. But there are thousands of anecdotes like that.

But the important thing was that Diaghilev was a marvellous man, and during his months of holidays, when he visited all the museums in Florence and Venice, there wasn't a single museum that Diaghilev hadn't been to ten times at least. He loved to look at things, and for us it was easy because without wasting any time we had the most extraordinary guide. We stopped in front of masterpieces. That was always extraordinary. And then he loved receptions. His last reception was in Paris, with Stravinsky, Prokofiev, Coco Chanel, all his artists, all the children of that age. And there was something extraordinary: he welcomed the world with simplicity, with gentleness, and with a sense of equality. He was never what you would call a dictator.

Nicholas Nabokov

1903 LYUBCHA, NOVOGRUDOK, NEAR MINSK–1978 NEW YORK

*Composer and arts administrator, Nabokov was a
distant cousin of Diaghilev, who in 1927
commissioned from him the music for a highly
experimental ballet called* Ode.

Tell me about the first time you met Diaghilev, when your mother introduced you to him.

I remember the restaurant. You had to go three steps down; it was somewhere near the Avenue d'Iéna, in one of those strange straight streets there which has no face, and it was called Moskva, and my mother pointed out to me Diaghilev, and, of course, I recognized him because he and his half-brother, whom I knew very well, Valentin Pavlovich Diaghilev, were face-wise very much alike. Otherwise they were completely different. Diaghilev was tall and had the strange stature of . . . In a way he resembled sort of a female Peter the Great, a high, big, tall Peter the Great, with this upper lip and so on. And the face was known to me, so when my mother introduced me to him and said that I am a striving young composer, I immediately felt the sort of *recul* of Diaghilev, faced with someone who was curiously enough a relative. My mother introduced me and insisted on the point and wanted Diaghilev immediately to see my music, and I tried to pull the sleeve of my mother and say, 'Oh, stop it for heaven's sake, I don't want to impose.' And Diaghilev was either with Dolin or with – no, it was Dolin. And Diaghilev said, '*Charmé*, very well, would like to meet you. Why don't you bring me your pieces?' And my mother thought it was a very successful meeting. My feeling was that it was unsuccessful in the sense that I felt that Diaghilev thought, there's another boring Russian lady who has this young man. On the other hand I also felt Diaghilev stare at me. I was young and not un-good-looking at that time, and he sort of looked me over: what is he like?

To me Diaghilev was already a legend, as to every young Russian. When I was a child with his nephews, the children of his half-brother, whose mother was a cousin of my stepfather, we played string ensembles. In fact, just returning from Moscow and Leningrad a few days ago, I had this extraordinary sort of tragic experience of meeting someone who was dead. I was in Leningrad at the house of a famous organist, a very elderly gentleman. I was told there is someone who wants to meet me. And there came in a smallish old man. And the smallish old man said to me, 'Don't you recognize me? I am Aleksei Valentovich Diaghilev.' I said, 'You're dead', and he said 'No, I'm not. I am alive and was taken prisoner by the Reds, and then I was in gaol and then I was many years away' – as they usually say in Russia – 'and then afterwards I came back, and I am here at the conservatory conducting the children's orchestra.' And it was exactly fifty years ago that I came to Leningrad, and approximately fifty years since we played together in the same chamber ensemble. And I suddenly saw in this old man's face certain features of Diaghilev, of Sergei Pavlovich, and they came back to me through these quick eyes, a little blasé, and yet suddenly darting at you through the blaséness, through the kind of societal manicure which eyes of people of his stature acquire through years of insistence and years of governing the world of the arts as he did. And I remember that somehow this meeting with this little old man now, barely ten days ago, and the meeting in the Restaurant Moskva the first time I saw Diaghilev in 1926 or 1925 had something in common. They were as strange and as anomalous to normal life as, well, probably as life is.

You said that as a young man, like every Russian, you knew the legend of Diaghilev. What was this legend?

There was this legend first of all of a man who, very young, became assistant to the director of the imperial theatres, Prince Volkonsky, and who had a big brawl with the then most famous dancer, who was, as everybody knew, high in favour at court, for obvious reasons. And Diaghilev didn't take her for the première. I think the ballet was *Fiametta* – God knows, I think it's Minkus's music, like *Don Quixote*. Diaghilev took another dancer and that made an enormous fuss. And there were pressures brought upon Diaghilev, and Diaghilev left what was for him a very high post. His answer to that was an extremely interesting one. First of all he took to Europe an exhibition of Russian painting, then an opera company and then a ballet company. And in each of them he brought the best of the technicians of their time, the best ballerinas, the best dancers, the best painters and the best singers. And, in fact, produced abroad also such extraordinary things as *Boris Godunov* for the first time at the Paris Opéra, which still remains a date in music history for the West.

What I would say the legend was based on was also partly family legend. We always played at Uncle Valentin's house and there was a picture on the wall of 'the half-brother' and there was always something about the half-brother which was never quite told and that something there was a mystery about. This something, which was connected with sort of conventional decency or conventional morals – one could never go into it because you would hit, like you would hit a pillow. There was also a great respect because he made this first great exhibition of Russian portraits when he went to, I don't know how many houses, and how many estates, where he found marvellous pieces of Russian portraiture, most of which are now hanging in the Tretyakov Gallery in Moscow, a marvel. The Russian portrait is a remarkable event in the history of Western painting. And Diaghilev did this. Then he took these companies abroad, then one heard all these strange stories about Nijinsky, the discovery of Nijinsky. Then there was Ida Rubinstein and *Joseph's Legend* and Richard Strauss, who came to conduct in Petersburg, then one knew Diaghilev was doing something with him, and the name of Hofmannsthal was mentioned. And then, of course, the name Stravinsky came very early in the game. I remember hearing the première of *Fireworks* in the summer music at Pavlovsk.

Hence there was round Diaghilev an aura of mystery and greatness which surrounded my childhood and the childhood of every thinking Russian, a kind of breakthrough from the usual rather tawdry diet which the Imperial theatres at that time served us, and one had the feeling, here is someone who is breaking loose, breaking out, showing the real sometimes, perhaps at times corny, but at other times great talent carried and brought to life by the nineteenth-century Russian people and the Russian writers and poets.

When you got to know Diaghilev, and went to work with the company in Monte Carlo, did his manner towards you change?

Yes, it did change, but in a very strange manner. It was the manner of someone who somehow owned you. You were somehow suddenly a piece of property. You had to work with Massine and Lifar. He would come to the rehearsals and, as a piece of property, you sat at the piano and played your music. He became sort of colder to you, more distant. Yet at the same time when you met him in town accidentally . . . I remember meeting him in the street. He always wore an overcoat, with the same sort of odour of violets, I don't know why, but he chewed little violet, sort of not gum, but *bonbons à la violette*. And I wasn't in an overcoat, and he said, 'You must wear an overcoat in Monte Carlo. It's the most dastardly climate. You think it's sunny', and so on.

Then he had tantrums, which he used quite openly. I remember that once he came to a rehearsal, and at that time he was not very well, and not on good terms with Massine. He didn't speak to Massine directly, but always through interposed persons, either through Mr Nouvel, Valich Nouvel, or through Boris Kochno. And Massine was doing a dance out of *Ode*, doing the choreography with Lifar. Diaghilev sat with his cane, and sat and sort of made as if he was asleep. And Massine said to me, 'He's gaga, he's fallen asleep.' Then suddenly, when I was back in my room about two or three hours later, I was frantically called by Grigoriev. I must come immediately. And there I saw this comic character that was always round Diaghilev, Pavel Korybut Kobytovich, his cousin, whom he called his uncle because he looked so old, and Pavel sat on the sofa and said, 'My God, we have a scandal, a scandal.' Apparently Diaghilev had hit the ceiling. He said that what Massine was doing was absolute nonsense, that Tchelitchev was doing total nonsense, and that my music was going to be nonsense, and the whole ballet was going to be a big flop, and he wanted everyone there immediately to see what Massine had done, but without Massine. Lifar had to come and everybody had to come, and then he looked at everything, and hit a table with his cane. Pavel said, 'The rats came out jumping', and Diaghilev said to me, 'Well, I wash my hands of your ballet. Do whatever you like', with his nasal, rather snobbish way of speaking, monocle on the face. And I was so upset that I went to a small hotel downstairs where the secretary of Diaghilev was living. What was her name? Troussevich. I forget her first name. She ended up as a nun – I saw her grave in Jerusalem – yes, Alexandrina. And Balanchine. And I said to Balanchine, 'It's all over. I have to pack up and go back to Paris. I think it's all over after this.' The next day I met Diaghilev at the hotel. He smiled at me as if nothing had happened. These tantrums were really tantrums. Partly it was an act, partly it was a real child's tantrum, partly it was a sort of ingrown hatred or sort of profound revenge he wanted to take on someone whom he loved very dearly and who had deserted, as had Massine.

I think one should never forget the fact that Diaghilev was an assertive homosexual, and the extraordinary thing about Diaghilev was that he was perhaps the first grand homosexual who asserted himself and was accepted as such by society. And I think this explains a great deal about Diaghilev, that people whom he loved, and to whom he gave his love, and who then deserted him, as Nijinsky did, as Massine did, then suddenly his love turned to a sense of frustration, not hatred, but a strange feeling of being deprived of the object or subject you love, because the subject and object were together in Diaghilev entwined. You never knew whether you were object or subject. I think the only relationships where the object and subject were kept separate was the relationship between Diaghilev and Stravinsky, and perhaps in the early days between Diaghilev and Benois. For everybody else who worked in his ballet – I'm not speaking of masters like Falla, sort of the old generation, or Debussy, because I didn't know Debussy – but for everybody else, like Rieti, Milhaud, Poulenc, Auric, Sauguet, any one of these people was part subject, part object. He used every one of us for his aim.

Now, what his aim was, that is the extraordinary mystery. And I think there again you have to go back to this assertion of what one would call, in the terms of St Paul's Christianity, a scandal; his homosexuality is the assertion of a scandal in terms of morality. And this revelation of a scandal was one of Diaghilev's qualities and at the same time weaknesses, and therefore everything he did was a desire, a little bit to shock but always to react. Part of it was showmanship, part of it was superficiality, but the core was a real, very deep and very profound understanding of what he was doing.

Do you think there's a danger that, looking back now, these possibly less successful qualities are more highly esteemed than his real powers, which were in organization and creativity?

It's a phenomenon when one thinks about it in terms of our age, where big managers manipulate large companies like the Bolshoi and bring them to the United States and make money out of them. When you think of Diaghilev – who always thought in terms of composer, painter, choreographer, always in terms of the creative artist, and went through the direst difficulties financially, always keeping, being kept, afloat by his friendships and occasional alliances with the Otto Khans and the Aga Khans and Chanel and La Comtesse Greffuhle and Madame d'Erlanger and La Princesse de Polignac – when one feels that he used all the society world for his aims, there's something magnificent about it. Nobody does that now. Mr Niarchos sails all over the seas, but I don't see anything produced by Mr Niarchos for the purposes of the arts. I know how difficult it is to get money for the arts unless you get it now from American foundations who take it off their taxes. Now, Diaghilev didn't have American foundations. He had to deal with the society and he had therefore to play their game of snobbishness.

Yet he never lost track in a certain sense of where the values lay. He knew very well that the *Fils Prodigue*, the *Prodigal Son*, of Prokofiev is a work of value. He knew perfectly well what *Apollo* is all about, and he did these things as a necessary reaction towards his earliest period, which everybody wanted him to repeat over and over and over again. I remember his voice in my ears saying, 'Now I finish nearly twenty-five years of my artistic life in Paris, and all over I hear "Give us *Schéhérazade*." I could do a *Schéhérazade* every year for them and they would all eat it, but I don't care for *Schéhérazade*.' And so therefore I think Diaghilev moved away from that by reaction against some former interest which he had. I think his reaction was in general very much stimulated by Satie against folklorism and any form of folklore. This is why Diaghilev never had any attachments, for instance, to Bartók. He never liked that. For him this was Hungarian csardas, *avec des mauvaises notes*.

Tell me about Diaghilev as a musician. How profound was his musicianship?

Diaghilev, as you know, had studied composition and wanted to be a composer. It is mentioned everywhere that he has actually written some music, and he himself found it not good enough. He was a tremendously perceptive and intuitive musician. I always think of Plato's distinction between *nous* and *dianoia* when I think of Diaghilev. Diaghilev was pure *nous*. I mean, immediate perception. An intuitive perception of a work of music, even though it may be played by a composer's ten odd fingers at the piano and on God knows what piano. Diaghilev immediately saw what is good, what is bad. As you know, he made composers like Prokofiev change and rewrite part of his score, and, as for me, I had to rewrite and add numbers to my *Ode* because Diaghilev didn't like certain things and liked other things. Every time his suggestions were correct. For example, at the end of *Ode*. He played it. After my playing it he came to the piano and started playing it – he could with a few fingers sort of play it – and he said, 'Musique tartare, musique tartare', and I understood what he meant. He meant there was some element of repetitiveness in the end of *Ode* which is a kind of Mongol side in Russian music, and which appears in the *Sacre du Printemps* and which comes in a lot of Russian musicians. I think his perceptiveness to music was absolutely intuitive and immediate.

He made a great deal of mistakes for fashion's sake. Fashion was important to him. He was a *grand couturier* of ballet and of the arts of music. He was *le grand couturier* of his period. He was above Chanel and all these girls and boys, and he dominated therefore the taste. And he played with this fashion side, but I'm afraid he knew what he was playing with. If he didn't know at once, he knew it was a merchandise which he could use for a few years. But when it came to serious works, and I will mention just one, the *Fils Prodigue*, the *Prodigal Son*, of Prokofiev, then he took great care in seeing that this piece would come out as best as the author could do it, not sort of as an approximation. What is the difference, for example, between Diaghilev and a contemporary Maecenas? There are many who commission works, orchestra directors, orchestra societies or foundations or so on. They commission a composer, and then the composer comes with his score and it is played and it is left for the public and the critics to judge. Not so with Diaghilev. Diaghilev wanted to see what he was buying, what he was getting, what he was producing. It was his property. It was his, and it then sort of acquired his stamp, and once he gave his stamp he wanted to be sure that this was what he approved of. There were many reasons which played for his approval, but he knew what he was doing and this is what made the great difference, and makes the great hole now, because there are very few people who I know who have the same intuitive perception of music which Diaghilev had.

Tell me about the time he met you backstage before the first night of Ode. *He said something to you. Didn't he say, 'Now it's up to you'?*

I don't remember. I only remember this awful moment when my score was written in pencil, was written badly, and was copied with an enormous amount of mistakes. And one day I was told suddenly, 'There is going to be a reading of your score.' And I said that I hadn't corrected the parts yet. 'Never mind, we have thirty-three minutes and the orchestra will read your score.' The score was thirty-five minutes long, so Diaghilev said, 'All right, we'll play it all allegretto.' And so they started playing and at every moment I would start up and try to stop the conductor and say, 'No, this is not so. The flute is playing wrong and this one is going wrong.' And Diaghilev would always stop me with his right hand and say, 'Asseyez-vous, calmez-vous.' And then after everything was over he turned to me and said to me in a very cold manner, 'You like that?' and walked out. So you felt, my God, what have I done?

Then you felt that everything is going topsy-turvy. Tchelitchev was doing his thing, Massine his thing, I my thing. Desormière is correcting the parts, and there were three or four days left before the première, and nobody knew how the thing would come together. Tchelitchev's set was the first time they had neon lights on the stage, and all sorts of lighting things for the very fancy sort of surrealist staging. Diaghilev, who the whole time was saying, 'I wash my hands of this ballet', then spent two whole nights looking after the lighting, looking after the costumes. Michel Larionov was running around. We were painting the last things, everybody was being directed by Diaghilev, like a horse is being directed in a circus by the circus master, and the music had to be played and replayed and replayed again, and additional rehearsals were done until he was satisfied that it would go. And I never had this in my life, saw this or experienced this in my life because in the last days suddenly he took it into his hands. The day after the first performance, where the press was divided, I came running to Diaghilev saying, 'Ah, I have just seen a marvellous article in a journal called *L'Excelsior* on the front page.' 'Well,' Diaghilev said, 'that cost me two lunches.' And he was very cynical about it, very relaxed. Then he told me that these things in my music are not good enough, these things are not good, these things are better and so on. He was quite relaxed after it was over.

PART 3

The Legacy

1 Spreading the Word

As Sokolova said, Diaghilev's death was the end of everything, at least for the Diaghilev company. No one was able to hold the enterprise together since the principal contenders were not readily compatible. It had only been Diaghilev's authority that had kept Massine and Balanchine as choreographers, or Dolin and Lifar as dancers, working side by side. Kochno, who probably had more skill and authority than the others in organizational matters, was on notably bad terms with many of his colleagues, and his influence proved insufficient. Above all, there was no money. After twenty extraordinary years the Ballets Russes de Serge Diaghilev simply ceased to exist.

But that very fact was the key to the next chapter in the history of ballet – the proliferation of classical dance companies all over the world, many of them created and led by former colleagues of Diaghilev. By the time I came to make the two Diaghilev films in the late 1960s the dancers had naturally all retired, although many were still influential as teachers, and of the choreographers only Balanchine was still working. But many of the younger generation of choreographers and directors had been formed as part of the diaspora that had followed Diaghilev's death. In a real sense the presence of Diaghilev still hung over the world of classical dance. Were it otherwise, I would never have been drawn to the subject or thought it so significant. Diaghilev's reputation may have faded in the years after his death, but something of his influence could still be sensed. That was what I had wanted to reveal through the interviews.

I have never thought that they achieved what I had originally hoped for or intended. Reading them now, it is clear that I had already, even before the filming, felt compelled to back away from trying to discover how things had happened and to substitute for that a lesser goal, to make the story as interesting and artistically telling as I could. On that level the films succeeded, but it was less than my original intention. The interviews became in a sense the evidence of failure. Not disaster, for at least a substantial number of important participants in the Diaghilev story had given their account. But I remained convinced that something more significant had happened, if it could only be pinned down. There was a degree of naïvety in this, since creativity is very hard to chart. No one is ever sure at what point an idea crystallizes, a design emerges or a musical motif is first heard in a composer's head, or who is responsible. The result is clear, but the process of gestation much harder to understand.

At various times over the past thirty years I have gone back to the interviews to find my reactions gradually changing. The passage of time has given me more confidence in what I did for, despite their largely anecdotal and descriptive nature, taken at length and not just in the small excerpts used in the films, the interviews contain, even if spread rather thinly, the clues to what I had wanted. Their subtexts show through more clearly than I had previously believed. Like a cipher which needs to be decoded, behind so many factual statements was the evidence of Diaghilev's policy. The interviews also highlight many of the differences between then and now, and suggest why it is so much harder to realize creative work today. This was something I had come to understand because of what happened to me as a result of the films.

A month or so before they were shown on television I was contacted by Peter Williams, the editor of *Dance and Dancers*, a monthly magazine about dance which at that time had considerable influence. He suggested meeting to discuss the films with a view to including something about them in the next issue of the magazine. We duly met and, after a long, gossipy lunch, recorded an extended interview about the programmes, sections of which appeared at the time of their transmission. It was good publicity, but it had wider repercussions. I had known Peter Williams by sight for many years. It was hard not to notice him, for he attended everything and, being extremely tall, was very visible. His height was accentuated by his willowy slimness, and in those days the long cigarette holder which wafted about above the heads of the crowd. He had started looking at dance in the 1920s and had seen the Diaghilev Ballet quite often. I would have done better to have interviewed him rather than Osbert Lancaster. He had become a designer, first of clothes and later of theatre, had been a colleague of Richard Buckle on his magazine *Ballet* immediately after the war, was closely associated with the creation of the Festival Ballet and worked as their press officer. He became the first editor of *D and D*, as it was known, a post he held for twenty-five years. Like many other prominent figures in the arts in those years, he was of independent means, and spent his money generously. Most evenings he bought dinner for someone after a performance, and often for whole groups.

I am not sure when he was first invited to join the Arts Council, but by the time I knew him he had become chairman of the Dance Committee. Together with Lord Harewood, he had written the Arts Council's influential report on opera and dance, which led to the creation of regional companies such as Opera North and Scottish Ballet. He was also chairman of the British Council's Dance and Drama Committee, and a key figure in the work of the Royal Ballet Benevolent Fund. He was involved in dance in a totally pervasive way and filled without strain a number of roles often thought to be contradictory. He could, as a member of the Arts Council of Great Britain, fund a company; as a friend advise that company on its repertory and development; and as a critic dispassionately review what they subsequently did. Only one or two inadequate ventures that lost their Arts Council funding found this unacceptable. For years any foreign company that came into London discussed what their programmes should be with him. He was a real power behind the scenes right across the world of dance.

Our lunch together was a success. I discovered that he had known who I was for years, but that the friend with whom he often saw me at the theatre, an Australian artist who drew dancers, was not on his list of favourite people. She had a tendency to telephone him at inconvenient moments and would go on for hours. I knew what he meant, for she did the same thing to me. But she also got complimentary tickets for performances, which was a help, for at that time I was not very well off. Once we had disposed of this seeming barrier, Peter and I got on famously. He could be very funny, was unusually tolerant, believed in the need for tradition, but was as committed as I was to dance in a much wider sense than just classical ballet. We saw each other frequently and by the late 1960s I counted him among my closest friends, something that continued until his death in 1995.

In 1969, no doubt due to him, I was invited to join the Dance Committee of the Arts Council, at that time a subcommittee of the Music Panel, which I also joined. It was my first experience of that particularly British system of arm's length arts administration – the invention of Maynard Keynes and Kenneth Clark – which still worked as effectively as it had done in the immediately post-war period. Membership of the committee not only brought me into contact with leading figures in the dance world, but meant that I was obliged to have views and justify them. My ticket of entry, as it were, was the Diaghilev films. Ever since that time I have been involved in one way or another with those organizations that are a hinge between state or local authority support and the artists themselves, ending up with a list of committees almost rivalling that of Peter Williams. The Diaghilev films were the moment of transition from being a spectator to having a more professional involvement. By the mid-1970s I was in charge of arts programmes on BBC2 and responsible for deciding which dance programmes would be shown on BBC Television. In Edinburgh, as director of the festival, I could invite companies to perform and even commission new works. Subsequently for nearly ten years I chaired the National Dance Coordinating Committee – an idea of mine to forge closer links between dance companies.

In those years there was little trouble in achieving an audience for dance. We were in the middle of what came to be called the dance explosion. But dance always had difficulty in finding people to join boards, launch appeals, assist foundations and so on. I became someone who, for a number of years, was pleased to be asked to undertake those roles. It was a time, if not of opulence, then certainly of aspiration, unlike today, when one feels that the original intention of the Arts Council to be an entirely supportive influence on the arts has become, through successive funding crises, almost entirely negated. Some of my contributons may have been useful, for example helping to draft the bid to raise dance from a subcommittee of music to a panel in its own right. Some were no doubt naïve or inappropriate. But nevertheless, in all that I did, I felt the influence of Diaghilev and his policy. His example and his achievements in the years from 1909 to 1929 had obviously influenced the next generation, the immediate successors such as Ninette de Valois and Balanchine. I had come to believe that Diaghilev's message could still be relevant in the 1970s and 1980s, despite the vast changes that had taken place since his time.

So dominant was Diaghilev's Ballets Russes that it is now hard to remember that it was not the only company operating in the early years of the century. Sokolova had made her mark in a group led by a dancer called Mordkin. The exotic and very rich Ida Rubinstein had run her own company in rivalry to Diaghilev during the 1920s. Massine and Nijinska had also led their own groups, while many of the French artists who collaborated with Diaghilev had worked with the Swedish Rolf de Maré and his Ballets Suedois from 1920 to 1925. But the principal influence on public taste in these years was a dancer whom Diaghilev rejected after one season: Anna Pavlova.

Everyone I knew when young had seen Pavlova, in Europe or America, in Australia or even, amazingly, Ceylon. She had gone everywhere on a permanent pilgrimage, fighting dreadful conditions to reach new audiences. I could never understand why she did it, why she never stayed in one place, running her company from there and founding a school as did so many other Russian dancers. I learned so much about Pavlova through accounts by my mother and her friends, and especially from Algeranoff, who had been a dancer in her company, that at times I feel I saw her myself, though she died before I was born. My mother first saw her in Melbourne, and never forgot the impact of her personality. In Lima the schoolboy Frederick Ashton saw her and always said it changed his life. Yet she only appeared with Diaghilev in his opening season in 1909. It is usually claimed that she was unprepared to submit to his will. Diaghilev's colleagues thought that she had dubious taste, preferring her little dance numbers to his great theatrical statements. She was certainly never very popular with her contemporaries. Even Karsavina, usually so generous, was cool about Pavlova's personality and severe in identifying technical shortcomings. Yet on and on she went, night after night, decade after decade, with her charming but artistically trivial little divertissements until her death in 1931, two years after Diaghilev. You could hardly expect her, with her small travelling circus, to be a focal point of creativity, but for a much wider public than Diaghilev ever reached she came to symbolize dance. The Dying Swan in my youth was as famous as any latter-day pop group. She was, and here we have the indisputable evidence of the film camera – something Diaghilev banned from his company – a mesmeric performer, able even at the age of fifty to give an illusion of girlish prettiness, or soulful Russian intensity. She was also tireless in a way that smacks of evangelism more than desperation.

Revealing dance to a live audience is something that mattered to Pavlova's generation. Even today the ghost of the idea still flickers fitfully in those oddly named groups of Russian dancers, popping up in the most unlikely places, calling themselves 'Stars of the Russian Ballet' or whatever. People still go to see them, though the dancers are of variable talent and the productions almost universally worthless in any terms Diaghilev would have recognized. But at least they dance, and often. Out on the road as Pavlova was, and as the Ballets Russes de Serge Diaghilev were for months a year, they danced just about every night. One of the reasons we fail to produce ballerinas today, let alone ones to whom the final accolade of *prima assoluta* can be given, is linked to that. All dancers complain about having to dance too often. Beware of a dancer who fails to complain if they dance too little.

No one talked of 'ballet' in the early years of the century, it was always 'Russian ballet'. Teachers and dancers had to have Russian names, however grotesque the results for non-Russians; for example Hilda Munnings was Munningsova before she became Sokolova, and Nottingham-born Hilda Boot in the Pavlova company was Butsova. It was the power of the words 'Ballets Russes' that eventually gave the rump of the Diaghilev company another two decades of life. A mysterious Russian businessman, Vassili Voskresensky, known to history as Colonel de Basil, brought a significant remnant of the Diaghilev Ballet together in 1932 and kept it going under one name or another until the late 1940s. Originally the Ballets Russes de Monte Carlo, it eventually became the Original Ballets Russes, just as meaningless a name. Although it kept a proportion of Diaghilev's creations in its repertory – *Les Sylphides, Carnaval, Petrushka, Spectre de la Rose* – it is primarily remembered today for Massine's later output, his symphonic ballets, *Les Présages, Choreartium* and *Symphonie Fantastique*, none of which was danced to an original score. Tchaikovsky, Brahms and Berlioz replaced Prokofiev and Stravinsky. Few new works created for the de Basil company remained in the repertory. *Beau Danube* and *Gaîté Parisienne* of Massine and *Graduation Ball* of Lichine are exceptions.

De Basil never claimed to be a creative artistic director like Diaghilev. He was a business manager, an impresario. I think it was Sacheverell Sitwell who told me how very much Diaghilev disliked the word 'impresario', with its implication of management rather than creativity. This was certainly true of de Basil and of a later example of a big international touring company with a wide repertory, the Grand Ballet du Marquis de Cuevas, which existed from 1947 to 1962. The de Cuevas company rivalled Diaghilev's in only one respect, the quality of its dancers. I saw them often during their visits to Britain in the 1950s and will never forget the impact of older members such as Markova and Toumanova, or the young American generation of Rosella Hightower and Marjorie Tallchief. But when it comes to creativity, practically nothing of those fifteen years remains. The only work I can recall with clarity is *Piège de Lumière*, and that only because of the designs. Peripatetic companies without a proper base were always vulnerable to changing attitudes, soaring costs and social upheaval. De Basil's Original Ballets Russes was stranded in Australia at the outbreak of the Second World War, while de Cuevas kept on running into money problems. The future in creative terms was to lie with those Diaghilev survivors who settled in one place, however improbable, founded a school, established a company and developed a repertory. Foremost among them were Ninette de Valois in London and George Balanchine in New York.

The way had been opened in London by Marie Rambert, who set up a school in 1920 and distinguished herself not just by training dancers, but by finding new choreographers, most notably Frederick Ashton and Anthony Tudor. By the time de Valois, in the aftermath of Diaghilev's death, started to assemble a company of her own, many of the necessary elements were already at her disposal: dancers such as Ursula Moreton, and even principals such as Alicia Markova and Anton Dolin, who had been stars of the later years of the Diaghilev Ballet. The story of British ballet's early years has been so frequently told, moving from Sunday Ballet Club to Camargo Society, from the Vic-Wells to the Sadler's Wells Ballet, that it looks in retrospect like an inevitable progression. Those who lived through it remember something quite different.

De Valois was very fortunate in her colleagues, most particularly in her music director, Constant Lambert, whose *Romeo and Juliet* had caused such a fuss with Diaghilev. Now almost entirely forgotten as a conductor, since he made very few recordings, and only of secondary importance as a composer, Lambert was nevertheless the brains behind the enterprise. Formidably well read and with a wonderfully unfashionable and wide-ranging taste in music (consider his Meyerbeer arrangements for *Les Patineurs*), he provided the intelligence behind the planning. De Valois knew that the *corps* dancers at her disposal were not at that time on a level with what people remembered from the Ballets Russes or continued to see through the regular visits of the de Basil company in the 1930s. What she worked towards was a new repertory geared to English taste and using the qualities of the people she had at her disposal. Her own ballets, among them *Checkmate*, with music by Arthur Bliss, or *Job*, to a Vaughan Williams score, are surviving examples of her ability as a choreographer. But she was most fortunate in the emerging talent of Frederick Ashton. Ashton, after studying with Rambert, had worked with Nijinska and Massine; he looked at everything going on in dance and had a sense of history and a love of the romantic era of the nineteeth century. His works have a natural lyric quality, as in *Les Patineurs*, while his sharp and slightly catty sense of humour and parody opened up in *Façade* a newer language than just the classical vocabulary.

Nothing helped the spread of ballet or its acceptance by a wider audience more than the Second World War. To an age of austerity it brought glamour; against a background of loss and deprivation it spoke of opulence and generosity not only through what one saw on the stage, but through its emotional impact. No one fought the war to save the modern movement; millions through it came to love the ballet. After the war the conquest of the empire was achieved by Ninette de Valois, sending her disciples out into the old dominions with a mission to graft classical dance on to any society that was reaching towards a cultural identity. Peggy van Praagh went to Australia, Celia Franca to Canada, David Poole to South Africa, Philip Chatfield to New Zealand. All of them set up national schools or companies which, to everyone's astonishment, flourished. Even Turkey was colonized for classical dance from Sadler's Wells.

Balanchine's career in the years following Diaghilev's death was at best unpredictable. He worked in France and Denmark, and even set up his own company in 1933. But in 1934, at the invitation of Lincoln Kirstein, he went to New York to found the School of American Ballet. As a performing group it made its début the following year with the still popular *Serenade*, to Tchaikovsky's Serenade for strings. Even though the company was taken under the wing of the Metropolitan Opera the following year, there were almost ten years of uncertainty before Balanchine was able to establish the New York City Ballet, whose director he remained until his death. It is only hindsight that gives the development of ballet in both London and New York a sense of inevitability.

Any family tree of the growth and development of these companies has Diaghilev as its progenitor, but whether his example was honoured varied considerably from company to company. They may have begun with established works, including some from the Diaghilev period, but, not surprisingly, they saw their primary role as finding a new approach and new repertory. In London Ninette de Valois's Vic-Wells Ballet, which became the Sadler's Wells Ballet, started off by including three works that the public had loved in Diaghilev's time: *Les Sylphides*, *Carnaval* and *Le Spectre de la Rose*. But no other Diaghilev ballets appeared in the Sadler's Wells repertory until after the Second World War. De Valois in the 1930s was building her own team, making her own ballets and, with Frederick Ashton as principal choreographer, creating works such as *Les Rendezvous* and *Wedding Bouquet*, which have remained in the repertory. Marie Rambert's company also pursued new talent, but often revived Nijinsky's *L'Après-midi d'un Faune*, which she adored and knew very well. In New York Balanchine never dropped *Apollo* from the repertory, though his first American success, the continuingly popular *Serenade*, came to have a similar place in his career as *Les Sylphides* had in that of Fokine, becoming what is now called a 'signature' work.

Fokine went on until his death in 1942, but never again found the form that had produced his early successes, for example *Petrushka* or the

Firebird. Nijinska settled in California and founded a school. Nothing in her later years equalled the achievement of *Les Noces* or *Les Biches*, but happily she lived long enough to supervise revivals of those works for the Royal Ballet in the 1960s. Massine had come back to London, invited by de Valois, immediately after the war to stage *La Boutique Fantasque* and later *Le Tricorne*. But he too suffered creative decline and his last years revolved around revivals, while he tried to assemble a visual and notated record of his earlier works. De Valois showed little interest in the early Diaghilev repertory until the 1950s, but eventually invited Grigoriev to revive *Petrushka* and Karsavina to coach Fonteyn in the *Firebird*. But Sokolova, with her extraordinary memory, was, with the single exception of the revival of *The Good-humoured Ladies*, in 1962, entirely overlooked.

Nevertheless, by the time I made my films in 1967 there was a network of companies across the world from London to Melbourne, and from New York to Cape Town, which in a real way owed their existence to Diaghilev and the legacy of the Ballets Russes. Few of them showed the extent of Diaghilev's insistence on involving composers and designers as well as choreographers in a collective theatrical statement, but elements of his influence remained, if only in that a substantial number of works he commissioned or revived were still danced. Even today, over sixty-five years after his death, the creative output of the Ballets Russes remains integral to the history of twentieth-century dance.

2 Looking after the Inheritance

The most obvious way in which Diaghilev's continuing influence can be felt across the world is in the survival in the repertory of ballets first given by his company. Although many have totally vanished, and some are only occasionally revived, others are so widely available that they have become a part of ballet's core tradition. Grigoriev lists in his book sixty-eight works as the output of the Diaghilev Ballet between 1909 and 1929. Breaking this list down produces a complicated picture, but the figures are nevertheless significant. Grigoriev omits from his list Diaghilev's early opera productions and also those operas presented in Monte Carlo during the 1920s. He does, however, include both *Le Coq d'Or*, which in 1914 was danced on the stage while the singers were placed in the orchestra pit, and *Le Rossignol*, whose first production had very little dancing but which re-emerged later in a new version by Massine, *Le Chant du Rossignol*. The early seasons contained a number of works previously seen in St Petersburg, and two sets of divertissements. Two of Massine's ballets were incorporated in later different versions: *Kikimora* became part of *Contes Russes*, and *Astuzie Femminili* was reshaped as *Cimarosiana*. *Cuadro Flamenco* was a set of Spanish traditional folk dances, and *Fireworks* had no performers at all, only moving lights. But even putting all those on one side, there were still forty-nine new ballets, and though thirty-one have vanished, eighteen still exist in something approaching their original version. There are three further works whose scores are well known and frequently played, *Daphnis and Chloe*, *Jeux* and *Renard*, but which as ballets exist only in versions unconnected with the Diaghilev Ballet.

It has therefore been possible for me during my years of looking at dance to see nearly a third of what Diaghilev produced, and helpfully those ballets cover the entire period of his activity, consisting of works by the five principal choreographers whom he engaged: Fokine, Nijinsky, Massine, Nijinska and Balanchine. It should be possible, then, to make some kind of assessment as to whether what the Diaghilev Ballet created can still be truly experienced theatrically in our time. Yet revivals bring problems as well as advantages, both as to the accuracy of the revival and how the work looks now in contrast to how it looked when it was first given. The passage of time has created more casualties than inadequate restaging.

Seventeen of Fokine's works were performed by the Diaghilev Ballet, fifteen of which were new. Of that seventeen, seven are still widely danced today. They represent comprehensively the range of Fokine's ideas, from the more classical language of *Les Sylphides*, *Carnaval* and *Le Spectre de la Rose* to the Russian qualities of *Firebird* and *Petrushka* and the exoticism of the two great successes of the first seasons, the *Polovtsian Dances* and *Schéhérazade*. It is not hard to appreciate the tremendous impact that the *Polovtsian Dances* must have made on that opening night of the Châtelet season in 1909. Borodin's music was hardly known and the sheer energy and vitality of the choreography was far removed from what was generally available in Western Europe at that time. The idea of the ballerina was, of course, familiar, but the role of the male dancer had been reduced to what was known as a *porteur*. Yet here was a stage full of whirling male dancers very convincingly representing warriors. The impact of *Schéhérazade* the following year was even greater. Here there was not only the riskiness of the girls' costumes and the daring of the final orgy, but the revelation for the first time of Bakst's genius as a designer. The contrast between what was seen on the stage and the tight-corseted society of pre-First World War Europe must have been extraordinary. Today the daring of the designs can still make an impression, but little is left of the rest. The music of *Schéhérazade* is very popular, and this no doubt conditions its revival as much as anything else. But in recent years I have not seen a production in which there was any sense of the drama, exoticism or danger that affected audiences when it was first danced. It has become one of those ballets that gets revived, but one has to ask why. Sokolova remembered that there were two kinds of male dancer in the Diaghilev company, known as the men and the boys, and that the men were all tall and virile, exuding real masculinity. Although the situation is changing today, for many years that is not how one would have described most male dancers. The sense of demonic activity and pent-up passion expressed by Fokine through dance was a revolutionary rejection of the pretty-pretty world of late nineteenth-century theatrical dance.

Once audiences had seen the *Polovtsian Dances* or *Schéhérazade*, a simple classical *pas de deux* was always going to look pale unless it was choreographed and danced with genius. That was certainly the case with *Le Spectre de la Rose*, remembered by everyone who saw it as the ideal vehicle for Karsavina's grace and Nijinsky's athleticism. It is revived for galas and occasional seasons, but it needs great dancers. In Diaghilev's time even revivals with soloists such as Idzikowski never equalled the impact made by Nijinsky and his famous leap through the window. *Carnaval* to Schumann's music was a charmer, and I remember in my youth loving its elegant flirtatiousness. The characterization drew on the old *commedia dell'arte* tradition, but with Fokine's special skill of creating character through movement. It is a fragile piece which again needs outstanding acting dancers to bring it off. But it should not be lost.

Much more complicated is the situation with *Les Sylphides*. An earlier version had been given in St Petersburg under the title still used in Russia, *Chopiniana*. It seemed that Fokine had taken all the language of the romantic tradition of nineteenth-century dance from *Giselle* onwards and transmuted it into a new kind of poetry. As I recalled earlier, it was the first ballet I saw, and I loved Benois's moonlit ruined chapel in the woods, and the sense of other-worldliness of the Sylphs. The problem in its revival lies not so much in understanding the style as in knowing which version to revive, for the question of accuracy is extremely complicated. There is no one agreed version of *Les Sylphides*. Fokine himself, in different places at different times over a period of nearly forty years, produced variants which contradict each other. Any production has to make choices. It provides a graphic example of the problem of conveying dance from one generation to another.

Today we have choreologists, dance notators, who, using one of several systems, write down as accurately as they can what the choreographer devises. But many things, particularly to do with expression, cannot be entirely written down. Fokine saw in different dancers individual possibilities that always led him to make slight changes. The original Schéhérazade, Ida Rubinstein, was not really a dancer. Fokine's wife, Vera, was an outstandingly good one, and exactly what Schéhérazade did tended to vary between performances according to which one of them was undertaking the role. Even when a second cast is taught by a choreographer at the same time as the creation of a work, small differences creep in. In a sense those differences are what make individuality important to dance. It is, of course, essential that *corps* movements should be identical and allow no latitude. From the older repertory, the great *défilé* at the opening of the 'Kingdom of the Shades' scene in *La Bayadère* is a testimony to the quality of Russian schooling and its uniformity of approach. Every movement of arm and leg of the *corps de ballet* as they move gradually to fill the stage has to be exactly the same, otherwise the impact is entirely lost. But when it comes to the solo dances that follow, something else must be present, something of the dancer's own personality. This is just as true of *Les Sylphides*, where the solos for the women and for the male dancer must show not just the steps, but something more. Yet how much variation can be allowed without distorting the original? I am sure that *Les Sylphides* will always remain in the repertory of most classical companies because it is in its way a perfect ballet. But although the many versions I have seen have all contained fundamentally the same movements, the different nuances can tremendously affect its capacity to involve and move an audience, preventing it from becoming a slightly faded museum piece.

The two profoundly Russian ballets of Fokine's early years with Diaghilev, *The Firebird* and *Petrushka*, show the full range of his dramatic as well as choreographic talent. But here too there are problems. *Firebird* is one of the rare examples in the story of the Diaghilev Ballet of a success being substantially revised. The original designs by Golovine and Korovine were much admired by C. W. Beaumont. I have never seen them except in rather pale sketches. The version danced today was designed by Natalia Goncharova in 1926, and so powerful is its impact that I can only think of *Firebird* in that form. Yet the redesigns demanded modification of the choreography, and that was done at a time when Fokine was no longer with the company. In the original designs the gates to Kashchei's Magic Kingdom were placed in the middle of the stage. As Beaumont recalled, when they swung open, his followers streamed on to the stage in their Infernal Dance. In the Goncharova version the gates are at the side of the stage, rather tucked away, and the whole impact is lessened. Yet there can hardly be anybody alive today who remembers the original. When it comes to the choreography of the leading roles one is on much safer ground. The Royal Ballet's version in London was, after all, staged by Grigoriev and his wife, and the role of the Firebird taught to Margot Fonteyn by Karsavina. The many photographs of the original production testify to how accurate the reproduction of the steps has been. I am convinced that a great deal of the magical atmosphere of Stravinsky's first ballet has survived, despite the change of scenery.

The situation with *Petrushka* is quite different and much less satisfactory. Stravinsky's music is one of the great masterpieces of musical theatre, while the story still has enough real drama to carry it, and it has leading roles to tempt good dancers. Why, then, does it usually fail in revival? Because, I believe, it has become fatally divorced from its original context. When Karsavina spoke of being moved by the Coachmen's Dance because it 'reminded me of my country' she pointed to a crucial fact. *Petrushka* is not just about puppets. It is about Russia. Fokine's and Benois's careful characterization of nurses, soldiers, itinerant vendors, performing bears and the rest of the crowd grows out of observation of the streets of St Petersburg in the nineteenth century. Modern Western companies attempt it without any sense of place; both characterization and mime have disappeared, leaving a gang of contemporary kids with funny costumes and totally inadequate make-up, giving hardly an idea of what they are meant to be or why. Unless this feeling of Russia is there in the crowd, none of the rest makes sense, however touching the Petrushka, dramatic the Moor or uncaring the Ballerina. One of the great moments in ballet, as the ghost of Petrushka appears on the roof of the magician's booth in the falling snow and fading light, goes for nothing. Why can its context not be effectively communicated to dancers of today? Is it simply because no one cares enough or tries hard enough? It may well require a considerable imaginative leap for a young dancer to appreciate a vanished world that he or she never knew, but what else are they trained for? Dance is not just steps. Benois may have made several different versions of the scenery, but Fokine's choreography remains unchanged, if only they could dance it. *Petrushka* is a priceless part of twentieth-century theatrical tradition. Yet few ballets have disappointed me so much in revival. We surely have a right to expect more with something of such quality.

Nijinsky made only four ballets for Diaghilev, two of which have disappeared without trace. As Karsavina recalled, *Jeux*, despite its extraordinary and prophetic Debussy score, was never a success and had very few performances. *Tyl Eulenspiegel*, choreographed during the Diaghilev Ballet's visit to America in 1916, was never seen by Diaghilev, and, according to Sokolova, never even completed. The dancers improvised the latter part of it owing to Nijinsky's incapacity to finish it. However, his two earlier works, *L'Après-midi d'un Faune* and the *Rite of Spring*, have left a mark on twentieth-century dance which has not been forgotten. Debussy was opposed to *L'Après-midi* being used in the theatre. He never intended it to be visualized in the way that Nijinsky wanted. Everyone involved found the style difficult and remembered the immense amount of time it took Nijinsky to convey the manner of movement. But it remains in the memory and also in performance. It is by far the best recorded of early Diaghilev ballets, through the many photographs, taken by Baron de Meyer, which reproduce almost all the stages of its action. Little more than ten minutes long and for a small group of dancers, it proved eminently revivable for people such as Marie Rambert, who had danced in it and knew it well. For contemporaries the furore that followed its first performance and Nijinsky's pose at the end, extending himself on the Nymph's scarf, imitating the thrusting movements of intercourse, may have given it a scandalous appeal, but today it seems timeless and extraordinarily beautiful. It no longer matters how long it took Nijinsky to realize it, it is a small masterpiece. Other choreographers have taken the music and used it in different ways, but Nijinsky's version still has power. Only Diaghilev would have given Nijinsky the chance to do it, insisting on his ability even though the company at the time thought he had no talent for choreography.

This was even more true of *The Rite of Spring*. I had always believed that this famous pretext for one of the greatest rows in theatrical history had vanished without trace. Dancers, such as Sokolova, who had appeared in it explained to me how little they remembered. And earlier attempts to call it out of memory had failed. However, a remarkable re-creation of it was eventually presented by the Joffrey Ballet in America in the 1980s, drawing on the recollections of all those survivors who knew it and the various notes that had been made at the time. It was subsequently televised and has been taken into the repertory of several companies. How can one assess it now? Rambert said that the music had become like 'a lovely prelude by Bach'. Even if one does not go that far, the greatness of the score is incontestable, a milestone in twentieth-century music, and many other dance versions have been made since which cannot be ignored. For myself, while I understand from what I have been told the scandal Nijinsky's choreography caused and the impact it made, in the reconstructed version it now looks rather small beer. Despite the best intentions of those who made the revival, it seems distanced from us in a way that gives it historical interest but very little actual power. It is like the completion of Mozart's Requiem, or Mahler's Tenth Symphony; something done with loving affection by people who understand, but which somehow feels not entirely genuine. Yet the fact that Diaghilev supported the production, even perhaps without understanding the importance of Stravinsky's music, is one of the things that has given him a permanent place in the history of the twentieth century. No one else at that time would have even considered something so outrageous and so likely to upset public taste. One of Diaghilev's more famous remembered remarks is 'There is no such thing as bad publicity. Scandal is good for the box office.' *The Rite of Spring* was a scandal. But today recordings abound, performances fill concert halls, and each time it is staged as a ballet the public responds with enthusiasm. In 1913 stamping one's feet and trembling may have been enough to upset the audience. Eighty years later other, more recent versions compel and convince in a way that the reconstructed Nijinsky does not. But I am nevertheless glad to have had a chance of seeing the attempt.

Of all Diaghilev's choreographers, Massine is the one whose reputation faded most quickly. A dominant figure in the 1920s and 1930s, he lived on into a bad-tempered old age in which his influence became negligible. Few choreographers made so many ballets which have been forgotten. In recent years revivals of some of his later ballets have won him renewed critical attention, but the works from the Diaghilev years seem to make less impact. This seems tremendously unfair, because Massine had qualities unlike any other choreographer of the century, an ability, which both Karsavina and Sokolova remembered in the interviews, to create character out of simple movements, and to tell stories often of extreme sophistication and wit through dance. Yet revivals have not served him well. *The Good-humoured Ladies* was given in 1962 by the Royal Ballet and was very enjoyable, but has not been seen since. A revival of *Le Tricorne* by the Birmingham Royal Ballet in 1995 drew weary reactions from the critics and a fair amount of apathy from the audience, who found it too long and too full of storytelling and narrative incidents between the dance sequences. But does this not say more about the quality of the acting than of the work itself? The sets and costumes for *Le Tricorne* were one of Picasso's great contributions to twentieth-century theatre. The score is masterly. Is not the problem perhaps that dancers today cannot suggest the real Spanishness of the work in the way that earlier companies did? *Le Tricorne* is closer to the reality of Spanish life and dancing than those many Spanish ballets that featured as part of Russian repertory in the nineteenth century, for example *Don Quixote*. But somehow or other it has lost its edge.

During his later years Massine made sure that all his major works were notated and claimed that they could all be easily revived, as his version of the *Rite of Spring* has been recently in France. One other that I would love to see is *Pulcinella*, again with a superb Stravinsky score and marvellous Picasso designs. But although occasionally given it has almost entirely disappeared. Once again, newer versions have taken its place by choreographers with a different approach. The Massine ballet which retained most of its oddness and originality when revived was *Parade*, that remarkable confection of Picasso designs and Satie music which presents on-stage all that was newest in the ideas that came out of Paris in the years around the First World War. *Parade*, with its cubist costumes and its *musique concrète* score, points to the future in a way that few other works did. It is not a substantial piece, either in length or in content, but it represents a ballet coming to terms with innovation in other areas as well as dance, and for that reason is, I believe, important. The most frequently performed Massine ballet from the Diaghilev years has been *La Boutique Fantasque*, a witty and entertaining work danced to a brilliant arrangement of Rossini by Respighi with décor by André Derain. The characterization of the visitors to the toy shop and the toys themselves remains clear and amusing. It is in most ways the least Russian of all Diaghilev's commissions, but it bears all the hallmarks of his policy in the close integration of music, design and choreography. I am sure that Massine's time will come again. His best works are so enjoyable.

Bronislava Nijinska, Nijinsky's sister, made seven works for the Diaghilev Ballet, two of them real masterpieces. Both *Les Noces* and *Les Biches* were revived by Nijinska herself for the Royal Ballet when Ashton was director of the company. They represent the two extremes of Diaghilev in the 1920s: *Les Noces* looks back to a Russia that Diaghilev and his associates had lost for ever, while *Les Biches* embraces the smart society world of the south of France in the post-war years. *Les Biches* is a fragile work, with many of its choreographic effects depending upon subtlety and nuance. In most of the revivals I have seen the comedy is played too broad, and the equivocal nature of relationships made too explicit. But nothing can diminish the exhilaration of Poulenc's music or the pale charm of Marie Laurencin's designs. It may be a period piece, but nothing better typifies the time in which it was created. *Les Noces*, on the other hand, is genuinely timeless. The Russia of which the music speaks so eloquently is without place or period, but somehow grasps the essence of the Russian soul. Nijinska created movements of matching, ritualistic grandeur. Over the years the Royal Ballet in London have revived it regularly and looked after it well. But I have often felt that the dancers have too little understanding of the background to the work.

In 1978 I collaborated with Bernstein and Nabokov in an extended television documentary about the music and the ballet. I suggested rather tentatively, while watching rehearsals with the Royal Ballet, supervised by Michael Somes, that it might be an idea if I were to speak to the company about the musical and literary sources of the work, which are curious and fascinating. The proposal was dismissed with contempt. Yet it is not entirely reasonable to expect that a group of young British dancers should understand the world *Les Noces* inhabits without some clues. They perform the steps with diligence and the version is marvellously accurate, as one can see from photographs, but it needs more than that, and raises again the question of whether it is possible to revive ballets across not only a wide expanse of time, but an even wider gap of cultural experience. There is no evidence that Stravinsky originally thought that *Les Noces* could be a ballet, any more than his original intentions for *Petrushka* were aimed at the stage, but Diaghilev somehow persuaded Stravinsky that it could be staged, and also found the right choreographer and in Goncharova the right designer. The whole development of Goncharova's ideas, at first very floral and pretty, finally refined to simple stark colours and lines, is real evidence of the care Diaghilev took in making sure that what he wanted to present should be realized at its best and not merely by the first response. By all accounts Nijinska was a difficult person. Dancers found it hard to understand what she wanted, and the integrity of her vision was hard to realize. Diaghilev took the trouble to do so. It contrasts strongly with how little Nijinska achieved in the years after the Diaghilev Ballet, although she went on working in various places for more than thirty years. As Markevich said, 'All these artists did their best to work for him', and happily that can still be appreciated today.

Diaghilev's last choreographer, Balanchine, went on for so long in the years following Diaghilev's death that it is very hard to reach back to his origins in the 1920s. Two of his Diaghilev ballets have survived, both with outstanding scores: *Apollo* by Stravinsky and *The Prodigal Son* by Prokofiev. In design terms *The Prodigal Son*, with its sinister sets by Rouault, is unchanged. *Apollo*, one of the most performed of twentieth-century ballets, very shortly after Diaghilev's death lost its original scenery. The spare, pared-down version in the repertory of so many companies today is not what Diaghilev presented when it had a very colourful décor by the French painter Bauchant. In this case I believe Balanchine was right to lose the Bauchant sets. The severely neoclassical mood of the ballet does not need clouds and prettiness. The starkness of what we see today is more in keeping with both music and choreography, which are in perfect balance.

All the Diaghilev works that survive in today's repertory provide clear evidence of his willingness to trust new ideas and new people. Only Fokine had any real reputation before working with Diaghilev, and even that was on a limited scale within the stuffy atmosphere of the imperial theatres. Nijinsky, Massine and Balanchine all did their first ballets for Diaghilev, and Nijinska, who had done some work elsewhere, had been a dancer in the Ballets Russes for years. Most striking of all, practically nothing else from the first thirty years of this century survives other than these Diaghilev works, so our whole view of the emergence of dance out of the Russian nineteenth-century tradition stems from Diaghilev and the people he chose. Time has not been kind to some of the things he presented. Exotic early works such as *Cléopâtre*, *Le Dieu Bleu* and *Thamar* from the Fokine years have gone, and I am sure rightly so. Massine in my view has been a casualty of the fact that although today's dancers are technically much better than their predecessors, they are not necessarily more impressive as actors. Even the leading roles in Massine ballets are often character parts, or demi-character, requiring the establishment of personality and not just the performance of steps, and this has proved a problem. I am sure also that Massine's intransigence and the difficulty of his personality did not encourage people to keep in touch with him or his work. So little of Nijinska's work is known at all that it is possible to overstate her abilities based on the evidence of only two incontestable masterpieces. But they are nevertheless masterpieces. *Les Noces* and *Les Biches* have enormously enriched the repertory. Balanchine's career moved in a different direction from works such as *The Prodigal Son*, which he rather disliked in later years, presumably because it contains narrative – something he had forsaken. But even if a bit dated, it still works, while *Apollo* has lost nothing of its impact after more than sixty years.

All these very varied new works have conditioned our view of the history of ballet in the twentieth century. So it is highly ironic that in the later years of the century programmes in companies across the world are dominated by exactly those full-length, three-act classical ballets from the nineteenth century that Diaghilev sought, for the most part, to avoid.

3 Preserving the Text

Diaghilev spent only a small part of his energy re-creating the past: *Giselle* in 1910, an intended revival for the great Spessivtseva; Act Two of *Swan Lake* in 1911 for Kchessinska, revived occasionally in the 1920s; and *The Sleeping Beauty* in the 1921 production that Diaghilev called *The Sleeping Princess*, and from which he salvaged a one-act version known as *Aurora's Wedding*. There is no doubt that Diaghilev, with his strong sense of history, honoured these great works from the nineteenth century, but he obviously felt them less important in his time than innovation. He can hardly have realized how the demands of later audiences would swing taste away from the evenings of short works that he presented to the massive three-act narrative ballets, for example *La Bayadère*, *Le Corsaire* and *Don Quixote*, which he had found so creatively stultifying in his early years working with the imperial theatres.

If full-length ballets become the centre of the repertory, there is an immediate problem. Unlike opera, ballet has very few bankable block-busters. It is claimed that the list of surefire successes in opera comprises about forty works. In the case of ballet it is fewer than ten. Five of those come from the nineteenth century: three Tchaikovsky ballets, *Swan Lake*, *The Sleeping Beauty* and *The Nutcracker*, and two French works, *Giselle* and *Coppélia*. The post-Diaghilev period has added maybe a few more, notably *Romeo and Juliet* and *Cinderella*. But it is with the older works that the principal problem arises: that of deciding what is the authentic text. Given the uncertainty, the response of most ballet companies today is not just to perform the classics, but to tinker with them.

In the strictest sense, none of the great works of the nineteenth century exists as a fixed entity. *Swan Lake* went through several versions before it settled in the form I knew as a child. Now every company feels the need to have its own *Swan Lake*, often substantially different from anyone else's. Many of these new versions not only fail to work in their own right, but go dangerously against the original intention of their composer and choreographer. So often it is reaction against the inherited experience rather than action on its behalf. Like Mahler's reorchestration of the symphonies of Schumann or Rimsky's modifications of Mussorgsky's harmonies, it places an opaque and unnecessary veil between the work as it originally was and the contemporary audience. Yet critics who dread yet another performance of *Giselle* or *Swan Lake* seem to admire changes of this kind. In Peter Darrell's 1960s version of *Swan Lake* the whole thing became the drug-induced dream of a drop-out Prince. Mark Morris's *Nutcracker*, vulgarly renamed *The Hard Nut*, is a post-Freudian evocation of abused childhood.

This constant tinkering requires examination. Why are we so flabby in not insisting that contemporary producers play fair with the work of their predecessors? No one would tolerate mucking about with Mozart, at least not with the notes. Perhaps it is because no one really believes that the Tchaikovsky classics or *Giselle* are on a par with Mozart or Verdi, so tinkering is somehow considered not only desirable, but artistically acceptable. The Royal Ballet's 1946 *Sleeping Beauty*, its signature production that won it world status, has gone through four reinterpretations over the past forty years, each of them visually weaker than the last, and not always with the clarity of storytelling that the original had so impressively retained. Later designers watered down Oliver Messel's Versailles-based vision without any apparent gain. The remarkable version produced by Peter Wright in 1968, designed by Lila de Nobili, transferred *Sleeping Beauty* from Perrault's France to a gothic Germany closer to the Brothers Grimm, at least a strong and dramatically original idea. It lasted for much less time than any hard-up company ought to envisage, given the vast cost of a new version. It was followed by new productions in 1973 by Kenneth MacMillan and in 1977 by Ninette de Valois, in what looked like a pastiche of the Messel sets of 1946. Maria Bjornson's most recent designs in the 1994 version produced by Anthony Dowell are, we are told, intended to last for twenty years. I can only hope that they do not. There is something deeply apologetic about our approach to the classics today, as if they need constant reworking, rather than loving preservation.

For *The Sleeping Princess*, which managed to be both Diaghilev's greatest success and his most damaging failure, Stravinsky rescored some of the music and Nijinska restaged some of the dances. Yet the whole project was intended to glorify both Petipa and Tchaikovsky – not Nijinska and Stravinsky. Bakst's striking scenery was to celebrate the influence of the great baroque designers, among them Bibiena. The costumes may have been difficult to dance in because they were so elaborate and heavy, but at least scenery was designed in a way that made the stage easy to use. Aurora was not expected to come down a very steep flight of steps for her first entry as she is in the current Royal Ballet production. Diaghilev's production was conceived as a homage to the greatness of the past, not as a 'Look at me!', 'How clever I am!' version for the present. Matthew Bourne's new *Swan Lake* for Adventures in Motion Pictures has an all-male cast of swans. It has been, of course, a huge success and in many ways deserves it, for it shows originality and intelligence. However, I am forced as so often to ask what impression something like this is making on someone who knows no history, no tradition, and is seeing the ballet for the first time? Much of the musical world in recent years has sought to reach back to the 'authenticity' of performances in the seventeenth or eighteenth century, however impossible that may be. When Mary Skeaping in her version of *Giselle* for the Royal Swedish Ballet restored the fugue that is normally cut from the scene with the Wilis, everybody fell about with laughter at such archaeological pedantry. But, so brain-washed are audiences by relentless revision, I doubt whether anyone today could tell you how the great classics were danced thirty, let alone sixty or a hundred, years ago. It all speaks of a lack of confidence in what was achieved by our predecessors.

But the reasons for change can be even shabbier. Companies today need sponsorship, and sponsorship can only be sought for new productions. Since no one can come up with good new ideas, especially in the case of the Royal Ballet since the death of Kenneth MacMillan, directors turn to revamping *Nutcracker* or *Swan Lake* or *Sleeping Beauty*, which at least have the virtue of being known quantities in an age that demands higher attendance for everything, so as to maximize box-office income and compensate for falling subsidy. It all lacks creative conviction and the sense that a strong artistic leadership is there to demand why the changes have been necessary. If that cannot be satisfactorily answered in artistic terms, then it should be refused, even if the commercial conditions suggest something different. I have never believed that theatre can be set in concrete, but, however many new ideas are brought to bear on Shakespeare by imaginative directors, very few have sought to rewrite the text, even though in some cases, as with *Macbeth*, the text is defective.

Early in 1982 I found myself in Peking improbably intervening in a class at the China Ballet. I had gone to China to try to acquire for the Edinburgh Festival the Western European première of the remarkable People's Art Theatre of Peking. Since the trip was partly funded by the British Council, I had volunteered to do anything I could to help reconnect culture in the West and what was emerging in China after the collapse of the so-called Cultural Revolution. Every day I went to theatre performances in the evening, but spent the mornings with a variety of professional groups: writers, film directors, drama teachers and, at my request, also dancers.

Classical ballet had arrived in China from Russia during the years of post-war cooperation. A number of teachers from the famous Vaganova school in Leningrad had gone to China to find and train dancers. Surprisingly, the school and the subsequent performing company that emerged survived the break with Russia. They felt very isolated, and in a sense represented the most extreme example of a museum culture that one could find, for the productions in their repertory of Russian classics such as *Swan Lake* or *Don Quixote* had no connection whatsoever to their past, present or future in terms of the mainstream of Chinese culture. It was something totally imported and grafted on from outside. My contact with this company had been one of the soloists, whom I had met earlier when he had been studying and performing in Houston with the company run there by the British choreographer Ben Stephenson.

This particular Chinese dancer, a likeable but rather pushy young man, was very keen for me to be impressed, and suggested after the general class a soloists' class, to which my advice and experience might be made available. Eight soloists remained behind and asked what I would like to see them do. It seemed a good idea to suggest something that I knew very well, which would give me a standard of comparison, and after some discussion we opted for the *pas de deux* from the last act of *Don Quixote*, a notorious showpiece of dance galas which gives a very strong technical challenge to both male and female soloists. Four couples danced together in the big rehearsal room. It was a very odd experience. I was struck by the curious imprecision of many of their movements, particularly of the hands and arms. How did they learn these steps, I asked. Well, from notation left by the Russian teachers. What did the circular revolving movements of the girls' hands mean, held just above their heads? Blank looks. 'Show me slowly,' I requested. The little short-fingered hands made a vague twisting gesture. 'But what are you actually *doing*?' I asked. Silence. I then volunteered, 'You are playing the castanets.' Total silence. The castanet was not something that had ever been heard of in China, and the notation gave no clue.

I cannot remember a clearer example of how easy it is to lose the meaning of something. Opera singers quite frequently perform in languages they do not speak, learning phonetically, but at least they have the dramatic sense of the passage to give them some clue. Here the whole experience of Spanish dancing, or the pastiche of Spanish dancing represented by the nineteenth-century choreography, fell outside their experience or their knowledge. It was no little wonder that what they were doing was enthusiastic, but, in the strictest sense, illiterate.

The dancers I saw in China had nothing to work from except a choreologist's notation. One or other method of notation is increasingly used – not merely as a record, but as a teaching text. Obviously notation has benefits since it can indicate a great deal where memory can be unreliable. Dancers have remarkable short-term memories. But after an interval of years remembering the solos comes more readily to them than ensemble or *corps* work. Algeranoff told me that when the original cast of that delightful ballet *Jeux d'Enfants*, created by the de Basil Ballet, came together a mere fifteen years after it had first been done, none of them could remember all of it. Vital links and transitions had somehow vanished. They had no notation. Yet dance notation even at its most subtle can never tell you what to feel. I remember Markova giving a master-class on the White Swan *pas de deux* from Act Two of *Swan Lake*, and insisting again and again that the Swan Queen should never look at the Prince in the early stages, so making marvellously telling the moment when she somehow ceases to fear capture and welcome involvement, which she reveals by, for the first time, looking directly at him. I always watch out for this when I see *Swan Lake*, and practically never see it reproduced. I am sure it could be traced back through Markova to earlier dancers and teachers who told her and who learned it from the original choreography of Ivanov. But many people have never been told this, and so it has generally disappeared. It may seem a very small, finicky point when one is looking at the survival of a major art form. Should one not just be pleased that *Swan Lake* still exists and is available to dance audiences across the world, rather than nit-picking about where someone's eyes are at a crucial moment? On the contrary. For *Swan Lake* to be worth remembering, detail of this kind is essential.

At their worst the problems of the transfer of choreography from one generation to another suggest that it can hardly be worth bothering. Something essential seems to disappear. The nearest analogy is in translating poetry into another language. But a very good translator can somehow convey the essential, as can a very good producer in dance. Time and again Peter Wright has shown his extraordinary skill in restaging classical masterpieces in a way which incorporates individual possibilities alongside the retention of the essential tradition. But with lesser people involvement of many different minds over years gives a bewildering feeling of multi-authorship.

This is perhaps less true of *Giselle* among dance classics, but *Swan Lake* has suffered greatly. To take another example, one of the big differences between productions is in how the Third Act, the Black Swan act, is presented. The structural sequence of the act is quite clear. There is a ball, at which Prince Siegfried is expected to choose a bride. Princesses are produced, but rejected. Just as it seems as if there is stalemate, the Enchanter von Rothbart appears with his daughter disguised to look like the White Swan that we have seen with Siegfried in the previous act, and with whom he has become enamoured. They dance; though dressed in black, she convinces him she is the same girl. We know she is not, though the same dancer performs both roles. He agrees to marry her; thunder and lightning strike the stage; there is a vision of the genuine Swan Queen; all is confusion, and Siegfried runs off to find the real girl.

It is dramatically quite straightforward, except for the fact that at some stage during the act there is a set of national dances – a Spanish dance, a Neapolitan dance, a Hungarian csardas – which inevitably hold up the action. What is their purpose, and at what point should they happen? It is a typical nineteenth-century theatrical device to put a set of dances of this kind in the middle of a story. In the old Sergeyev version von Rothbart arrives, presents his daughter, she goes off with the Prince and von Rothbart sits down with the Prince's mother and watches the dances. A number of versions today suggest the national dances are a kind of entertainment provided by von Rothbart rather than the Prince's mother. They come as part of his retinue. Beryl Grey did a production for London Festival Ballet which moved the dances back to the earlier scene with the Princesses. Their famous waltz was interrupted to interpolate the national dances as if they represented the countries from which the Princesses came. It sounds quite sensible, but it had the most dreadful effect on the music, constantly interrupting one of Tchaikovsky's finest waltzes. I do not think there is any real answer to this problem. In Act One of *Giselle* there is a moment when a peasant *pas de deux* or *pas de trois* is inserted into the action of the villagers. This is, in the strictest sense, an irrelevance, since it even uses music by a different composer, Burgmüller, rather than Adolphe Adam. But somehow after 150 years it has become part of the tradition. The national dances in Act Three of *Swan Lake* are there just to fill time and provide a spectacle, so there is little point in trying to make sense of them in a narrative way. They are a convention.

If that seems a weak and an unimaginative response, I would question how much of the story is intelligible anyhow, given another distortion which has happened through later production attitudes, where fashion has played a part. It became normal at a relatively recent stage to remove passages of pure mime from classical ballet, though, of course, they had been an integral part of dance from the seventeenth century onwards. The language of mime within classical dance is often the one clear indication of the story. The plot is advanced through mime and then reacted to in dance, as an aria is in a sense a reaction to a recitative in a Mozart opera. For a long time cutting recitatives in opera was standard practice. In almost every case they are now restored. But not so with mime in the dance classics. If you remove mime from *Swan Lake*, for instance, what little logic the story has disappears completely. I think it matters in Act Two that you know why Odette has been turned into a swan, and also what is the origin of this lake. Ivanov's choreography in the version that I first saw and memorized showed this quite clearly. There was a short musical section in an agitated minor key which accompanied a mimed dialogue between Odette and Siegfried, with a visual representation of Odette's mother's royal rank, the loss of her daughter to the Enchanter von Rothbart and the fact that it was her tears which formed the lake. Very few contemporary versions of the ballet include it. Yet it surely matters – otherwise how does the Prince know whether these birds are birds or women, or why they seem to regain human form at night? Some contemporary critics will say, 'Who cares? It is only a fairy story.' But I would counter by saying that fairy stories are not just fairies but stories, and stories need telling.

Once again, *Giselle* has fared better. If the sword is not left in the cottage opposite Giselle's mother's home, how can the gamekeeper Hilarion produce it to prove that Albrecht is not a jolly peasant but an aristocrat slumming? The sword is also essential because otherwise Giselle has nothing to kill herself with. It is a crucial element in the action. But then so are knitting needles in *Sleeping Beauty*. Older productions of *Sleeping Beauty* had the knitting women prominently present at the start of the scene where Aurora appears for the first time. The needles are discovered and the women thrown out. In some more recent versions they have gone entirely, and no one sees a knitting needle until Carabosse produces one with which the Princess spikes her finger. Removing the *tricoteuses* weakens the whole dramatic structure of that act.

These may seem like small details, but they are exactly the kinds of detail which Diaghilev insisted on. When he said to Karsavina, 'Let's go and re-create *Giselle* in the Paris Opéra' the place where it was born, I am sure there were substantial ways in which *Giselle* differed from how it had been danced in the mid-nineteenth century. But the decisions on details, as is quite clear from the accounts of the dancers, came out of close study of the past, and a real understanding of the dramatic demands of the situation. That is why people were moved and why it was remembered. Not the dead hand of the past, but a living tradition.

The essence of the transmission of dance from one who knows to one who is learning must always go far beyond just steps and music. If the message is truly learned and understood in theatrical as well as technical terms, it will always show. Moira Shearer told me that, thrown in at very short notice for her first performance of *Giselle*, she panicked, and rushed up to Hampstead to get Karsavina's advice. A very sensible thing to do, one would think. Not so. After the First Act at her initial performance Ninette de Valois came thundering round to her dressing room to complain violently about what she had seen her do. So what it was that Karsavina had passed on to Moira Shearer was instantly visible. She never forgot this incident or, indeed, ever forgave de Valois for her reaction. Sokolova, who danced *Le Spectre de la Rose* a few times with Nijinsky, told me that she always tried to imagine herself as Karsavina when dancing it – no mean feat, since they were very different in height, temperament and technical skills. Sokolova, a much sturdier dancer, had to reach for fragility. When I asked if there wasn't another way, her way perhaps, of dancing the role, she looked at first shocked and then for a rare moment almost angry that I should so singularly fail to understand that changes of that kind were not acceptable, and would be a betrayal of what had been devised by Fokine. If she was to dance the girl in *Le Spectre de la Rose*, she had to get as close to Karsavina as she could.

So how, I asked her, did *Le Tricorne* seem to her, choreographed on her body but permanently associated by the public with Karsavina, who danced the première? 'Well,' she said, 'Tamara was more of a lady than I was. I felt it more as a peasant.' When I questioned Massine about this, he did not remember anything other than how very quickly Karsavina had picked up the steps, given the fact that she had less experience than Sokolova of the kind of Spanish dancing which had inspired the role. But experienced dancers learn steps with a facility that is astonishing to the outsider. What is less clear is how long it takes them to feel more than the steps, and whether that depends on more and more thorough rehearsals or more and more performances. We all want to see solo dancers bring something of themselves to their performances, but the range of personal adjustment or elaboration is, or should be, very small when it comes to steps. The difference comes from within. And that is where so much ballet training today falls short. The brilliant musical and choreographic diversity of the Fairy Variations in the Prologue to *Sleeping Beauty* tells the audience, or should, exactly what quality each fairy is bestowing on the infant Princess. Diaghilev thought it worth Ninette de Valois's crossing Europe to prove this point, in the Fairy Violante Variation, where, with her sharpness of attack, she made the point better than any other available dancer. It was a typical Diaghilev response; he wanted the best, even at considerable expense. De Valois thought it was too much to expect her to cross Europe for a dance lasting less than a minute. So often these days the fairies in *Sleeping Beauty* seem to have been handed their roles according to no better system than seniority or Buggins's turn. The connection between their own qualities as dancers and the qualities they are bestowing on the baby have become so tenuous that the whole original point is lost.

But who should tell dancers not just what to do, but what it should mean? Watching Frederick Ashton or Kenneth MacMillan at work always took one to the core of the dancer's individuality. However well others may dance the role of Natalia Petrovna in Ashton's *A Month in the Country*, for those of us with long memories the role belongs to Lynn Seymour. Yet in earlier years she had been the victim of a cast change just as personally saddening as Sokolova had experienced with *Le Tricorne*. MacMillan's *Romeo and Juliet* was choreographed on Seymour, but for the same box-office reasons that led Diaghilev to use Karsavina in *Le Tricorne* the première of *Romeo and Juliet* went to Fonteyn. It became one of Fonteyn's most famous roles, additionally touching for the insight this 46-year-old brought to the embodiment of teenage love. But I can never forget that it was Seymour's vulnerability that had stimulated the steps that MacMillan had produced.

The *pas de deux* in MacMillan's ballets were always the core of his work. Nowhere is this more true than with *Mayerling*, in which a series of intense, erotic *pas de deux* charts a whole range of sexual and sensual response with an urgent originality that in my view is truly great. Set in the middle of a vast historical canvas, impossible to follow without copious notes and access to the *Almanach de Gotha*, they justify the ballet by bypassing history to become profound statements about the human condition. Yet today, only twenty years after they were created, in the persons of other dancers the edge has been blunted. They are still extraordinary, but no longer for me disturbing. Is it any wonder that the legacy of Diaghilev, after anything between sixty and ninety years, seems frequently vague and distant?

If you accept the line of thought that you cannot preserve things exactly as they were, then the logical extension is that only the new should be presented to the public and nothing revived or retained. I cannot go that far. But I am sure that much more needs to be done in the communication of dance across the years to justify most revivals, and to re-create more than a shadow of the original creative impulse. We need teachers with real understanding, not glorified physical education instructors. We need choreologists with modesty about what notation leaves out, and company directors with much clearer ideas about casting. Beyond that, I want artistic directors who are just that – who know about art and who are not afraid to direct. But is that possible in our present times?

4 Who Directs the Directors?

Had Diaghilev lived as long as Ninette de Valois, he would still have been alive in the 1960s to be interviewed for my films. His early death meant that I had to depend on the views of others and my own judgement. But one thing, above all, struck me during the research. Diaghilev was responsible for everything as director of the Ballets Russes. Artistic director first and foremost, but many other things as well, in areas today covered by additional people: finance, administration, publicity, planning. It is rare to find anyone since his time who has attempted, let alone succeeded in, all these roles. Of course, Diaghilev had 'the committee', that small group whom he trusted and presumably at times even allowed to make policy, though evidence of that is hard to come by. Composers, choreographers and designers all seemed to bend to his will, as the interviews show. Projects began with his encouragement and existed only with his continuing support. Even the influence of the public, as expressed through the box office, took a lower place, as one sees in his refusal to revive past successes just because there was continuing public demand. The company policy was his policy – it was, after all, as Dolin said, his company, his initiative. His authority prevailed because he knew more about more things than any of his colleagues. That meant that the policy which stemmed from it usually justified itself in artistic terms. He had the normal problems of any company director at any time – finding talent, bringing it on in the best possible way and then retaining it when it became successful. He realized how crucial to this was the role of the choreographer. Ballets did not succeed because of their décor or their music, however distinguished. Diaghilev's willingness to woo Fokine back after Nijinsky's departure, and even to bring Massine back after his marriage, showed the practical flexibility that any artistic director must have, overriding his own emotional involvement. But the choreographer is only part of the story, however important.

If since Diaghilev's death the focus has been most sharply on the choreographer, it is not just as dance maker but as artistic director. Almost all the classical companies of the past fifty years have been led by former dancers who became choreographers, and inevitably the work of these companies centred on their own creations. While Balanchine's New York City Ballet or Cranko's Stuttgart Ballet can be seen as the positive side of this situation, there are more numerous examples where the lesser talents of the choreographer/director have led to stagnation and decline. Nowhere is this more true than in the cases of those two, as it were, 'parent' companies of classical dance, the Bolshoi in Moscow and the Kirov in St Petersburg. Both have schools which perpetuate the Russian classical tradition and the continued involvement of great dancers of the older generation, so the ability of Russian-trained dancers to dance well has rarely been in doubt at any stage since the Revolution. But what they were dancing was a different matter.

Communist regimes required heroic spectacle. The dancer was seen as a supreme physical embodiment of the people, in the same way as the Olympic athlete. They were used to justify the political system when it came to creating new works. Ideological requirements took precedence over imagination. The two directors, Vinogradov and Grigorovich, who have dominated Russian ballet for the past quarter of a century, have failed entirely to find a new repertory or to renew the creative spirit of Russian dance. The relentless tinkering with the classics so prevalent in the West has been just as evident and damaging in Russia, although more so in Moscow than in Leningrad. These directors had quite extraordinary power, but it was an authority not justified by artistic achievement. Both have now been pushed aside, but nothing and no one have yet emerged in their place to suggest a new spirit at work. Meanwhile, the economic conditions which surrounded the companies under communism have disappeared so that new work cannot be contemplated because no money can be found for the costumes or designs. All the energy is expended on just keeping going, undertaking lengthy foreign tours to earn hard currency, with increasingly desperate attempts to retain their best dancers, many of whom prefer a less prestigious role in the West, where they can at least pay their rent. Russia has certainly not been the place to look for artistic directors with vision.

Of the Western countries, France continues to produce outstanding dancers, and has demonstrated several different approaches to the quest for artistic significance. Both Lifar and Kochno went on to run companies after Diaghilev's death, Lifar at the Paris Opéra and Kochno rather later with the small but influential Ballets des Champs-Élysées. Lifar's reputation was virtually destroyed by the war, and he never had the intelligence to be a second Diaghilev. Kochno was more interesting, for, like Diaghilev, he was not a performer, but had a certain creative vision. He went on devising scenarios for choreographers, commissioning composers and designers until the 1950s, but it all fizzled out and, ironically, his achievements were eventually overtaken by the success of the choreographer he had put his faith in, Roland Petit. Petit is archetypally French, with a long theatrical career that has ranged indiscriminately from the classics to revue. Despite the success of his early and middle years, it was never for the choreography that one remembered his ballets, but rather for their theatricality. There is a kind of French approach to ballet which depends on what is called the *coup de théâtre*, a dramatic and effective moment, often in tableau, which sets a scene or achieves some kind of apotheosis. The result of this is to give you brilliant moments, but what have often been called *mauvais quarts d'heures*. Petit had a particular gift for tableau, while his wife, the dancer Renée, later Zizi, Jeanmaire, became as famous as any great classical dancer, but for a kind of repertory closer to the music hall. Petit's creative career has long been in decline, though he is still at work. I remember so well being enchanted by *Les Forains*, with its lovely Sauguet score, in the late 1940s, and also being thrilled with his dance version of *Carmen*. But there were always dreadful vulgarities along the way and odd reworkings of the classics, notably *Coppélia*. In the end Petit seems to me more clever than important, more entertaining than significant and, despite his survival running companies in different cities in France for over forty years, no Diaghilev.

A variant of the Petit approach is that of the Marseilles-born choreographer Maurice Béjart, one of the most successful company directors of our time, in Brussels with his Ballets du Vingtième Siècle and later in Lausanne. Like Petit, Béjart is a master of the *coup de théâtre*, but sadly, like Petit, he also has not maintained the choreographic originality that made his early reputation. Béjart was not afraid to take a score such as *Firebird* and give it a new and very effective scenario. He was open to non-European influences, both in music and in movement. But over the years the effect became more and more just that – effect, hollow at the centre and straining for a significance it rarely achieved. His company was, however, for many years extremely popular, and Béjart proved highly ingenious, delighting in filling improbable spaces such as the Cirque Royale in Brussels or the Piazza San Marco in Venice with dancers, using brilliant lighting effects and adopting a sort of camp chic which I find fundamentally fraudulent. It is as if dance were being *used* and the dancer's body merely an object forced into ever more improbable contortions.

Practically everyone has had a go at running the Paris Opéra Ballet, from

Lifar to Nureyev, via a number of French dancers and choreographers of differing ability. Paris's strength has lain in an eclecticism of repertory allied to the quality of its dancers. It has taken works from all over the place, using Russians such as Bourmeister to restage classics, importing American ballets, notably from Balanchine, and even British ones from MacMillan. It has flirted with modern dance choreographers, including Lucinda Childs and Carolyn Carlson, and through its great size maintained a wider repertory than many other companies. But no one has succeeded in putting a creative stamp on its output. They may have commissioned Chagall to design *Daphnis et Chloé*, and at the same time to repaint the ceiling of the Garnier Opera House, but how many can now recall who did the choreography? I never fail to enjoy watching the Paris Opéra Ballet, but it is the performers rather than the works which give the pleasure.

For fifty years the American scene was dominated by Balanchine. But it is important to recall the man who persuaded him to go to New York and, indeed, to stay there at a time when the lure of Hollywood and its high fees was very strong. This was Lincoln Kirstein, in many ways the most Diaghilev-like figure to be involved in dance since Diaghilev's death, but with a difference. Kirstein operated much more behind the scenes than in the public eye. A man of great culture, unusually, for a rich young American, passionately committed to the new, he was a force behind much that proved important in the American art world in the middle years of this century. Not only did he fund the Balanchine school when it opened, he was a founding figure of the Museum of Modern Art. Sadly, though the opportunity presented itself on two occasions that I recall, I never met Kirstein, who died only in 1995, but I have a suspicion that I would not have got much out of him had we talked. The image I always received from both his writing and his public manner was aloof and Olympian. There was no argument about the depth of his culture, but he certainly did not seem to have the kind of personality that would go out and lead a public enterprise in the way that Diaghilev had done. Kirstein used his authority and to a great extent his fortune in the service of the arts. But it is an open question as to how much influence he had over his closest colleague, George Balanchine.

Balanchine was an extraordinary man from any point of view. He never made great claims for his career as a dancer, but he had a quirky originality in character parts that allowed him to use his imagination. Markova remembers him going on as the Cat in *La Chatte* (presumably everybody else was injured as usual), and reducing the company to giggling incompetence. There is a marvellous photograph of him as the Enchanter Kashchei in the *Firebird*. But it was his choreographic talent rather than his dancing that singled him out from the very start of his time with Diaghilev. He had a solid grounding both in dance and in music, and his friendship with Stravinsky was, together with that with Kirstein, the most important and fruitful of his life. Yet his ultimate achievement in choreographing virtually everything that Stravinsky ever wrote, and then doing the same for Ravel, seems almost wilful given how much in his youth he had been involved in creating entirely new works to new scores. I have never been a total subscriber to the New York view of Balanchine as 'the greatest genius in the history of twentieth-century dance', though it is understandable why New York thought that. He certainly showed an aspect of genius in the way he extended the vocabulary of classical dance into whole new areas of movement which not only work theatrically, but look as natural as anything Fokine devised.

Yet along the way there were losses. After early successes such as *The Prodigal Son* he moved implacably away from narrative, and with it went scenery, costumes and characterization. Time and again I would come out of performances by the New York City Ballet, especially in its great years, the 1950s and 1960s, knocked out by the quality of the choreography and the dancing, but unsatisfied by the event as theatre. On the rare occasions when he sought something more traditionally theatrical, as in his full-length ballet *Jewels*, I was even more disappointed. Today, when it is fairly difficult to find any great originality in the work of younger choreographers who still retain the classical vocabulary, the Balanchine legacy looks superb. But is not the theatrical impact of classical dance reduced when almost always danced in front of a plain backcloth in all-over tights or practice clothes? Even so you only have to look at the work of Balanchine's imitators to see how superior he was in his capacity to devise steps and produce a new kind of dancer to perform them. Balanchine liked dancers with long legs and very small heads. It never seemed to me that he liked dancers who had much in those heads. He went on working as long as Petipa, and in a sense the whole American classical dance scene stems from what he did. But although it may seem ungrateful to carp even in a quiet way, I could never survive on a diet of Balanchine alone. The only other American choreographer of comparable quality is Jerome Robbins, versatile in that he could move from *West Side Story* on Broadway to *Dancers at a Gathering* for the New York City Ballet without difficulty. But Robbins's output has been disappointingly small, and although still alive he has become, like Nijinska, a name to be invoked rather than a continuing and powerful influence.

The combined talents of Kirstein, Balanchine, Stravinsky and Robbins would suggest that the New York City Ballet was in its great years the nearest thing in artistic terms to the Ballets Russes de Serge Diaghilev. But it certainly never felt like that. It felt like a company which revolved almost exclusively around its founder choreographer: his taste, his judgement, his talent, but also his limitations.

The other leading American company of the post-war years, American Ballet Theatre, had grown out of a group led by Mordkin, who had been with both Diaghilev and Pavlova and staged *Swan Lake* in New York as early as 1927. ABT was quite the opposite of NYCB, eclectic in its choice of choreographers, highly dramatic in its creations and the retention of narrative work and with a strong sense of the value of the past. It presented Fokine's last works and the new American talents of Agnes de Mille and later Twyla Tharp. It was for many years the home base of the great Anthony Tudor, the Rambert protégé, who moved to New York in the late 1930s and spent the rest of his life there, and whose work is today sadly underrated and neglected. ABT was very influential, particularly through constant touring and travel, and it certainly won a new audience for dance in America. It was kept afloat for many years by its director, Lucia Chase, who had not only good taste, but considerable sums of money with which to fund a policy. It had a range comparable to that of the Diaghilev Ballet, but eventually fell victim to the full-length classic virus that has infected all classical companies except Paris and the New York City Ballet. Today, sadly, ABT is hardly a force to be reckoned with, despite its heritage.

In Great Britain the person who has always paid warmest tribute to Diaghilev for teaching her everything she knew is Ninette de Valois, and it is therefore important to examine whether the Diaghilev policy survived in the company she created and its off-shoots, both in the United Kingdom and elsewhere. In 1996 de Valois, at the age of nearly ninety-eight, was present at a gala to mark the fiftieth anniversary of Sadler's Wells Ballet moving permanently to the Royal Opera House, Covent Garden. It was a grand and touching occasion. Thirty former members of her company who had appeared on that night in 1946 joined today's Royal Ballet in the final act of *Sleeping Beauty*: not only ballerinas such as Nadia Nerina, Beryl Grey and Violetta Elvin, but others whose careers had taken dance in different directions, among them Margaret Dale (to television) and Gillian Lynne (to the West End musical theatre). In 1946 the founding triumvirate of de Valois, Constant Lambert and Frederick Ashton was still there. But Lambert died in 1951. The following year Ashton became co-director and in 1963 he took over as director, remaining in that position for seven years. De Valois officially retired in 1968, but in a real sense has always been present. Since Lambert's death no one has occupied as prominent a role in the musical planning of the House, and one of the criticisms made of the Royal Ballet is how relatively rarely it has commissioned new scores. Henze's *Ondine* and Britten's *Prince of the Pagodas* were the only full-length ballets with new scores in the post-war years. Most of Ashton's big successes were danced to existing music: *La Fille Mal Gardée* (1960), *The Dream* (1964), *Enigma Variations* (1968). As director of the company Ashton gave little impression of confident authority or that he had a clear vision of the future.

He never spoke with ease about his own work, but he could be fascinating on the subject of others. A few days after the death of Balanchine I spent an evening with Ashton when he talked with wonderful percipience about the differences between their work. Put simply, Ashton felt that Balanchine's work was the continuation of a school, while his own ballets were the continuation of a tradition. Even when Ashton made a purely abstract ballet, such as *Symphonic Variations*, it had somehow a stronger sense of continuity with the past than the harder (as in *Diamonds*), more brilliant style of Balanchine's work. Ashton hugely admired Balanchine, but doubted if that admiration was reciprocated. But it was Ashton's talent that was the key to the eventual success of the Royal Ballet. He and de Valois, working together, cherished the great classics of the Russian and French tradition and also created a new repertory of their own, based on a school that put elegance of line as high in the priorities as brilliance or virtuosity. I wrote earlier about how much less impressed I was when young with British dancers as compared with Russian or French. Yet the gentler British school has had the more wide-ranging influence, especially in the Commonwealth.

When the Sadler's Wells Ballet moved to the Royal Opera House, Covent Garden, in 1946, a second group remained behind called the Sadler's Wells Theatre Ballet. That small operation proved amazingly fertile, since its members included Kenneth MacMillan, John Cranko and Peter Wright, all destined to make important contributions as choreographers or company directors. Kenneth MacMillan succeeded Ashton as director of the Royal Ballet in 1970, and once again a major choreographic talent seemed unhappy with executive authority. He did go on worrying away at the problem of creating new full-length works. His version of *Romeo and Juliet* had proved as popular as Ashton's *Cinderella*, demonstrating as in other countries that these two Prokofiev scores could extend the list of nineteenth-century classics. The two full-length works MacMillan created as director, *Anastasia* and *Manon*, have both lasted in the repertory. But MacMillan grew increasingly uncomfortable with the London situation, and many of his best later works were made for other companies.

Meanwhile, the 'Second Company', as it unhelpfully came to be called, expanded and became a touring group. In 1970 it was reduced to an experimental body, but in 1977 returned to its original base as the Sadler's Wells Royal Ballet with Peter Wright as its director. Once again it has expanded and has now moved to Birmingham, where it appears as the Birmingham Royal Ballet. Peter Wright became one of the outstanding artistic directors of our time. Considering the limitations of his company in both size and budget, his achievements are remarkable. He did all the things Diaghilev did, bringing on new choreographers, restaging the classics with taste and high intelligence and rescuing important works from the past for reassessment. He also created an extraordinary feeling of family within the company which reminded many of the way people remembered the Ballets Russes. He showed an impressive loyalty to his dancers, refusing offers to move elsewhere, and his dancers reciprocated, many of them making whole careers with his company. It is impossible not to wonder what Wright might have achieved had he become director of the main company of the Royal Ballet rather than the reluctant Kenneth MacMillan or the outsider Norman Morrice. Birmingham Royal Ballet consistently produced the most interesting programmes of the classical companies in Britain and, if only they had had not just good but great dancers, I feel the impact could have been limitless. As it was, Peter Wright set standards as an artistic director matched by very few of his contemporaries.

The other main British classical company has traded under a variety of names: Festival Ballet, London Festival Ballet, London's Festival Ballet or, as it now is, English National Ballet. It was founded by Markova and Dolin in 1949 and took its name from the forthcoming Festival of Britain of 1951. It was run on similar lines to the de Basil company, with a businessman of sorts, Julian Braunsweg, as manager. Braunsweg showed considerable ingenuity, but with finance rather than creativity. From 1969 London Festival Ballet was run for ten years by the English ballerina Beryl Grey. It always had good dancers and became the workhorse of the British classical dance scene, without a theatre or base of its own, giving seasons in the barely suitable Royal Festival Hall in London, but mostly on the road. It was and still is very popular, and in a way that popularity has been its problem. They never seem to have had the time or, indeed, the audience's expectation to do much in the way of experimentation. Their staple diet has been the full-length classics, in serviceable versions for the most part, but rarely at the highest level. They have never had a first-rate choreographer associated with them for any length of time, as the Royal Ballet did with Ashton and MacMillan. Neither did other off-shoots from London, among them the National Ballet of Canada and the Australian Ballet. But a new company was created in the 1960s which had just the right characteristics, and in the most unlikely of places, Germany.

The Stuttgart Ballet was to all intents and purposes the creation of one man, the South African choreographer John Cranko. Cranko's career was in itself an indictment of the British dance establishment in the 1950s. He should have run a major company in the United Kingdom, having spent all his adult life as a dancer, choreographer and theatre director in Britain, largely with the Royal Ballet. But his quirky diversity and openly declared homosexuality terrified timid Britain, and from 1961 he found a grateful home in Stuttgart. There he created a brilliant international company: Marcia Haydee from Brazil, Richard Cragun from the United States, Egon Madsen from Denmark and even some good German dancers. Germany has never shown the aptitude for classical ballet that it has for modern dance. There is no classical equivalent of Pina Bausch. Cranko's achievement was nearest in my view to a newly invented Ballets Russes. Within a few years he had not only found new choreographers such as the very young William Forsythe, but built a new image for established figures such as Kenneth MacMillan. In his own work he created instant classics: *Romeo and Juliet, Eugene Onegin, The Taming of the Shrew*. He died tragically young in an aeroplane returning from New York after a triumphant season with his company at the Metropolitan Opera, but during his Stuttgart years he and his company showed a creative vitality which in my view is on the level of Diaghilev and the Ballets Russes. Whether he could have gone on at that level is impossible to tell. After twelve years in Stuttgart success was already becoming a problem as well as an advantage for the company. But during those years there was an excitement and focus to the Stuttgart Ballet which I found irresistible.

By the 1970s it was not only dancers and choreographers trained in London who ran companies around the world, but ex-London productions that dominated their stages. Pleasing as it was to see the creations of Ashton, MacMillan or Cranko travelling widely, it gave in the long run a static feeling of sameness to the world dance scene. I spent several visits to the United States of America in 1979 and 1980 looking for a classical company that was not based in New York to bring to the Edinburgh Festival, for none had been seen here. It was depressing to find few of them with much original repertory of their own. If they were not sub-Balanchine, they were almost entirely ex-London: Houston with a repertory almost entirely from London Festival or the Royal Ballet; Joffrey with, apart from his own rather second-rate creations, a great deal of Ashton; while American Ballet Theatre was at that time deep in a long relationship with Kenneth MacMillan. Eventually I chose the San Francisco Ballet, less because of a sense of their real achievement, than because they could offer a considerable number of works which were new to Europe. But when it came to full-length works, it was inevitably yet another version of *Romeo and Juliet*.

Yet it was in the 1970s that dance made its biggest breakthrough in finding new audiences. Part of it came from the star partnership of Fonteyn and Nureyev, and later defecting dancers such as Natalia Makarova and Mikhail Baryshnikov. But the principal successes of dance came almost entirely from the other side of the fence, the modern school, headed by the truly original figure of Martha Graham. Graham had imposed on the world her own dance language and attitudes, growing out of a new technique based on the interplay between psychological preoccupations and the movements of the human body. However odd and dated much of it may seem today, in its heyday it was thrilling. She had, in just the same way as Ninette de Valois, sent out into the world her disciples to convert other territories. Glen Tetley had gone to Amsterdam to work with Hans Van Manen for Netherlands Dance Theatre, Robert Cohan came to London to establish London Contemporary Dance Theatre and the American companies run by her former pupils were regularly to be seen all over the world, with a new interpretation of the Graham message.

When Graham herself, through age and alcohol, lost her creative leadership, the brilliantly exhibitionist company of Paul Taylor may have had the most popular success, but the most influential was that led by Merce Cunningham. Graham had learned from her predecessors in modern dance, Ruth St Denis and Ted Shawn, and from her long-time collaborator, the musician Louis Horst, how important new music and new design was. She had in her younger years championed the American talents of Aaron

Copland and Samuel Barber. She had supported the timeless oriental visions of the sculptor Isamo Noguchi. Merce Cunningham went much further, through his lifelong association with the composer John Cage, and with the newest talents from the New York art scene: Robert Rauschenberg, Andy Warhol and Jasper Johns. It is perhaps not surprising that American dancers should show a kind of frontier spirit and freedom in movement, but even more remarkable is that choreographers such as Graham and her successors should absorb the legacy of Freud. In many ways myth found renewal in the New World. It is understandable that a young generation found all this a great deal more exciting than yet another *Swan Lake.*

It took several visits for Graham to have anything like a success in London, where the work and attitudes of the Royal Ballet very much dominated the scene. De Valois was more than lucky in her successors, at least from a choreographic point of view. Despite nods in the direction of Balanchine or Robbins, and occasional flirtations with the likes of Petit, the core of the Royal Ballet's repertory in both its companies from the 1940s onwards was British, and none the worse for that, given the talent at their disposal. But at the end of the 1990s the situation looks less secure. Ashton died in glory at a great age festooned with honours and much love. Cranko, MacMillan and Peter Darrell, another former Sadler's Wells dancer, who created first Western Theatre Ballet and then Scottish Ballet, did not live long enough to achieve totally accepted classic status. No one yet, not even the prolific David Bintley, has taken their place.

What differentiates all these choreographers from their Diaghilev-period predecessors is that they became company directors, with responsibilities for a whole company and its output, not just for their own works. Many of them expressed often enough, even publicly, the sense of frustration this led to. I knew all of them well, and since I was in no way either a rival or a critic I could become a confidant, and from the late 1960s through to the 1980s was in regular receipt of confidences, indiscretions and anxieties. All of them felt that they had become a cog – necessary, but by no means the most important element in a great bureaucratic structure which provided them with the company on which they worked, but which sapped their creative vitality by expecting them to be also outstanding administrators, impartial judges of their own work and that of others, fund-raisers, ambassadors, public relations officers and understanding employers. All of them felt that this involved a degree of artistic compromise which carried with it not just the risk, but the near certainty of diminishing their own creativity. It is hardly surprising that MacMillan made some of his strongest choreographic statements when he worked elsewhere, in Stuttgart, for instance, with *Requiem* and *Song of the Earth*, or in Berlin, with the one-act version of *Anastasia*. Darrell rarely in later years regained the thrilling vitality of *Sun into Darkness*, a powerful full-length ballet he made to a scenario by playwright David Rudkin, set in an all too contemporary world of bikers and violence.

The irony of the Diaghilev legacy is that the success of ballet has created dance machines which need to be tended by factory managers, and these choreographer/managers have had their time and energy sapped by administration. Few of them had guru figures to advise or restrain them in the mysterious way that Lincoln Kirstein related to Balanchine as a kind of *alter ego*. Ashton enjoyed the invigorating friendship of many of the most intelligent men and women of his time, but he still had to cope daily with the board of the Royal Opera House and, at one remove, with the Arts Council.

The strings attached to the money Diaghilev raised were straightforward. Lord Rothermere's support was conditional on the casting of Nikitina, a dancer whom he fancied. Chanel gave Diaghilev money out of friendship, although not without commercial intuition. Today money comes attached to obligations and quotas. These can range from politically correct theories of equal opportunity to requirements for regional touring. Other god-parents have even more specific demands. The government's insistence on part-funding from the private sector demands sponsorship. Sponsorship may be available, provided that the work proposed does not frighten the chairman's wife, or the chairman's colleagues on the board. Local authority money may depend on education programmes, community projects or other neo-political requirements. There is no such thing as a free grant. Privately funded companies in the past could bend the world to their vision. State-funded establishments today have to serve stricter masters. I do not believe that Diaghilev could have operated in this climate. He did only what he wanted, with a weather eye on some degree of continuity and an instinctive understanding of the box office. He was not compelled to announce six months in advance a 'New Work', as yet untitled, or commit to foreign tours in which the funding agent for the tour dictated the repertory, usually rejecting anything controversial, allowing only so much or so little that was new and thereby inhibiting both the development of the company and the growth of the audience.

If market research counts for more than artistic planning, there is an inevitable loss of daring, while nothing inhibits creativity like under-funding. If everything is calculated on a narrow balance of income and expenditure, the accountants (usually the board members) will go for playing safe rather than playing brave. Increasingly these timorous would-be supporters, and I cannot exclude from this stricture the Arts Council, shelter behind words such as 'accessibility' and 'accountability'. They justify their own lack of vision by refusing it to others. But if giving the public what it already knows is all that can be done, you are already in a spiral of decline. Ballet ends up with everybody dancing the *Nutcracker* for months of the year. Is it surprising that the audience is becoming restless and bored, and will only be lured by the cult of stars or shock tactics? Sylvie Guillem dancing *In the Middle Somewhat Elevated* to a heavy metal score on the stage of the Royal Opera House, Covent Garden, certainly sells seats. But what does it tell us about the Royal Ballet, and how does it point the way forward? In Frankfurt you get a whole evening of Forsythe's choreography, and I feel even more frustrated. Is this what everybody has worked so hard to achieve?

The lessons of Diaghilev are plain to see, but it is much less clear how, in the present climate, they can be applied.

5 Without Authority

One evening during my years as director of the Edinburgh Festival I ran into a group of friends who were also in charge of major arts organizations: the director of the National Theatre, the general administrator of the Royal Opera House and the director of the Royal Shakespeare Compnay. We all knew each other quite well, since the arts community is a small one, and it was Trevor Nunn, of the Royal Shakespeare Company, who put to Peter Hall, John Tooley and me a simple but crucial question. 'How many days this week', he asked, 'have you spent doing the job for which you were hired?' His point was that we had all been hired to be artistic directors, but our conversation up to that point had demonstrated the reality of the 1980s, that we had become arts administrators rather than artistic directors. We had spent the week raising money, dealing with the unions, seeking to repair ageing buildings, writing papers for the board, lobbying local authorities, seeking sponsorship and a dozen other things – almost anything, in fact, except devoting ourselves single-mindedly to the artistic planning of the opera, the theatre or the festival for which we were responsible. Against this background, none of us could claim to have spent more than two days of the previous seven (we all worked seven-day weeks) being an artistic director.

We do not expect to live in an Arcadian grove where one talks only of art, but we all felt that we had been reduced to being part-time artistic directors and almost full-time businessmen. None of us could see an alternative. In an inexorable way the very support systems that have grown up around arts organizations with the intention of giving them stability and long-term security have come to overwhelm us with administrative distractions. Year by year the demands made on us administratively and the need to operate without financial or artistic loss within a steadily shrinking budget were dictating to us what our artistic policy was to be. Diaghilev never knew where the next year's income was coming from. He lived an entirely *ad hoc* existence, taking real risks and suffering occasional disasters. But he remained a free agent. His policy was made by him and executed by his associates. Not even the bank intervened. Today hardly any organization in the arts, except perhaps the Getty Museum, has more money than it needs, and most have much less than they would like. Over the past fifty years in countries such as France and Germany government policy has resulted in huge cultural expenditure, but today the accountants have moved in, bringing mutual distrust. All arts organizations in Western civilization exist in a society which doubts the capacity of the artist to understand money. Time and again they are treated like potential criminals, likely to make off with the takings. Yet in Britain arts organizations have shown a capacity to deal with the immensely complicated financial demands of multiple funding with greater flexibility than many industrial or commercial enterprises. A highly complex organization such as the Royal National Theatre or a largely peripatetic one such as English National Ballet has been infinitely better at dealing with money than British Leyland or British Aerospace, whose subsidies from the government so far outrun anything this country has ever spent on the arts. Predicting audience response in the arts is just as tricky as launching any new product, but the arts have shown time and again a readiness to embrace new ideas and find new audiences. Their reward is a strait-jacket of monitoring bodies who patently do not trust what they call their 'clients'.

There is something about the Arts Council today which radiates a lack of confidence between the two sides, rather than constructive cooperation. The council will claim that its own shortage of funds, and the need to be sure that what it has is spent intelligently, demands close supervision. But this is a relatively new view. In the early days the Arts Council's role was only advisory. Money for the Royal Ballet bypassed the Arts Council and came as a grant in aid from the Treasury. Ninette de Valois was given her money and allowed to get on with it, and make her own policy. Now the Royal Ballet, treated often with exasperated irritation, has its budget closely scrutinized by both the Royal Opera House board and the Arts Council, and is obliged to respond to quotas such as the percentage of employees from ethnic minorities. Given that we live in a society where black classical dancers are very few in number, this has led to some curious appointments in other areas. I am not suggesting that the arts should not show an awareness of national policy, such as equal opportunities, merely that imposing and monitoring these policies puts the Arts Council and its clients in a very different relationship to that of the past. Diaghilev wanted the best people for the job, and if that meant taking on an extraordinary Jewish millionairess who could barely dance but had real glamour, so be it. He chose Ida Rubinstein for *Schéhérazade,* unafraid of the reactions of a largely anti-Semitic society, or of a company of dancers who resented her limited skills. He thought she was right for the part. She was not part of a quota.

State support for the arts is opposed by many on the right as a waste of money. Even many moderates believe it unfairly subsidizes a middle-class audience that could afford the arts without it. Many artists, especially experimental ones, dislike the idea, believing that it inhibits and controls their creativity. On all sides something that seemed a huge step forward fifty years ago is questioned. Yet anyone who understands the reality of the contemporary world knows that no large-scale organization could exist without subsidy or, indeed, ever has. The choir of the Sistine Chapel for which Palestrina wrote, Haydn's orchestra at Eszterháza and the Russian Imperial Ballet were all subsidized in much the same way as their descendants today. The patronage has simply passed from monarch, aristocrat or pope to the state. But neither then nor now could the artistic enterprise have existed without the subsidy. Our own Arts Council was created largely to bridge the gap between the income and the expenditure of large arts organizations, such as orchestras, opera companies, ballet companies and theatres, unable to balance the books in any other way. For reasons that can be questioned but are hard to dismiss the council has reacted to the expansion of activity and diversification by moving into other areas: education, architecture, disability. This has spread the available funds even more thinly.

In these circumstances, is it reasonable to demand higher and higher levels of creativity from organizations that are less and less well funded to accept the risks of innovation? Karsavina remembered Diaghilev speculating on whether a new work would succeed. 'Can't tell, one can never tell,' he said, but added, 'I believe in it.' Is it possible today for whoever is running the Royal Ballet to allow themselves the luxury of such blind faith? What has happened at Covent Garden is a good example of intended help turning to control. When Ninette de Valois moved the company from Sadler's Wells to the Royal Opera House, she was entirely in control of the operation. But who controls it today? Anthony Dowell may be director of the Royal Ballet, but the company is a subsidiary of the Royal Opera House and, it would seem, of the Royal Opera, both of whom have their own boards, structures and priorities. One explanation of the fact that no director since de Valois has had real authority is that none of her successors has had the degree of control that she had. I indicated earlier that the personalities of Ashton and MacMillan were not ideally suited to executive authority, but even had they been, I doubt whether they would have had the freedom de Valois had in deciding in which direction the company should go. Becoming part of a larger organization, far from enhancing and encouraging creativity, has tended to restrict it, just as the Imperial Ballet in St Petersburg suffered from the closeness of the conservative court bureaucracy.

The costs involved in running a large company have also escalated, with results both good and bad. Today people are at least paid better, but the network of contractual agreements that conditions the way staff can be used has limited flexibility. When Nabokov recalled extra orchestral rehearsals for his ballet *Ode* and people staying up all night to finish painting the scenery, one knows instinctively that there were no union shop stewards around. The unionization of the arts was inevitable and necessary, for the exploitation of theatre workers and performers was intolerable. Even today many stage staff work in conditions which would be unacceptable in a factory. I once invited the Edinburgh Festival Council to hold a meeting in the room below the stage of the King's Theatre in Edinburgh, where orchestras had to change and spend intervals or rehearsal breaks. Of course, they refused; it would never do for them to experience the nightmare conditions in which great art was expected to flourish. Time and again local authorities repair and improve the front of house of theatres long before any attention is paid to the areas in which the artists and the supporting staff are working. If the theatrical unions have taken up reactionary postures, or instituted restrictive practices and inflexible schedules, the reasons can be readily understood, even if the resulting costs are harder to accept. In no circumstances can one imagine Diaghilev coping with today's employment regulations, for they inevitably mean a loss of control and less time in which to achieve the desired results. In our necessarily money-led operations, everything comes with a price-tag, and one of the highest is the cost of new stagings and their operation. The television series about Covent Garden, *The House*, however questionable in some ways, at least allowed a wide public to understand the complexity of staging a new production of something as elaborate as *The Sleeping Beauty*. Diaghilev's response to overtime was a shrug, a few bottles of wine and an improvised picnic, as Karsavina remembered from the rehearsals in th Châtelet. No one could get away with that today. In Diaghilev's company choreographers were not paid royalties, and often not even given a contract. It is perhaps not surprising that Massine became so obsessed with money matters in later years.

External controls and internal obstacles can be blamed for much of the tentativeness with which companies today confront innovation and risk-taking. But this surely cannot be accepted as inevitable. Some arts organizations have succeeded, and not just by throwing money at the problems. The winners have been people with real authority to create and embody an artistic policy. In dance this has happened relatively rarely, although it certainly did with Balanchine in New York and with Cranko in Stuttgart, and in a different way with Peter Wright at Sadler's Wells and in Birmingham. All of them achieved remarkable things in the face of difficulties. Smaller, more innovative companies such as those of Martha Graham or Merce Cunningham have avoided many of the problems by not being building based. They have not had to share with opera companies, or be subject to the boards that control those buildings. I am convinced that it is not just the emergence of new ideas or new kinds of movement that has led to greater creativity in modern dance, but the lack of top-heavy superstructures that bedevil traditional ballet companies, almost all of them part of a larger unit revolving around an ageing shared building, whether it be the Bolshoi Theatre in Moscow, the Paris Opéra or the Royal Opera House, Covent Garden.

Yet the fact that Cranko could achieve what he did in a city such as Stuttgart with little or no dance audience in a shared house, and in a country without much tradition, cannot be dismissed as the exception which proves the rule. It happened because Cranko willed it, despite the problems – all of which he overcame. The city of Stuttgart became immensely proud of its ballet, and everything was done to keep them there and to get them established. Today, without Cranko and in thinner times, Stuttgart has the same problems as anyone else. Perhaps it is only the beginnings of things that show sufficient drive to realize the ambitions which produce the great leap forward. For so many today it is simply a question of somehow keeping going. New York City Ballet since Balanchine has continued to dance splendidly, but without any sense of a new direction or fresh energy to renew the past. It risks, as do so many companies, becoming a museum with a few half-hearted gestures towards innovation.

The vast expansion of arts activity in this century across the world has not necessarily produced the leaders that are required. Having a ballet company at your disposal no more creates a great choreographer or artistic director than the existence of an opera house leads to the creation of great operas. Without the institution nothing can happen, but its existence is no guarantee that talent will emerge, especially since so much is left to chance.

We are always told that you cannot train artistic directors, they have to learn by trial and error and occasionally by example. Changing conditions require constantly changing responses, and it is a matter of luck as to whether someone really able emerges, they say.

I cannot find such a passive attitude acceptable. I want more, and as so often it goes back to education and the cultural climate in which we grow up. One of the most depressing aspects of the late twentieth century has been the lack of belief, even among practitioners of the arts, in the importance of the new. How many, or rather how few, conductors of eminence have a real commitment to new music? The theatre has always depended more on new writing, and actors have a trusting enthusiasm about new ventures, even if shakily based. In ballet the omnipresence of the older repertory has given young dancers a belief that to succeed they have to be Giselles or Auroras, and that newer works will not give them the same benchmark by which they can be judged. Yet you have only to look at the reputation of the New York City Ballet to realize that that is hardly true.

Students of the piano today still regard Bach and Beethoven as the Himalayas, but many will admit that Bartók and beyond have their peaks as well. Yet, as in all the arts, our musical education is alarmingly rooted in the past. It is as if the late twentieth century were merely a depressing appendix to the great epic of European culture, downhill all the way from the Impressionists or Wagner or Ibsen, the titans of a hundred years ago. Most societies have some difficulty in coming to terms with the sharp edge of innovation, but they have been quicker to absorb it than we are now. Diaghilev found his public. Today we are surrounded by the achievements of the past and constantly reminded of them through books, photographs, television or recordings. It is possible to live one's whole life actively interested in the arts and yet never be challenged by the new. The usual response of a sceptical audience is to blame the creative artist, yet I find this intolerable. We seem to have forgotten that any form of understanding requires an effort. We are lazy and allow prejudice to raise barriers to receptivity. Children plunge in without anxiety. If only the natural creative enthusiasm of the child in words, sound and movement could be harnessed to an education system that believed in contemporary culture as much as the past, then the spirit of the child could be carried over into more creative adulthood, leading to more demanding and responsive audiences, as well as more confident creators.

The divisive architecture of the arts in our society, with the different art forms often locked into quite separate buildings, leads to a climate in which it is possible to become a successful musician without ever having read a book or looked at a picture. I have always been struck by how deeply read and widely travelled were those artistic directors whom I much admire, among them Diaghilev, Reinhardt or Stanislavsky. They were unwilling to accept that specialization in one area let one off the hook of knowing about anything else. This was also true of the outstanding creators. The sensitivity of Ashton's choreographic version of the *Enigma Variations*, on the face of it an extraordinarily daring proposition risking sentimentality and inappropriateness, grew out of his profound musicality, his understanding of Elgar's time and its social nuances and his observation of English attitudes to friendship and affection. It was the product of a mature mind, well versed in history and humanity. More recent attempts to turn *Cyrano de Bergerac*, *Peter Pan* or *La Ronde* into ballets have shown how shallow were the choreographers' understanding of literature and history.

We need to educate our artists in more than one chosen discipline. Dancers are going to spend their lives working with music, and yet for many years the history of music was not even on the curriculum of the Royal Ballet School. Twenty years ago, at the height of the Cold War, a young Russian pianist I met in London asked me how to get to the Tate Gallery. He could not go back to his home in St Petersburg, he said, without having seen the Turners. I have always been amazed at the depth of culture of Russian artists, whether musicians, film makers or writers, as if understanding the arts were a way of combating the dreariness of a communist society. In the West material comfort allows us to be more superficial. There can also be a deeper interest in culture in countries where the artist has a hard time achieving acceptance, as in Australia, where the arts in recent years have done much to provide a new nation with a necessary past.

Truly great artists are steeped in cultural information. Alfred Brendel may be an archetypal product of his Viennese intellectual background, but he has a remarkable collection of ethnography from other societies. Pina Bausch may have grown up in the shadow of the Holocaust, but she has responded to the theatrical arts of Asia with comparable intensity. Artists need the wider vision not just to interpret, but to create and to lead. The arts can be led by those who do not have the ability to create or perform themselves, but only if they understand its importance. This has never been more true than in the case of Diaghilev – not a musician, not a dancer, not a painter, but someone with the ability to feel the power of the creative impulse, sense its future direction and devise a context for its expression.

Some of Diaghilev's achievements may have been accidental. He could hardly have known that the Great War and the Russian Revolution would lead him into a permanent exile that expanded his influence far beyond Russia. But whatever the circumstances, his actions were always harnessed to a set of values which underpinned all his work. Those values were based in literature, in painting, in music and in poetry as much as in dance. This sort of talent is rare, but the fact of its existence, even occasionally, allows for hope. You cannot plan for a Diaghilev any more than you can plan for a Goethe, whose knowledge and interests were similarly wide, but you can work towards a society in which it is more likely that one might emerge.

The regulation-infested, rigorously budgeted, accountant-led world of the 1990s seems less likely to produce such figures than that of any previous decade. Yet it can still happen. On a small but important scale Pierre Audi's achievement at the Almeida Theatre in London showed that. A cultivated director in a new place suddenly filled all kinds of voids of which nobody was conscious. Yet what then happened to Audi is dreadfully instructive. Regularly refused support by the Arts Council, the Almeida was threatened with losing the small sum it received from the Greater London Arts Association, because of the ethnic composition of its board, rather than the quality of its work. Audi, a true independent, who had put much of his own money into the enterprise, left for the Netherlands, a country that still has a belief in innovation and is prepared to fund it. Audi's budget at the Netherlands Opera today would make any British intendant jealous. His inspiration came from Peter Brook, who also found the attitudes of Great Britain hostile, not to his work, but to his need to be unconventional in the way he achieved it. We are a society of conformists, and happy to reject those who are not. But Russia was the same, and Diaghilev and Stravinsky left for the same reasons. Why can we not make a society in which leading figures wish to remain and work in the world they know best?

Lightning, it is said, never strikes twice in the same place. It is unlikely that the next real leap forward in the arts will come from the world of classical ballet. But the Diaghilev years show what can be achieved. This is why what he did still matters, and not only to those interested in dance. Somewhere, inevitably, there is a new Diaghilev figure in embryo. Will that person, whoever he or she is, find a world in which they can grow and flourish? I believe we all have a responsibility to improve that likelihood, not by forming committees, but by opening our minds as well as our pockets. That is what happened in the past, and what we tend to call civilization. There is no reason to believe that in fundamental ways the world has changed. Despite all today's problems and the siren-calls of nostalgia, I have a degree of optimism. I have spent a good part of my life and want to continue working towards the wider understanding which brings more enduring rewards. And in that quest it is still worth speaking of Diaghilev.

APPENDIX
Productions of the Ballets Russes

Date of première	Title	Composer/ conductor	Choreographer	Designer	Author of plot/text	Principal dancers at première
19 May 1909 Paris, Théâtre du Châtelet	*Le Pavillon d'Armide* ballet, three scenes	Tcherepnin cond. Tcherepnin	Fokine	Benois	Benois, after Gautier	Pavlova, Fokine, Nijinsky, Bulgakov
	Polovtsian Dances (from *Prince Igor*)	Borodin cond. Cooper	Fokine	Roerich	—	Bolm, Fedorova, Smirnova
	Le Festin	Glinka Tchaikovsky Mussorgsky Glazunov Rimsky-Korsakov cond. Tcherepnin	Petipa Gorsky Fokine Foltz Kchessinsky	scenery: Korovin costumes: Bakst, Benois, Bilibin, Korovin	—	Karsavina, Nijinsky
2 June 1909 Paris, Théâtre du Châtelet	*Les Sylphides* ballet (one act)	Chopin cond. Tcherepnin	Fokine	Benois	Fokine	Pavlova, Karsavina, Baldina, Nijinsky
	Cléopâtre choreographic drama (one act)	Arensky, Taneyev, Rimsky-Korsakov, Glinka, Glazunov, Mussorgsky, Tcherepnin cond. Tcherepnin	Fokine	Bakst	Fokine, after Pushkin	Pavlova, Rubinstein, Karsavina, Fokine, Nijinsky, Bulgakov, Bolm
20 May 1910 Berlin, Theater des Westens	*Le Carnaval* ballet-pantomime (one act)	Schumann (orchestrated Rimsky-Korsakov, Liadov, Glazunov, Tcherepnin, Arensky) cond. Tcherepnin	Fokine	Bakst	Fokine and Bakst	Lopokova, Piltz, Leontier, Bolm, Nijinsky, Fokine

4 June 1910 Paris, Grand Opéra	*Schéhérezade* choreographic drama (one act)	Rimsky-Korsakov cond. Tcherepnin	Fokine	Bakst	Bakst, Benois and Fokine	Rubinstein, Nijinsky, Bulgakov
18 June 1910 Paris, Grand Opéra	*Giselle* ballet-pantomime (two acts)	Adam and Burgmüller cond. Vidal	After Coralli, Perrot and Petipa; produced by Fokine	Benois	Gautier and Saint-Georges, after Heine	Karsavina, Nijinsky
25 June 1910 Paris, Grand Opéra	*The Firebird* Russian fairy-tale (two scenes)	Stravinsky cond. Pierné	Fokine	Golovin; some costumes by Bakst	Fokine	Karsavina, Fokina, Fokine, Bulgakov
	Les Orientales choreographic sketches	Grieg, Sinding arr. Arensky, Glazunov, Borodin cond. Tcherepnin	various, including Nijinsky	Korovin and Bakst	Diaghilev	Geltzer, Karsavina, Fokina, Nijinsky, Volinin, Orlov
19 April 1911 Monte Carlo	*Le Spectre de la Rose* choreographic tableau	Weber cond. Tcherepnin	Fokine	Bakst	Vaudoyer, after Gautier	Karsavina, Nijinsky
26 April 1911 Monte Carlo	*Narcisse* mythological poem (one act)	Tcherepnin cond. Tcherepnin	Fokine	Bakst	Bakst	Karsavina, Nijinska, Nijinsky, Fokine, Bolm
6 June 1911 Paris, Théâtre du Châtelet	*Sadkô* ('au royaume sous-marin')	Rimsky-Korsakov cond. Tcherepnin	Fokine	Anisfeldt	—	—
13 June 1911 Paris, Théâtre du Châtelet	*Petrushka* burlesque scenes (four tableaux)	Stravinsky cond. Monteux	Fokine	Benois	Stravinsky and Benois	Karsavina, Nijinsky, Orlov, Cecchetti

Date of première	Title	Composer/ conductor	Choreographer	Designer	Author of plot/text	Principal dancers at première
30 November 1911 London, Theatre Royal, Covent Garden	*Swan Lake* ballet-pantomime (two acts, three tableaux)	Tchaikovsky cond. Monteux	Petipa and Ivanov; produced by Fokine	Korovin and Golovin	Begitchev and Geltzer libretto: M. Tchaikovsky	Kchessinskaya, Nijinsky
13 May 1912 Paris, Théâtre du Châtelet	*Le Dieu Bleu* Hindu legend (one act)	Hahn cond. Inghelbrecht	Fokine	Bakst	Cocteau and de Madrazo	Karsavina, Nelidova, Nijinsky
20 May 1912 Paris, Théâtre du Châtelet	*Thamar* choreographic drama (one act)	Balakirev cond. Monteux	Fokine	Bakst	Bakst, after Lermontov	Karsavina, Bolm
29 May 1912 Paris, Théâtre du Châtelet	*L'Après-midi d'un Faune* choreographic tableau	Debussy cond. Monteux	Nijinsky	Bakst	Nijinsky, after Mallarmé	Nelidova, Nijinsky
8 June 1912 Paris, Théâtre du Châtelet	*Daphnis and Chloe* ballet (one act, three tableaux)	Ravel cond. Monteux	Fokine	Bakst	Fokine	Karsavina, Nijinsky, Bolm
January 1913 Vienna Opera House	*L'Oiseau d'Or* classic pas de deux	Tchaikovsky cond. Monteux	Petipa	—	—	Karsavina, Nijinsky
15 May 1913 Paris, Théâtre des Champs-Élysées	*Jeux* 'poème dansé'	Debussy cond. Monteux	Nijinsky	Bakst	Blanche	Karsavina, Schollar, Nijinsky
29 May 1913 Paris, Théâtre des Champs-Élysées	*The Rite of Spring* tableau (two acts)	Stravinsky cond. Monteux	Nijinsky	Roerich	Stravinsky and Roerich	Piltz

12 June 1913 Paris, Théâtre des Champs-Élysées	The Tragedy of Salome	Schmidt cond. Monteux	Romanov	Soudeikin	d'Humières	Karsavina
16 April 1914 Monte Carlo	Papillons ballet (one act)	Schumann (orchestrated Tcherepnin) cond. Monteux	Fokine	scenery: Doboujinsky costumes: Bakst	Fokine	Karsavina, Schollar, Fokine
17 May 1914 Paris, Grand Opéra	The Legend of Joseph ballet (one act)	Richard Strauss cond. Strauss	Fokine	scenery: Sert costumes: Bakst	von Kessler and von Hoffmannsthal	Kuznetsova, Massine, Bulgakov
24 May 1914 Paris, Grand Opéra	Le Coq d'Or opera produced as ballet (three tableaux)	Rimsky-Korsakov cond. Monteux	Fokine	Goncharova	production devised by Benois	Karsavina, Jezierska, Bulgakov, Cecchetti, Kovalski
26 May 1914 Paris, Grand Opéra	Le Rossignol opera with ballet (three tableaux)	Stravinsky cond. Monteux	Romanov	Benois	Stravinsky, after H. C. Andersen	Karsavina
2 June 1914 Paris, Grand Opéra	Midas mythological comedy (one act)	Steinberg cond. Baton	Fokine	Doboujinsky	Bakst	Karsavina, Bolm, Frohman
20 December 1915 Geneva, Grand Théâtre	Le Soleil de Nuit Russian scenes and dances	Rimsky-Korsakov cond. Ansermet	Massine	Larionov	—	Massine, Zverev
21 August 1916 San Sebastian (Spain), Eugenia-Victoria Theatre	Las Meninas pavane	Fauré cond. Ansermet	Massine	scenery: Socrate costumes: Sert	after Velazquez	Sokolova, Khoklova, Massine, Woizikowski

Date of première	Title	Composer/conductor	Choreographer	Designer	Author of plot/text	Principal dancers at première
25 August 1916 San Sebastian, Eugenia-Victoria Theatre	*Kikimora* Russian fairy-tale	Liadov cond. Ansermet	Massine	Larionov	–	Shabelska, Idzikowski
August 1916	*Sadkô* (new version)	Rimsky-Korsakov	Bolm	Goncharova	–	–
23 October 1916 New York, Manhattan Opera House	*Till Eulenspiegel* 'comico-dramatic' ballet	Richard Strauss cond. Goetz	Nijinsky	Jones	Nijinsky after D. Coster	Nijinsky
12 April 1917 Rome, Costanza Theatre	*Fireworks* symphonic poem	Stravinsky cond. Ansermet	none	Balla	production devised by Diaghilev	none
	The Good-humoured Ladies	Scarlatti, arr. Tommasini cond. Ansermet	Massine	Bakst	Massine, after Goldoni	Lopokova, Tchernicheva, Mme Cecchetti, Massine, Cecchetti, Idzikowski, Woizikowski
11 May 1917 Paris, Théâtre du Châtelet	*Contes Russes* suite of scenes and dances	Liadov cond. Ansermet	Massine	Sets: Larionov Costumes: Goncharova	Massine	Tchernicheva, Sokolova, Woizikowski, Jazvinsky, Idzikowski
18 May 1917 Paris, Théâtre du Châtelet	*Parade*	Satie cond. Ansermet	Massine	Picasso	Cocteau	Lopokova, Shabelska, Massine, Zverev

Date / Place	Title	Music	Choreography	Design	Libretto	Dancers
5 July 1919 London, Alhambra Theatre	*La Boutique Fantasque* ballet (one act)	Rossini, arr. Respighi cond. Defosse	Massine	Derain	Massine	Lopokova, Massine, Idzikowski
22 July 1919 London, Alhambra Theatre	*The Three-cornered Hat* ballet (one act)	de Falla cond. Ansermet	Massine	Picasso	Sierra, after Alcarcón	Karsavina, Massine, Woizikowski
2 February 1920 Paris, Grand Opéra	*Le Chant du Rossignol* ballet (one act); adapted from opera *Le Rossignol*	Stravinsky cond. Ansermet	Massine	Matisse	Stravinsky, after H. C. Andersen	Karsavina, Idzikowski, Sokolova, Grigoriev
15 May 1920 Paris, Grand Opéra	*Pulcinella* ballet (one act)	Stravinsky, after Pergolesi cond. Ansermet	Massine	Picasso	Massine	Karsavina, Tchernicheva, Nemchinova, Massine, Idzikowski, Cecchetti
27 May 1920 Paris, Grand Opéra	*Le Astuzie Femminili* (opera-ballet)	Cimarosa, arr. Respighi cond. Ansermet	Massine	Sert	—	Karsavina, Tchernicheva, Nemchinova, Sokolova, Idzikowski, Woizikowski
15 December 1920	*The Rite of Spring* (new production)	Stravinsky cond. Ansermet	Massine	Roerich	Stravinsky and Roerich	Sokolova
17 May 1921 Paris, Gaieté Lyrique Theatre	*Chout* Russian legend (six scenes)	Prokofiev cond. Ansermet	Larionov and Slavinsky	Larionov	—	Devillier, Slavinsky, Jazvinsky

Date of première	Title	Composer/conductor	Choreographer	Designer	Author of plot/text	Principal dancers at première
	Cuadro Flamenco suite of Andalusian dances	traditional Spanish, arr. De Falla	traditional Spanish	Picasso	—	Dalbaicín, de Jerez, del Gorrotín, La Lopez, El Tejero, El Moreno
2 November 1921 London, Alhambra Theatre	*The Sleeping Princess* ballet (four acts)	Tchaikovsky cond. Fitelberg	Petipa, produced by Sergeev, with additions by Nijinska	Bakst	Vsevolozhsky and Petipa, after Perrault	Spessivtseva, Lopokova, Brianza, Vladimirov, Idzikowski
18 May 1922 Paris, Grand Opéra	*Aurora's Wedding* (from *The Sleeping Princess*) ballet (one act)	Tchaikovsky cond. Fitelberg	Petipa and Nijinska	costumes: Benois and Goncharova	Vsevolozhsky, after Perrault	Trefilova, Vladimirov
	Renard burlesque ballet with song	Stravinsky cond. Ansermet	Nijinska	Goncharova	Stravinsky	Nijinska, Idzikowski, Jazvinsky, Fedorov
13 July 1923 Paris, Gaieté Lyrique Theatre	*Les Noces* choreographic movements (four scenes)	Stravinsky cond. Ansermet	Nijinska	Goncharova	Stravinsky	Tchernicheva, Doubrovska, Semenov, Woizikowski
3 January 1924 Monte Carlo	*Les Tentations de la Bergère* (or *L'Amour Vainqueur*) ballet (one act)	Monteclair, edited Casadesus cond. Ansermet	Nijinska	Gris	text: Kochno	Nemchinova, Nijinska, Tchernicheva, Woizikowski, Vilzak
6 January 1924 Monte Carlo	*Les Biches* ballet (one act)	Poulenc cond. Flament	Nijinska	Laurençin	—	Nemchinova, Nijinska, Vilzak, Woizikowski

Date & Place	Title	Music	Choreographer	Designer	Libretto	Dancers
8 January 1924 Monte Carlo	*Cimarosiana* suite of dances (from *Le Astuzie Femminili*)	Cimarosa, arr. Respighi cond. Flament	Massine	Sert	—	Nemchinova, Tchernicheva, Sokolova, Idzikowski, Woizikowski, Vilzak
19 January 1924 Monte Carlo	*Les Fâcheux* ballet (one act)	Auric cond. Flament	Nijinska	Braque	Kochno, after Molière	Tchernicheva, Vilzak, Dolin, Nijinska
13 April 1924 Monte Carlo	*Night on the Bare Mountain* choreographic tableau	Mussorgsky cond. Flament	Nijinska	Goncharova	—	Sokolova, Fedorov
20 June 1924 Paris, Théâtre des Champs-Elysées	*Le Train Bleu* danced operetta (one act)	Milhaud cond. Monteux	Nijinska	scenery: Laurens costumes: Chanel curtain: Picasso	Cocteau	Dolin, Nijinska, Sokolova, Woizikowski
28 April 1925 Monte Carlo	*Zéphyre et Flore* ballet (three tableaux)	Dukelsky cond. Scotto	Massine	Braque	Kochno	Nikitina, Dolin, Lifar
17 June 1925 Paris, Gaieté Lyrique Theatre	*Les Matelots* ballet (five tableaux)	Auric cond. Scotto	Massine	Pruna	Kochno	Nemchinova, Sokolova, Woizikowski, Lifar, Slavinsky
	Le Chant du Rossignol (new production)	Stravinsky	Balanchine	Matisse	Stravinsky	Markova, Sokolova
11 December 1925 London, Coliseum Theatre	*Barabau* ballet with vocal chorus	Rieti cond. Desormière	Balanchine	Utrillo	Rieti	Woizikowski, Lifar, Chamié, Nikitina

Date of première	Title	Composer/ conductor	Choreographer	Designer	Author of plot/text	Principal dancers at première
4 May 1926 Monte Carlo	*Romeo and Juliet* 'rehearsal, without scenery, in two parts'	Lambert cond. Scotto	Nijinska and Balanchione	Ernst and Miró	Kochno, after Shakespeare	Karsavina, Lifar
29 May 1926 Paris, Théâtre Sarah Bernhardt	*La Pastorale*	Auric cond. Desormière	Balanchine	Pruna	Kochno	Doubrovska, Danilova, Lifar, Woizikowski
3 July 1926 Paris, Théâtre Sarah Bernhardt	*Jack-in-the-Box*	Satie, orch Milhaud cond. Desormière	Balanchine	Derain	—	Danilova, Tchernicheva, Doubrovska, Idzikowski
3 December 1926 London, Lyceum Theatre	*The Triumph of Neptune* English pantomime (twelve tableaux)	Berners cond. Defosse	Balanchine	Shervashidze, after Pollock's collection of prints by G. and R. Cruikshank, Tofts, Honigold and Webb	Sacheverell Sitwell	Danilova, Tchernicheva, Sokolova, Lifar, Balanchine
30 April 1927 Monte Carlo	*La Chatte* ballet (one act)	Sauguet cond. Scotto	Balanchine	Gabo and Pevsner	'Sobeika' (Kochno), after Aesop	Spessivtseva, Lifar
3 May 1927	*Les Facheux* (new production)	Auric	Massine	Braque	Kochno, after Molière	Massine
2 June 1927 Paris, Théâtre Sarah Bernhardt	*Mercure 'poses plastiques'*	Satie cond. Desormière	Massine	Picasso	Cocteau	Petrova, Massine, Lissanevich
7 June 1927 Paris, Théâtre Sarah Bernhardt	*Le Pas d'Acier* ballet (two tableaux)	Prokofiev cond. Desmorière	Massine	Yakoulov	Prokofiev and Yakoulov	Tchernicheva, Danilova, Petrova, Massine, Lifar, Woizikowski

Date / Place	Title	Music	Choreography	Design	Book / Text	Dancers
6 June 1928, Paris, Théâtre Sarah Bernhardt	*Ode* spectacle (two acts)	Nabokov, cond. Desormière	Massine	Tchelichiv, with Charbonnier	book: Kochno text: Lomonosov	Doubrovska, Nikitina, Massine, Lifar
12 June 1928, Paris, Théâtre Sarah Bernhardt	*Apollon Musagète* ballet (two scenes)	Stravinsky, cond. Desormière	Balanchine	Bauchant	Stravinsky	Nikitina, Tchernicheva, Doubrovska, Lifar
16 July 1928, London, His Majesty's Theatre	*The Gods Go A'Begging* pastorale	Handel, arr. Beecham cond. Beecham	Balanchine	scenery: Bakst costumes: Gris	'Sobeika' (Kochno)	Danilova, Woizikowski, Doubrovska, Tchernicheva
9 May 1929, Monte Carlo	*Le Bal* ballet (two tableaux)	Rieti cond. Scotto	Balanchine	de Chirico	Kochno	Danilova, Dolin, Doubrovska, Woizikowski, Balanchine, Lipkovska, Lifar
21 May 1929, Paris, Théâtre Sarah Bernhardt	*Renard* (new production)	Stravinsky cond. Desormière	Lifar	Larionov	—	Woizikowski, Efimov, Hoyer, Lissanevich
	The Prodigal Son scenes in three tableaux	Prokofiev cond. Desormière	Balanchine	Rouault	Kochno	Doubrovska, Lifar, Woizikowski, Dolin

Index

371